ISBN: 9781313430524

Published by:
HardPress Publishing
8345 NW 66TH ST #2561
MIAMI FL 33166-2626

Email: info@hardpress.net
Web: http://www.hardpress.net

Janice Meredith

A STORY OF THE AMERICAN REVOLUTION

By

PAUL LEICESTER FORD

Author of "The Honorable Peter Stirling," "The Story of an Untold Love," "The Many-Sided Franklin," "The True George Washington," etc.

NEW YORK · · DODD, MEAD AND COMPANY · MDCCCXCIX

TO

GEORGE W. VANDERBILT

My dear George,

Into the warp and woof of every book an author weaves much that even the subtlest readers cannot suspect, far less discern. To them it is but a cross and pile of threads interlaced to form a pattern which may please or displease their taste. But to the writer every filament has its own association: How each bit of silk or wool, flax or tow, was laboriously gathered, or was blown to him; when each was spun by the wheel of his fancy into yarns; the colour and tint his imagination gave to each skein; and where each was finally woven into the fabric by the shuttle of his pen. No thread ever quite detaches itself from its growth and spinning, dyeing and weaving, and each draws him back to hours and places seemingly unrelated to the work.

And so, as I have read the proofs of this book I have found more than once that the pages have faded out of sight and in their stead I have seen Mount Pisgah and the French Broad River, or the ramp and terrace of Biltmore House, just as I saw them when writing the words which served to recall them to me. With the visions, too, has come a recurrence to our long talks, our work among the books, our games of chess, our cups of tea, our walks, our rides, and our drives. It is therefore a pleasure to me that the book so naturally gravitates to you, and that I may make it a remembrance of those past weeks of companionship, and an earnest of the present affection of

PAUL LEICESTER FORD.

Contents

JANICE MEREDITH

A Story of the Revolution

I

A HEROINE OF MANY POSSIBILITIES

"*ALONZO now once more found himself upon an element that had twice proved destructive to his happiness, but Neptune was propitious, and with gentle breezes wafted him toward his haven of bliss, toward Amaryllis. Alas, when but one day from happiness, a Moorish zebec —*"

"Janice!" called a voice.

The effect on the reader and her listener, both of whom were sitting on the floor, was instantaneous. Each started and sat rigidly intent for a moment; then, as the sound of approaching footsteps became audible, one girl hastily slipped a little volume under the counterpane of the bed, while the other sprang to her feet, and in a hurried, flustered way pretended to be getting something out of a tall wardrobe.

Before the one who hid the book had time to rise, a woman of fifty entered the room, and after a glance, cried: —

"Janice Meredith! How often have I told thee that it is ungenteel for a female to repose on the floor?"

"Very often, mommy," said Janice, rising meekly, meantime casting a quick glance at the bed, to see how far its smoothness had been disturbed.

"And still thee continues such unbecoming and vastly indelicate behaviour."

"Oh, mommy, but it is so nice!" cried the girl. "Did n't you like to sit on the floor when you were fifteen?"

"Janice, thou 't more careless every day in bed-making," ejaculated Mrs. Meredith, making a sudden dive toward the bed, as if she desired to escape the question. She smoothed the gay patchwork quilt, seemed to feel something underneath, and the next moment pulled out the hidden volume, which was bound, as the bookseller's advertisements phrased it, in "half calf, neat, marbled sides." One stern glance she gave the two red-faced culprits, and, opening the book, read out in a voice that was in itself an impeachment, "The Adventures of Alonzo and Amaryllis!"

There was an instant's silence, full of omen to the culprits, and then Mrs. Meredith's wrath found vent.

"Janice Meredith!" she cried. "On a Sabbath morning, when thee shouldst be setting thy thoughts in a fit order for church! And thou, Tabitha Drinker!"

"It 's all my fault, Mrs. Meredith," hurriedly asserted Tabitha. "I brought the book with me from Trenton, and 't was I suggested that we go on reading this morning."

"Six hours of spinet practice thou shalt have to-morrow, miss," announced Mrs. Meredith to her daughter, "and this afternoon thou shalt say over the whole catechism. As for thee, Tabitha, I shall feel it my duty to write thy father of his daughter's conduct. Now hurry and make ready for church." And Mrs. Meredith started to leave the room.

"Oh, mommy," cried Janice, springing forward and laying a detaining hand on her mother's arm in an imploring manner, "punish me as much as you please, — I know 't was very, very wicked, — but don't take the book away! He and Amaryllis were just —"

"Not another sight shalt thou have of it, miss. My daughter reading novels, indeed!" and Mrs. Meredith departed, holding the evil book gingerly between her fingers, much as one might carry something that was liable to soil one's hands.

The two girls looked at each other, Tabitha with a woebegone expression, and Janice with an odd one, which might mean many things. The flushed cheeks were perhaps due to guilt, but the tightly clinched little fists were certainly due to anger, and, noting these two only, one would have safely affirmed that Janice Meredith, meekly as she had taken her mother's scolding, had a quick and hot temper. But the eyes were fairly starry with some emotion, certainly not anger, and though the lips were pressed tightly together, the feeling that had set them so rigidly was but a passing one, for suddenly the corners twitched, the straight lines bent into curves, and flinging herself upon the tall four-poster bedstead, Miss Meredith laughed as only fifteen can laugh.

"Oh, Tibbie, Tibbie," she presently managed to articulate, "if you look like that I shall die," and as the god of Momus once more seized her, she dragged the quilt into a rumpled pile, and buried her face in it, as if indeed attempting to suffocate herself.

"But, Janice, to think that we shall never know how it ended! I could n't sleep last night for hours, because I was so afraid that Amaryllis would n't have the opportunity to vindicate herself to — and 't would have been finished in another day."

"And a proper punishment for naughty Tibbie Drinker it is," declared Miss Meredith, sitting up and assuming a judicially severe manner. "What do you mean, miss, by tempting good little Janice Meredith into reading a wicked romance on Sunday?"

"'Good little Janice!'" cried Tibbie, contemptuously. "I could slap thee for that." But instead she threw her arms about Janice's neck and kissed her with such rapture and energy as to overbalance the judge from an upright position, and the two rolled over upon the bed laughing with anything but discretion, considering the nearness of their mentor. As a result a voice from a distance called sharply: —

"Janice!"

"O gemini!" cried the owner of that name, springing off the bed and beginning to unfasten her gown, — an example promptly followed by her room-mate.

"Art thou dressing, child?" called the voice, after a pause.

"Yes, mommy," answered Janice. Then she turned to her friend and asked, "Shall I wear my light chintz and kenton kerchief, or my purple and white striped Persian?"

"Sufficiently smart for a country lass, Jan," cried her friend.

"Don't call me country bred, Tibbie Drinker, just because you are a modish city girl."

"And why not thy blue shalloon?"

"'T is vastly unbecoming."

"Janice Meredith! Can't thee let the men alone?"

"I will when they will," airily laughed the girl.

"Do unto others —" quoted Tabitha.

"Then I will when thee sets me an example," retorted Janice, making a deep curtsey, the absence of drapery and bodice revealing the straightness and suppleness of the slender rounded figure, which still had as much of the child as of the woman in its lines.

"Little thought they get from me," cried Tabitha, with a toss of her head.

> "'Tell me where is fancy bred,
> In the heart or in the head?'"

hummed Janice. "Of course, one does n't think about men, Mistress Tabitha. One feels." Which remark showed perception of a feminine truth far in advance of Miss Meredith's years.

"Unfeeling Janice!"

"'T is a good thing for the oafs and ploughboys of Brunswick. For there are none better."

"Philemon Hennion?"

"'Your servant, marms,'" mimicked Janice, catching up a hair brush and taking it from her head as if it were a hat, while making a bow with her feet widely spread. "'Having nothing better ter do, I've made bold ter come over ter drink a dish of tea with you.'" The girl put the brush under her arm, still further spread her feet, put her hands behind some pretended coat-tails, let the brush slip from under her arms, so that it fell to the floor with a racket, stooped with an affectation of clumsiness which seemed impossible to the lithe figure, while mumbling something inarticulate in an apparent paroxysm of embarrassment, — which quickly became a genuine inability to speak from laughter.

"Janice, thee should turn actress."

"Oh, Tibbie, lace my bodice quickly, or I shall burst of laughing," breathlessly begged the girl.

"Janice," said her mother, entering, "how often must I tell thee that giggling is missish? Stop, this moment."

"Yes, mommy," gasped Janice. Then she added, after a shriek and a wriggle, "Don't, Tabitha!"

"What ails thee now, child? Art going to have an attack of the megrims?"

"When Tibbie laces me up she always tickles me, because she knows I'm dreadfully ticklish."

"I can't ever make the edges of the bodice meet, so I tickle to make her squirm," explained Miss Drinker.

"Go on with thy own dressing, Tabitha," ordered Mrs. Meredith, taking the strings from her hand. "Now breathe out, Janice."

Miss Meredith drew a long breath, and then expelled it, instant advantage being taken by her mother to strain the strings. "Again," she said, holding all that had been gained, and the operation was repeated, this time the edges of the frock meeting across the back.

"It hurts," complained the owner of the waist, panting, while the upper part of her bust rose and fell rapidly in an attempt to make up for the crushing of the lower lungs.

"I lose all patience with thee, Janice," cried her mother. "Here when thou hast been given by Providence a waist that would be the envy of any York woman, that thou shouldst object to clothes made to set it off to a proper advantage."

"It hurts all the same," reiterated Janice; "and last year I could beat Jacky Whitehead, but now when I try to run in my new frocks I come nigh to dying of breathlessness."

"I should hope so!" exclaimed her mother. "A female of fifteen run with a boy, indeed! The very idea is indelicate. Now, as soon as thou hast put on thy slippers and goloe-shoes, go to thy father, who has been told of thy misbehaviour, and who will reprove thee for it." And with this last damper on the "lightness of young people," as Mrs. Meredith phrased it, she once more left the room. It is a regrettable fact that Miss Janice, who had looked the picture of submission as her mother spoke, made a mouth, which was far from respectful, at the departing figure.

"Oh, Janice," said Tabitha, "will he be very severe?"

"Severe?" laughed Janice. "If dear dadda is really angry, I'll let tears come into my eyes, and then he'll say he's sorry he hurt my feelings, and kiss me; but if he's only doing it to please mommy, I'll let my eyes shine, and then he'll laugh and tell me to kiss him. Oh, Tibbie, what a nice time we could have if women were only as easy to manage as men!" With this parting regret, Miss Meredith sallied forth to receive the expected reproof.

The lecture or kiss received, — and a sight of Miss Meredith would have led the casual observer to opine that the latter was the form of punishment adopted, — the two girls mounted into the big, lumbering coach along with their elders, and were jolted and shaken over the four miles of ill-made road that separated Greenwood, the "seat," as the "New York Gazette" termed it, of the Honourable Lambert Meredith, from the village of Brunswick, New Jersey. Either this shaking, or something else, put the two maidens in a mood quite unbefitting the day, for in the moment they tarried outside the church while the coach was being placed in the shed, Miss Drinker's face was frowning, and once again Miss Meredith's nails were dug deep into the little palms of her hands.

"Yes," Janice whispered. "She put it in the fire. Dadda saw her."

"And we'll never know if Amaryllis explained that she had ever loved him," groaned Tabitha.

"If ever I get the chance!" remarked Janice, suggestively.

"Oh, Jan!" cried Tabitha, ecstatically. "Would n't it be delightsome to be loved by a peasant, and to find he was a prince and that he had disguised himself to test thy love?"

"'T would be better fun to know he was a prince and torture him by pretending you did n't care for him," replied Janice. "Men are so teasable."

"There's Philemon Hennion doffing his hat to us, Jan."

"The great big gawk!" exclaimed Janice. "Does he want another dish of tea?" A question which set both girls laughing.

"Janice! Tabitha!" rebuked Mrs. Meredith. "Don't be flippant on the Sabbath."

The two faces assumed demureness, and, filing into the Presbyterian meeting-house, their owners apparently gave strict heed to a sermon of the Rev. Alexander McClave, which was later issued from the press of Isaac Collins, at Burlington, under the title of: —

"The Doleful State of the Damned, Especially such as go to Hell from under the Gospel."

II

THE PRINCE FROM OVER THE SEAS

ACROSS the water sounded the bells of Christ Church as the anchor of the brig "Boscawen," ninety days out from Cork Harbour, fell with a splash into the Delaware River in the fifteenth year of the reign of George III., and of grace, 1774. To those on board, the chimes brought the first intimation that it was Sunday, for three months at sea with nothing to mark one day from another deranges the calendar of all but the most heedful. Among the uncouth and ill-garbed crowd that pressed against the waist-boards of the brig, looking with curious eyes toward Philadelphia, several, as the sound of the bells was heard, might have been observed to cross themselves, while one or two of the women began to tell their beads, praying perhaps that the breadth of the just-crossed Atlantic lay between them and the privation and want which had forced emigration upon them, but more likely giving thanks that the dangers and suffering of the voyage were over.

Scarcely had the anchor splashed, and before the circling ripples it started had spread a hundred feet, when a small boat put off from one of the wharfs lining the water front of the city, with the newly arrived ship as an evident destination; and the brig had barely swung to the current when the hoarse voice of the mate was heard ordering the ladder over the side. The preparation to receive the boat drew the attention of the crowd, and they stared at its occupants with an intentness which implied some deeper interest than mere curiosity; low words were exchanged, and some of the poor frightened creatures seemed to take on a greater cringe.

Seated in the sternsheets of the approaching boat was a

plainly dressed man, whose appearance so bespoke the mercantile class that it hardly needed the doffing of the captain's cap and his obsequious "your servant, Mr. Cauldwell, and good health to you," as the man clambered on board, to announce the owner of the ship. To the emigrants this sudden deference was a revelation concerning the cruel and oath-using tyrant at whose mercy they had been during the weary weeks at sea.

"A long voyage ye 've made of it, Captain Caine," said the merchant.

"Ay, sir," answered the captain. "Another ten days would have put us short of water, and —"

"But not of rum? Eh?" interrupted Cauldwell.

"As for that," replied the captain, "there 's a bottle or two that 's rolled itself till 't is cruelty not to drink it, and if you 'll test a noggin in the cabin while taking a look at the manifests —"

"Well answered," cried the merchant, adding, "I see ye set deep."

"Ay," said the captain as they went toward the companionway; "too deep for speed or safety, but the factors care little for sailors' lives."

"And a deep ship makes a deep purse."

"Or a deep grave."

"Wouldst die ashore, man?"

"God forbid!" ejaculated the mariner, in a frightened voice. "I 've had my share of ill-luck without lying in the cold ground. The very thought goes through me like a dash of spray in a winter v'y'ge." He stamped with his foot and roared out, "Forrard there: Two glasses and a dipper from the rundlet," at the same time opening a locker and taking therefrom a squat bottle. "'T is enough to make a man bowse himself kissing black Betty to think of being under ground." He held the black bottle firmly, as if it were in fact a sailor's life preserver from such a fate, and hastened, so soon as the cabin-boy appeared with the glasses and dipper, to mix two glasses of rum and water. Setting these on the table, he took from the locker a bundle of papers, and handed it to the merchant.

Twenty minutes were spent on the clearances and manifests, and then Mr. Cauldwell opened yet another paper.

"Sixty-two in all," he said, with a certain satisfaction in his voice.

"Sixty-three," corrected the captain.

"Not by the list," denied the merchant.

"Sixty-two from Cork Harbour, but we took one aboard ship at Bristol," explained the captain.

"Ye must pack them close between decks."

"Ay. The shoats in the long boat had more room. Mr. Bull-dog would none of it, but slept on deck the whole v'y'ge."

"Mr. Bull-dog?" queried Cauldwell.

"The one your factor shipped at Bristol," explained Caine, and running over the bundle, he spread before the merchant the following paper: —

This Indenture, Made the Tenth Day of March in the fifteenth Year of the Reign of our Sovereign Lord George the third King of Great Britain, etc. And in the Year of our Lord One Thousand Seven Hundred and seventy-four, Between Charles Fownes of Bath in the County of Somerset Labourer of the one Part, and Frederick Caine of Bristol Mariner of the other part Witnesseth That the said Charles Fownes for the Consideration hereinafter mentioned, hath, and by these Presents doth Covenant, Grant and Agree to, and with the said Frederick Caine, his Executors, Administrators and Assigns, That the said Charles Fownes shall and will, as a Faithful Covenant Servant well and truly serve said Frederick Caine his Executors, Administrators or Assigns, in the Plantations of Pennsylvania and New Jersey beyond the Seas, for the space of five years next ensuing the Arrival in the said Plantation, in the Employment of a servant. And the said Charles Fownes doth hereby Covenant and declare himself, now to be of the age of Twenty-one Years and no Covenant or Contract Servant to any Person or Persons. And the said Frederick Caine for himself his Executors, and Assigns, in Consideration thereof do hereby Covenant, Promise and Agree to and with the said Charles Fownes his Executors and Administrators, that he the said Frederick Caine his Executors, Administrators or Assigns, shall and will at his or their own proper Cost and Charges, with what Convenient Speed they may, carry and convey or cause to be carried and conveyed over unto the said Plantations, the said Charles Fownes and also during the said Term, shall and will at the like Cost and Charges, provide and allow the said Charles Fownes all necessary Cloaths, Meat, Drink, Washing, and Lodging, and Fitting and Convenient for him as Covenant Servants in such Cases are usually provided for and allowed. And for the true Performance of the Premises, the said Parties to these Presents, bind themselves their Executors and Administrators, the either to the other, in the Penal Sum of Thirty Pounds Sterling, by these Presents. In Witness whereof they have hereunto interchangeably set their Hands and Seals, the Day and Year above written.

The mark of
CHARLES × FOWNES [Seal].

Sealed and delivered in
the presence of
J. PATTISON, C. CAPON.

These are to certify that the above-named Charles Fownes came before me Thomas Pattison Deputy to the Patentee at Bristol the Day and Year above written, and declared himself to be no Covenant nor Contracted Servant to any Person or Persons, to be of the Age of Twenty-one Years, not kidnapped nor enticed, but desirous to serve the above-named or his assigns five Years, according to the Tenor of his Indenture above written. All of which is Registered in the office for that Purpose appointed by the Letters Patents. In witness whereof I have affixed the common Seal of the said office.

THOMAS PATTISON, D. P.

"And why Mr. Bull-dog?" asked Cauldwell, after a glance at the paper.

"By the airs he takes. Odd's life! if we 'd had the Duke of Cumberland aboard, he'd not have carried himself the stiffer. From the day we shipped him, not so much as a word has he passed with one of us, save to threat Mr. Higgins' life, when he knocked him down with a belaying pin for his da—for his impertinence. And he nothing but an indentured servant not able to write his name and like as not with a sheriff at his heels." The captain's sudden volubility could mean either dislike or mere curiosity.

"Dost think he's of the wrong colour?" asked the merchant, looking with more interest at the covenant.

"'T is the dev — 't is beyond me to say what he is. A good man at the ropes, but a da — a Dutchman for company. 'Twixt he and the bog-trotters we shipped at Cork Harbour 't was the dev — 't was the scuttiest lot I ever took aboard ship." The rum was getting into the captain's tongue, and making his usual vocabulary difficult to keep under.

"Have ye no artisans among the Irish?"

"Not so much as one who knows the differ between his two hands."

"'T is too bad of Gorman not to pick better," growled the merchant. "There's a great demand for Western settlers, and Mr. Lambert Meredith writes me to pick him up a good man at horses and gardening, without stinting the price. 'T would be something to me to oblige him."

"'T is a parcel of raw teagues except for the Bristol man."

"And ye think he's of the light-fingered gentry?"

"As for that," said the captain, "I know nothing about him. But he came to your factor and wanted to take the first ship that cleared, and seemed in such a mortal pother that Mr. Horsley suspicioned something, and gave me a slant to look out for him. And all the time we lay off Bristol, my fine fellow kept himself well out of sight."

"Come," said the merchant, rising, "we'll have a look at him. Mr. Meredith is not a man to be disappointed if it can be avoided."

Once on deck the captain led the way to the forepart of the ship, where, standing by himself, and, like the other emigrants, looking over the rail, but, unlike them, looking not at the city, but at the water, stood a fellow of a little over medium height, with broad shoulders and a well-shaped back, despite the ill form his ragged coat tried to give it. At a slap on the shoulder he turned about, showing to the merchant a ruddy, sea-tanned skin, light brown hair, gray eyes, and a chin and mouth hidden by a two months' beard, still too bristly to give him other than an unkempt, boorish look.

"Here's the rogue," announced the captain, with a suggestion of challenge in the speech, as if he would like to have the epithet resented. But the man only regarded the officer with steady, inexpressive eyes.

"Now, my good fellow," asked the merchant, "to what kind of work have ye been bred?"

The steady gray eyes were turned deliberately from the captain until the questioner was within their vision. Then, after a moment's scrutiny of his face, they were slowly dropped so as to take in the merchant from head to foot. Finally they came back to the face again, and once more studied it with intentness, though apparently without the slightest interest.

"Come," said the merchant a little heatedly, and flushing at the man's coolness. "Answer me. Are ye used to horses and gardening?"

As if he had not heard the question, the man turned, and resumed his staring at the water.

"None of your damned impertinence!" roared the captain, catching up the free part of a halyard coiled on the deck, "or I'll give you a taste of the rope's end."

The young fellow faced about in sudden passion, which strangely altered him. "Strike me at your peril!" he challenged, his arm drawn back, and fist clinched for a blow.

"None but a jail-bird would be so afraid of telling about himself," cried the captain, though ceasing to threaten. "The best thing you can do will be to turn the cursed son of a sea cook over to the authorities, Mr. Cauldwell."

"Look ye, my man," warned the merchant, "ye only bring suspicion on yourself by such conduct, and ye know best how far ye want to have your past searched into —"

The man interrupted the merchant.

"Ar bain't much usen to gardening, but ar knows —" he hesitated for a moment and then went on, "but ar bai willin' to work."

"Ay," bawled the captain. "Fear of the courts has made him find his tongue."

"Well," remarked the merchant, "'t is not for my interest to look too closely at a man I have for sale." Then, as he walked away with the captain, he continued: "Many a convict or fugitive has come to the straightabout out here, but hang me if I like his looks or his manner. However, Mr. Meredith knows the pot-luck of redemptioners as well as I, and he can say nay if he chooses." He stopped and eyed the group of emigrants sourly, saying, "I 'll let Gorman hear what I think of his shipment. He knows I don't want mere bog cattle."

"'T is a poor consignment that can't be bettered in the advertisement," comforted the captain, and apparently he spoke truly, for in the "Pennsylvania Gazette" of September 7th appeared the following: —

"*Just arrived on board the brig 'Boscawen,' Alexander Caine, Master from Ireland, a number of likely, healthy, men and women Servants; among whom are Taylors, Barbers, Joiners, Weavers, Shoemakers, Sewers, Labourers, etc., etc., whose indentures are to be disposed of by Cauldwell & Wilson, or the master on board the Vessel off Market Street Wharff— Said Cauldwell & Wilson will give the highest prices for good Pot-Ashes and Bees-Wax.*"

III

MISS MEREDITH DISCOVERS A VILLAIN

BREAKFAST at Greenwood was a pleasant meal at a pleasant hour. For some time previous to it, the family were up and doing, Mr. Meredith riding over his farm directing his labourers, Mrs. Meredith giving a like supervision to her housekeeping, and Janice, attired in a wash dress well covered by a vast apron, with the aid of her guest, making the beds, tidying the parlour, and not unlikely mixing cake or some dessert in the kitchen. Before the meal, Mr. Meredith replaced his rough riding coat by one of broadcloth, with lace ruffles, while the working gowns of the ladies were discarded for others of silk, made, in the parlance of the time, "sack" fashion, or without waist, and termed "an elegant *négligée*," — this word being applied to any frock without lacing strings.

Thus clothed, they gathered at seven o'clock in the pleasant, low-ceiled dining-room whose French windows, facing westward, gave glimpses of the Raritan, over fields of stubble and corn-stacks, broken by patches of timber and orchard. On the table stood a tea service of silver, slender in outline, and curiously light in weight, though generous in capacity. Otherwise, a silver tankard for beer, standing at Mr. Meredith's place beside a stone jug filled with home brew, balanced by another jug filled with buttermilk, was all that tended to decoration, the knives and forks being of steel, and the china simplicity itself. For the edibles, a couple of smoked herring, a comb of honey, and a bunch of water-cress, re-enforced after the family had taken their seats by a form of smoking cornbread, was the simple fare set forth. But the early rising, and two hours of work, brought hunger to the table which required nothing more elaborate as a fillip to tempt the appetite.

While the family still lingered over the meal one warm

September morning, as if loth to make further exertion in the growing heat, the sound of a knocker was heard, and a moment later the coloured maid returned and announced: —

"Marse Hennion want see Marse Meredith."

"Bring him in here, Peg," said Mr. Meredith. "Like as not the lad 's not breakfasted."

Janice hunched her shoulders and remarked, "Never fear that Master Hennion is not hungry. He is like the roaring lion, who 'walketh about seeking whom he may devour.'"

"Black shame on thee, Janice Meredith, for applying the Holy Word to carnal things," cried her mother.

"Then let me read novels," muttered Miss Meredith, but so indistinctly as not to be understood.

"Be still, child!" commanded her mother.

"And listen to Philemon glub-glub-bing over his victuals?"

"Philemon is no pig," declared Mrs. Meredith.

"No," assented Janice. "He 's too old for that," — a remark which set Mr. Meredith off into an uproarious haw-haw.

"Lambert," protested his wife, "I lose patience with thee for encouraging this stiff-necked and wayward girl, when she should be thankful that Providence has made one man who wants so saucy a Miss Prat-a-pace for a wife."

Miss Meredith, evidently encouraged by her father's humour, made a mouth, and droned in a sing-song voice: "'What doth every sin deserve? Every sin deserveth God's wrath and curse, both in this life and that which is to come.'" Such a desecration of the Westminster Assembly of Divines' "Shorter Catechism" would doubtless have produced further and severer reproof from Mrs. Meredith, but the censure was prevented by the clump of heavy boots, followed by the entrance of an over-tall, loosely-built fellow of about eighteen years, whose clothes rather hung about than fitted him.

"Your servant, marms," was his greeting, as he struggled to make a bow. "Your servant, squire. Mr. Hitchins, down ter Trenton, where I went yestere'en with a bale of shearings, asked me ter come araound your way with a letter an' a bond-servant that come ter him on a hay-sloop from Philadelphia. So — "

"Having nothing better to do, you came?" interrupted Janice, with a gravely courteous manner.

"That 's it, Miss Janice; I 'm obleeged ter you for sayin' it better nor I could," said the young fellow, gratefully, while manifestly straining to get a letter from his pocket.

"Hast breakfasted, Phil?" asked the squire.

Producing the letter with terrible effort, and handing it to Mr. Meredith, Hennion began, "As for that —"

Here Janice interrupted by saying, "You breakfasted in Trenton — what a pity!"

"Janice!" snapped her mother, warningly. "Cease thy clack and set a chair for Philemon this instant."

That individual tried to help the girl, but he was not quick enough, except to get awkwardly in the way, and bring his shins in sharp contact with the edge of the chair. Uttering an exclamation of pain, he dropped his hat, — a proceeding which set the two girls off into ill-suppressed giggles. But finally, relieved of his tormenting head-gear, he was safely seated, and Janice set the dishes in front of him, from all of which he helped himself liberally. Meanwhile, the squire broke the seal of the letter and began to read it.

"Wilt have tea or home brew?" asked Mrs. Meredith.

"Beer for me, marm, thank you. An' I think it only kindly ter say I 've hearn talk concernin' your tea drinkin'."

"Let 'em talk," muttered the squire, angrily, looking up from the letter. "'T is nothing to me."

"But Joe Bagby says there 's a scheme ter git the committee of Brunswick township ter take it up."

"Not they," fumed Mr. Meredith. "'T is one thing to write anonymous letters, but quite another matter to stand up and be counted. As for that scamp Joe —"

"Anonymous letters?" questioned Philemon.

"Ay," sputtered the squire, taking from his pocket a paper which he at once crushed into a ball, and then as promptly smoothed out again as a preliminary to handing it to the youth. With difficulty, for the writing was bad, and the paper old and dirty, Philemon read out the following: —

MISTER MURIDITH, —

Noing that agenst the centyments of younited Amurika you still kontinyou to youse tea, thairfor, this is to worn you that

we konsider you as an enemy of our kuntry, and if the same praktises are kontinyoud, you will shortly receeve a visit from the kommitty of TAR AND FETHERS,
Brunswick Township.

"The villains!" cried Janice, flushing. "Who can have dared to send it?"

"One of my tenants, like as not," snapped the squire.

"They 'd never dare," asserted Janice.

"Dare!" cried the squire. "What daring does it take to write unsigned threats and nail 'em at night on a door? They get more lawless every day, with their committees and town meetings and mobs. 'T is next to impossible to make 'em pay their rents now, and to hear 'em talk ye 'd conclude that they owned their farms and could not be turned off. A pretty state of things when a man with twenty thousand acres under lease-holds has to beg for his rentals, and then does n't get 'em."

"You 'd find it easier ter git your rents, squire, if you only sided more with folks, an' wa'n't so stiff," suggested the youth. "A little yieldin' now an' then —"

"Never!" roared Mr. Meredith. "I 'll have no Committee of Correspondence, nor Sons of Liberty, nor Town Meeting telling me what I may do or not do at Greenwood, any more than I let the ragtag and bobtail tell me what I was to buy in '69. Till I say nay, tea is drunk at Greenwood," and the squire's fist came down on the table with a bang.

"Folks say that Congress will shut up the ports," said the young man.

"Ay. And British frigates will open 'em. The people are mad, sir, Bedlam mad, with the idea of liberty, as they call it. Liberty, indeed! when they try to say what a man shall do in his own house; what he shall eat; what he shall wear. And this Congress! We, A and B, elect C to say what the rest of the alphabet shall do, under penalty of tar and feathers, burned ricks, or — don't talk to me, sir, of a Congress. 'T is but an attempt of the mobility to override the nobility of this land, sir." Once again the plates rattled on the table from the squire's fist, and it became evident that if Miss Meredith had a temper it came by inheritance.

"Now, Lambert," interposed his wife, "stop banging the table and getting hot about nothing. Remember how thee hadst the colonies ruined in Stamp Act times, and again during the Association, and it all went over, just as this will. Pour thy father another tankard of small beer, Janice."

Clearly, what the Committee of Correspondence, and even the approaching Congress could not do, Mrs. Meredith could, for the squire settled back quietly into his chair, took a long swallow of beer, and resumed his letter.

"What does Mr. Cauldwell say, dadda?" inquired the daughter.

"Hmm," said Mr. Meredith. "That he sends me the likeliest one from his last shipment. What sort of fellow is he, Phil?"

Hennion paused to swallow an over-large mouthful, which almost produced a choking fit, before he could reply. "He han't a civil word about him, squire — a regular sullen dog."

"Cauldwell writes guardedly, saying it was the best he could do. Where d' ye leave him, lad?"

"Outside, in my waggon."

"Peg, bid him to come in. We'll have a look at —" Mr. Meredith consulted the covenant enclosed and read, "Charles Fownes, heigh?"

A moment later, preceded by the maid, Fownes entered. He took a quick, almost furtive, survey of the room, then glanced in succession at each of those seated about the table, till his eyes rested on Janice. There they fixed themselves in a bold, unconcealed scrutiny, to the no small embarrassment of the maiden, though the man himself stood in an easy, unconstrained attitude, quite unheeding the five pairs of eyes staring at him, or, if conscious, entirely unembarrassed by them.

"Well, Charles, Mr. Cauldwell writes me that ye don't know much about horses or gardening, but he thinks ye have parts and can pick it up quickly."

Still keeping his eyes on Miss Meredith, Fownes nodded his head, with a short, quick jerk, far from respectful.

"But he also says ye are a surly, hot-tempered fellow, who may need a touch of a whip now and again."

Without turning his head, a second time the man gave a jerk

of it, conveying an idea of assent, but it was the assent of contempt far more than of accord.

"Come, come," ordered the squire, testily. "Let 's have a sound of your tongue. Is Mr. Cauldwell right?"

Still looking at Miss Meredith, the man shrugged his shoulders, and replied, "Bain't vor the loikes of ar to zay Mister Cauldwell bai a liar." Yet the voice and manner left little doubt in the hearers as to the speaker's private opinion, and Janice laughed, partly at the implication, but more in nervousness.

"What kind of work are ye used to?" asked Mr. Meredith.

The man hesitated for a moment and then muttered crossly, "Ar indentured vor to work, not to bai questioned."

"Then work ye shall have," cried the squire, hotly. "Peg, show him the stable, and tell Tom —"

"One moment, Lambert," interjected his wife, and then she asked, "Hast thou had breakfast, Charles?"

Fownes shook his head sullenly.

"Take him to the kitchen and give him some at once, Peg," ordered Mrs. Meredith.

For the first time the fellow looked away from Janice, fixing his eyes on Mrs. Meredith. Then he bowed easily and gracefully, saying, "Thank you." Apparently unconscious that for a moment he had left the Somerset burr off his tongue and the rustic pretence from his manner, he followed Peg to the kitchen.

If he were unconscious of the slip, it was more than were his auditors, and for a moment they all exchanged glances in silent bewilderment.

"Humph!" finally growled the squire. "I like the look of him still less."

"He holds himself like a gentleman," asserted Tabitha.

"This fellow will need close watching," predicted Mr. Meredith. "He 's no yokel. He moves like a gentleman or a house-servant. Yet he had to make his mark on the covenant."

"I think, dadda," said Miss Meredith, in her most calmly judicial manner, "that the new man is a born villain, and has committed some terrible crime. He has a horrid, wicked face, and he stares just as — as — so that one wants to shiver."

Mrs. Meredith rose. "Janice," she chided, "thou 't too young to make thy opinions of the slightest value. Go to thy spinet, child, and don't let me hear any more such foolish babble. Charles has a good face, and will make a good servant."

"I don't care what mommy thinks," Miss Meredith confided to Tabitha in the parlour, as the one took her seat at an embroidery frame and the other at the spinet. "I know he 's a bad man, and will end by killing one of us and stealing the silver and a horse, just as Mr. Vreeland's bond-servant did. He makes me think of the villain in 'The Tragic History of Sir Watkins Stokes and Lady Betty Artless.' "

IV

AN APPLE OF DISCORD

IN the week following his advent the new servant was the cause of considerable discussion, and, regrettably, of not a little controversy, among the members of the household of Greenwood. The squire maintained that "the fellow is a bad-tempered, lazy, deceitful rogue, in need of much watching." Mrs. Meredith, on the contrary, invariably praised the man, and promptly suppressed her husband whenever he began to rail against him. To Janice, with the violent prejudices of youth still unmodified by experience and reason, Charles was almost a special deputy of the individual she heard so unmercifully thrashed to tatters each Sunday by the Rev. Mr. McClave. And again, to the contrary, Tabitha insisted with growing fervour that the servant was a gentleman, possessed of all the qualities that word implied, plus the most desirable attribute of all others to eighteenth-century maidens, a romantic possibility.

As a matter of fact, these diverse and contradictory views had a crossing-point, and accepting this as their mean, Charles proved himself to be a knowing man with horses, an entirely ignorant and by no means eager labourer in the little farm work there was to do, a silent though easily angered being with every one save Mrs. Meredith, and so clearly above his station that he was viewed with disfavour, tinctured by not a little fear, by house-servants, by field hands, and even by Mr. Meredith's overseer.

For the most part, Fownes spoke in the West of England dialect; but whenever he became interested, this instantly slipped from him, as did his still more ineffective attempt to move and act the rustic. Indeed, the ease of his movements and the straightness of his carriage, with a certain indefinable precision of manner, led to a common agreement among his fellow-labourers that he had earlier in life accepted the king's shilling. Granting him to be but one and twenty years of age, as his covenant stated, and as in fact he looked, his service must have been shorter than the act of Parliament allowed, and this seeming bar to their hypothesis caused many winks and shrugs over the tankards of ale consumed of an evening at the King George tavern in the village of Brunswick. Furthermore, for some months the deserter columns of such stray numbers of the "London Gazette" as occasionally drifted to the ordinary were eagerly scanned by the loungers, on the possibility that they might contain some advertisement of a fellow standing five feet ten, with broad shoulders, light brown hair, straight nose, and gray eyes, whose whereabout was of interest to His Majesty's War Office, Whitehall. Neither from this source, however, nor from any other, did they gain the slightest clue to the past history of the bond-servant, spy upon the fellow who would.

Nor was talk of the man limited to farm hands and tavern idlers, for dearth of new topics in the little community made him a subject of converse to the two girls during the hours of spinet practice, embroidery, and sewing, which were their daily occupations between breakfast and dinner, and, even extended into the afternoon, if the stint was not completed. Yet all their discussion brought them no nearer to agreement, Janice maintaining that Fownes was a villain *in posse*, if not *in esse*, while Tabitha contended that Charles had been disappointed in a love which he still, none the less, cherished, and which to her mind accounted in every particular for his conduct. As such a theory allowed considerable scope to the imagination, she promptly created several romances about him, in all of which he was of noble birth, with such other desirable factors as made him a true hero; and having thus endowed him with a halo of romance, she could not find words strong enough to express her thorough-going contempt for the woman whose disregard and cruelty had driven him across the seas.

"Thee knows, Janice," she argued, when the latter expressed scepticism, "that the Earl of Anglesey was kidnapped, and sold in Maryland, so it 's perfectly possible for a nobleman to be a bond-servant."

"That 's the one case," answered Janice, sagely.

"But things like it are very common in novels," insisted Tabitha. "And what is more likely for a man disappointed in love than, in desperation, to indenture himself?"

"I can easily credit a female of taste — yes, any female — refusing the ill-mannered, bold-staring rogue," said Janice, giving the coarse osnaburg shirt she was working upon a fretted jerk; "but to suppose him to be capable of a grand, devoted passion is as bad as expecting — expecting faithfulness in a dog like Clarion."

"Clarion?" questioned Tabitha.

"Yes. Have n't you seen how — how — that he — the man, has taken possession of him? Thomas says the two sneak off together every chance they get, and sometimes are n't back till eleven or twelve. I wish dadda would put a stop to it. Like as not, 't is for pilfering they are bound." Miss Meredith began anew on the buttonhole, and had she been thrusting her needle into either man or dog, she could not have sewed with a more vicious vigour.

"That must be the way he got those rabbits for thy mother."

"I should know he had been a poacher," asserted Janice, as she contemptuously held up and surveyed at arms-length the completed shirt. Then she laid it aside with another, and sighed a weary, "Heigh-ho, those are done. Here I have to work my fingers to the bone making shirts for him, just because mommy says he has n't enough clothes," — a sentence which perhaps partly accounted for the maiden's somewhat jaundiced view of Charles.

"Are those for him?" cried Tabitha. "Why didst thou not tell me? I would have helped thee with them."

"You 'd have been welcome to the whole job. As it is, I 've done them so carelessly that I know mommy will scold me. But I was n't going to work myself to death for him!"

"I should have loved — I like shirt-making," fibbed Tabitha.

"And I hate it! Forty-two have I made this year, and mommy has six more cut out."

There was a moment's silence, and then Tabitha said, "Janice." For some reason the name seemed to embarrass her, for the moment it was spoken she coloured.

"What?"

"Dost thee not think — perhaps — if we steal out and take the shirts to the stable, thy mother will never — ?"

"Tibbie Drinker! Go out of the house in a sack? I'd as soon go out in my night-rail."

"Thee breakfasts in a *négligée*, even when Philemon is here," retorted Miss Drinker. "Wouldst as lief breakfast in thy shift?"

"No," said Miss Janice, with a wicked sparkle in her eyes, "because if I did Philemon would come oftener than ever."

"Fie upon thee, Janice Meredith!" cried her friend, "for a froward, indelicate female."

"And why more indelicate than the men who'd come?" demanded Janice.

> "'Immodest words admit of no defence,
> For want of modesty is want of sense,'"

quoted Miss Drinker.

"Rubbish!" scoffed Janice, but whether she was referring to the stanza of the reigning poet of the eighteenth century, or simply to Miss Tabitha's application of it, cannot be definitely known. "You know as well as I, Tibbie, that I'd rather have Philemon, or any other man, see me in my shroud than in my rail. Come, we'll change our frocks and take a walk."

A half hour later, newly clothed in light dimity gowns, cut short for walking, and which, in combination with slippers, then the invariable footgear of ladies of quality, served to display the "neatly turned ankles" that the beaux of the period so greatly admired, the girls sallied forth. First a visit was paid to the stable, to smuggle the shirts from the criticism of Mrs. Meredith, as well as to entice Clarion's companionship for the walk. But Thomas, with a grumble, told them that Fownes had stolen away from the job that had been set for him after dinner, and that the hound had gone with him.

Their rambling walk brought the girls presently to the river, but just as they were about to force their way through the fringe of willows and underbrush which hid the water from view, a sudden loud splashing, telling of some one in swimming, gave them pause. Yelps of excitement from Clarion a moment later served to tell the two who it probably was, and the probability was instantly confirmed by the voice of Charles, saying:

"'T is sport, old man, is 't not? To get the dirt and transpiration off one! 'S death! What a climate! 'Twixt the sun and osnaburg and fustian my skin feels as if I 'd been triced up and had a round hundred."

Exchanging glances, the girls stole softly away from the bank, neither venturing to speak till out of hearing. As they retired they came upon a heap of coarse garments, and Tabitha, catching the arm of her friend, exclaimed: —

"Oh, Jan, look!"

What had caught her eye was the end of a light gold chain that appeared among the clothes, and both girls halted and gazed at it as if it possessed some quality of fascination. Then Tabitha tip-toed forward, with but too obvious a purpose.

"Tibbie!" rebuked Janice, "you should n't!"

"Oh, but Jan!" protested Eve, junior. "'T is such a chance!"

"Not for me," asserted Miss Meredith, proudly virtuous, as she walked on.

If Miss Drinker had searched for a twelve-month she could scarce have found a more provoking remark than her spontaneous exclamation, "Oh! how beautiful she is!"

Janice halted, though she had the moral stamina not to turn.

"What? The chain?" she asked.

"No! The miniature," responded her interlocutor, in a tone expressing the most unbounded admiration and delight. "Such an elegant creature, Jan, and such —"

Her speech ended there, as a crashing in the bushes alarmed her, and she darted past Janice, who, infected by the guilt of her companion, likewise broke into a run, which neither ceased till they had covered a goodly distance. Then Tabitha, for want of breath, came to a stop, and allowed her friend to overtake her.

She held up the chain and miniature in her hand. "What shall I do?" she panted.

"Tibbie, how could you?" ejaculated her horrified friend.

"His coming frighted me so that — oh, I did n't drop it!"

"You must take it back!"

"I'd never dare!"

"Black shame on —!"

"A nice creature, thou, Jan!" interrupted Miss Drinker, with a sudden carrying of the war into the enemy's camp. "To tell me to go back when he's sure to be dressing! No wonder thee makes indelicate speeches."

Miss Meredith, without deigning to reply to this shameful implication, walked away toward the house.

That Tibbie intended to shirk the consequences of her misdemeanour was only too clearly proved to Janice, when later she went to her room to prink for supper, for lying on her dressing stand was the miniature. Shocked as Miss Meredith was at the sight, she lifted and examined the trinket.

Bred in colonial simplicity, it seemed to the maid that she had never seen anything quite so exquisite. A gold case, richly set with brilliants, encompassed the portrait of a girl of very positive beauty. After a rapt dwelling on the portrait for some minutes, further examination revealed the letters W. H. J. B. interlaced on the back.

Taking the miniature when her toilet had been perfected, Janice descended to the parlour. As she entered, Tabitha, already there, jumped up from a chair, in which, a moment previous she had been carrying on a brown study that apparently was not enjoyable, and tripped nonchalantly across the room to the spinet. Seating herself, she struck the keys, and broke out into a song entitled, "Taste Life's Glad Moments as They Glide."

Not in the least deflected from her intention, Miss Meredith marched up to the culprit, the bondsman's property in her hand, and demanded, "Dost intend to turn thief?"

"Prithee, who's curious now?" evaded Tibbie. "I knew thee'd look at it, for all thy airs."

"Very well, miss," threatened Janice, with much dignity. "Then I shall take it to him, and narrate to him all the circumstances."

"Tattle-tale, tattle-tale!" retorted Tabitha, scornfully.

With even greater scorn her friend turned her back, and leaving the house, walked toward the stable. This took her through the old-fashioned, hedge-begirt kitchen garden, in which flowers were grown as if they were vegetables, and vegetables were grown as if they were flowers. The moment Janice had passed within the tall row of box, her expression of mingled haughtiness and determination ended; she came to a sudden halt, said "Oh!" and then pretended to be greatly interested in a butterfly. The bravest army can be stampeded by a surprise, and after having screwed up her spirit to the point of facing Fownes in his fortress, the stable, Miss Meredith's courage deserted her on almost stumbling over him a hundred yards nearer than she expected. So taken aback was she that all the glib explanation she had planned was forgotten, and she held out the miniature to him without a single word.

Charles had been walking to the house, and only paused at meeting Miss Meredith. He glanced at the outstretched hand, and then let his eyes come back to the girl's face, without making the slightest motion to take his property.

Tongue-tied and doubly embarrassed by his calm scrutiny, the young lady stood with flushed cheeks, and with long black lashes dropped to hide a pair of very shamed eyes, the personification, in appearance, of guilt.

Whether the girl would have found her tongue, or would have ended the incident as she was longing to do by taking to her heels, it is impossible to say. Ere she had time to do either, the angry voice of the squire broke in upon them.

"Ho, there ye are! Twice have I looked for ye this afternoon, and I warn ye I'm not the man to take such conduct from any one, least of all from one of my own servants," he said as he came toward the pair, the emphasis of his walking stick and his heels both telling the story of his anger. "What mean ye, fellow," he continued, "by neglecting the work I set ye?"

Absolutely unmoved by the reproof, Charles stood as heedless of it as he had been of the outstretched hand of the daughter, a hand which had promptly disappeared in the folds of Miss Meredith's skirt at the first sound of her father's voice.

"A taste of my walking stick ye should have if ye had your deserts!" went on the squire, now face to face with the servant.

Without taking his eyes from the girl, Charles laughed. "Is it fear of me," he challenged, "or fear of the law that prevents you?"

"What know ye of the law, sirrah?" demanded Mr. Meredith.

"Nothing, when I was fool enough to indenture myself," snapped the servant; "but Bagby tells me that 't is forbidden, under penalty of fine, for a master to strike a servant."

"Joe Bagby!" roared the squire, more angry than ever. "And how come ye to have anything to do with that scampy lawyer! Hast been up to some mischief already?"

Again the man laughed. "That is for His Majesty's Justices of the Peace to discover. Till they do, I shall maintain that I consulted him concerning the laws governing bond-servants."

"A pretty state the country 's come to!" raged the squire. "No wonder there is no governing the land, when even servants think to have the law against their masters. But, harkee, my fine fellow. If I may not punish ye myself, the Justices may order ye whipped, and unless ye change your manners I will have ye up before their next sitting. Meantime, saddle Joggles as soon as supper is done, and take this paper over to Brunswick, and post it on the proclamation board of the Town Hall. And no tarrying, and consulting of tricky lawyers, understand. If ye are not back by nine, ye shall hear from me."

Striking a sunflower with his cane as a slight vent to his anger, the master strode away to the house.

His back turned, Janice once again held out the miniature. "Won't you please take it?" she begged.

"Art tired of it already?" jeered the man.

"I did not take it, Charles," she stammered, "but I knew of its taking and so brought it back to you."

The man shrugged his shoulders. "'T is not mine, nor is it aught to me," he said, and passing the girl, walked to the house.

V

THE VALUE OF HAIR

AT the evening meal the farm hands and negro house-servants remarked in Fownes not merely his customary unsocial silence, but an abstraction more obvious than usual. A gird or two from the rougher of his fellow-labourers was wholly unnoted by him, and though he ate heartily, it was with such entire unconsciousness of what he was eating as to make the cook, Sukey, who was inclined to favour him, question if after all he deserved special consideration at her hands.

The meal despatched, Charles took his way to the stable, but some motive caused him to stop at the horse trough, lean over it, and examine the reflection of his face. Evidently what he saw was not gratifying, for he vainly tried to smooth down his short hair, and then passed his hand over the scrub of his beard. "'T is said clothes make the gentleman," he muttered, "but methinks 't is really the barber. How many of the belles of the Pump Room and the Crescent would take me for other than a clodhopper? 'T was not Charles Lor — Charles what? — to whom they curtesied and ogled and smirked, 't was to a becoming wig and a smooth chin." Snapping his fingers contemptuously, he went in and began to saddle the horse.

A half-hour later, the man rode up the village street of Brunswick. Hitching Joggles to a post in front of the King George tavern, he walked to the board on the side of the Town Hall and Court House. Here, over a three months' old proclamation, he posted the anonymous note recently received by the squire, which had been wafered to a sheet of *pro patria* paper, and below which the squire had written: —

This is to give notice that I despise too much the cowardly villain who wrote and nailed this on my door to pay any attention to him. A Reward of two pounds will be given for any information leading to the discovery of said cowardly villain.

LAMBERT MEREDITH.

For a moment the servant stood with a slight smile on his face at the contradiction; then, with a shrug of his shoulders, he entered the public room of the tavern. Within the air was so thick with pipes in full blast, and the light of the two dips was so feeble, that he halted in order to distinguish the dozen figures of the occupants, all of whom gave him instant attention.

"Ar want landlord," he said, after a pause.

"Here I be," responded a man sitting at a small table in the corner, with two half-emptied glasses and a bowl of arrack punch before him. Opposite to mine host was a thick-set man of about forty, attired in a brown suit and heavy top-boots, both of which bore the signs of recent travel.

The servant skirted the group at the large table in the centre of the room, and taking from his pocket a guinea, laid it on the table. "Canst 'e give change for thiccy?" he asked.

"I vum!" cried the landlord, as he picked up the coin and rang it on the table. "'T ain't often we git sight o' goold here. How much do yer want fer it?"

"Why, twenty-one shillings," replied the servant, with some surprise in his voice.

"I 'll givit you dirty-two," spoke up a Jewish-looking man at the big table, hurriedly pulling out his pouch and counting down a batch of very soiled money from it, which he held out to the servant just as the landlord, too, tendered him some equally ragged bills.

"Trust Opper to give a shilling less than its worth," jeered one of the drinkers.

"Bai thiccy money, Bagby?" questioned Charles, looking suspiciously at both tenders.

"Not much," answered Bagby from the group about the large table, not one of whom had missed a word of the foregoing conversation. "'T is shaved beef,"—a joke which called forth not a little laughter from his companions.

"Will it buy a razor?" asked Fownes, quickly, turning to the lawyer with a smile.

"Keep it a week and 't will shave you itself," retorted the joker, and this allusion to the steady depreciation of the colony paper money called forth another laugh.

"Then 't is not blunt?" responded Charles, but no one save the traveller at the small table caught the play on words, the Cockney cant term for money being unfamiliar to American ears. He smiled, and then studied the bond-servant with more interest than he had hitherto shown.

Meanwhile, at the first mention of razor, the Jew had left the room, and he now returned, carrying a great pack, which he placed upon the table.

"Sir," he said, in an accent which proved his appearance did not belie his race, while beginning to unstrap the bundle, "I haf von be-utiful razor, uf der besd —" but here his speech was interrupted by a roar of laughter.

"You 've a sharper to deal with now," laughed the joker, and another called, "Now ye 'll need no razor ter be shaved."

"Chentlemen, chentlemen," protested the peddler, "haf n't I always dealt fair mit you?" He fumbled in his half-opened pack, and shoving three razors out of sight, he produced a fourth, which he held out to the servant. "Dot iss only dree shillings, und it iss der besd of steel."

"You can trust Opper to know pretty much everything 'bout steals," sneered Bagby, who was clearly the local wit. "It 's been his business for twenty years."

"I want a sharp razor, not a razor sharp," said Charles, good-naturedly, while taking the instrument and trying its edge with his finger.

"What business hez a bond-servant tew spend money fer a razor?" demanded the tavern-keeper, for nothing then so marked the distinction between the well-bred and the unbred as the smooth faces of the one and the hairy faces of the other.

"Has n't he a throat to cut?" demanded one of the group, "an' has n't a covenant man reason to cut it?"

"More likes he 's goin' a sparkin'," suggested one of the idlers. "The gal up ter the squire's holds herself pooty high an' mighty, but like as not she 's as plaguey fond of bundling with a good-looking man on the sly as most wenches."

"If she 's set on that, I 'm her man," remarked Bagby.

"Bundling?" questioned the covenant servant. "What 's that?"

The question only produced a roar of laughter at his ignorance, during which the traveller turned to the publican and asked: —

"Who is this hind?"

"'T is a new bond-servant o' Squire Meredith's, who I hearn is no smouch on horses. Folks think he 's a bloody-back who 's took French leave."

"A deserter, heigh?" said the traveller, once more looking at the man, who was now exchanging with the peddler the three-shilling note for the razor. He waited till the trade had been consummated, and then suddenly said aloud, in a sharp, decisive way, "Attention! To the left — dress!"

Fownes' body suddenly stiffened itself, his hands dropped to his sides, and his head turned quickly to the left. For a second he held this position, then as suddenly relaxing himself, he turned and eyed the giver of the order.

"So ho! my man. It seems ye have carried Brown Bess," said the traveller, giving the slang term for the musket.

Flushed in face, Fownes wheeled on the man hotly, while the whole room waited his reply in silence. "Thou liest!" he asserted.

"Thou varlet!" cried the man so insulted, flushing in turn, as he sprang to his feet and caught up from the table a heavy riding-whip.

As he did so, the bond-servant's right hand went to his hip, as if instinctively seeking something there. The traveller's eyes followed the impulsive gesture, even while he, too, made a motion more instinctive than conscious, by stepping backward, as if to avoid something. This motion he checked, and said: —

"No. Bond-servants don't wear bayonets."

Again the colour sprang to Fownes' face, and his lips parted as if an angry retort were ready. But instead of uttering it, he turned and started to leave the room.

"Ay," cried the traveller, "run, while there 's time, deserter."

Fownes faced about in the doorway, with a smile on his face not pleasant to see, it was at once so contemptuous and so lowering. Yet when he spoke there was an amused, almost merry note in his voice, as if he were enjoying something.

"Ar bain't no more deserter than thou baist spy," he retorted, as he left the tavern and went to where his horse was tethered. Unfastening him, he stood for a moment stroking the animal's nose.

"Joggles," he confided, "I fear, despite the praise the fair ones gave of my impersonation of 'The Fashionable Lover,' that I am not so good an actor as either Garrick or Barry. I forget, and I lose my temper. So, a bond-servant should cut his throat," he continued, as he swung lightly into the saddle. "I fear 't is the only way I can go undiscovered. Fool that I was to do it in a moment of passion. Five years of slavery!" Then he laughed. "But then I 'd never have seen her! Egad, if she could be painted as she looked to-day by Reynolds or Gainsborough, 'twould set more than my blood glowing! There 's a prize, Joggles! Beauty, wealth, and freedom, all in one. She 'd be worth a tilt, too, if for nothing but the sport of it. We 'll shave, make a dandy of ourselves, old man —" Then the servant paused — "and, like a fool, be recognised by some fellow like Clowes — what does he here? — but for my beard, and that he'd scarce expect to meet Charles —" Fownes checked himself, scowling. "Charles Nothing, a poor son of a gun of a bond-servant. Have done with such idiot schemes, man," he admonished. "For what did you run, if 't was not to bury yourself? And now you 'd risk all for a petticoat." Taking from his pocket the razor, he threw it into the bushes that lined the road, saying as he did so, "Good-by, gentility."

VI

MEN ARE DECEIVERS EVER

THE departure of the bond-servant, leaving the sting of innuendo behind him, had turned all eyes toward the traveller, and Bagby but voiced the curiosity of the roomful when he inquired, "What did Fownes call you spy for?"

"Nay, man, he called me not that," denied the stranger, "unless he meant to call himself a deserter as well. Landlord, a bowl of swizzle for the company! Gentlemen, I am Lincolnshire born and bred. My name is John Evatt, and I am travelling through the country to find a likely settling place for six solid farmers, of whom I am one. Whom did you say was yon rogue's master?"

"Squire Meredith," informed mine host, now occupied in combining the rum, spruce beer, and sugar at the large table.

"And what sort of man is he?" asked Evatt, bringing his glass from the small table and taking his seat among the rest.

"He 's as hot-tempered an' high an' mighty as King George hisself," cried one of the drinkers. "But I guess his stinkin' pride will come down a little afore the committee of Brunswick 's through with him."

"Let thy teeth keep better guard over thy red rag, Zerubbabel," rebuked Joe Bagby, warningly. "We want no rattlepates to tell us — or others — what 's needed or doing."

"This Meredith 's a man of property, eh?" asked Evatt.

"He 's been so since he married Patty Byllynge," replied the publican. "Afore then he war n't nothin' but a poor young lawyer over tew Trenton."

"And who was Patty Byllynge?"

"You don't know much 'bout West Jersey, or I guess you 'd have heard of her," surmised Bagby. "'T is n't every girl brings her husband a pot of money and nigh thirty thousand acres of land. Folks tell that before the squire got her, the men was about her like — " the speaker used a simile too coarse for repetition.

"So ho!" said the traveller. "Byllynge, heigh? Now I begin to understand. A daughter — or granddaughter — of one of the patentees?"

"Just so. In the old man's day they held the lands all along this side of the Raritan, nigh up to Baskinridge, but they sold a lot in the forties."

"Then perhaps this is the place to bargain about a bit? The land looked rich and warm as I rode along this afternoon."

"'T ain't no use tryin' ter buy of the new squire," remarked one man. "He won't do nothin' but lease. He don't want no freemen 'bout here."

"Yer might buy o' Squire Hennion. He sells now an' agin," suggested the innkeeper."

"Who's he?" demanded Evatt.

"Another of the monopolisers who got a grant in the early days, before the land was good for anything," explained Bagby. "His property is further down."

"Ye'd better bargain quick, if ye want any," spoke up an oldster. "Looks like squar's son was a-coortin' squar's daughter, an' mayhaps her money 'll make old Squar Hennion less put tew it fer cash."

"So Squire Meredith is n't popular?"

"He 'll find out suthin' next time he offers fer Assembly," asserted one of the group.

"He 's a member of Assembly, is he?" questioned Evatt. "Then he 's all right on — he belongs to the popular party?"

"Not he!" cried several.

"He was agin the Association, tried tew prevent our sendin' deputies tew Congress, an' boasts that tea 's drunk at his table," said the landlord.

"'T won't be for long," growled Bagby.

"Then how comes it that ye elect him Assemblyman?"

"'T is his tenants do it," spoke up the lawyer. "They don't have the pluck to vote against him for fear of their leaseholds. And so 't is with the rest. The only way we can get our way is by conventions and committees. But get it we will, let the gentry try as they please."

"Well, gentlemen," said Evatt, "here 's the swizzle. Glasses around, and I 'll give ye a toast ye can all drink: May your freedom never be lessened by either Parliament or Congress!"

Two hours of drinking and talking followed, and when the last of the tipplers had staggered through the door, and Evatt, assisted by the publican, had reeled rather than walked upstairs to his room, if he was not fully informed as to the locality of which the tavern was the centre, it was because his brain was too fuddled by the mixed drink, and not because tongues had been guarded.

Eighteenth-century heads made light of drinking bouts, and Evatt ate a hearty breakfast the next morning. Thus fortified, he called for his horse, and announced his intention of seeing Squire Meredith "about that damned impertinent varlet."

Arrived at Greenwood, it was to find that the master of the house was away, having ridden to Bound Brook to see some of his more distant tenants; but in colonial times visitors were such infrequent occurrences that he was made welcome by the hostess, and urged to stay to dinner. "Mr. Meredith will be back ere nightfall," she assured him, "and will deeply regret having missed thee if thou rides away."

"Madam," responded Evatt, "American hospitality is only exceeded by American beauty."

It was impossible not to like the stranger, for he was a capital talker, having much of the chat of London, tasty beyond all else to colonial palates, at his tongue's tip. With a succession of descriptions or anecdotes of the frequenters of the Park and Mall, of Vauxhall and Ranelagh, he entertained them at table, the two girls sitting almost open-mouthed in their eagerness and delight.

The meal concluded, the ladies regretfully withdrew, leaving Evatt to enjoy what he chose of a decanter of the squire's best Madeira, which had been served to him, visitors of education being rare treats indeed. Like all young peoples, Americans ducked very low to transatlantic travellers, and, truly colonial, could not help but think an Englishman of necessity a superior kind of being.

The guest filled his glass, unbuttoned the three lower buttons of his waistcoat, and slouched back in his chair. Then he put the wine to his lips, and holding the swallow in his mouth to prolong the enjoyment, a look of extreme contentment came over his visage. And if he had put his thoughts into words, he would have said: —

"By Heavens! What wine and what women! The one they smuggle, but where get they the other? In a rough new country who 'd think to encounter greater beauty and delicacy than can be seen skirting the Serpentine? Such eyes, such a waist, and such a wrist! And those cheeks — how the colour comes and goes, telling everything that she would hide! And to think that some bumpkin will enjoy lips fit for a duke. Burn it! If 't were not for my task, I 'd have a try for Miss Innocence and —" The man glanced out of the window and let his eyes wander over the landscape, while he drained his glass — "Thirty thousand acres of land!" he said aloud, with a smack of pleasure.

His eyes left off studying the fields to fix themselves on Janice, who passed the window, with the garden as an evident destination, and they followed her until she disappeared within the opening of the hedge. "There 's a foot and ankle," he exclaimed with an expression on his face akin to that it had worn as he tasted the Madeira. "'T would fire enough sparks in London to set the Thames all aflame!" He reached for the Madeira once more, but after removing the stopper, he hesitated a moment, then replacing it, he rose, buttoned his waistcoat, and taking his hat from the hall, he slipped through the window and walked toward the garden.

Finding that Janice was not within the hedge-row, Evatt passed across the garden quickly and discovered the young lady standing outside the stable, engaged in the extremely undignified occupation of whistling. Her reason for the action was quickly revealed by the appearance of Clarion; and still unconscious that she was watched, after a word with the dog, they both started toward the river.

A few hasty strides brought the man up with the maiden, and as she slightly turned to see who had joined her, he said, "May I walk with you, Miss Meredith? I intended a stroll about the farm, and it will be all the pleasanter for so fair a guide."

Shyly but eagerly the girl assented, and richly rewarded was she in her own estimate by what the visitor had to tell. More gossip of court, of the lesser world of fashion, and of the theatre, he retailed: how the king walked and looked, of the rivalry between Mrs. Barry and Mrs. Baddeley, of Charles Fox's debts and eloquence, of the vogue of Cecilia Davis, or "L'Inglesina." To Janice, hungry with the true appetite of provincialism, it was all the most delicious of comfits. To talk to a man who could imitate the way the Duke of Gloucester limped at a levee when suffering from the gout, and who was able to introduce a story by saying, "As Lady Rochford once said to me at one of her routs —" was almost like meeting those distinguished beings themselves. Janice not merely failed to note that the man paid no heed whatever to the land they strolled over, but herself ceased to give time or direction the slightest thought.

"Oh!" she broke out finally, in her delight, "won't Tibbie be sorry when she knows what she's missed? And, forsooth, a proper pay out for her wrong-doing it is!"

"What mean ye by that?" questioned Evatt.

"She deserves to have it known, but though she called me tattle-tale, I'm no such thing," replied Janice, who in truth was still hot with indignation at Miss Drinker, and wellnigh bursting to confide her grievance against her whilom friend to this most delightful of men. "Doubtless, you observed that we are not on terms. That was why I came off without her."

Evatt, though not till this moment aware of the fact, nodded his head gravely.

"'T is all her doings, though she'd be glad enough to make it up if I would let her. A fine frenzy her ladyship would be in, too, if she dreamt he'd given me the miniature."

"A miniature!" marvelled the visitor, encouragingly. "Of whom?"

"'T is just what — Oh, I think I'll tell thee the whole tale and get thy advice. I dare not go to mommy, for I know she'd make me give it up, and dadda being away, and Tibbie in a snip-snap, I have no one to — and perhaps — I 'd never tell thee to shame Tibbie, but because I need advice and — "

"A man with half an eye would know you were no talebearer, Miss Janice," her companion assured her.

Thus prompted and enticed, the girl poured out the whole story. "I wish I could show you the picture," she ended. "She is the most beautiful creature I ever saw."

"Hast never looked in a mirror, Miss Janice?"

"Now thou 't just teasing."

"I' faith, 't is the last thought in my mind," said Evatt, heartily.

"You really think me pretty?" questioned the girl, with evident delight if uncertainty.

Evatt studied the eager, guileless face questioningly turned to him, and had much ado to keep from smiling.

"'T is impossible not to think it," he replied.

"Even after seeing the court beauties?" demanded Janice, half doubtful and half joyous.

"Not one but would have to give the *pas* to ye, Miss Janice," protested Evatt, "could ye but be presented at St. James's."

"How lovely!" cried Janice, ecstatically, and then in sudden abasement asserted, "Oh, I know you are — you are only making fun of me!"

"Now, burn me, if I am!" insisted the man, with such undoubted admiration in his manner as to confirm his words to the girl. "By Heaven!" he marvelled to himself. "Who 'd have believed such innocence possible? 'T is Mother Eve before the fall! She knows nothing." A view of woman likely to get Mr. Evatt into trouble. There is very little information concerning the ante-prandial Eve, but from later examples of her sex, it is safe to affirm that the mother of the race knew several things before partaking of the tree of knowledge. Man only is born so stupid as to need education.

"Why canst thou not let me have sight of this wondrous female?" he went on aloud. "Surely thou art not really fearsome to brave comparison."

"'T is not that, indeed," denied Janice, colouring, "but — well — in a moment." The girl turned her back to Mr. Evatt, and in a moment faced him once more, the miniature in her hand. "Is n't she beautiful?"

Evatt looked at the miniature. "That she is," he assented. "And strike me dumb, but she reminds me of some woman I 've once seen in London."

"Oh, how interesting!" exclaimed the girl. "What was her name?"

"'T is exactly that I am asking myself."

"He must be well-born," argued Janice, "to have her miniature; look at the jewels in her hair."

"Ah, my child, there 's more than the well-born wear —" the man stopped short. "How know ye," he went on, "that the bondsman comes by it rightly? The frame is one of price."

"I don't," the girl replied, "and the initials on the back are n't his."

"'W. H. J. B.,'" read Evatt.

"He may have changed his name," suggested Janice.

"True," assented the man, with a slight laugh; "that 's a mighty clever thought and gives us a clue to his real one."

"Perhaps you 've heard of a man in London with a name to fit W. H. J. B.?" said the maid, inquiringly.

Evatt turned away to conceal an unsuppressable smile, while thinking, "The innocent imagines London but another Brunswick!"

"Dost think I should make him take it back?" asked Janice.

"Certainly not," replied her adviser, responding to the only too manifest wish of the girl.

"Then dost think I should speak to mommy or dadda?"

"'T is surely needless! The fellow refuses it, and so 't is yours till he demands it."

"How lovely! Oh, I 'd like to be home this instant, to see how 't would appear about my neck. Last night I crept out of bed to have a look, but Tibbie turned over, and I thought me she was waking. I think I 'll go at once and —"

"And end our walk?" broke in Evatt, reproachfully.

"'T is nearly tea-time," replied Janice, pointing to the sun. "How the afternoon has flown!"

"Thanks to my charming companion," responded the man, bowing low.

"Now you are teasing again," cried Janice. "I don't like to be made fun —"

"'Tis my last thought," cried Evatt, with unquestionable earnestness, and possessing himself of Janice's hand, he stooped and kissed it impetuously and hotly.

The colour flooded up into the maiden's face and neck at the action, but still more embarrassing to her was the awkward pause which ensued, as they set out on their return. She could think of nothing to say, and the stranger would not help her. "Let her blush and falter and stammer," was his thought. "Every minute of embarrassment is putting me deeper in her thoughts."

VII

SPIDER AND FLY

FORTUNATELY for the girl, the distance to the house was not great, and the rapid pace she set in her stress quickly brought them to the doorway, which she entered with a sigh of relief. The guest was at once absorbed by her father, and Janice sought her room.

As she primped, the miniature lay before her, and occasionally she paused for a moment to look at it. Finally, when properly robed, she picked it up and held it for a moment. "I wonder if she broke his heart?" she soliloquised. "I don't see how he could help loving her; I know I should." Janice hesitated for a moment, and then tucked the miniature into her bosom. "If only Tibbie was n't — if — we could talk about it," she sighed, as she pinned on her little cap of lace above the hair dressed high *à la Pompadour*. "Why did she have to be — just as so many important things were to happen!" Miss Meredith looked at her double in the mirror, and sighed again. "Mr. Evatt must have been laughing at me," she said, "for she is so much prettier. But I should like to know why Charles always stares so at me."

In the meantime, Evatt, without so much as an allusion to the bond-servant, had presented a letter from a New Yorker, introducing him to the squire, and by the confidence thus established he proceeded to question Mr. Meredith long and carefully, not about farming lands and profits, but concerning the feeling of the country toward the questions then at issue between Great Britain and America. He made as they talked an occasional note, and the interview ended only with Peg's announcement of supper. Nor was this allowed to terminate the inquiry, for the squire, as Mrs. Meredith had foreseen, insisted on Evatt's spending the night, and Charles was accordingly ordered to ride over to the inn for the traveller's saddlebags. After the ladies had left the two men at the table, the questioning was resumed over the spirits and pipes, and not till ten o'clock was passed did Evatt finally rise. Clearly he must have pleased the squire as well as he had the dames, for Mr. Meredith, with the hospitality of the time, pressed him heartily to stay for more than the morrow, assuring him of a welcome at Greenwood for as long as he would make it his abiding spot.

"Nothing, sir, would give me greater pleasure," responded Evatt, warmly, "but in confidence to ye, as a friend of government, I dare to say that my search for a farm is only the ostensible reason for my travels. I am executing an important and delicate mission for our government, and having already journeyed through the colonies to the northward, I must still travel through those of the south. 'T is therefore quite impossible for me to tarry more than the night. I should, in fact, not have dared to linger thus long were it not that your name was on the list given me by Lord Dartmouth of those to be trusted and consulted. And the information ye have furnished me concerning this region has proved that his Lordship did not err in his opinion as to your knowledge, disposition, and ability."

This sent the squire to his pillow with a delightful sense of his own importance, and led him to confide to the nightcap on the pillow beside him that "Mr. Evatt is a man of vast insight and discrimination." Regrettable as it is to record, the visitor, before seeking his own pillow, mixed some ink powder in a mug with a little water and proceeded to add to a letter already begun the following paragraph: —

"*From thence I rode to Brunswick, a small Town on the Raritan. Here I find the same division of Sentiment I have already dwelt upon to your Lordship. The Gentry, consisting hereabouts of but two, are sharply opposed to the small Farmers and Labourers, and cannot even rely upon their own Tenantry for more than a nominal support. Neither of the great Proprietors seem to be Men of sound Judgment or natural Popularity, and Mr. Lambert Meredith — a name quite unknown to your Lordship, but of some consequence in this Colony through a fortunate Marriage with a descendant of one of the original Patentees — at the last Election barely succeeded in carrying the Poll, and is represented to be a Man of much impracticality, hot-tempered, a stickler over trivial points, at odds with his Neighbours, and not even Master of his own Household. To such Men, my Lord, has fallen the Contest, on behalf of Government, while opposed to them are self-made Leaders, of Eloquence, of Force, and, most of all, of Dishonesty. Issues of Paper Money, escape from all Taxation, free Lands, suspensions of Debts — such and an hundred other tempting Promises they ply the People with, while the Gentry sit helpless, save those who, seeing how the Tide sets, throw Principles to the Wind, and plunge in with the popular Leaders. Believe me, my Lord, as I have urged already, a radical change of Government, and a plentiful sprinkling of Regiments, will alone prevent the Disorders from rising to a height that threatens Anarchy."*

Though the visitor was the last of the household abed, he was early astir the next morning, and while Charles was beginning his labours of the day, by leading each horse to the trough in the barnyard, Evatt joined him.

"We made a bad start at our first meeting, my man," he said in a friendly manner, "and I have only myself to blame for 't. One should keep his own secrets."

"'T is a sorry calling yours would be if many kept to that," replied Fownes, with a suggestion of contempt.

Evatt bit his lip, and then forced a smile. "The old saying runs that three could keep a secret if two were but dead."

Charles smiled. "My two will never trouble me," he said meaningly, "so save your time and breath."

"Hadst best not be so sure," retorted Evatt, in evident irritation. "'Twixt thine army service, the ship that fetched thee on, and that miniature, I have more clues than have served to ferret many a secret."

"And entirely lack the important one. Till you have that, I don't fear you. What is more, I'll tell you what 't is."

"What?" asked the man.

"A reward," sneered Fownes.

"I see I've a sly tyke to deal with," said the man. "But

if ye choose not —" The speaker checked himself as Janice came through the opening in the hedge, and the two stood silently watching her as she approached.

"Charles," she said, when within speaking distance, while holding out the miniature, "I 've decided you must take this."

Charles smiled pleasantly. "Then 't is your duty to make me, Miss Meredith," he replied, folding his arms.

"Won't you please take it?" begged Janice, not a little nonplussed by her position, and that Evatt should be a witness of it. "We know it belongs to you, and 't is too valuable for me to —"

"How know you that?" questioned the man, still smiling pleasantly.

"Because 't was with your clothes when you went in swimming," said Janice, frankly.

"Miss Meredith," replied Charles, "the word of a poor devil of a bond-servant can have little value, but I swear to you that that never belonged to me, and that I therefore have no right to it. If it gives you any pleasure, keep it."

"That is as good as saying ye stole it," asserted Evatt.

Charles smiled contemptuously. "'All are not thieves whom dogs bark at,'" he retorted. "Nor are all of us sneaks and spies," he added, as, turning, he led away the horse toward the stable.

"Yon fellow does n't stickle at calling ye names, Miss Meredith," said Evatt.

"He has no right to call me a spy," cried the girl, indignantly.

"His words deserve no more heed than what he said t'other night at the tavern of ye."

"What said he at the tavern?" demanded Janice.

"'T is best left unspoken."

"I want to know what he said of me," insisted Miss Meredith.

"'T would only shame ye."

"He — he told of — he did n't tell them I took the miniature?" faltered Janice.

Again Evatt bit his lip, but this time to keep from smiling. "Worse than that, my child," he replied.

"Why should he insult me?" protested Janice, proudly, but still colouring at the possibility.

"Ye do right to suppose it unlikely. Yet 't is so, and while I can hardly hope that my word will be taken for it, his lies to us a moment since prove that he is capable of any untruth."

Evatt spoke with such honesty of manner, and with such an apparent lack of motive for inventing a tale, that Janice became doubtful. "He could n't insult me," she said, "for I — I have n't done anything."

"'T is certain that he did. Had I but known ye at the time, Miss Janice, he should have been made to swallow his coarse insult. 'T was for that I sought him this morning. Had ye not interrupted us, 't would have fared badly for him."

"You were very kind," said Janice, dolefully, beginning, more from his manner than his words, to believe Evatt. "I did n't know there were such bad men in the world. And for him to say it at the tavern, where 't will be all over the county in no time! Was it very bad?"

"No one would believe a redemptioner," replied Evatt. "Yet had I the right — "

"Marse Meredith send me to tell youse come to breakfast," interrupted Peg from the gateway in the box.

"Why!" exclaimed the girl. "It can't be seven."

"The squire ordered it early, that I might be in the saddle betimes," explained Evatt, and then as the girl started toward the house, he checked the movement by taking her hand. "Miss Janice," he said, "in a half-hour I shall ride away — not because 't is my wish, but because I 'm engaged in an important and perilous mission — a mission — can ye keep a secret — even from — from your father and mother?"

Janice was too young and inexperienced to know that a secret is of all things the most to be avoided, and though her little hand, in her woman's intuition that all was not right, tried feebly to free itself, she none the less answered eagerly if half-doubtfully, "Yes."

"I am sent here under an assumed name — by His Majesty. Ye — I was indiscreet enough with ye, to tell — to show that I was other than what I pretend to be, but I felt then and now that I could trust ye. Ye will keep secret all I say?"

Again Janice, with her eyes on the ground, said, "Yes."

"I must do the king's work, and when 't is done I return to

England and resume my true position, and ye will never again hear of me — unless — " The man paused, with his eyes fixed on the downcast face of the girl.

"Unless?" asked Janice, when the silence became more embarrassing than to speak.

"Unless ye — unless ye give me the hope that by first returning here — as your father has asked me to do — that I may — may perhaps carry ye away with me. Ah, Miss Janice, 't is an outrage to keep such beauty hidden in the wilds of America, when it might be the glory of the court and the toast of the town."

Again a silence ensued, fairly agonising to the bewildered and embarrassed girl, which lengthened, it seemed to her, into hours, as she vainly sought for some words that she might speak.

"Please let go my hand," she begged finally.

"Not till you give me a yea or nay."

"But I can't — I don't — " began Janice, and then as footsteps were heard, she cried, "Oh, let me go! Here comes Charles."

"May I come back?" demanded Evatt.

"Yes," assented the girl, desperately.

"And ye promise to be secret?"

"I promise," cried Janice, and to her relief recovered her hand, just as Charles entered the garden.

Like many another of her sex, however, she found that to gain physical and temporary freedom she had only enslaved herself the more, for after breakfast Evatt availed himself of a moment's interest of Mrs. Meredith's in the ordering down of his saddle-bags, and of the squire's in the horse, to say to Janice, aside: —

"I gave ye back your hand, Janice, but remember 't is mine," and before the girl could frame a denial, he was beside Mr. Meredith at the stirrup, and, ere many minutes, had ridden away, leaving behind him a very much flattered, puzzled, and miserable demoiselle.

VIII

SEVERAL BURNING QUESTIONS

THE twenty-four hours of Evatt's visit troubled Janice in recollection for many a day, and marked the beginning of the most distinct change that had come to her. The experience was in fact that which befalls every one somewhere between the ages of twelve and thirty, by which youth first learns to recognise that life is not mere living, but is rather the working out of a strange problem compounded of volition and necessity, accident and fatality. The pledge of secrecy preyed upon her, the stranger's assumption that she had bound herself distressed her, and the thought that she had been the subject of tavern talk made her furious. Yet she had promised concealment, she was powerless to write to Evatt denying his pretension, and she could not counteract a slander the purport of which was unknown to her. Had she and Tibbie but been on terms, she might have gained some relief by confiding her woes to her, but that young lady's visit came to an end so promptly after the departure of Evatt that restoration of good feeling was only obtained in the parting kiss. For the first time in her life, Janice's head would keep on thinking after it was resting on its pillow, and many a time that enviable repository was called upon to dry her tears and cool her burning cheeks. Never, it seemed to her, had man or woman borne so great a burden of trouble.

The change in the girl was too great not to be noticed by the household of Greenwood. Mrs. Meredith joyfully confided to the Rev. Mr. McClave that she thought an "effectual calling" had come to her daughter, and that Janice was in a most promising condition of unhappiness. Thus encouraged, the divine, who was a widower of forty-two, with five children sadly needing a woman's care, only too gladly made morning calls on the daughter of his wealthiest parishioner, and in place of the discussions with Tibbie over romance in general, and the bond-servant in particular, as they sewed or knitted, Janice was forced to attend to long monologues specially prepared for her benefit, on what to the presbyter were the truly burning questions of justification, adoption, and sanctification. What is more, she not only listened dutifully, but once or twice was even moved to tears, to the enormous encouragement of Mr. McClave. The squire, who highly resented the lost vivacity and the new seriousness, insisted that the "girl sha'n't be made into a long-faced, psalm-singing hypocrite;" but not daring to oppose what his wife approved, he merely expressed his irritation to Janice herself, teasing and fretting her scarcely less than did Mr. McClave.

Not the least of her difficulties was her bearing toward the bondsman. Conditions were still so primitive that the relations between master and servant were yet on a basis that made the distinctions between them ones of convenience rather than convention, and thus Janice was forced to mark out a new line of conduct. At first she adopted that of avoidance and proud disregard of him, but his manner toward her continued to convey such deference that the girl found her attitude hard to maintain, and presently began to doubt if he could be guilty of the imputation. Nor could she be wholly blind to the fact that the groom had come to take a marked interest in her. She noted that he made occasion for frequent interviews, and that he dropped all pretence of speaking to her in his affected Somerset dialect. When now she ventured out of doors, she was almost certain to encounter him, and rarely escaped without his speaking to her; while he often came into the kitchen on frivolous pretexts when she was working there, and seemed in no particular haste to depart.

Several times he was detected by Mrs. Meredith thus idling within doors, and was sharply reproved for it. Neither to this, nor to the squire's orders that he should put an end to his "night-walking" and to his trips to the village, did he pay the slightest heed.

Fownes entered the kitchen one morning in November while Janice and Sukey were deep in the making of some grape jelly, carrying an armful of wood; for the bond-servant for once had willingly assumed a task that had hitherto been Tom's Putting the logs down in the wood-box, he stood with back to the fire, studying Miss Meredith, as, well covered with a big apron, with rolled up sleeves, flyaway locks, and flushed cheeks, she pounded away in a mortar, reducing loaf sugar to usable shape.

"Now youse clar right out of yar," said Sukey, who, though the one servant who was fond of Charles, like all good cooks, was subject to much ferment of mind when preserving was to the fore. "We uns doan want no men folks clutterin' de fire."

"Ah, Sukey," besought Charles, appealingly, "there 's a white frost this morning, and 't is bitter outside. Let me just warm my fingers?"

Sukey promptly relented, but the chill in Fownes' fingers was clearly not unendurable, for in a moment he came to the table, and putting his hand over that of Janice, which held the pestle, he said: —

"Let me do the crushing. 'T is too hard work for you."

"I wish you would," Miss Meredith somewhat breathlessly replied. "My arms are almost ready to drop off."

"'T would set the quidnuncs discussing to which of the Greek goddesses they belonged," remarked Fownes. Then he was sorry he had said it, for Miss Meredith promptly unrolled her sleeves; not because in her secret heart she did not like the speech, but because of a consciousness that Charles was noticing what the Greek goddesses generally lack. A low-cut frock was almost the unvarying dress of the ladies, there was nothing wrong in the display of an ankle, and elbow sleeves were very much the vogue, but to bare the arms any higher was an immodesty not permitted to those who were then commonly termed the "bon ton."

This addition to the working staff promptly produced an order from Sukey for Janice to assume the duty of stirring a pot just placed over the fire, "while I 'se goes down cellar an' clars a shelf for them jellies to set on. Keep a stirrin', honey, so 's it won't burn," was her parting injunction.

No sooner was the cook out of hearing than Charles spoke: "For two days," he said in a low voice, "I have tried to get word with you. Won't you come to the stable when I am there?"

"Are you going to crush that sugar?" asked Miss Meredith.

"Art going to come to the stable?" calmly questioned Charles.

"Give me the pestle!" said Janice, severely.

"Because if you won't," continued the groom, "I shall have to say what I want now."

"I prefer not to hear it," Janice announced, moving from the fire.

"You must keep on stirring, or 't will burn, Miss Janice," the man reminded her, taking a mean advantage of the situation.

Janice came back and resumed her task, but she said, "I don't choose to listen."

"'T is for thy father's sake I ask it."

"How?" demanded the girl, looking up with sudden interest.

"I went to the village t' other night," replied the man, "to drill —" Then he checked himself, in evident disconcertion.

"Drill?" asked Janice. "What drill?"

"Let us call it quadrille, since that is not the material part," said Charles. "What is to the point is that after — after doing what took me, I stayed to help in Guy Fawkes' fun on the green."

"Well?" questioned the girl, encouragingly.

"The frolickers had some empty tar barrels and an effigy of the Pope, and they gave him and a copy of the Boston Port Bill each a coat of tar and leaves, and then burned them."

"What fun!" cried Janice, ceasing to stir in her interest. "I wish mommy would let me go. She says 't is unbecoming in the gentility, but I don't see why being well born should be a reason for not having as good a time as —"

"As servants?" interrupted Fownes, hotly, as if her words stung him.

"I 'm afraid, Charles," reproved Janice, assuming again a severe manner, "that you have a very bad temper."

Perhaps the man might have retorted, but instead he let

the anger die from his face, as he fixed his eyes on the floor. "I have, Miss Janice," he acknowledged sadly, after a moment's pause, "and 't is the curse of my life."

"You should discipline it," advised Miss Meredith, sagely. "When I lose my temper, I always read a chapter in the Bible," she added, with a decidedly "holier than thou" in her manner.

"How many times hast thou read the good book through, Miss Janice?" asked Fownes, smiling, and Miss Meredith's virtuous pose became suddenly an uncomfortable one to the young lady.

"You were to tell me something about Mr. Meredith," she said stiffly.

"After burning the Pope and the bill, 't was suggested by some to empty the pot of tar on the fire. But objection was made, because — "

"Because?" questioned Janice.

"Someone said 't would be needed shortly to properly season *green wood*, and therefore must not be wasted."

"You don't think they — ?" cried Janice, in alarm.

The servant nodded his head. "The feeling against the squire is far deeper than you suspect. 'T will find vent in some violence, I fear, unless he yield to public sentiment."

"He 'll never truckle to the country licks and clouted shoons of Brunswick," asserted Janice, proudly.

"'T will fare the worse for him. 'T is as sensible to run counter to public opinion as 't is to cut roads over mountains."

"'T is worse still to be a coward," cried Janice, contemptuously. "I fear, Charles, you are very mean-spirited."

Fownes shrugged his shoulders. "As a servant should be," he muttered bitterly.

"Even a servant can do what is right," answered the girl.

"'T is not a question of right, 't is one of expediency," replied the bondsman. "A year at court, Miss Janice, would teach you that in this world 't is of monstrous importance to know when to bow."

"What do you know of court?" exclaimed Janice.

"Very little," confessed the man. "But I know it teaches

one good lesson in life, — that of submission, — and an important thing 't is to learn."

"I only bow to those whom I know to be my superiors," said Janice, with her head held very erect.

"'T is an easy way for you to avoid bowing," asserted the groom, smiling.

Again Janice sought a change of subject by saying, "Think you that is why we are being spied upon?"

"Spied?" questioned the bondsman.

"Last week dadda thought he saw a face one evening at the parlour window, and two nights ago I looked up suddenly and saw — Well, mommy said 't was only vapours, but I know I saw something."

The servant turned his face away from Janice, and coughed. Then he replied, "Perhaps 't was some one watching you. Didst make no attempt to find him?"

"Dadda went to the window both times, but could see nothing."

"He probably had time to hide behind the shrubs," surmised Charles. "I shall set myself to watching, and I 'll warrant to catch the villain at it if he tries it again." From the savageness with which he spoke, one would have inferred that he was bitterly enraged at any one spying through the parlour window on Miss Meredith's evening hours.

"I wish you would," solicited Janice. "For if it happened again, I don't know what I should do. Mommy insisted it was n't a ghost, and scolded me for screaming; but all the same, it gave me a dreadful turn. I did n't go to sleep for hours."

"I am sorry it frightened you," said the servant, and then after a moment's hesitation he continued, "'T was I, and if I had thought for a moment to scare you — "

"You!" cried Janice. "What were you doing there?"

The man looked her in the eyes while he replied in a low voice, "Looking at paradise, Miss Janice."

"Janice Meredith," said her mother's voice, sternly, "thou good-for-nothing! Thou 'st let the syrup burn, and the smell is all over the house. Charles, what dost thou mean by loafing indoors at this hour of the day? Go about thy work."

And paradise dissolved into a pot of burnt syrup.

IX

PARADISE AND ELSEWHERE

WHILE Charles was within hearing, Mrs. Meredith continued to scold Janice about the burnt syrup, but this subject was ended with his exit.

"I 'm ashamed that a daughter of mine should allow a servant to be so familiar," Mrs. Meredith began anew. "'T is a shame on us all, Janice. Hast thou no idea of what is decent and befitting to a girl of thy station?"

"He was n't familiar," cried Janice, angrily and proudly, "and you should know that if he had been I — he was telling me — "

"Yes," cried her mother, "tell me what he was saying about paradise? Dost think me a nizey, child, not to know what men mean when they talk about paradise?"

Janice's cheeks reddened, and she replied hotly, "If men talked to you about paradise, why should n't they talk to me? I 'm sure 't is a pleasant change after the parson's everlasting and eternal talk of an everlasting and eternal — "

"Don't thee dare say it!" interrupted Mrs. Meredith. "Thou fallen, sin-eaten child! Go to thy room and stay there for the rest of the day. 'T is all of a piece that thou shouldst disgrace us by unseemly conduct with a stable-boy. Fine talk 't will make for the tavern."

The injustice and yet possible truth in this speech was too much for Janice to hear, and without an attempt at reply, she burst into a storm of tears and fled to her room.

Deprived of a listener, Mrs. Meredith sought the squire, and very much astonished him by a prediction that, "Thy daughter, Mr. Meredith, is going to bring disgrace on the family."

"What 's to do now?" cried the parent.

"A pretty to do, indeed," his wife assured him. "Dost want her running off some fine night with thy groom?"

"Tush, Matilda!" responded Mr. Meredith. "'T is impossible."

"Just what my parents said when thou camest a-courting."

"I was no redemptioner."

"'T was none the less a step-down for me," replied Mrs. Meredith, calmly. "And I had far less levity than —"

"Nay, Matilda, she often reminds me very —"

"Lambert, I never was light! Or at least never after I sat under Dr. Edwards and had a call. The quicker we marry Janice to Mr. McClave, the better 't will be for her."

"Now, pox me!" cried the squire, "if I'll give my lass to be made the drudge of another woman's children."

"'T is the very discipline she needs," retorted the wife. "But for my checking her a moment ago I believe she'd have spoken disrespectfully of hell!"

"Small wonder!" muttered her husband. "Is't not enough to ye Presbyterians to doom one to everlasting torment in the future life without making this life as bad?"

"'T is the way to be saved," replied Mrs. Meredith. "As Mr. McClave said to Janice shortly since, 'Be assured that doing the unpleasant thing is the surest road to salvation, for tho' it should not find grace in the eyes of a righteously angry God, yet having been done from no carnal and sinful craving of the flesh, it cannot increase his anger towards you.' Ah, Lambert, that man has the true gift."

"Since he's so damned set on being uncarnal," snapped the squire, "let him go without Janice."

"And have her running off with an indentured servant, as Anne Loughton did?"

"She'll do nothing of the kind. If ye want a husband for the lass, let her take Phil."

"A bankrupt."

"Tush! There are acres enough to pay the old squire's debts three times over. She'd bring Phil enough ready money to clear it all, and 't is rich mellow land that will double in value, give it time."

"I tell thee her head 's full of this bond-servant. The two were in the kitchen just now, talking about paradise, and I know not what other foolishness."

"That," said Mr. Meredith, with a grin of enjoyment, "sounds like true Presbyterian doctrine. The Westminster Assembly seem to have left paradise out of the creation."

"Such flippancy is shameful in one of thy years, Mr. Meredith," said his wife, sternly, "and canst have but one ending."

"That is all any of us can have, Patty," replied the squire, genially.

Mrs. Meredith went to the door, but before leaving the room, she said, still with a stern, set face, though with a break in her voice, "Is 't not enough that my four babies are enduring everlasting torment, but my husband and daughter must go the same way?"

"There, there, Matilda!" cried the husband. "'T was said in jest only and was nothing more than lip music. Come back —" the speech ended there as a door at a distance banged. "Now she 'll have a cry all by herself," groaned the squire. "'T is a strange thing she took it so bravely when the road was rough, yet now, when 't is easy pulling, she lets it fret and gall her."

Then Mr. Meredith looked into his fire, and saw another young girl, a little more serious than Janice, perhaps, but still gay-hearted and loved by many. He saw her making a stolen match with himself; passed in review the long years of alienation from her family, the struggle with poverty, and, saddest of all, the row of little gravestones which told of the burial of the best of her youth. He saw the day finally when, a worn, saddened woman, she at last was in the possession of wealth, to find in it no pleasure, yet to turn eagerly, and apparently with comfort, to the teachings of that strange combination of fire and logic, Jonathan Edwards. He recalled the two sermons during Edwards's brief term as president of Nassau Hall, which moved him so little, yet which had convinced Mrs. Meredith that her dead babies had been doomed to eternal punishment and had made her the stern, unyielding woman she was. The squire was too hearty an animal, and lived too much in the open air, to be given to introspective thought, but he shook his head. "A strange warp and woof we weave of the skein," he sighed, "that sorrow for the dead should harden us to the living." Mr. Meredith rose, went upstairs, and rapped at a door. Getting no reply, after a repetition of the knock, he went in.

A glance revealed what at first sight looked like a crumpled heap of clothes upon the bed, but after more careful scrutiny the mass was found to have a head, very much buried between two pillows, and the due quantity of arms and legs. Walking to the bed, the squire put his hand on the bundle.

"There, lass," he said, "'t is nought to make such a pother about."

"Oh, dadda," moaned Janice, "I am the most unhappy girl that ever lived."

It is needless to say after this remark that Miss Meredith's knowledge of the world was not of the largest, and the squire, with no very great range of experience, smiled a little as he said: —

"Then 't will not make you more miserable to wed the parson?"

"Dadda!" exclaimed the girl, rolling over quickly, to get a sight of his countenance. When she found him smiling, the anxious look on the still red and tear-stained face melted away, and she laughed merrily. "Think of the life I'd give the good man! How I would wherrit him! He'd have to give up his church to have time enough to preach to me." Apparently the deep woe alluded to the moment before was forgotten.

"I've no manner of doubt he'd enjoy the task," declared the father, with evident pride. "Ah, Jan, many a man would enter the ministry, if he might be ordained parson of ye."

"The only parson I want is a father confessor," said Janice, sitting up and giving him a kiss.

"Then what's this maggot your mother has got in her head about ye and Charles and paradise?" laughed her father.

"Indeed, dadda," protested the girl, eagerly, "mommy was most unjust. I was to stir some syrup, and Charles came into the kitchen and would talk to me, and as I could n't leave the pot, I had to listen, and then — well — "

"I thought as much!" cried the squire, heartily, when Janice paused. "Where the syrup is, there 'll find ye the flies. But we 'll have no horse-fly buzzing about ye. My fine gentleman shall be taught where he belongs, if it takes the whip to do it."

"No, dadda," exclaimed Janice. "He spoke but to warn me of danger to you. He says there 's preparation to tar and feather you unless you — you do something."

"Foo!" sniffed the squire. "Let them snarl. I 'll show them I 'm not a man to be driven by tag, long tail, and bobby."

"But Charles — " began the girl.

"Ay, Charles," interrupted Mr. Meredith. "I 've no doubt he 's one of 'em. 'T is always the latest importations take the hottest part against the gentry."

"Nay, dadda, I think he — "

"Mark me, that 's what takes the tyke to the village so often."

"He said 't was to drill he went."

"To drill?" questioned the squire. "What meant he by that?"

"I asked him, and he said 't was quadrille. Dost think he meant dancing or cards?"

"'T is in keeping that he should be a dancing master or a card-sharper," asserted Mr. Meredith. "No wonder 't is a disordered land when 't is used as a catchall for every man not wanted in England. We 'll soon put a finish to his night-walking."

"I don't think he 's a villain, dadda, and he certainly meant kindly in warning us."

"To make favour by tale-bearing, no doubt."

"I 'm sure he 'd not a thought of it," declared Janice, with an unconscious eagerness which made the squire knit his brows.

"Ye speak warmly, child," he said. "I trust your mother be not justified in her suspicion."

The girl, who meanwhile had sprung off the bed, drew herself up proudly. "Mommy is altogether wrong," she replied. "I'd never descend so low."

"I said as much," responded the squire, gleefully.

"A likely idea, indeed!" exclaimed Janice. "As if I'd have aught to do with a groom! No, I never could shame the family by that."

"Wilt give me your word to that, Jan?" asked the squire.

"Yes," cried the girl, and then roguishly added, "Why, dadda, I'd as soon, yes, sooner, marry old Belza, who at least is a prince in his own country, than see a Byllynge marry a bond-servant."

X

A COLONIAL CHRISTMAS

FOR some weeks following the pledge of Janice, the life at Greenwood became as healthily monotonous as of yore. Both Mr. and Mrs. Meredith spoke so sharply to both Sukey and Charles of his loitering about the kitchen that his visits, save at meal times, entirely ceased. The squire went further and ordered him to put an end to his trips to the village, but the man took this command in sullen silence, and was often absent.

One circumstance, however, very materially lessened the possible encounters between the bond-servant and the maiden. This was no less than the setting in of the winter snows, which put a termination to all the girl's outdoor life, excepting the attendance at the double church services on Sundays, which Mrs. Meredith never permitted to be neglected. From the window Janice sometimes saw the groom playing in the drifts with Clarion, but that was almost the extent of her knowledge of his doings. It is to be confessed that she eagerly longed to join them or, at least, to have a like sport with the dog. Eighteenth-century etiquette, however, neither countenanced such conduct in the quality, nor, in fact, clothed them for it.

A point worth noting at this time was connected with one window of the parlour. Each afternoon as night shut down, it was Peg's duty to close all the blinds, for colonial windows not being of the tightest, every additional barricade to Boreas was welcome, and this the servant did with exemplary care. But every evening after tea, Janice always walked to a particular window and, opening the shutter, looked out for a moment, as if to see what the night promised, before she took her seat at her tambour frame or sewing. Sometimes one of her parents called attention to the fact that she had not quite closed the shutters again, and she always remedied the oversight at once. Otherwise she never looked at the window during the whole evening, glance where she might. Presumably she still remembered the fright her putative ghost had occasioned her, and chose not to run the chance of another sight of him. Almost invariably, however, in the morning she blew on the frost upon the window of her own room and having rubbed clear a spot, looked below, much as if she suspected ghosts could leave tracks in the snow. In her behalf it is only fair to say that the girls of that generation were so shut in as far as regarded society or knowledge of men that they let their imaginations question and wander in a manner difficult now to conceive. At certain ages the two sexes are very much interested in each other, and if this interest is not satisfied objectively, it will be subjectively.

Snow, if a jailer, was likewise a defence, and apparently cooled for a time the heat of the little community against the squire. Even the Rev. Mr. McClave's flame of love and love of flame were modified by the depth of the drifts he must struggle through, in order to discourse on eternal torment while gazing at earthly paradise. Janice became convinced that the powers of darkness no longer had singled her out as their particular prey, and in the peaceful isolation of the winter her woes, when she thought of them, underwent a change of grammatical tense which suggested that they had become things of the past.

One of her tormenting factors was not to be so treated. Philemon alone made nothing of the change of season, riding the nine miles between his home and Greenwood by daylight or by moonlight, as if his feeling for the girl not merely warmed but lighted the devious path between the drifts. Yet it was not to make love he came; for he sat a silent, awkward figure when once within doors, speaking readily enough in response to the elders, but practically inarticulate whenever called upon to reply to Janice. Her bland unconsciousness was a barrier far worse than the snow; and never dreaming that he was momentarily declaring his love for her in a manner far stronger than words, he believed her wholly ignorant of what he felt, and stayed for hours at a time, longing helplessly for a turn of events which should make it possible for him to speak.

Philemon was thus engaged or disengaged one December morning when Peg entered the parlour where the family were sitting as close to the fire as the intense glow of the hickory embers would allow, and handing Janice a letter with an air of some importance, remarked, "Charles he ask me give you dat." Then, colonial servants being prone to familiarity, and negro slaves doubly so, Peg rested her weight on one foot, and waited to learn what this unusual event might portend. All present instantly fixed their eyes upon Janice, but had they not done so it is probable that she would have coloured much as she did, for the girl was enough interested and enough frightened to be quite unconscious of the eyes upon her.

"A letter for thee, lass!" exclaimed the squire. "Let's have the bowels of it."

The necessity for that very thing was what made the occurrence so alarming to Janice, for her woman's intuition had at once suggested, the moment she had seen the bold handwriting of the superscription, that it could be from none other than Evatt, and she had as quickly surmised that her father and mother would insist upon sight of the missive. Unaware of what it might contain, she sat with red cheeks, not daring to break the seal.

"Hast got the jingle brains, child?" asked her mother, sharply, "that thou dost nothing but stare at it?"

Janice laid the letter in her lap, saying, "'Twill wait till I finish this row." It was certainly a hard fate which forced her to delay the opening of the first letter she had ever received.

"'Twill nothing of the sort," said her mother, reaching out for the paper. "Art minded to read it on the sly, miss? There shall be no letters read by stealth. Give it me."

"Oh, mommy," begged the girl, desperately, "I'll show it to you, but — oh — let me read it first, oh, please!"

"I think 't is best not," replied her mother. "Thy anxiety has an ill look to it, Janice."

The girl handed the letter dutifully, and with an anxious attention watched her mother break it open, all pleasure in the novelty of the occurrence quite overtopped by dread of what was to come.

"What nonsense is this?" was Mrs. Meredith's anything but encouraging exclamation. Then she read out:—

"*'Tis unworthy of you, and of your acceptance, but 't is the fairest gift I could think of, and the best that I could do. If you will but put it in the frame you have, it may seem more befitting a token of the feelings that inspired it.*"

Janice, unable to restrain her curiosity, rose and peered over her mother's shoulder. From that vantage point she ejaculated, "Oh, how beautiful she is!"

What she looked at was an unset miniature of a young girl, with a wealth of darkest brown hair, powdered to a gray, and a little straight nose with just a suggestion of a tilt to it, giving the mignon face an expression of pride that the rest of the countenance by no means aided. For the remaining features, the mouth was still that of a child, the short upper lip projecting markedly over the nether one, producing not so much a pouty look as one of innocence; the eyes were brilliant black, or at least were shadowed to look it by the long lashes, and the black eyebrows were slender and delicately arched upon a low forehead.

"Art a nizey, Janice," cried her mother, "not to know thine own face?"

"Mommy!" exclaimed the girl. "Is — am I as pretty as that?"

"'T is vastly flattered," said her mother, quickly. "I should scarce know it."

"Nay, Matilda," dissented the squire, who was now also gazing at the miniature. "'T is a good phiz of our lass, and but does her justice. Who ever sent it ye, Jan?"

"I suppose 't was Mr. Evatt," confessed Janice.

"Let 's have sight of the wrapper," said the father. "Nay, Jan. This has been in no post-rider's bag or 't would bear the marks."

"Peg, tell Charles to come here," ordered Mrs. Meredith, and after a five minutes spent by the group in various surmises, the bond-servant, followed by the still attentive Peg, entered the room.

"Didst find this letter at the tavern?" demanded the squire.

The groom looked at the wrapper held out to him, and replied, "Mayhaps."

"And what took ye there against my orders?"

Charles shrugged his shoulders, and then smiled. "Ask Hennion," he said.

"What means he, Phil?" questioned the squire.

"Now you 've been an' told the whole thing," exclaimed Philemon, looking very much alarmed.

"Not I," replied the servant. "'T is for you to tell it, man, if 't is to be told."

"Have done with such mingle-mangle talk," ordered Mr. Meredith, fretfully. "Is 't not enough to have French gibberish in the world, without —"

"Charles," interrupted Mrs. Meredith, "who gave thee this letter?"

"Ask Miss Meredith," Fownes responded, again smiling.

"It must be Mr. Evatt," said Janice. Then as the bond-servant turned sharply and looked at her, she became conscious that she was colouring. "I wish there was no such thing as a blush," she moaned to herself, — a wish in which no one seeing Miss Meredith would have joined.

"'T was not from Mr. Evatt," denied the servant.

Without time for thought, Janice blurted out, "Then 't is from you?" and the groom nodded his head.

"What nonsense is this?" cried Mr. Meredith. "Dost mean to say 't is from ye? Whence came the picture?"

"I was the limner," replied Charles.

"What clanker have we here?" exclaimed the squire.

"'T is no lie, Mr. Meredith," answered the servant. "In England I 've drawn many a face, and 't was even said in jest that I might be a poor devil of an artist if ever I quitted the ser — quitted service."

"And where got ye the colours?"

"When I went to Princeton with the shoats I found Mr. Peale painting Dr. Witherspoon, and he gave me the paints and the ivory."

"Ye 'll say I suppose too that ye wrote this," demanded the squire, indicating the letter.

"I'll not deny it."

"Though ye could not sign the covenant?"

Fownes once more shrugged his shoulders. "'T is a fool would sign a bond," he asserted.

"Better a fool than a knave," retorted Mr. Meredith, angered by Charles' manner. "Janice, give the rogue back the letter and picture. No daughter of Lambert Meredith accepts gifts from her father's bond-servants."

The man flushed, while evidently struggling to control his temper, and Janice, both in pity for him, as well as in desire for possession of the picture, for gifts were rare indeed in those days, begged: —

"Oh, dadda, mayn't I keep it?"

"Mr. Meredith," said Charles, speaking with evident repression, "the present was given only with the respect —" he hesitated as if for words and then continued — "the respect a slave might owe his — his better. Surely on this day it should be accepted in the same spirit."

"What day mean ye?" asked Mr. Meredith.

The servant glanced at each face with surprise on his own. When he read a question in all, he asked in turn, "Hast forgotten 't is Christmas?"

Mrs. Meredith, who was still holding the portrait, dropped it on the floor, as if it were in some manner dangerous. "Christmas!" she cried. "Janice, don't thee dare touch the —"

"Oh, mommy, please," beseeched the girl.

"Take it away, Charles," ordered Mrs. Meredith. "And never let me hear of thy being the devil's deputy again. We'll have no papish mummery at Greenwood."

The servant sullenly stooped, picked up the slip of ivory without a word, and turned to leave the room. But as he reached the door, Philemon found tongue.

"I'll trade that 'ere for the fowlin'-piece you set such store by," he offered.

The bondsman turned in the doorway and spoke bitterly. "This is to be got for no mess of pottage, if it is scorned," he said.

"I don't scorn —" began Janice, but her father broke in there.

"Give it me, fellow!" ordered the squire. "No bond-servant shall have my daughter's portrait."

An angry look came into the man's eyes as he faced his master. "Come and take it, then," he challenged savagely, moving a step forward,—an action which for some reason impelled the squire to take a step backward.

"Oh, dadda, don't," cried Janice, anxiously. "Charles, you would n't!"

Fownes turned to her, with the threat gone from his face and attitude. "There's my devil's temper again, Miss Janice," said he, in explanation and apology.

"Please go away," implored the girl, and the man went to the door. As he turned to close it, Janice said, "'T was very pretty, and — and — thank you, just the same."

The formalism of bygone generations was no doubt conducive to respectful manners, but not to confidential relations, and her parents knew so little of their daughter's nature as never to dream that they had occasioned the first suggestion of tenderness for the opposite sex the young girl's heart had ever felt. And love's flame is superior to physical law in that the less ventilation it has, the more fiercely it burns.

XI

"'T IS AN ILL WIND THAT BLOWS NOBODY GOOD"

THE next ripple in the Greenwood life was due to more material circumstances, being inaugurated by the receipt of the Governor's writ, convening the Assembly of New Jersey. A trivial movement of a petty pawn on the chess-board of general politics, it nevertheless was of distinct importance in several respects to the Meredith family. Apparently the call meant only a few weeks' attendance of the squire's at Burlington, in the performance of legislative duties, and Janice's going with him to make a return visit to the Drinkers at Trenton. These, however, were the simplest aspects of the summons, and action by the citizens of Middlesex County quickly injected a more serious element into the programme.

The earliest evidence of this was the summoning by the Committee of Observation and Correspondence of a gathering to "instruct" the county representatives how they should vote on the question as to indorsing or disapproving the measures of the recent Congress. The notice of the meeting was read aloud by the Rev. Mr. McClave before his morning sermon one Sunday, and then he preached long and warmly from 2 Timothy, ii. 25, — "Instructing those that oppose themselves," — the purport of his argument being the duty of the whole community to join hands in resisting the enemies of the land. The preacher knew he was directly antagonising the views of his wealthiest parishioner and the father of his would-be wife, but that fact only served to make him speak the more forcefully and fervently. However hard and stern the old Presbyterian faith was, its upholders had the merit of knowing what they believed, and of stating that belief without flinch or waver.

As he sat and listened, not a little of the squire's old Madeira found its way into his face, and no sooner were the family seated in the sleigh than the wine seemed to find expression in his tongue as well.

"'T is the last time I set foot in your church, Mrs. Meredith," he declared, loudly enough to make it evident that he desired those filing out of the doors to hear. "Never before have I —"

"Hold thy tongue, Lambert!" interrupted Mrs. Meredith, in a low voice. "Dost think to make a scene on the Sabbath?"

"Then let your parson hold his," retorted Mr. Meredith, but like a well-trained husband, in so low a voice as to be inaudible to all but the occupants of the sleigh. "Ge wug, Joggles! What is the land coming to, when such doctrines are preached in the pulpits; when those in authority are told 't is their duty to do what the riff-raff think best? As well let their brats and bunters tell us what to do. They 'll not force me to attend their meeting, nor to yield a jot."

In fulfilment of his assertion, the squire sat quietly at home on the afternoon that the popular opinion of the county sought to voice itself, nodding his head over a volume of "Hale's Compleat Body of Husbandry." But as night drew near he was roused from his nap by the riding up of Squire Hennion and Philemon. Let it be confessed that, despite Mr. Meredith's contempt for what he styled the "mobocracy," his first question concerned the meeting.

"A pooty mess yer 've made of it, Meredith," growled Mr. Hennion.

"I!" cried the squire, indignantly. "'T is naught I had to do with it."

"An' 't is thet 'ere keepin' away dun the harm," scolded the elder Hennion. "Swamp it, yer let the hotheads control! Had all like yer but attended, they 'd never hev bin able to carry some of them 'ere resolushuns. On mor 'n one resolve a single vote would hev bin a negative."

"Pooh!" sneered the squire. "Sit down and warm thy feet while thee cools thy head, man. Ye 'll not get me to believe that one vote only was needed to prevent 'em indorsing the Congress association."

"Sartin they approved the Congress doins, *nemine contradicente*, as they wuz baound ter do since all aginst kep away, but —"

"Dost mean to say ye voted for it?" demanded Mr. Meredith.

Squire Hennion's long, shrewd face slightly broadened as he smiled. "I wuz jest stepped over ter the ordinary ter git a nipperkin of ale when thet ere vote wuz took."

"Who let the hotheads control, then?" jerked out Mr. Meredith.

"'T ain't no sort of use ter hev my neebours set agin me."

"And ye 'll vote at Burlington as they tell ye?" fumed the squire.

"I 'm rayther fearsome my rheumatiz will keep me ter hum this winter weather. I 've had some mortal bad twinges naow an' agin."

"Now damn me!" swore the squire, rising and pacing the room with angry strides. "And ye come here to blame me for neglecting a chance to check 'em."

"I duz," responded Hennion. "If I go ter Assembly, 't won't prevent theer votin' fer what they wants. But if yer had attended thet 'ere meetin', we could hev stopped them from votin' ter git up a militia company an' ter buy twenty barrels —"

"Dost mean to say they voted rebellion?" roared Mr. Meredith, halting in his angry stride.

"It duz hev a squint toward it, theer ain't no denyin'. But I reckon it wuz baound ter come, vote ay or vote nay. Fer nigh three months all the young fellers hev been drillin' pooty reg'lar."

"Oh!" spoke up Janice. "Then that 's what Charles meant when he said 't was drill took him to the village."

"What?" demanded the squire. "My bond-servant?"

"Ay. 'T is he duz the trainin', so Phil tells me."

Mr. Meredith opened the door into the hall, and bawled, "Peg!" Without waiting to give the maid time to answer the summons he roared the name again, and continued to fairly bellow it until the appearance of the girl, whom he then ordered to "find Charles and send him here." Slightly relieved, he stamped back to the fire, muttering to himself in his ire.

A pause for a moment ensued, and then the elder Hennion spoke: "Waal, Meredith, hev yer rumpus with yer servant, but fust off let me say the say ez me and Phil come fer."

"And what 's that?"

"I rayther guess yer know areddy," continued the father, while the son's face became of the colour of the hickory embers. "My boy 's in a mighty stew about yer gal, but he can't git the pluck ter tell her; so seein' he needed some help an' since I 'd come ez far ez Brunswick, says I we 'll make one ride of it, an' over we comes ter tell yer fair an ' open what he 's hangin' araound fer."

Another red face was hurriedly concealed by its owner stooping over her tambour-frame, and Janice stitched away as if nothing else were worth a second thought. It may be noted, however, that, as a preliminary to further work the next morning, a number of stitches had to be removed.

"Ho, ho!" laughed the squire, heartily, and slapping Phil on the shoulder. "A shy bird, but a sly bird, eh? Oh, no! Mr. Fox thought the old dogs didn 't know that he wanted little Miss Duck."

Already in an agony of embarrassment, this speech reduced Phil to still more desperate straits. He could look at his father only in a kind of dumb appeal, and that individual, seeing his son 's helplessness, spoke again.

"I'd hev left the youngsters ter snook araound till they wuz able ter fix things by themselves," Mr. Hennion explained. "But the times is gittin' so troublous thet I want ter see Phil sottled, an' not rampin' araound as young fellers will when they hain't got nuthin' ter keep them hum nights. An' so I reckon thet if it ever is ter be, the sooner the better. Yer gal won't be the wus off, hevin' three men ter look aout fer her, if it duz come on ter blow."

"Well said!" answered the squire. "What say ye, Matilda?"

"Oh, dadda," came an appeal from the tambour-frame, "I don't want to marry. I want to stay at home with —"

"Be quiet, child," spoke up her mother, "and keep thine

opinion to thyself till asked. We know best what is for thy good."

"He, he, he!" snickered the elder Hennion. "Gals hain't changed much since I wuz a-courtin'. They allus make aout ter be desprit set agin the fellers an' mortal daown on marryin', but, lordy me! if the men held off the hussies 'ud do the chasin'."

"Thee knows, Lambert," remarked his better half, "that I think Janice would get more discipline and greater godliness in —"

"I tell ye he sha'n't have her," broke in the squire. "No man who preaches against me shall have my daughter; no, not if 't were Saint Paul himself."

"For her eventual good I —"

"Damn her eventual —"

"I fear 't will come to that."

"Well, well, Patty, perhaps it will," acceded the squire. "But since 't is settled already by foreordination, let the lass have a good time before it comes. Wouldst rather marry the parson than Phil, Janice?"

"I don't want to marry any one," cried the girl, beginning to sob.

"A stiff-necked child thou art," said her mother, sternly. "Dost hear me?"

"Yes, mommy," responded a woful voice.

"And dost intend to be obedient?"

"Yes, mommy," sobbed the girl.

"Then if thee 'll not give her to the parson, Lambert, 't is best that she marry Philemon. She needs a husband to rule and chasten her."

"Then 't is a bargain, Hennion," said Mr. Meredith, offering a hand each to father and son.

"Yer see, Phil, it 's ez I told yer," cried the elder. "Naow hev dun with yer stand-offishness an' buss the gal. Thet 'ere is the way ter please them."

Philemon faltered, glancing from one to another, for Janice was bent low over her work and was obviously weeping, — facts by no means likely to give courage to one who needed that element as much as did the suitor.

"A noodle!" sniggered Mr. Hennion. "'T ain't ter be wondered at thet she don't take ter yer. The jades always snotter first off, but they 'd snivel worse if they wuz left spinsters — eh, squire?"

Thus encouraged, Phil shambled across the room and put his hand on the shoulder of the girl. At the first touch Janice gave a cry of desperation, and springing to her feet she fled toward the hall, her eyes still so full of tears that she did not see that something more than the door intervened to prevent her escape. In consequence she came violently in contact with Charles, and though to all appearance he caught her in his arms only to save her from falling, Janice, even in her despair, was conscious that there was more than mere physical support. To the girl it seemed as if an ally had risen to her need, and that the moment's tender clasp of his arms was a pledge of aid to a sore-stricken fugitive.

"How now!" cried the squire. "Hast been listening, fellow?"

"I did not like to interrupt," said Charles, drily.

"I sent for ye, because I 'm told ye 've been inciting rebellion against the king.

The man smiled. "'T is little inciting they need," he answered.

"Is 't true that ye 've been drilling them?" demanded the squire.

"Ask Phil Hennion," replied the servant.

"What mean ye?"

"If 't is wrong for me to drill, is 't not wrong for him to be drilled?"

"How?" once more roared the squire. "Dost mean to say that Phil has been drilling along with the other villains?"

"Naow, naow, Meredith," spoke up the elder Hennion. "Boys will be boys, yer know, an' —"

"That 's enough," cried the father. "I 'll have no man at Greenwood who takes arms against our good king. Is there no loyalty left in the land?"

"Naow look here, Meredith," Mr. Hennion argued. "Theer ain't no occasion fer such consarned highty-tighty airs. Yer can't keep boys from bein' high-sperited. What 's more —"

"High-spirited!" snapped the squire. "Is that the name ye give rebellion, Justice Hennion?"

"Thet 'ere is jest what I wuz a-comin' ter, Meredith," went on his fellow-justice. "Fust off I wuz hot agin his consarnin' himself, an' tried ter hold him back, but, lordy me! young blood duz love fightin', an' with all the young fellows possest, an' all the gals admirin', I might ez well a-tried ter hold a young steer. So, says I, 't is the hand of Providence, fer no man kin tell ez what 's ahead of us. There ain't no good takin' risks, an' so I 'll side in with the one side, an' let Phil side in with t' other, an' then whatsomever comes, 't will make no differ ter us. Naow, ef the gal kin come it over Phil ter quit trainin', all well an' good, an' — "

"I 'll tell ye what I think of ye," cried Mr. Meredith. "That ye 're a precious knave, and Phil 's a precious fool, and I want no more of either of ye at Greenwood."

"Now, squire," began Phil, " 't ain't — "

"Don't attempt to argue!" roared Mr. Meredith. "I say the thing is ended. Get out of my house, the pair of ye!" and with this parting remark, the speaker flung from the room, and a moment later the door of his office banged with such force that the whole house shook. Both the elder and younger Hennion stayed for some time, and each made an attempt to see the squire, but he refused obstinately to have aught to do with them, and they were finally forced to ride away.

Though many men were anxiously watching the gathering storm, a girl of sixteen laid her head on her pillow that night, deeply thankful that British regiments were mustering at Boston, and that America, accepting this as an answer to her appeal, was quietly making ready to argue the dispute with something more potent than petitions and associations.

XII

A BABE IN THE WOOD

THE following morning the squire went to the stable, and after soundly rating Charles for his share in the belligerent preparation of Brunswick, ordered him, under penalty of a flogging, to cease not only from exercising the would-be soldiers, but from all absences from the estate "without my order or permission." The man took the tirade as usual with an evident contempt more irritating than less passive action, speaking for the first time when at the end of the monologue the master demanded: —

"Speak out, fellow, and say if ye intend to do as ye are ordered, for if not, over ye go with me this morning to the sitting of the justices."

"I'm not the man to take a whipping, that I warn you," was the response.

"Ye dare threaten, do ye?" cried the master. "Saddle Jumper and Daisy, and have 'em at the door after breakfast. One rascal shall be quickly taught what rebellion ends in."

Fuming, the squire went to his morning meal, at which he announced his intention to ride to Brunswick and the purport of the trip.

"Oh, dadda, he — please don't!" begged Janice.

"And why not, child?" demanded her mother.

"Because he — oh! he is n't like most bondsmen and —"

"What did I tell thee, Lambert?" said Mrs. Meredith.

"Nonsense, Matilda," snorted the squire. "The lass gave me her word for 't — "

"Word!" ejaculated the wife. "What's a word or anything else when — Since thee 's sent Phil off, the quicker thee comes to my mind, and gives her to the parson, the better."

"What mean ye by objecting to this fellow being flogged, Jan?" asked the father.

Poor Janice, torn between the two difficulties, subsided, and meekly responded, "I — Well, I don't like to have things whipped, dadda. But if Charles deserves it, of course he — he — 't is right."

"There!" said Mr. Meredith, "ye see the lass has the sense of it."

The subject was dropped, but after breakfast, as the crunch of the horse's feet sounded, Janice left the spinet for a moment to look out of the window, and it was a very doleful and pitiful face she took back to her task five minutes later.

When master and man drew rein in front of the Brunswick Court-house, it was obvious to the least heedful that something unusual was astir. Although the snow lay deep in front of the building and a keen nip was in the air, the larger part of the male population of the village was gathered on the green. Despite the chill, some sat upon the steps of the building, others bestowed themselves on the stocks in front of it, and still more stood about in groups, stamping their feet or swinging their arms, clearly too chilled to assume more restful attitudes, yet not willing to desert to the more comfortable firesides within doors.

Ordering the bond-servant to hitch the two horses in the meeting-house shed and then to come to the court-room, the squire made his way between the loafers on the steps, and attempted to open the door, only to discover that the padlock was still fast in the staple.

"How now, Mr. Constable?" he exclaimed, turning, and thus for the first time becoming conscious that every eye was upon him. "What means this?"

The constable, who was one of those seated on the stocks, removed a straw from between his lips, spat at the pillory post, much as if he were shooting at a mark, and remarked, "I calkerlate yer waan't at the meetin', squire?"

"Not I," averred Mr. Meredith.

"Yer see," explained the constable, "they voted that there should n't be no more of the king's law till we wuz more sartin of the king's justice, an' that any feller as opposed that 'ere resolution wuz ter be held an enemy ter his country an' treated as such. That ain't the persition I 'm ambeetious ter hold, an' so I did n't open the court-house."

"What?" gasped Mr. Meredith. "Are ye all crazy?"

"Mebbe we be," spoke up one of the listeners, "but we ain't so crazy by a long sight as him as issued that." The speaker pointed at the king's proclamation, and then, either to prove his contempt for the symbol of monarchy, or else to show the constable how much better shot he was, he neatly squirted a mouthful of tobacco juice full upon the royal arms.

"And where are the other justices?" demanded the squire, looking about as if in search of assistance.

"The old squire an' the paason wuz at the meetin', an' I guess they knew it 'ud only be wastin' time to attend this pertiklar sittin' of the court."

"Belza take them!" cried the squire. "They 're a pair of cotswold lions, and I 'll tell it them to their faces," he added, alluding to a humorous expression of the day for a sheep. "Here I have a rebellious servant, and I 'd like to know how I 'm to get warrant to flog him, if there is to be no court. Dost mean to have no law in the land?"

"I guess," retorted Bagby, "that if the king won't regard the law, he can't expect the rest of us to, noways. What 's sauce for the goose is sauce for the gander, and if there ever was a gander it 's him." — a *mot* which produced a hearty laugh from the crowd.

"As justice of the peace I order ye to open this door, constable," called the squire.

The constable pulled out a bunch of keys and tossed it in the snow, saying, "'T ain't fer me to say there sha'n't be no sittin' of the court, an' if yer so set on tryin', why, try."

The squire deliberately went down two steps to get the keys, but the remaining six he took at one tumble, having received a push from one of the loafers back of him which sent his heavy body sprawling in the snow, his whip, hat, and, worst of all, his wig, flying in different directions. In a moment he had risen, cleared the snow from his mouth and eyes, and recovered his scattered articles, but it was not so easy to recover his dignity, and this was made the more difficult by the discovery that the bunch of keys had disappeared.

"Who took those keys?" he roared as soon as he could articulate, but the only reply the question produced was laughter.

"Don't you wherrit yourself about those keys, squire," advised Bagby. "They 're safe stowed where they won't cause no more trouble. And since that is done with, we 'd like to settle another little matter with you that we was going to come over to Greenwood about to-day, but seeing as you 're here, I don't see no reason why it should n't be attended to now."

"What 's that?" snapped the squire.

"The meeting kind of thought things looked squawlish ahead, and that it would be best to be fixed for it, so I offered a resolution that the town buy twenty half-barrels of grain, and that —"

"Grain!" exclaimed the squire. "What in the 'nation can ye want with grain?"

"As we are all friends here, I 'll tell you confidential sort, that we put it thataways, so as the resolutions need n't read too fiery, when they was published in the 'Gazette.' But the folks all knew as the grain was to be a black grain, that 's not very good eating."

"Why, this is treason!" cried Mr. Meredith. "Gunpowder! That 's —"

"Yes. Gunpowder," continued the spokesman, quite as much to the now concentrated crowd as to the questioner. "We reckon the time 's coming when we 'll want it swingeing bad. And the meeting seemed to think the same way, for they voted that resolution right off, and appointed me and Phil Hennion and Mr. Wetman a committee to raise a levy to buy it."

"Think ye a town meeting can lay a tax levy?" contemptuously demanded Mr. Meredith. "None but the —"

"'T is n't to be nothing but a voluntary contribution," interrupted Bagby, grinning broadly, "and no man 's expected to give more than his proportion, as settled by his last rates."

"An' no man 's expected ter give less, nuther," said a voice back in the crowd.

"So if you 've nine pounds seven and four with you, squire," went on Bagby, "'t will save you a special trip over to pay it."

"I 'll see ye all damned first!" retorted the squire, warmly. "Why don't ye knock me down and take my purse, and have done with it?"

"'T would be the sensible thing with such a tarnal cross tyke," shouted some one.

"Everything fair and orderly is the way we work," continued the committee man. "But we want that nine pounds odd, and 'twill be odd if we don't get it."

"You 'll not get it from me," asserted the squire, turning to walk away.

As he did so, half a dozen hands were laid upon his arms from behind, and he was held so firmly that he could not move.

"Shall we give him a black coat, Joe?" asked some one.

"No," negatived Bagby. "Let 's see if being a 'babe in the wood' won't be enough to bring him to reason."

The slang term for occupants of the stocks was quite suggestive enough to produce instant result. The squire was dragged back till his legs were tripped from under him by the frame, the bunch of keys, which suddenly reappeared, served to unlock the upper board, and before the victim quite realised what had transpired he was safely fastened in the ignominious instrument. Regrettable as it is to record, Mr. Meredith began to curse in a manner highly creditable to his knowledge of Anglo-Saxon, but quite the reverse of his moral nature.

So long as the squire continued to express his rage and to threaten the bystanders with various penalties, the crowd stood about in obvious enjoyment, but anger that only excites amusement in others very quickly burns itself out, and in this particular case the chill of the snow on which the squire was sitting was an additional cause for a rapid cooling. Within two minutes his vocabulary had exhausted itself, and he relapsed into silence. The fun being over, the crowd began to scatter, the older ones betaking themselves indoors while the youngsters waylaid Charles, as he came from hitching the horses, and suggested a drill.

The bondsman shook his head and walked to the squire. "Any orders, Mr. Meredith?" he asked.

"Get an axe and smash this —— thing to pieces."

"They would not let me," replied the man, shrugging his shoulders. "Hadst best do as they want, sir. You can't fight the whole county."

"I 'll never yield," fumed the master.

Charles again shrugged his shoulders, and walking back to the group, said, "Get your firelocks."

In five minutes forty men were in line on the green, and as the greatest landholder of the county sat in the stocks, in a break-neck attitude, with a chill growing in fingers and toes, he was forced to watch a rude and disorderly attempt at company drill, superintended by his own servant. It was a clumsy, wayward mass of men, and frequent revolts from orders occurred, which called forth sharp words from the drill-master. These in turn produced retorts or jokes from the ranks that spoke ill for the discipline, and a foreign officer, taking the superficial aspect, would have laughed to think that such a system could make soldiers. Further observation and thought would have checked his amused contempt, for certain conditions there were which made these men formidable. Angry as they became at Fownes, not one left the ranks, though presence was purely voluntary, and scarce one of them, ill armed though he might be, but was able to kill a squirrel or quail at thirty paces.

When the drill had terminated, a result due largely to the smell of cooking which began to steal from the houses facing the green, Charles drew Bagby aside, and after a moment's talk, the two, followed by most of the others, crossed to the squire.

"Mr. Meredith," said Charles, "I 've passed my word to Bagby that you 'll pay your share if he 'll but release you, and that you won't try to prosecute him. Wilt back up my pledge?"

The prisoner, though blue and faint with cold, shook his head obstinately.

"There! I told you how it would be," sneered Bagby.

"But I tell you he 'll be frosted in another hour. 'T will be nothing short of murder, man."

"Then let him contribute his share," insisted Bagby.

"'T is unfair to force a man on a principle."

"Look here," growled Bagby. "We are getting tired of

your everlasting hectoring and attempting to run everything. Just because you know something of the manual don't make you boss of the earth."

The bondsman glanced at the squire, and urged, "Come, Mr. Meredith, you 'd better do it. Think how anxious Mrs. Meredith and — will be, aside from you probably taking a death cold, or losing a hand or foot."

At last the squire nodded his head, and without more ado Bagby stooped and unlocked the log. Mr. Meredith was so cramped that Charles had to almost lift him to his feet, and then give him a shoulder into the public room of the tavern, where he helped him into a chair before the fire. Then the servant called to the publican: —

"A jorum of sling for Mr. Meredith, and put an extra pepper in it."

"That sounds pretty good," said Bagby. "Just make that order for the crowd, and the squire 'll pay for it."

While the favourite drink of the period was sizzling in the fire, Mr. Meredith recovered enough to pull out his purse and pay up the debatable levy. A moment later the steaming drink was poured into glasses, and Bagby said: —

"Now, squire, do the thing up handsome by drinking to the toast of Liberty."

"I 'll set you a better toast than that," offered the bondsman.

"'T ain't possible," cried one of the crowd.

The servant raised his glass and with an ironical smile said: —

"Here 's to liberty and fair play, gentlemen."

"That 's a toast we can all drink," responded Bagby, "just as often as some one 'll pay for the liquor."

XIII

THE WORLD IN MINIATURE

THE exposure of the squire brought on a sharp attack of the gout which confined him to the house for nigh a month. Incidentally it is to be noted that his temper during this period was not confined, and when Philemon appeared one morning he was met with a reception that drove him away without a chance to plead his cause. Mrs. Meredith and Janice were compelled to listen to many descriptions as to what punitive measures their particular lord of creation intended to set in motion against the villagers when he should attend the Assembly, or when King George had reduced the land to its old-time order.

One piece of good fortune the attack brought its victim was its putting him in bed on the particular day selected for the committee of the town meeting to inform the squire as to the instruction voted by that gathering for his conduct in the Assembly. In default of an interview, they merely left an attested copy of the resolution, and had to rest satisfied, without knowing in what way their representative received it. Mrs. Meredith, Janice, and Peg did not remain in any such doubt.

Another unfortunate upon whom the vials of his wrath were poured out was the parson, who came a-calling one afternoon. News that he was in the parlour was sufficient to bring Mr. Meredith downstairs prematurely, where he enacted a high scene, berating the caller, and finally ordering him from the house.

A relapse followed upon the exertion and outburst, but even gout had its limitations, and finally the patient was sufficiently convalescent for preparations to begin for the journey to Trenton and Burlington.

It did not take Janice long one morning to pack her little leather-covered and brass-nail studded trunk, and, this done, her conduct became not a little peculiar. After dinner she spent some time in spinet practice, and then rising announced to the elders that she must pack for the morrow's journey. Her absence thus explained, she left the room, only to steal through the kitchen, and catch Sukey's shawl from its hook in the passage to the wood-shed. Regardless of slippers and snow, she then sped toward the concealing hedge, and behind its friendly protection walked quickly to the stable. The door was rolled back enough to let the girl pass in quietly, and when she had done so, she glanced about in search of something. For an instant a look of disappointment appeared on her face, but the next moment, as a faint sound of scratching broke upon her ear, she stole softly to the feed and harness room, and peeked in.

The groom was sitting on a nail barrel, in front of the meal-bin, the cover of which was closed and was thus made to serve for a desk. On this were several sheets of what was then called *pro patria* paper, or foolscap, and most of these were very much bescribbled. An ink-horn and a sand-box completed the outfit, except for a quill in the hands of the bond-servant, which had given rise to the sound the girl had heard. Now, however, it was not writing, for the man was chewing the feather end with a look of deep thought on his face.

"O Clarion," he sighed, as the girl's glance was momentarily occupied with the taking in of these details, "why canst thou not give me a word to rhyme with morn? 'T will not come, and here 't is the thirteenth."

A low growl from Clarion, sounding like anything more than the desired rhyme, made the servant glance up, and the moment he saw the figure of some one, he rose, hastily bunched together the sheets of paper, and holding them in his hand cried, "Who 's that?" in a voice expressing both embarrassment and anger. Then as his eyes dwelt on the intruder, he continued in an altered tone, "I ask your pardon, Miss Janice; I thought 't was one of the servants. They are everlastingly spying on me. Can I serve you?" he added, rolling the papers up and stuffing them into his belt.

Janice's eyes sought the floor, as she hesitatingly said, "I —I came to—to ask a favour of you."

"'T is but for you to name," replied the man, eagerly.

"Will you let me — I want — I should like Tibbie to see the — the picture of me, and I wondered if — if you would let me take it to Trenton — I'll bring it back, you know, and —"

"Ah, Miss Janice," exclaimed the servant, as the girl halted, "if you'd but take it as a gift, 't would pleasure me so!" While he spoke, without pretence of concealment he unbuttoned the top button of his shirt and taking hold of a string about his neck pulled forth a small wooden case, obviously of pocket-knife manufacture. Snapping the cord, he offered its pendant to Janice.

"I — I would keep it, Charles," replied Janice, "but you know mommy told me —"

"And what right has she to prevent you?" broke in Charles, warmly. "It does her no wrong, nor can it harm you to keep it. What right have they to tyrannise over you? 'T is all of a piece with their forcing you to marry that awkward, ignorant put. Here, take it." The groom seized her hand, put the case in her palm, closed her fingers over, and held them thus, as if striving to make her accept the gift.

"Oh, Charles," cried the girl, very much flustered, "you should n't ask —"

"Ah, Miss Janice," he begged, "won't you keep it? They need never know."

"But I only wanted to show it to Tibbie," explained the girl, "to ask her if mommy was right when she said 't was monstrous flattered."

"'T is an impossibility," responded the man, earnestly, though he was unable to keep from slightly smiling at the unconscious naïveté of the question. "I would she could see it in a more befitting frame, to set it off. If thou 't but let me, I'd put it in the other setting. Then 't would show to proper advantage."

"Would it take long?"

"A five minutes only."

The girl threw open the shawl, and thrusting her hand under her neckerchief into the V-cut of her bodice, produced the miniature.

The servant recoiled a step as she held it out to him.

Then snatching rather than taking the trinket from her hand, he said, "That is no place for this."

"Why not?" asked Janice.

"Because she is unfit to rest there," cried the man. He pulled out a knife, and with the blade pried up the rim, and shook free the protective glass and slip of ivory. "Now 't is purged of all wrong," he said, touching the setting to his lips. "I would it were for me to keep, for 't has lain near your heart, and 't is still warm with happiness."

The speech and act so embarrassed Janice that she hurriedly said, "I really must n't stay. I 've been too long as 't is, and —"

"'T will take but a moment," the servant assured her hastily. "Wilt please give me t' other one?" Throwing the miniature he had taken from the frame on the floor, he set about removing that of Janice from its wooden casing and fitting it to its new setting.

"Don't," cried Janice, in alarm, stooping to pick up the slip of ivory. "'T is not owing to you that 't was n't spoiled," she added indignantly, after a glance at it.

"Small loss if 't were!" responded the man, bitterly. "Promise me, Miss Janice, that you 'll not henceforth carry it in your bosom?"

"'T is a monstrous strange thing to ask."

"I tell thee she 's not fit to rest near a pure heart."

"How know you that?"

"How know I?" cried the man, in amazement. "Why —" There he stopped and knit his brows.

"I knew thou wert deceiving us when thee said 't was not thine," charged the girl.

"Nay, Miss Janice, 't was the truth I told you, though a quibble, I own. The miniature never was mine, tho' 't was once in my possession."

"Then how came you by it?"

"I took it by force from — never mind whom." The old bitter look was on the man's face, and anger burned in his eyes.

"You stole it!" cried the girl, drawing away from him.

"Not I," denied the man. "'T was taken from one who had less right to 't than I."

"You knew her?" questioned the girl.

"Ay," cried the man, with a kind of desperation. "I should think I did!"

"And — and you — you loved her?" she asked with a hesitancy which might mean that she was in doubt whether to ask the question, or perhaps that she rather hoped her surmise would prove wrong.

The young fellow halted in his work of trimming the ivory to fit the frame, and for a moment he stood, apparently looking down at his half-completed job, as it lay on the top of the meal-box. Then suddenly he put his hand to his throat as if he were choking, and the next instant he leaned forward, and, burying his face in his arms, as they rested on the whilom desk, he struggled to stifle the sobs that shook his frame.

"Oh, I did n't mean to pain you!" she cried in an agony of guilt and alarm.

Charles rose upright, and dashing his shirt sleeve across his eyes, he turned to the girl. "'T is over, Miss Janice," he asserted, "and a great baby I was to give way to 't."

"I can understand, and I don't think 't was babyish," said Janice, her heart wrung with sympathy for him. "She is so lovely!"

The man's lips quivered again, despite of his struggle to control himself. "That she is," he groaned. "And I — I loved her — My God! how I loved her! I thought her an angel from heaven; she was everything in life to me. When I fled from London, it seemed as if my heart was — was dead for ever."

"She was untrue?" asked Janice, with a deep sigh.

The servant's face darkened. "So untrue — Ah! 'T is not to be spoken. The two of them!"

"You challenged and killed him!" surmised Janice, excitedly. "And that 's why you came to America."

The groom shook his head sadly. "Not that, Miss Janice. They robbed me of both honour and revenge. I was powerless to punish either — except by — Bah! I 've done with them for ever."

"Foh mussy's sakes, chile," came Sukey's voice, "what

youse doin' hyar? Run quick, honey, foh your mah is 'quirin' foh youse."

"Oh, Luddy!" cried the girl, reaching out for the miniature.

"'T is not done, but I 'll see to 't that you get it this evening," exclaimed Charles.

The girl turned and fled toward the house, closely followed by Sukey.

"Peg she come to de kitchen foh youse," the cook explained; "an' 'cause I dun see youse go out de back do', I specks whar youse gwine, an' I sens her back to say dat young missus helpin' ole Sukey, an' be in pretty quick, an' so dey never know."

"Oh, Sukey, you 're a dear!"

"But, missy dear, doan youse do nuthin' foolish 'bout dat fellah, 'cause I 'se helped youse. Doan youse—"

"Of course I won't," asserted the girl. "I could n't, Sukey. You know I could n't."

"Dat 's right, honey. Ole Sukey knows she can trust youse. Now run right along, chile."

"What have you been doing, Janice?" asked her mother, as the girl entered the parlour.

"I 've been in the kitchen with Sukey, mommy," replied Janice. And if there was wrong in the quibble, both father and mother were equally to blame with the girl, for "Ole Sukey" was actually better able to enter into her feelings and thoughts than either of them; and where obedience is enforced from authority and not from sympathy and confidence, there will be secret deceit, if not open revolt.

Left to himself, the bondsman finished trimming the ivory to a proper size, and neatly fitted it into the frame. Then he spread the papers out, and in some haste, for the winter's day was fast waning, he resumed his scribbling, varied by intervals of pen-chewing and knitting of brows. Finally he gave a sigh of relief, and taking a blank sheet he copied in a bold handwriting what was written on the paper he had last toiled over. Then picking up the miniature, he touched it to his lips. "She was sent to give me faith again in women," he said, as he folded the miniature into the paper.

"Well, old man," he remarked, as he passed from the stable,

to the dog, who had followed in his footsteps, and sought to attract his attention by fawning upon him, "has blindman's holiday come at last? Wait till I bestow this, and get a bite from Sukey to put in my pocket, and we 'll be off for a look at the rabbits. 'T is a poor sport, but 't will do till something better comes. Oh for a war!"

The bondsman passed into the kitchen, and made his plea to Sukey for a supper he could take away with him. The request was granted, and while the cook went to the larder to get him something, Charles stepped into the hall and listening intently he stole upstairs and tapped gently on a door. Getting no reply, he opened it, and tiptoeing hastily to the dressing-stand, he tucked the packet under the powder-box. A minute later he was back in the kitchen, and erelong was stamping through the snow, whistling cheerfully, which the hound echoed by yelps of excited delight.

Janice was unusually thoughtful all through supper, and little less so afterwards. She was sent to her room earlier than usual, that she might make up in advance for the early start of the journey, and she did not dally with her disrobing, the room being almost arctic in its coldness. But after she had put on the short night-rail that was the bed-gown of the period, the girl paused for a moment in front of her mirror, even though she shivered as she did so.

"I really thought 't was for me he cared," she said. "But she is so much more beautiful that —" Janice tucked the fly-away locks into the snug-fitting nightcap, which together with the bed-curtains formed the protections from the drafts inevitable to leaky windows and big chimneys, and having thus done her best to make herself ugly, she blew out her candle, and as she crept into bed, she remarked, "'T was very foolish of me."

XIV

A QUESTION CONCERNING THALIA

ALL was animation at Greenwood the next morning, while yet it was dark, and as Janice dressed by candle-light, she trembled from something more than the icy chill of the room. The girl had been twice in her life to New York, once each to Newark and to Burlington, and though her visits to Trenton were of greater number, the event was none the less too rare an occurrence not to excite her. Her mother had to order her sharply to finish what was on her plate at breakfast, or she would scarce have eaten.

"If thou dost not want to be frozen, lass, before we get to Trenton," warned the squire, "do as thy mother says. Stuff cold out of the stomach, or 't is impossible to keep the scamp out of the blood."

"Yes, dadda," said the girl, obediently falling to once more. After a few mouthfuls she asked, "Dadda, who was Thalia?"

"'T was a filly who won the two-year purse at the Philadelphia races in sixty-eight," the squire informed her, between gulps of sausage and buckwheat cakes.

"Was she very lovely?" asked Janice, in a voice of surprise.

"No. An ill-shaped mare, but with a great pace."

The girl looked thoughtful for a moment and then asked, "Is that the only one there is?"

"Only what?" demanded her mother.

"The only Thalia?"

"'T is the only one I 've heard of," said the squire.

"Thou 'rt wrong, Lambert," corrected his spouse, in wifely fashion. "'T was one of those old heathens with horns, or tail, or something, I forget exactly. What set thy mind on that, child? Hast been reading some romance on the sly?"

"No, mommy," denied the girl.

"Put thy thoughts to better uses, then," ordered the mother. "Think more of thy own sin and corruption and less of what is light and vain."

It had been arranged that Thomas was to drive the sleigh, the squire preferring to leave Fownes in care of the remaining horses. It was Charles, however, who brought down the two trunks, and after he had put them in place he suggested, "If you 'll take seat, Miss Janice, I 'll tuck you well in." Spreading a large bearskin on the seat and bottom of the sleigh, he put in a hot soapstone, and very unnecessarily took hold of the little slippered feet, and set them squarely upon it, as if their owner were quite unequal to the effort. Then he folded the robe carefully about her, and drew the second over that, allowing the squire, it must be confessed, but a scant portion for his share.

"Thank you, Charles," murmured the girl, gratefully. "Of course he 's a bond-servant and he has a horrid beard," she thought, "but it is nice to have some one to — to think of your comfort. If he were only Philemon!"

The bondsman climbed into the rear of the sleigh, that he might fold the back part of the skin over her shoulders. The act brought his face close to the inquirer, and she turned her head and whispered, "Who was Thalia?"

"'T was one of — "

"Charles, get out of that sleigh," ordered Mrs. Meredith, sharply. "Learn thy place, sir. Janice, thou 'rt quite old enough to take care of thyself. We 'll have no whispering or coddling, understand."

The bondsman sullenly obeyed, and a moment later the sleigh started. The servant looked wistfully after it until the sound of the bells was lost, and then, with a sigh, he went to his work.

With all the vantage of the daylight start, it took good driving among the drifts to get over the twenty-eight miles that lay between Greenwood and Trenton before the universal noon dinner, and as the sleigh drew up at the Drinkers' home on the main street of the village, the meal was in the air if not on the table.

For this reason the two girls had not a chance for a moment's confidence before dinner; and though Janice was fairly bursting with all that had happened since Tibbie's visit, the departure of the squire for Burlington immediately the meal was ended, and the desire of Tabitha's father and aunt to have news of Mrs. Meredith and of the doings "up Brunswick way," filled in the whole afternoon till tea time — if the misnomer can be used, for, unlike the table at Greenwood, tea was a tabooed article in the Drinker home. One fact worth noting about the meal was that Janice asked if any of them knew who Thalia was.

"Ay," said Mr. Drinker, "and the less said of her the better. She was a lewd creature that —"

"Mr. Drinker!" cried Tabitha's aunt. "Thee forgets there are gentlewomen present. Wilt have some preserve, Janice?"

"No, I thank you," said the girl. "I'm not hungry." And she proved it by playing with what was on her plate for the rest of the meal.

Not till the two girls retired did they have an opportunity to exchange confidences. The moment they were by themselves, Tabitha demanded, "What made thee so serious to-night?"

"Oh, Tibbie," sighed Janice, dolefully, "I'm very unhappy!"

"What over?"

"I — he — Charles — I'm afraid he — and yet — 'T is something he wrote, but whether in joke or — Mr. Evatt said he insulted me at the tavern — Yet 't is so pretty that — and mommy interrupted just —"

"What art thou talking about, Jan?" exclaimed Tibbie.

Janice even in her disjointed sentences had begun to unlace her travelling bodice, — for with a prudence almost abnormal this one frock was not cut low, — and she now produced from her bosom a paper which she unfolded, and then offered to Tibbie with a suggestion of hesitation, asking "Dost think he meant to insult me?"

Tabitha eagerly took the sheet, and read —

TO THALIA

These lines to her my passion tell,
Describe the empire of her spell;
A love which naught will e'er dispel,
That flames for sweetest Thalia.

The sun that brights the fairest morn,
The stars that gleam in Capricorn,
Do not so much the skies adorn
As does my lovely Thalia.

The tints with which the rose enchants,
The fragrance which the violet grants;
Each doth suggest, but ne'er supplants,
The charms of dainty Thalia.

To gaze on her is sweet delight:
'Tis heaven whene'er she's in my sight,
But when she's gone, 't is endless night —
All 's dark without my Thalia.

I vow to her, by God above,
By hope of life, by depth of love,
That from her side I ne'er will rove,
So much love I my Thalia.

"How monstrous pretty!" cried Tabitha. "I 'm sure he meant it rightly."

"I thought 't was a beautiful valentine," sighed Janice, — "and 't was the first I ever had — but dadda says she was an ill-shaped mare — and mommy says 't was something with a tail — and 't is almost as bad to have her a wicked woman — so I 'm feared he meant it in joke — or worse —"

"I don't believe it," comforted Tibbie. "He may have made a mistake in the name, but I 'm sure he meant it; that he — well — thee knows. And if thee copies it fair, and puts in 'Delia,' or 'Celia,' 't will do to show to the girls. I wish some one would send me such a valentine."

Made cheerful by her friend's point of view, Janice went on with more spirit, —

"Nor is that the end." She took from her trunk a handkerchief and unwrapping it, produced the unset miniature. "He let me keep it," she said.

"How mighty wonderful!" again exclaimed Tibbie, growing big-eyed. "Who —"

"Furthermore, and in continuation, as Mr. McClave always says after his ninthly," airily interrupted Janice, drawing from her bosom the portrait of herself. "Who 's that, Tibbie Drinker?"

"Janice!" cried the person so challenged. "How lovely! Who — Did Mr. Peale come to Greenwood?"

"Not he. Who, think you, did it?"

"I vow if I can guess."

"Charles!"

"No!" gasped Tibbie, properly electrified. "Thee is cozening me."

"Not for a moment," cried Janice, delightedly.

"Tell me everything about *all*," was Tabitha's rapturous demand.

It took Janice many minutes, and Tibbie was called upon to use many exclamation and question marks, ere the tale of all these surprises was completed. Long before it had come to a finish, the two girls were snuggled together in bed, half in real love, as well as for the mutual animal heat, and half that they might whisper the lower. The facts, after many interruptions and digressions, having been narrated, Janice asked, —

"Whom, think you, Charles loves, Tibbie?"

"'T is very strange! From his valentine and miniature I should think 't was thee. But from what he told thee —"

"'T is exactly that which puzzles me."

"Oh, Janice! He — Perhaps thee was right. He may be a villain who is trying to beguile thee."

"For what could — Then why should he tell me about her?"

"That — well — 't is beyond me."

"If 't had not been for coming away, I — that is —" The girl hesitated and then said, "Tibbie?"

"What?"

"Dost think — I mean —" The girl drew her bedfellow closer, and in an almost inaudible voice asked, "Would it be right, think you — when I go back, you know — to — to encourage him — that is, to give him a chance to tell me — so as to find out?"

The referee of this important question was silent for long enough to give a quality of consideration to her opinion, and then decided, "I think thee shouldst. 'T is a question that thou hast a right to know about." Having given the ruling, this most upright judge changed her manner from one conveying thought to one suggesting eagerness, and asked, "Oh, Janice, if he does — if thee finds out anything, wilt thee tell it me?"

"Ought I?" asked Janice, divided between the pleasure of monopolising a secret and the enjoyment of sharing it.

"Surely thee ought," cried Tabitha. "After telling me so much, thou shouldst — for Charles' sake. Otherwise I might misjudge him."

"Then I 'll tell you everything," cried Janice, clearly happy in the decision.

"And if he does love you, Jan?" suggestively remarked Tibbie.

"'T will be vastly exciting," said Janice. "You know, Tibbie, it frightens me a little, for he 's just the kind of man to do something desperate."

"And — and you would n't — "

"Tibbie Drinker! A redemptioner!"

"But Janice, he must have been a gentle —"

"What he was, little matters," interrupted the girl. "He 's a bond-servant now, and even if he were n't, he 'd have a bristly beard — Ugh!"

"Poor fellow," sighed Tabitha. "'T is not his fault!"

"Nor is 't mine," retorted Janice.

A pause of some moments followed and then Janice asked: "Dost think I am promised to Mr. Evatt, Tibbie?" — for let it be confessed that every incident of what she had pledged herself not to tell had been poured out to her confidant.

"I think so," whispered the girl, "and he being used to court ways would surely know."

"He 's — well, he 's a fine figure of a man," owned Janice. "And tho' I ne'er intended it, I 'd rather 't would be he than Philemon Hennion or the parson."

"What if thy father and mother should not consent?" said Tabitha.

"'T would be lovely!" cried Janice, ecstatically. "Just like a romance, you know. And being court-bred, he 'd know how to — well — how to give it *éclat*. Oh, Tibbie, think of making a runaway match and of going to court!"

Much as Tabitha loved her friend, the little green-eyed monster gained possession of her momentarily. "He may be deceiving thee," she suggested. "Perhaps he never was there."

"Nay. He knows all the titled people. He was at one of Lady Grafton's routs, Tibbie, and was spoke to by the Duke of Cumberland!"

For a man falsely to assert acquaintance with a royal duke seemed so impossible to the girl that this was accepted as indisputable proof; driven from her first position, Tibbie remarked, "Perhaps he won't return. Many 's the maid been cozened and deserted by the men."

For a moment, either because this idea did not please Janice or because she needed time to digest it, there was silence.

"Oh, Janice," sighed Tibbie, presently, "'t is almost past belief that thee has had so much happen to thee."

But a few weeks before the girl thought the chief part of her experiences the most cruel luck that had ever befallen maiden. Yet so quickly does youth put trouble in the past, and so respondent is it to the romantic view of things, that she now promptly answered,—

"Is 't not, Tibbie! Am I not a lucky girl? If I only was certain about Thalia, I should be so happy.

XV

QUESTIONS OF DELICACY

OF the time Janice spent at Trenton little need be said. Compared with Greenwood, the town was truly almost riotous. Neither Presbyterian nor Quaker approved of dancing, and so the regular weekly assemblies were forbidden fruit to the girls, and Janice and Tibbie were too well born to be indelicately of the throng who skated long hours on Assanpink Creek, or to take part in the frequent coasting-parties. But of other amusements they had, in the expression of the day, "a great plenty." Four teas, — but without that particular beverage, — two quilting-bees, one candy-pulling and one corn-popping, three evenings at singing-school, and a syllabub party supplied such ample social dissipation to Janice that life seemed for the time fairly to whirl.

Not the least of the excitement, it must be confessed, was the conquest by Janice of a young Quaker cousin of Tabitha's named Penrhyn Morris. Two other of the Trenton lads, too, began to behave in a manner so suspicious to the girls as to call for much discussion. Tibbie as well had several swains, who furnished still further subjects of conversation after sleeping hours had come. Several times sharp reproofs were shouted through the partition from Miss Drinker's room, but the whispering only sank in tone and not in volume.

One incident not to be omitted was the appearance of Philemon, nominally on business, in Trenton; but he called upon the Drinkers, and remained to dinner when asked. He stayed on and on after that meal, wearying the two girls beyond measure by the necessity of maintaining a conversation, until, just as the desperation point was reached, Tibbie introduced a topic which had an element of promise in it.

"Hast thou seen Charles Fownes of late?" she asked of the mute awkward figure; and though Janice did not look up, there was a moment's flicker of her eyelashes.

"All I wants ter," said Phil, sulkily. "An' I guess that ere 's the feelin' pretty generally."

"Why?" demanded Tabitha, after a glance at Janice.

"'Cause of the airs he takes. He called me a put because I was a bit slow — ter his mind — in learnin' the manual, an' he 's got a tongue an' a temper like a hedgehog. But the fellers paid him off come Saturday week."

"How?" asked Janice, dropping her pose of indifference.

"He 's been expectin' ter be appointed captain of the Brunswick Invincibles, when they was trained, but he put on such airs, an' was so sharp an' bitin' with his tongue, that when they voted for officers last week I 'll be dinged if they did n't drop him altogether. He did n't get a vote for so much as a corporal's rank. He was in a stew, I tells you."

"What did he do?" questioned Tabitha.

"He was so took aback," snickered Philemon, "that he up and says 't was the last he 'd have ter do with 'em, an' that they was a lot of clouts an' clodpates, an' they 'd got a captain ter match."

"Was that you?" cruelly asked Janice.

"No. 'T was Joe Bagby," replied Phil, not so much as seeing the point.

"The village loafer and ne'er-do-weel," exclaimed Janice, reflecting her father's view.

"He ain't idlin' much these-a-days," asserted Philemon, "and the boys all like him for his jokes an' good-nature. I tell you 't was great sport ter see him an' your redemptioner give it ter each other. Fownes, he said that if 't were n't better sport ter catch rabbits, he 'd mightily enjoy chasin' the whole company of Invincibles with five grenadiers of the guard, an' Bagby he sassed back by sayin' that Charles need n't be so darned cocky, for he 'd run from the regulars hisself, an' then your man tells Joe ter give his red rag a holiday by talkin' about what he know'd of, for then he 'd have ter be silent, an' then the captain says he was a liar, and Charles knocks him down, an' stood over him and made him take it back. An' Bagby he takes it back, sayin' as how his own words was very good eatin' anyways. I tell you, the whole town enjoyed that 'ere afternoon."

"I suppose they made you an officer?" said Miss Meredith, with unconcealed contempt.

"No, Miss Janice," Philemon eagerly denied, "an' that's what I come over to tell you. Seein' that you an' the squire did n't like my drillin', I 've left the company, an' I won't go back, I pass you my word."

"'T is nothing to me what you do," responded Janice, crushingly.

"Don't say that, Miss Janice," entreated Phil.

"Is thee not ashamed," exclaimed Tabitha, "to seek to marry a girl against her wishes? If I were Janice, I'd never so much as look at thee."

"She never said as how she —" stammered Hennion.

"That was nothing," continued Tibbie. "Thee shouldst have known it. The idea of asking the father first!"

"But that's the regular way," ejaculated Phil, in evident bewilderment.

"To marry a girl when she does n't choose to!" snapped Tibbie. "A man of any decency would find out — on the sly — if she wanted him."

"She never would — "

"As if the fact that she would n't was n't enough!" continued Tibbie, with anything but Quaker meekness. "Dost think, if she wanted thee, she'd have been so offish?"

Phil, with a sadly puzzled look on his face, said, "I know I ain't much of a sharp at courtin', Miss Janice, an' like as not I done it wrong, but I loves you, that's certain, an' I would n't do anything ter displeasure you, if I only know'd what you wanted. Dad he says that I was n't rampageous enough ter suit a girl of spirit, an' that if I'd squoze you now an' again, 'stead of — "

"That's enough," said Janice. "Mr. Hennion, there is the door."

"Thou art a horrid creature!" added Tibbie.

"I ain't goin' till I've had it all out with you," asserted Phil, with a dogged determination.

"Then you force us to leave you," said Janice, rising.

Just as she spoke, the door was thrown open, and Mr. Meredith entered. His eye happened to fall first on Philemon, and without so much as a word of greeting to the girls, he demanded angrily, "Ho! what the devil are ye doing here? 'T is all of a piece that a traitor to his king should work by stealth."

Even the worm turns, and Philemon, already hectored to desperation by the girls, gave a loose to his sense of the wrong and injustice that it seemed to him every one conspired to heap upon him. "I 've done no hugger-muggery," he roared, shaking his fist in the squire's face, "an' the man 's a tarnal liar who says I have."

"Don't try to threaten me, sir!" roared back the squire, but none the less retiring two steps. "Your father's son can't bully Lambert Meredith. But for his cowardice, and others like him, but for the men of all sides and no side, we 'd have prevented the Assembly's approving the damned resolves of the Congress. Marry a daughter of mine! I 'll see ye and your precious begetter in hell first. Don't let me find ye snooking about my girl henceforth, or 't will fare ill with ye that I warn ye."

"If 't war n't that you are her father an' an old man, I 'l teach you a lesson," growled Phil, as he went to the door; "as 't is, look out for yourself. You has enemies enough without makin' any more."

"There 's a good riddance to him," chuckled the squire. "Well, hast a kiss for thy dad, Jan?"

"A dozen," responded the girl. "But what brought you back? Surely the Assembly has not adjourned?"

"'T is worse than that," asserted the squire. "For a week we held the rascals at bay, but yesterday news came from England that the ministry had determined not to yield, and in a frenzy the Assembly indorsed the Congress's doings on the spot. As a consequence this morning the king's governor dissolved us, and the writs will shortly be out for a new election. So back I must get me to Brunswick to attend to my poll. I bespoke a message to Charles by Squire Perkins, who rid on to Morristown, telling him to be here with the sleigh to-morrow as early as he could; and meanwhile must trust to some Trenton friend or to the tavern for a bed, if thy father, Tabitha, can't put me up."

Charles reported to the squire at an hour the following morning which indicated either a desire for once to please his master, or some other motive, for an obedience so prompt must have necessitated a moonlight start from Greenwood in order to reach Trenton so early. He was told to bait his horses at the tavern, and the time this took was spent by the girls in repeating farewells.

"'T is a pity thee hast to go before Friend Penrhyn hath spoken," said Tibbie, regretfully.

"Is n't it?" sighed Janice. "I did so want to see how he 'd say it."

"You may — perhaps Charles — " brokenly but suggestively remarked Tibbie.

"Perhaps," responded Janice, "but 't will be very different. I know he 'll — well, he 'll be abrupt and — and excited, and will — his sentences will not be well thought out beforehand. Now Penrhyn would have spoken at length and feelingly. 'T would have been monstrously enjoyable."

"At least thee 'll find out who Thalia is."

"Oh, Tibbie, I fear me I sha'n't dare. I tried to ask Mr. Taggart, who, being college-bred, ought to know, but I was so afraid she was a wicked woman, that I began to blush before I 'd so much as got out the first word. I wish I was pale and delicate like Prissy Glover. 'T is mortifying to be so healthy."

"Thy waist is at least two inches smaller than hers, when 't is properly laced."

"But I have red cheeks," moaned Janice, "and, oh, Tibbie, at times I have *such* an appetite!"

"Oh, Jan! so have I," confided Miss Drinker in the lowest of whispers, as if fearing even the walls. "Sometimes when the men are round, I 'd eat twice as much but for the fear they 'd think me coarse and — "

"Gemini, yes!" assented Janice, when the speaker paused. "Many and many 's the time I 've wanted more. But 't is all right as long as the men don't know that we do."

"Here 's the sleigh," interrupted Tabitha, going to the door. "Come out quickly, while thy father is having the stirrup cup, and I 'll ask him about Thalia."

"Oh, will you?" joyfully cried Janice. "Tibbie, you 're a —"

Miss Meredith's speech was stopped by the two coming within hearing of the redemptioner, who promptly removed his cap. "'T will be good to have you back at Greenwood, Miss Janice," he said with a bow.

"How gracefully he does it!" whispered Tabitha, as they approached the sleigh. Then aloud she asked, "Charles, wilt tell me who — who — who was chosen captain of the 'Invincibles'?"

The question brought a scowl to the man's face, and both girls held their breath, expecting an outbreak of temper, while Tabitha to herself bemoaned that so unfortunate a subject sprang first into her thoughts to replace the question she dared not put. But before the groom replied, the scowl changed suddenly into a look of amusement, and when he spoke, it was to say, —

"'T is past belief, Miss Tabitha, except they want to save their skins by never fighting. 'T was Joe Bagby the bumpkins chose — a fellow I 've knocked down without his resenting it. A cotswold lion, who works his way by jokes and by hand-shakes. He 's the best friend of every one who ever lived, and I make no doubt, if a British regiment appears, he 'll say he loves the lobsters too much to lead the 'Invincibles' against them."

"No doubt," agreed Tibbie. "Canst tell me also who — who — how Clarion is?"

But this question was never answered, for the squire appeared at this point, and the sleigh was quickly speeding towards Greenwood. It was after dark when it drew up at its destination, for the spring thaw was beginning, and the roads soft and deep. Janice was so stiff with the long sitting and the cold that she needed help both in alighting and in climbing the porch steps. This the groom gave her, and when she was safely in front of the parlor fire, he assisted in the removing of her wraps, while Mrs. Meredith performed a like service for the squire in the hallway.

"Dost remember your question, Miss Janice," asked Charles, "just as you drove away from Greenwood?"

"Yes."

"She was one of the three graces."

"Was she very beautiful?"

"The ancients so held her, but they had never seen you, Miss Janice."

The girl had turned away as she nonchalantly asked the last question, and so Charles could not see the charmingly demure smile that her face assumed, nor the curve of the lips, and perhaps it was fortunate for him that he did not. Yet all Miss Meredith said was, —

"Not that I cared to know, but I knew Tibbie would be curious."

XVI

A VARIETY OF CONTRACTS

THE spring thaw set in in earnest the day after the squire's return to Greenwood, and housed the family for several days. No sooner, however, did the roads become something better than troughs of mud than the would-be Assemblyman set actively to work for his canvass of the county, daily riding forth to make personal calls on the free and enlightened electors, in accordance with the still universal British custom of personal solicitation. What he saw and heard did not tend to improve his temper, for the news that the Parliament was about to vote an extension to the whole country of the punitive measures hitherto directed against Massachusetts had lighted a flame from one end of the land to the other. The last election had been with difficulty carried by the squire, and now the prospect was far more gloomy.

When a realising sense of the conditions had duly dawned on the not over-quick mind of the master of Greenwood, he put pride in his pocket and himself astride of Joggles, and rode of an afternoon to Boxley, as the Hennions' place was named. Without allusion to their last interview, he announced to the senior of the house that he wished to talk over the election.

"He, he, he!" snickered Hennion. "Kinder gettin' anxious, heigh? I calkerlated yer 'd find things sorter pukish."

"Tush!" retorted Meredith, making a good pretence of confidence. "'T is mostly wind one hears, and 't will be another matter at the poll. I rid over to say that tho' we may not agree in private matters, 't is the business of the gentry to make head together against this madness."

"I see," snarled Hennion. "My boy ain't good enuf fer yer gal, but my votes is a different story, heigh?"

"Votes for votes is my rule," rejoined the squire. "The old arrangement, say I. My tenants vote for ye, and yours for me."

"Waal, this year theer 's ter be a differ," chuckled Hennion. "I 've agreed ter give my doubles ter Joe, an' he 's ter give hisn ter me."

"Joe! What Joe?"

"Joe Bagby."

"What!" roared the squire. "Art mad, man? That good-for-nothing scamp run for Assembly?"

"Joe ain't no fool," asserted Hennion. "An' tho' his edication and grammer ain't up ter yers an' mine, squire, he thinks so like the way folks ere jest naow a-thinkin' thet it looks ter me as if he wud be put in."

"The country is going to the devil!" groaned Mr. Meredith. "And ye 'll throw your doubles for that worthless—"

"I allus throw my doubles fer the man as kin throw the most doubles fer me," remarked Hennion. "An' I ain't by no means sartin haow many doubles yer kin split this year."

"Pox me, the usual number!"

"Do yer leaseholds all pay theer rents?"

"Some have dropped behind, but as soon as there 's law in the land again they 'll come to the rightabout."

"Exactly," sniggered Hennion. "As soon as theer 's law. But when 's thet 'ere goin' ter be? Mark me, the tenants who dare refuse ter pay theer rent, dare vote agin tneer landlord. An' as Joe Bagby says he 'll do his durndest ter keep the courts closed, I guess the delinquents will think he 's theer candidate. Every man as owes yer money, squire, will vote agin yer, come election day."

"And ye 'll join hands with these thieves and vote with Bagby in Assembly?"

"Guess I mought do wus. But if thet 'ere 's displeasin' ter yer, jest blame yerself for 't."

"How reason ye that, man?"

"Cuz I had it arranged thet I wuz ter side in with the king, and Phil wuz ter side in with the hotheads. But yer gal hez mixed Phil all up, so he 's turned right over an' talks ez ef he wuz Lord North or the Duke of Bedford. Consumaquently, since I don't see no good of takin' risks, I hed ter swing about an' jine the young blood."

What the squire said in reply, and continued to say until he had made his exit from the Hennion house, is far better omitted. In his wrath he addressed a monologue to his horse, long after he had passed through the gate of Boxley; until, in fact, he met Phil, to whom, as a better object for them than Joggles, the squire at once transferred his vituperations.

Instead of going on in his original direction, Philemon turned his horse and rode along with the squire, taking the rating in absolute silence. Only when Mr. Meredith had expressed and re-expressed all that was in him to say did the young fellow give evidence that his dumbness proceeded from policy.

"Seems ter me, squire," he finally suggested, "like you 're layin' up against me what don't suit you 'bout dad. I 've done my bestest ter do what you and Miss Janice set store by, an' it does seem ter me anythin' but fairsome ter have a down on me, just because of dad. 'T ain't my fault I 've got him for a father; I had n't nothin' ter do with it, an' if you have any one ter pick a quarrel with, it must be with God Almighty, who fixed things as they is. I 've quit drillin'; I 've spoke against the Congress; an' there ain't nothin' else I would n't do ter get Miss Janice."

"Go to the devil, then," advised the squire. "No son of—" There the squire paused momentarily, and after a brief silence ejaculated, "Eh!" After another short intermission he laughed aloud, as if pleased at something which had occurred to him. "Why, Phil, my boy," he cried, slapping his own thigh, "we 'll put a great game up on thy dad. We 'll show him he 's not the only fox hereabout."

"And what 'ere 's that?"

"What say ye to being my double in the poll, lad?"

"Run against father?" ejaculated Phil.

"Ay. We 'll teach him to what trimming and time-serving come. And be damned to him!"

"That 'ere 's all very well for you," responded Hennion, "but he hain't got the whip hand of you like he has of me. He would n't stand my —"

"He 'd have to," gleefully interrupted the squire. "Join hands with me, lad, and I 'll fix it so ye can snap your fingers at him."

"But —" began Phil.

"But," broke in the squire. "Nonsense! No but, lad. Butter — ay, and cream it shall be. Let him turn ye off. There 's a home at Greenwood for ye, if he does — and something better than that too. Sixteen, ye dog! Sweet sixteen, rosy sixteen, bashful sixteen, glowing sixteen, run-away-and-want-to-be-found sixteen!"

"She don't seem ter want me ter find her," sighed Phil.

"Fooh!" jeered the father. "There 's only two kinds of maids, as ye 'd know if ye 'd been out in the world as I have — those that want a husband and those that don't. But six months married, and ye can't pick the one from t' other, try your best. There 's nothing brings a lass to the round-about so quick as having to do what she does n't want. They are born contrary and skittish, and they can't help shying at fences and gates, but give 'em the spur and the whip, and over they go, as happy as a lark. And I say so, Janice will marry ye, and mark my word, come a month she 'll be complaining that ye don't fondle her enough."

Mr. Meredith's pictorial powers, far more than his philosophy, were too much for Philemon to resist. He held out his hand, saying, "'T is a bargain, squire; an' I 'll set to on a canvass to-day."

"Well said," responded the elder, heartily. "And that 's not all, Phil, that ye shall get from it. I 've a tidy lot of money loaned to merchants in New York, and I 'll get it from 'em, and we 'll buy the mortgages on your father's lands. Who 'll have the whip hand then, eh? Oh! we 'll smoke the old fox before we 've done with him. His brush shall be well singed."

The compact thus concluded to their common satisfaction, the twain separated, and the squire rode the remaining six miles in that agreeable state of enjoyment which comes from the sense of triumphing over enemies. His very stride as he stamped through the hall and into the parlour had in it the suggestion that he was planting his heel on some foe, and it was with evident elation that he announced: —

"Well, lass, I 've a husband for ye, so get your lips and blushes ready for him against to-morrow!"

"Oh, dadda, no!" cried the girl, ceasing her spinet practice.

"Oh, yes! And no obstinacy, mind. Phil 's a good enough lad for any girl. Where 's your mother that I may tell her?"

"She 's in the attic, getting out some whole cloth," answered the girl; and as her father left the room, she leaned forward and rested her burning cheek on the veneer of the spinet for an instant as if to cool it. But the colour deepened rather than lessened, and a moment later she rose, with her lips pressed into a straight line, and her eyes shining very brightly. "I 'll not marry the gawk. No! And if they insist I 'll —" Then she paused.

"How did Janice take it?" asked Mrs. Meredith, when the squire had broken his news to her.

"Coltishly," responded the father, "but no blubbering this time. The filly 's getting used to the idea of a bit, and will go steady from now on." All of which went to show how little the squire understood the nature of women, for the lack of tears should have been the most alarming fact in his daughter's conduct.

When Phil duly put in an appearance on the following day, he was first interviewed by what Janice would have called the attorney for the prosecution, who took him to his office and insisted, much to the lover's disgust, in hearing what he had done politically. Finally, however, this all-engrossing subject to the office-seeker was, along with Philemon's patience, exhausted, and the squire told his fellow-candidate that the object of his desires could now be seen.

"The lass jumped to her feet as ye rid up, and said she 'd some garden matters to tend, so there 's the spot to seek her." Then the father continued, "Don't shilly-shally with her, whate'er ye do, unless ye are minded to have balking and kicking for the rest of your days. I took Matilda — Mrs. Meredith — by surprise once, and before she knew I was there

I had her in my arms. And, egad! I never let her go, plead her best, till she gave me one of my kisses back. She began to take notice from that day. 'T is the way of women."

Thus stimulated, Phil entered the garden, prepared to perform most valiant deeds. Unfortunately for him, however, the bondsman had been summoned by Janice to do the digging, and his presence materially altered the situation and necessitated a merely formal greeting.

Having given some directions to Charles for continuation of the work, Janice walked to another part of the garden, apparently quite heedless of Philemon. Her swain of course followed, and the moment they were well out of hearing of the servant, Janice turned upon him and demanded: —

"Art thou gentleman enough to keep thy word?"

"I hope as how I am, Miss Janice," stuttered Phil, very much taken aback.

"Wilt give me your promise, if I tell thee something, to repeat it to no one?"

"Certain, Miss Janice, I 'll tell nothin' you don't want folks ter know."

"Even dadda and mommy?"

"Cross my heart."

"You see that man over there?"

"Yer mean Charles?"

"Yes. He is desperately in love with me," announced the girl.

"Living jingo! He 's been a-troublin' you?"

"No. He loves me too much to persecute me, and, besides, he 's a gentleman."

"Now, Miss Janice, you know as how I —"

"Am trying to marry me against my will."

"But the squire says you 'll be gladsome enough a month gone; that —"

"Ugh!"

"Now please don't —"

"And what I am going to tell you and what you 've given your word not to repeat is this: If you persist in trying to marry me, if you so much as try to — to — to be familiar, that moment I 'll run off with him — there!"

"You never would!"

"In an instant."

"You 'd take a bondsman rather than me?"

The girl coloured, but replied, "Yes."

"I 'll teach him ter have done with his cutty-eyed tricks," roared Phil, doubling up his fists, and turning, "I 'll — "

"Mr. Hennion!" exclaimed the girl, her cheeks gone very white. "You gave me your word that — "

"I never gave no word 'bout not threshing the lick."

"Most certainly you did, for you — you would have to tell him before — and if you do that, I 'll — "

"But, Miss Janice, you must n't disgrace — Damn him! Then Bagby was n't lyin' when he told me how there 'd been talk at the tavern of his bundlin' with you."

For a moment Janice stood speechless, everything about her suggesting the shame she was enduring. "He — he never said that!" she panted more than spoke, as if she had ceased to breathe.

"I told Bagby if he said that he was lyin'; but after — "

"Mr. Hennion, do you intend to insult me as well?"

"No, no, Miss Janice. I don't believe it. 'T was a lie for certain, and I 'm ashamed ter have spoke of it."

With unshed tears of mortification in her eyes Janice turned to go, every other ill forgotten in this last grief.

"Miss Janice," called Phil, "you can't go without — "

The girl faced about. "You men are all alike," she cried, interrupting. "You tease and worry and torture a girl you pretend to care for, till 't is past endurance. I hate you, and before I 'll — "

"Now, Miss Janice, say you 'll not run off with him. I 'll — I 'll try ter do as you ask, if only you — "

"So long as you — as you don't — don't bother me, I won't," promised Janice; "but the instant — "

And leaving the sentence thus broken, the girl left Philemon, and fled to her room.

XVII

IN THE NAME OF LIBERTY

THE scheme devised by Janice to keep Philemon at arm's length would hardly have succeeded for long, had not the squire been so preoccupied with the election and with the now active farm work that he paid little heed to the course of true love. Poor Phil was teased by him now and again for his "offishness;" but Janice carefully managed that their interviews were not held in the presence of her parents, and so the elders did not come to a realising sense of the condition, but really believed that the courtship was advancing with due progress to the port of matrimony.

Though this was a respite to Janice, she herself knew that it was at best the most temporary of expedients, and that the immediate press of affairs once over, her marriage with Philemon was sure to be pushed to a conclusion. Already her mother's discussions of clothes, of linen, and of furniture were constant reminders of its imminence, and the mere fact that the servants of Greenwood and the neighbourhood accepted the matter as settled, made allusions to it too frequent for Janice not to feel that her bondage was inevitable. A dozen times a day the girl would catch her breath or pale or flush over the prospect before her, frightened, as the bird in the net, not so much by the present situation, as by what the future was certain to bring to pass.

A still more serious matter was further to engross her parents' thoughts. One evening late in April, as the squire sat on the front porch resting from his day's labour, Charles, who had been sent to the village on some errand, came cantering up the road, and drew rein opposite.

"Have better care how ye ride that filly, sir," said the

squire, sharply. "I'll not have her wind broke by hard riding."

"I know enough of horses to do her no harm," answered the man, dismounting easily and gracefully; "and if I rode a bit quick, 't is because I've news that needs wings."

"What's to do?" demanded the master, laying down the "Rivington's Royal Gazette" he had been reading.

"As I was buying the nails," replied the servant, speaking with obvious excitement, "Mr. Bissel rode up to the tavern with a letter from the Massachusetts Committee of Safety to the southward; and as 't was of some moment, while he baited, I took a copy of it." The groom held out a paper, his hand shaking a little in his excitement, and with an eager look on his face he watched the squire read the following:—

Water Town Wednesday Morning near 11 of Clock.

To all friends of american liberty, be it known, that this morning before break of day, a Brigade, consisting of about 1,000 or 1,200 Men, landed at Phipp's Farm at Cambridge and marched to Lexington, where they found a Company of our Militia in Arms, upon whom they fired without any provocation and killed 6 Men & wounded 4 others — By an express from Boston we find another Brigade are now upon their march from Boston, supposed to be about 1,000 — The bearer Israel Bissel is charged to alarm the Country quite to Connecticut; and all Persons are desired to furnish him with fresh Horses, as they may be needed — I have spoken with several, who have seen the dead & wounded.

J. Palmer one of the Committee of safety.

Forwarded from Worcester April 19, 1775.

Brooklyn — Thursday	*11 o Clock*
Norwich	*4 o Clock*
New London	*7 o Clock*
Lynne — Friday Morning	*1 o Clock*
Say Brook	*4 o Clock*
Shillingsworth	*7 o Clock*
E. Gillford	*8 o Clock*
Guilford	*10 o Clock*
Bradford	*12 o Clock*
New Haven — April 21	

Recd & fowarded on certain Intelligence
Fairfield April 22d *8 o Clock*
New York Committee Chamber *4 o Clock*
23d April 1775 P. M.

Recd the within Acct by Express, forwd by Express to N Brunswick with directions to stop at Elizabeth Town & acquaint the Committee there with the foregoing particulars by order

J. S. Low, *Chairman.*

"Huh!" grunted the squire. "I said the day would come when British regulars would teach the scamps a lesson. The rapscallions are getting their bellyful, no doubt; 't is to be hoped that it will bring law and quiet once again in the land."

"'T will more likely be the match that fires the mine. You 've little idea, Mr. Meredith, how strong and universal the feeling is against Great Britain."

"'T is not as strong as British bayonets, that ye may tie to, fellow."

The servant shook his head doubtfully. "'T will take a long sword to reach this far, and Gage is not the man to handle it."

"Odd's life!" swore the squire. "What know ye of Gage? If every covenant man does n't think himself the better of a major-general or a magistrate!"

"Had you ever made the voyage from England, you 'd appreciate the difficulties. 'T is as big a military folly to suppose that if America holds together she can be conquered by bayonets, as 't is to suppose that she 'll allow a rotten Parliament, three thousand miles away, to rule her."

"Have done with such talk! What does a rogue like ye know of Parliament, except that it passes the laws ye run from? 'T is the like of ye — debtors, runaways, and such trash — that is making all this trouble."

The servant laughed ironically. "Fools do more harm in the world than knaves."

"What mean ye by that?" demanded the squire, hotly.

"'T is as reasonable to hold the American cause bad because a few bad men take advantage of it as 't is to blame the flock of sheep for giving the one wolf his covering. What the Whigs demand is only what the English themselves fought for under Pym and Hampden, and to-day, if the words 'Great Britain' were but inserted in the acts of Parliament of which America complains, there 'd be one rebellion from Land's End to Duncansby Head."

"Didst not hear my order to cease such talk?" fumed the squire. "Go to the stable where ye belong, fellow!"

The man coloured and bit his lip in a manifest attempt to keep his temper, but he did not move, saying instead, "Mr. Meredith, wilt please tell me what you paid for my bond?"

"Why ask ye that?"

"If I could pay you the amount — and something over — wouldst be willing to release me from the covenant?"

"And why should I?" demanded the squire.

The servant hesitated, and then said in a low voice: "As a gentleman, you must have seen I 'm no groom — and think how it must gall me to serve as one."

"Thou shouldst have thought of that before thou indentured, rather —"

"I know," burst out the man, "but I was crazed — was wild with — with a grief that had come to me, and knew not what I was doing."

"Fudge! No romantics. Every redemptioner would have it he is a gentleman, when he 's only caught the trick by waiting on them."

"But if I buy my time you —"

"How 'd come ye by the money?"

"I — I think I could get the amount."

"Ay. I doubt not ye know how money 's to be got by hook or by crook! And no doubt ye want your freedom to drill more rebels to the king. Ye 'll not get it from me, so there 's an end on 't." With which the squire rose, and stamped into the hall and then to his office.

Charles stood for a moment looking at the ground, and then raised his head so quickly that Janice, who had joined the two during the foregoing dialogue and whose eyes were upon him, had not time to look away. "Can't you persuade him to let me go, Miss Janice?" he asked appealingly.

"Why do you want your freedom?" questioned Janice, letting dignity surrender to curiosity.

"I want to get away from here — to get to a place where there's a chance for a quicker death than eating one's heart by inches."

"How beautifully he talks!" thought Janice.

"Nor will I bide here to see — to see —" went on the bondsman, excitedly, "I must run, or I shall end by — 'T will be better to let me go before I turn mad."

"'T is as good as a romance," was Janice's mental opinion. "How I wish Tibbie was here!"

"'T is no doubt a joke to you — oh! you need not have avoided me as you've done lately to show me that I was beneath you. I knew it without that. But who is this put you are going to marry?"

"Mr. Hennion is of good family," answered Janice, with spirit.

"Good family!" laughed the man, bitterly. "No doubt he is. Think you Phil Hennion is less the clout because he has a pedigree? There are hogs in Yorkshire can show better genealogies than royalty."

"'T is quite in keeping that a bond-servant should think little of blood," retorted Janice, made angry by his open contempt.

"Blood! Yes, I despise it, and so would you if you knew it as I do," exclaimed Charles, hotly, cutting the air with his whip. "*That* for all the blood in the world, unless there be honour with it," he said.

"The fox did n't want the grapes."

"'T is no case of sour grapes, as you'd know if I told you my story."

"Oh! I should monstrous like to hear it," eagerly ejaculated Janice.

The man dropped the bridle and came to the porch. "I swore it should die with me, but there's one woman in the world to whom —" he began, and then checked himself as a figure came into view on the lawn out of the growing darkness. "Who's there?" Charles demanded.

"It's me — Joe Bagby," was the answer, as that individual

came forward. "Is the squire home, miss?" he asked; and, receiving the reply that he was in his office, Joe volunteered the information that a wish to talk with the lord of Greenwood about the election was the motive of his call. "I want to see if we can't fix things between us."

Scarcely had he spoken when there was a sudden rush of men, who seemed to appear from nowhere, and at the same instant Joe gave a shove to the bond-servant, which, being entirely unexpected, sent him sprawling on the grass, where he was pinioned by two of the party.

"Keep your mouth shut, or I 'll have to choke you," said Bagby to Janice, as she opened her mouth to scream. "Two of you stand by her and keep her quiet. Sharp now, fellows, he 's in his office. Have him out, and some of you start a fire, quick."

The orders were obeyed with celerity, and as some rushed into the hall and dragged forth the squire, struggling, the scene was lighted by the blazing up of a bunch of hay, which had appeared as if by magic, and on which sticks of wood were quickly burning. Over the fire a pot, swung on a stick upheld by two men, was placed, telling a story of intention only too obvious.

"There is n't any sort of use swearing like that, squire," said Bagby. "We 've got a thing or two to say, and if you won't listen to it quiet, why, we 'll fill your mouth with a lump of tar, to give you something to chew on while we say it. Cussing did n't prevent your being a babe in the wood, and it won't prevent our giving you a bishop's coat; so if you don't want it, have done, and listen to what we have to propose."

"Well?" demanded the squire.

"We 've stood your conduct just as long as it was possible, squire," went on Bagby, "and been forbearing, hoping you 'd mend your ways. But it 's no use, and so we 've come up this evening to give you a last chance to put yourself right, for we 're a peace-loving, law-abiding lot, and don't want to use nothing but moral suasion, as the parson puts it, unless you make us."

"That 's it. Give it to him, Joe," said some one, approvingly.

"Now that the regulars of old Guelph have begun slaughtering the sons of liberty, we have decided to put an end to snakes in the grass, and so you can come to the face-about, or you can have a coat of tar and a ride on a rail out of the county. And what's more, when you're once out, you're to stay out, mind. Which is your choice?"

"What do you want me to do?" demanded the squire, sullenly.

"First off, we're tired of your brag that tea's drunk on your table. You're to give us all you've got, and you're not to get any new, whether 't is East India or smuggled."

"I agree to that."

"Secondly," went on Bagby, in a sing-song voice, much as if he was reading a series of resolutions, "you're to sign the Congress Association, and live up to it."

The squire looked to right and left, as if considering some outlet; but there were men all about him, and after a pause he merely nodded his head.

"You're getting mighty reasonable, squire," remarked Bagby, with a grin. "Lastly, we don't want to be represented in Assembly by such a king's man, and so you're to decline a poll."

"If the electors don't want me, let them say so at the election."

"Some of your tenants are 'feared to vote against you, and we intend that this election shall be unanimous for the friends of liberty. Will you decline a poll?"

"Now damn me if —" began the squire.

"Come, come, squire," interrupted an elderly man. "Yer 've stud no chance of election from the fust, so what's the use of stickling?"

"I wash my hands of ye," roared the squire. "Have whom ye want for what ye want. I've done with serving a lot of ingrates. Ye can come to me in the future on your knees, but ye'll not get me to —"

"That's just what we wants," broke in Joe. "If you'd always been so open to public opinion, we'd have had no cause for complaint against you. And now, squire, since a united land is what we wants, while your daughter gets the tea and a pen to sign the Association, do the thing up handsome by singing us the liberty song."

"Burn me if I will," cried the owner of Greenwood, like many another yielding big points without much to-do, but obstinate over the small ones.

"Is that tar about melted?" inquired Bagby.

"Jest the right consistency, Joe," responded one of the pole-holders.

"Better sing it, squire," advised Bagby. "We know you 're not much at a song, but the sentiments is what we like."

Once again the beset man looked to right and left, rage and mortification united. Then, with a remark below his breath, he sang in a very tuneless bass, that wandered at will between flat and sharp, with not a little falsetto: —

"Come join Hand in Hand, brave Americans all,
And rouse your bold Hearts at fair Liberty's Call;
No tyrannous Acts shall suppress your just Claim
Or stain with Dishonour America's Name —
In Freedom we 're born and in Freedom we 'll live
Our Purses are ready —
Steady, Friends, Steady —
Not as Slaves, but as Freemen our Money we 'll give."

"That 's enough!" remarked the ringleader. "Now, Watson, let the squire sign that broadside. Take the pot off, boys, and dump the tea on the fire. Good-evening, squire, and sweet dreams to you; I hope 't will be long before you make us walk eight miles again. Fall in, Invincibles. You 've struck your first blow for freedom."

For a moment the steady tramp of the departing men was all that broke the stillness of the night; but as they marched they fell into song, and there came drifting back to the trio standing silent about the porch the air of "Hearts of Oak," and the words: —

"Then join Hand in Hand, brave Americans all!
To be free is to live, to be Slaves is to fall;
Has the Land such a Dastard, as scorns not a Lord,
Who dreads not a Fetter much more than a Sword?
In Freedom we 're born, and, like Sons of the Brave,
We 'll never surrender,
But swear to defend her,
And scorn to survive, if unable to save."

XVIII

FIGUREHEADS AND LEADERS

THE squire's mood in the next few days was anything but genial, and his family, his servants, his farm-hands, his tenants, and in fact all whom he encountered, received a share of his spleen.

His ill-nature was not a little increased by hearing indirectly, through his overseer, that it was the elder Hennion who had planned the surprise party; and in revenge Mr. Meredith set about the scheme, already hinted at, of buying assignments of the mortgages on Boxley. For this purpose he announced his intention of journeying to New York, and ordered Philemon to be his travelling companion that he might have the advantage of his knowledge of the holders of the elder Hennion's bonds. The would-be son-in-law at first objected to being made a cat's-paw, but the squire was obstinate, and after a night upon it, Phil acceded. No other difficulty was found in the attainment of Mr. Meredith's purpose, the money-lenders in New York being only too glad, in the growing insecurity and general suspension of law, to turn their investments into cash. It was a task of some weeks to gather them all in, but it was one of the keenest enjoyment to the squire, who each evening, over his mulled wine in the King's Arms Tavern, pictured and repictured the moment of triumph, when, with the growing bundle of mortgages completed, he should ride to Boxley and inform its occupant that he wished them paid.

"We 'll show the old fox that he 's got a ferret, not a goose, to deal with," he said a dozen times to Phil, — a speech which always made the latter look very uneasy, as if his conscience were pricking.

This absence of father and lover gave Janice a really restful breathing space, and it was the least eventful time the girl had known since the advent of the bondsman nearly a year before. Even he almost dropped out of the girl's life, for the farm-work was now at its highest point of activity, and he was little about house or stable. Furthermore, though twenty thousand minutemen and volunteers were gathered before Boston, though the thirteen colonies were aflame with war preparations, and though the Continental Congress was voting a declaration on taking up arms and appointing a general, nothing but vague report of all this reached Greenwood.

In Brunswick, however, Dame Rumour was more precise, and one afternoon as the bondsman rode into the town, with some horses that needed shoeing, he was hailed by the tavern-keeper.

"Say! Folks tells that yer know how tew paint a bit?" And, when Charles nodded, he continued: "Waal, we 've hearn word that the Congress has appinted a feller named George Washington fer ginral, who 's goin' tew come through here tew-morrer on his way tew Boston, an' I want tew git that ere name painted out and his'n put in its place. Are yer up tew it, and what 'ud the job tax me?" As the publican spoke he pointed at the lettering below the weather-beaten portrait of George the Third, which served as the signboard of the tavern.

"Get me some colours, and bide till I leave these horses at the smith's, and I 'll do it for nothing," said Charles, smiling; and ten minutes later, sitting on a barrel set in a cart, he was doing his share toward the obliteration of kinghood and the substitution of a comparatively unknown hero.

"'T is good luck that they both is called George," remarked the tavern-keeper; "fer yer 've only got tew paint out the 'King' an' put in a 'Gen.' in the first part, which saves trouble right tew begin on."

Charles smilingly adopted the suggestion, and then measured off "the III." "'T is a long name to get into such space," he said.

"Scant it is," assented the publican. "I 'll tell yer what. Jist leave the 'the' an' paint in 'good' after it. That 'll make it read slick." Pleased with this solution of the difficulty, the hotel-keeper retired to the "public," with a parting invitation to the painter to drink something for his trouble.

While Charles was doing the additional work, he was interrupted by a roar of laughter, and, twisting about on his barrel, he found a group of horsemen, who had come across the green and drawn rein just behind him, looking at the newly lettered sign. From the one of the three who rode first came the burst of laughter — a man of medium size and thinly built, perhaps fifty years of age, with a nose so out of proportion to his face, in its size and heaviness, that it came near enough to caricature to practically submerge all his other features. The second man was evidently trying not to smile, and as Charles glanced at him, he found him looking at the third of the trio, as if to ascertain his mood. This last, a man of extreme tallness, and in appearance by far the youngest of the group — for he looked not over thirty at most — was scrutinising the signboard gravely, but his eyes had a gleam of merriment in them, which neutralised the set firmness of the mouth. All the party were in uniform, save for a couple of servants in livery, and all were well mounted.

"Haw, haw, haw!" laughed the noisy one. "Pray God mine host be not as chary with his spit as he is with his paint or 't will be lean entertainment."

"I said 't was best to make a push for 't to Amboy," remarked the second.

"Nay, gentlemen," responded the third, smiling pleasantly. "A man so prudent and economical must keep a good ordinary. Better bide here for dinner and kill a warm afternoon, and then push on to Amboy, in the cool of the evening, with rested cattle."

"Within there!" shouted the noisy rider, "hast dinner and bait for a dozen travellers?"

The call brought the publican to the door, and at first he gasped a startled "By Jingo!" Then he jerked his cap off, and ducked very low, saying: "'T was said, yer — yer — Lordship, that yer 'd not come till the morrow. But if yer 'll honour my tavern, yer shall have the bestest in the house." He kept bowing between every word to the man with the big nose.

"Then here we tarry for dinner," said the young-looking

man, gracefully swinging himself out of the saddle, a proceeding imitated by all the riders. "Take good heed of the horses, Bill," he said, as a coloured servant came forward. "Wash Blueskin's nose and let him cool somewhat before watering him." He turned toward the door of the tavern, and this bringing Charles into vision again, he looked up at the painter to find himself being studied with so intent a gaze that he halted and returned the man's stare.

"Art struck of a heap by the resemblance?" demanded the noisy officer.

"Go in, gentlemen," replied the tall one. "Well, my man," he continued to Charles, "ye change figureheads easily."

"Ay, 't is easier to get new figureheads than 't is to be true to old ones."

A grave, almost stern look came into the officer's face, making it at once that of an older man. "Then ye think the old order best?" he asked, scanning the man with his steady blue eyes.

The bondsman put his hand on the signboard. "'T is safest to stick to an old figurehead until one can find a true leader," he answered.

"And think you he is one?" demanded the officer, pointing at the signboard.

Charles laughed and laid a finger on the chin of royalty. "No man with so little of that was ever a leader," he asserted. He reached down and picked up a different pot of paint from the one he had been using, dipped his brush in it, and with one sweep over the lower part of the face cleverly produced a chin of character. Then he took another colour and gave three or four deft touches to the lips, transforming the expressionless mouth into a larger one, but giving to it both strength and expression. "There is a beginning of a leader, I think," he said.

"Thou art quick with thy brush and quick with thy eyes," replied the man, smiling slightly and starting to go. In the doorway he turned and said with a sudden gravity, quite as much to himself as to the bondsman: "Please God that thou be as true in opinion."

Left alone, the bondsman once more took his brush and broadened and strengthened the nose and forehead. Just as he had completed these, the tavern-keeper came bustling out of the door. "Wilt seek Joe Bagby an' tell him tew git the Invincibles tewgether?" he cried. "He intended tew review 'em tew-morrer fer the ginral, an' their Lordships says they 'll see 'em go through — Why, strap me, man, what hast thou been at?"

"I 've been making it a better portrait of the general than it ever was of the king."

"But yer 've drawn the wrong man!" exclaimed the publican. "That quiet young man is not him. 'T is the heavy-nosed man is his Excellency."

"Nonsense!" retorted the bondsman. "That loud-voiced fellow is Leftenant-Colonel Lee, a half-pay officer. Many and many 's the time I 've seen him — and if I had n't, I 'd have known the other for the general in a hundred."

"I tell yer yer 're wrong," moaned the hotel-keeper. "Any one can see he 's a ginral, an' 't is he gives all the orders fer victuals an' grog."

Charles laughed as he descended from the barrel and the cart. "'T is ever the worst wheel in the cart which makes the most noise," he said, and walked away.

Two hours later the Invincibles were bunched upon the green. As the diners issued from the inn, Bagby gave an order. With some slight confusion the company fell in, and two more orders brought their guns to "present arms."

"Bravo!" exclaimed Lee. "Here are some yokels who for once don't hold their guns as if they were hoes."

Joe, fairly swelling with the pride of the moment, came strutting forward. When he was within ten feet of the officers he took off his hat and bowed very low. "The Invincibles is ready to be put through their paces, your honour," he announced.

"Damme!" sneered Lee, below his breath. "Here 's a mohair in command who does n't so much as know the salute."

The tall officer, despite his six feet and three inches of height, swung himself lightly into the saddle without using a stirrup, and rode forward.

"Proceed with the review, sir," he said to Joe.

"Yes, sir — that is, I mean — your honour," replied Joe; and, turning, he roared out, "Get ready to go on, fellows. Attention! Dress!"

Instant disorder was visible in the ranks, some doing one thing, and some another, while a man stepped forward three or four steps and shouted: "Yer fergot ter git the muskets back ter the first persition, Joe."

"Get into line, durn you!" shouted Joe; "an' I'll have something to say to you later, Zerubbabel Buntling."

"O Lord!" muttered Lee to the other officers, most of whom were laughing. "And they expect us to beat regulars with such!"

"Attention!" once more called Joe. "To the right face — no — I mean, shoulder firelocks first off. Now to the left face." But by this time he was so confused that his voice sank as he spoke the last words, and so some faced right and some left; while altercations at once arose in the ranks that broke the alignment into a number of disputing groups and set the captain to swearing.

"Come," shouted one soldier, "cut it, Joe, an' let Charles take yer place. Yer only mixes us up."

The suggestion was greeted by numerous, if various, assenting opinions from the ranks, and without so much as waiting to hear Bagby's reply, Charles sprang forward. Giving the salute to the mounted officers, he wheeled about, and, with two orders, had the lines in formation, after which the manœuvres were gone through quickly and comparatively smoothly.

The reviewing officer had not laughed during the confusion, watching it with a sternly anxious face, but as the drill proceeded this look changed, and when the parade was finished, he rode forward and saluted the Invincibles. "Gentlemen," he said, "if you but conduct yourselves with the same steadiness in the face of the enemy as you have this afternoon, your country will have little to ask of you and much to owe." He turned to Joe, standing shamefaced at one side, and continued: "You are to be complimented on your company, sir. 'T is far and away the best I have seen since I left Virginia."

"And that is n't all, your honour," replied Joe, his face brightening and his self-importance evidently restored. "We are a forehanded lot, and we 've got twenty half-barrels of powder laid in against trouble."

After a few more words with Bagby, which put a pleased smile on his face, the officer wheeled his horse. "Well, gentlemen, we 'll proceed," he called to the group; and, as they were mounting, he rode to where Charles stood. "You have served?" he said.

Charles, with the old sullen look upon his face, saluted, and replied bitterly: "Yes, general, and would give an eye to be in the ranks again."

The general looked at him steadily. "If ye served in the ranks, how comes it that ye give the officer's salute?" he asked.

Charles flushed, but met the scrutinising eye to eye, as he answered: "None know it here, but I held his Majesty's commission for seven years."

"You look o'er young to have done that," said the general.

"I was made a cornet at twelve."

"How comes it that you are here?"

"My own folly," muttered the man.

"'T is a pity thou 'rt indentured, for we have crying need of trained men. But do what you can hereabouts, since you are not free to join us."

"I will, general," said Charles, eagerly, and, as the officer wheeled his horse, he once more saluted. Then as the travellers rode toward the bridge, the bondsman walked over and looked up at his crude likeness of the general.

"Yer wuz right," remarked the innkeeper. "The young-lookin' feller wuz Ginral Washington."

"Ay," exclaimed the man; "and, mark me, if a face goes for aught, he 's general enough to beat Gage — and that —" the man paused, and then added: "that sluggard Howe. And would to God I could help in it!"

XIX

SPIES AND COUNTER-SPIES

IT was the middle of July when the squire and Phil returned from New York, bringing with them much news of the war preparations, of Washington's passing through the city, and of the bloody battle of Bunker Hill. Of far more importance, however, to the ladies of Greenwood, were two pieces of information which their lord and master promptly announced. First, that he wished the marriage to take place speedily, and second, that at New York he had met Mr. Evatt, just landed from a South Carolina ship, and intending, as soon as some matter of business was completed, to repeat his former visit to Greenwood, — an intention that the squire had heartily indorsed by the warmest of invitations. Both brought the colour to the cheeks of Janice, but had the parents been watchful, they would have noted that the second bit of news produced the higher tint.

Although Phil was still on apparently good terms with his father, he was, from the time of his return, much at Greenwood; and, his simple nature being quite incapable of deceit, Janice very quickly perceived that his chief motive was not so much the lover's desire to be near, as it was to keep watch of her. Had the fellow deliberately planned to irritate the girl, he could have hit upon nothing more certain to enrage her, and a week had barely elapsed when matters reached a crisis.

Janice, who, it must be confessed, took pleasure in deliberately arousing the suspicion of Philemon, and thus forcing him to reveal how closely he spied upon her, one evening, as they rose from the supper-table, slipped out of the window and walked toward the stable. Her swain was prompt in pursuit; and she, quite conscious of this, stepped quickly to one side as she passed through the last opening in the box, and stood half-buried in the hedge. Ignorant of her proximity, Philemon came quickly through the hedge, and was promptly made aware of it by her hot words.

"'T is past endurance. I 'll not be spied on so."

"I — I — Why, Janice, you know how I likes ter be with you," falteringly explained Hennion.

"Spy, spy, spy — nothing but spy!" rebuked Janice; "I can't so much as — as go to pick a flower but you are hiding behind a bush."

"'Deed, Janice, you 're not fairsome ter me. After you sayin' what you did about that rake-helly bondsman, 't is only human ter — "

"To treat me as if I was a slave. Why, Peg has more freedom than I have. If you — I 'm going to the stable — to see Charles — and if you dare to follow me, I 'll — " The girl walked away and disappeared through the doorway, leaving Philemon standing by the box, the picture of indecision and anxiety. "He does n't know that Charles was sent to the village," thought Janice, laughing merrily to herself as she went to a stall, and pulling the horse's head down put her cheek against it. "Oh, Joggles dear," she sighed, "they are all against me but you." She went from one horse to another, giving each a word and a caress. Then she stole back to the door and peeked through the crack, to find that her shadow had disappeared; this ascertained, she went and sat down on the hay. "If he tortures me, I 'll torture him," was her thought.

Janice waited thus for but a few minutes, when she heard the rapid trot of a horse, which came to a halt at the stable door. As that sound ceased, the voice of Charles broke the silence, saying, "You stall the horse, while I see the squire;" and, in obedience to this direction, some one led Daisy into the stable. The gloom of nightfall made the interior too dark for the girl to recognise the man, and, not wishing it to be known that she was there, she sat quiet.

For a good ten minutes the man waited, whistling softly the while, before Charles returned.

"Waal, what luck?" asked the stranger ere Charles had come through the doorway.

"Luck!" growled the bondsman. "The devil's own, as mine always is, curse it!"

"From which I calkerlate that old Meredith wuz obstinate and wud n't set yer free."

"Not he, plead my best. But that's the last I ask of him; and 't would have served him as well to let me go, for go I will."

"You 'll go off without —"

"I will."

"Yer know what it means if brought back?"

"Double the time. Well, treble it, and still I'll do it. I gave my word I'd help, and the general shall have the powder, if for nothing else than to spite that dirty coward Bagby, though I serve thrice five years for' t. Tell the lads I 'll lead them, and if they 'll meet me at Drigg's barn to-morrow evening at ten we 'll scheme out how to do it."

Without further parley the stranger walked away, and no sooner had the crunch of his boots ceased than Janice came forward.

Charles gave a startled exclamation as she appeared, and caught the girl roughly by the wrist. "Who's this?" he exclaimed.

"You hurt," complained Janice.

The bondsman relaxed but not released his hold at the sound of her voice. "You 've heard all I said?" he demanded.

"Yes. I — I did n't like to come out while the man was here."

"And you 'll tell your father?"

"No," denied the girl. "I did n't want to listen by stealth, but since I did, I 'm no tale-bearer."

Raising the hand he held by the wrist, Charles kissed it. "I should have known you were no eavesdropper, Miss Janice," he said, releasing his hold.

"But — Oh, what is it you are going to do?" asked Janice.

"I have your word that it goes no further?"

"Yes."

"A secret letter came to the Brunswick Committee yestermorn from General Washington, saying that it had just been discovered that their powder account was a lie, and that there were less than ten rounds to each man in stock. He knew by some means of what is here, and he begged the committee to send it to him; for if the British attacked him in his present plight, 't would be fatal. And yet what think you the committee did?"

"They asked you to take it to him?"

"Not they, the — Ah! there 's no words to fit them. Old Hennion, mean hunks that he is, wanted them to write and offer to sell it at double what had been paid for 't, while Bagby would n't part with it on any terms, because he said 't was needed by the 'Invincibles' to defend the town. The two voted down Parson McClave, who declared that Brunswick should be laid in ashes rather than that Washington should not be helped. Ah, Miss Janice, that 's a man for these times."

"Then what dost intend?"

"The parson came to me to counsel what was best, and 'tween us we concocted a plan to outwit the time-servers. There are plenty of fellows of spirit in the 'Invincibles,' and 't is our scheme to steal the powder some night, put it on a sloop, and be to sea before daylight."

"How monstrous exciting!" exclaimed Janice, her eyes sparkling. "And you —"

"I 'll lead them. I 'm desperate enough to do anything that has risk. There 's real fighting there, if the accounts speak true, and perhaps a bullet will cancel both my shame and my bond — ay, and my — my love for you. For I love you, Miss Janice, love you more —"

Though taken very much by surprise, Janice drew herself up proudly, and interrupted: "You forget —" she began.

"Of course I forget!" broke in the groom. "What would love be worth if it did n't forget everything but itself? I forget I 'm a bond-servant, you 'd say. So I should if I were a king. But you are too heartless to know what love is," he ended bitterly.

"'T is not so," denied Janice, angrily; "but I 'll love no redemptioner, though he be as good-looking and good-tempered as you are ill-natured and ugly."

"And who are you," demanded the man, passionately, "to

take such mighty airs? A daughter of a nobody, dubbed Esquire because he is the biggest bubble in a pint pot."

"I shall not stay here to be insulted," cried Janice, moving away. But in the doorway her exasperation got the better of her dignity, and she faced about and said: "You evidently don't know that my great-grandfather was Edward Byllynge."

The man laughed contemptuously. "Why, you little ninny," he retorted, "my great-grandfather was king of England!"

Janice caught hold of the lintel, and stood as if transfixed for a moment, even the mortifying epithet of the groom forgotten in her amazement. "A likely tale!" she ejaculated finally when the first mute surprise was conquered.

The bond-servant had gained control of himself in the pause, for he quietly rejoined: "'T is true enough, though nothing to make boast of, save to those who set great store by grandfathers." Then, in a sadder tone, he added: "'T was a foolish brag I never thought to make, for it carries more shame than honour, and 't is therefore best forgotten. Moreover, I ask your pardon for saying what else I did; 't was my tongue and not my heart which spoke."

The insult being atoned, Janice came back. "You said you would tell me your history."

"But then — that was when I hoped — a fool I was." The redemptioner paused, and then took a quick step toward Janice with an eager look on his face and his hand outstretched. "There is but one woman in the world can gain the right to hear my sorry tale. May I tell it to you?"

Young and inexperienced as the girl was, the implication of the question was too obvious for her to miss, and she replied, "No."

The man dropped his arm and stood quietly for a moment, then gave a short, abrupt laugh. "Either 't is my lot to worship clay idols," he said, "or no woman is worth loving."

"Small blame to them for not loving you," rejoined Janice.

"Electing to marry a put like Hennion! There 's a husband of whom to be proud."

"At least he is no indentured servant," retorted the girl, in her irritation, walking away from the stable. Once through the garden and in sight of the house, she halted, her attention attracted by some to-do about the porch. Coming swiftly forward, it was to discover the squire there, candle in hand, to light the dismounting of a horseman, and that no less than Mr. Evatt.

"A welcome to ye," the host was saying. "Peg, tell Charles to come and take this horse. Get ye into the house, man; I'll hold him. Ah! Jan. Take Mr. Evatt in, lass, and tell your mother we've a visitor."

Janice, feeling strangely shy, led the way to the parlour, and when her mother, after the briefest of greetings, promptly bustled off to order a glass of wine and to inspect the best lodging-room — as guest chambers were then termed — her embarrassment was sufficient to bring the blood glowing into her cheeks, while, not daring so much as to meet Evatt's eye, she hung her head and had much ado to keep from trembling.

Evatt stood with a broad smile on his face and unconcealed pleasure in his eyes, for in truth the girl made a picture to charm any man; and not till Janice lifted her eyes, and shot a furtive look at him, did he move toward her. He took her hand and whispered: "For nine months I've thought me of those lips and wondered when I should have taste of them. Quickly, or thy father will —"

"You must n't!" gasped Janice, hanging her head more than ever. "I'm to marry Philemon."

"Tush!" exclaimed the man. "I heard that tarradiddle in York City. Why, thou 'rt promised to me, dost not remember, and I'll not release thee, that I bind to. Wouldst rather have that clout than me, Janice?"

Very falteringly and still with downcast face the girl murmured, "No."

"Then I'll save ye from him, mark my word. Come, up with your lips, and give me a kiss for the promise. What! still frightened? 'Tis nothing so terrible. A court lady would have had a dozen kisses in the time I've pleaded. And ye are no mere country hoyden, without manners or —"

Already Janice was raising her head, the possibility of seeming countrified being worse even than a man's caress; but her intended submission and Evatt's speech were both interrupted by the clump of boots in the hall, and the pair had barely time to assume less tell-tale attitudes when the squire and Phil were standing in the doorway.

"Friend Evatt," ejaculated Mr. Meredith, "come to my office at once. I 've a matter needing your advice. Lass, tell your mother to send us the Madeira and rum, with some hot water, but let us not be disturbed."

Evatt made a grimace as he followed, and threw himself into a chair with a suggestion of irritation.

"This lad, for a reason he won't tell," began the squire, as he closed the door, "has kept eye on a bondsman of mine, and this evening, as luck would have it, he stood upon a barrel, by one of the stable windows, and overheard a pretty story the fellow told to some one whom Phil could n't see. Tell it o'er, lad, as ye told it me."

Hennion, thus admonished, retold the story of the powder, as the bond-servant had related it to Janice. But two omissions he made: the first being a failure to mention the connection of his father with the matter, and the second the presence of Janice in the stable.

"Here 's news indeed!" exclaimed Evatt.

"Ay. But what to do with it is the question."

"Do! Why, get word of it to Howe as quick as may be, so that he may take advantage of their plight. We must send him a letter."

"'T is easier said than done. Boston is encompassed, and no man can get through the lines."

"I have it. The 'Asia' frigate, with her tender, lies in the lower bay at New York; the latter can be sent round with a letter to Boston. And ye shall bear it, lad," added Evatt, turning to Phil.

"'T ain't no wish of mine," ejaculated Philemon.

"There is no one else we can trust. 'T will be but a month's affair, at worst."

"But I don't care ter go," dissented Hennion. "I want ter get married ter Miss Janice right off, an' not — "

"Come, squire, tell the fellow he must n't shirk his duty to his king. He can marry your daughter any time, but now 's the moment to do a service to his country. Why, man, if it ends this rebellion, as it seems like to, they 'll give ye a title — and ye, too, squire, I doubt not."

"He speaks true, Phil. Here 's a chance, indeed. Put the girl out of thy head for a time, and think a man's thoughts."

"Ay," cried Evatt. "Don't prove the old saying:

'He who sighs for a glass without G,
Take away L and that is he.'"

It took much more urging to get Phil to yield, but finally, on a promise of the master of Greenwood that he should wed so soon as he returned, he gave a half-hearted consent. Over the rum a letter to Sir William Howe was written by Evatt, and he and Phil arranged to be up and away betimes in the morning.

"That gets him well out of the way," remarked Evatt, as in his bedroom he stripped off his clothes. "Now to be as successful with Miss Blushing Innocence."

XX

THE LOGIC OF HONOURED PARENTS AND DUTIFUL CHILDREN

PHILEMON and Evatt were in the saddle by five the next morning and a little more than an hour later held consultation with Bagby. Everything except Phil's intended mission was quickly told him.

"Jingo!" he remarked, and then whistled. "Why, 't is stealing? Is n't there to be no law in the land? When do they plot to rob us?"

"They meet this evenin' ter scheme it, an' a body can't tell when they 'll act."

"'T won't likely be to-night, but I'll keep guard myself, all the same, and some of the Invincibles shall watch every night."

This warning given, and a bite taken at the tavern by way of breakfast, the ride to Amboy was made in quick time. Here a boat was secured, and the two were rowed off to the "Asia" as she lay inside the Hook. Evatt had a long conference with her captain in his cabin, and apparently won consent to his plan; for when he returned on deck, a cutter was cleared away, and Phil was told it would put him on the tender which was to carry him to Boston. With many a longing glance at the shore, he bade good-by to Evatt, who cheered him by predictions of reward and speedy return.

Philemon gone, Evatt remained a short time in conference with the chaplain of the man-of-war, and then returned to Amboy. Once more taking horse, he set off on his return to Greenwood, arriving there in the heat of the afternoon. He was forced, by the absence of all the working force in the hayfield, to stable his horse himself, and then he walked toward what he had already observed from the saddle, — Janice, seated upon a garden bench under a poplar on the lawn, making artificial flowers. Let it be acknowledged that until the appearance of Evatt the girl had worked languidly, and had allowed long pauses of idleness while she meditated, but with his advent she became the embodiment of industry.

"Odd's life!" the man ejaculated as he sat down beside the worker. "'Twixt love's heat and an August sun, your lover, Janice, has come nigh to dissolving."

Janice, with hands that shook, essayed to snip out a rose petal which her own cheeks matched in tint.

Evatt removed first his hat and then his wig, that he might mop his head. Having replaced the hirsute ornament, he continued: "And thy father is as hot for thy marriage with that yokel. He set the day yestere'en."

"When?" demanded the girl, looking up anxiously.

"What say ye to this day week?"

"Oh!" cried Janice. "Was ever maid born under such a ha'penny planet?"

"Don't make outcry 'gainst your star when it has sent ye a lover in the nick of time, ready to save ye from the bumpkin."

Janice took a shy come-and-go glance at him and said: "You mean —"

"What say ye to an elopement?"

"Oh!" exclaimed the girl, meeting Evatt's gaze eagerly. "'T would be monstrous delightsome to be run off with, of course; but —"

"But what?"

"Well — I — Mommy told me that in the province no maid could be lawfully wed without her parents' consent."

"True," assented the tempter, "if she wed where the colony law holds good. But we 'll get round that by having the knot tied on royal ground."

"Not in England?" said the girl, drawing back a little.

"Think ye I 'd treat the lass I love like that?" responded Evatt, reproachfully. "Nay. A friend of mine is chaplain on the 'Asia' man-of-war, and he 'll make no bones about helping us. And as the king's flag and broad arrow puts the ship out of the colony jurisdiction, 't will make the thing legal despite the law."

"How romantic!" exclaimed Janice. "To think of making a stolen match, and of being wed on a king's ship!"

"Now dost want to rail at thy star?"

"'T is great good fortune," ecstatically sighed the girl. "Think you 't would be right?"

"Would I ask it if 't were not?" rejoined Evatt, heartily.

"But dadda and mommy —" began the falterer.

"Will be pleased enough when the job 's done. Think ye, if they were n't bound they 'd not rather have a titled son-in-law than that gawk?"

"A what?" cried Janice.

"Thou dost not know thy lover's true name, Janice. 'T is John Ombrey, Lord Clowes, who sits beside thee."

Janice sprang to her feet. "And I 've spoke to you as if you were just — just a man," she cried in a horrified voice. "'T was not fair so to beguile me!"

Evatt looked at the ground to hide the smile he could not suppress. "'T was done for the king, Janice," he said. "And 't is all the more romantic that I 've won ye without your knowing. Sit down again; if 't were not in view of the house I should be kneeling to ye."

Janice sank back on the garden seat. "I can't believe it yet!" she gasped breathlessly. "I knew of course thou wast a court gentleman, but —"

"And now I suppose ye 'll send me packing and wed the yokel?" suggested the lover.

"Oh, no!" cried Janice. "If you — if you really —" the girl gave a glance at the man, coloured to the temples, and, springing to her feet, fled toward the house. She did not stop till she reached her room, where she flung herself on the bed and buried her cheeks in the pillow. Thus she lay for some time, then rose, looked at herself in the mirror, and finding her hair sadly disordered, she set about the task of doing it over. "'T is beyond belief!" she murmured. "I must be very beautiful!" She paused in her task, and studied her own face. "Now I know why he always makes me feel so uncomfortable — and afraid — and — and gawky. 'T is because he is a lord. Sometimes he does look at me as if — as if he were hungry — ugh! It frights me. But he must know what 's the mode.

'Lady Janice Clowes.' 'T is a pity the title is not prettier. Whatever will Tibbie say when she hears!"

It was a little after ten that evening when the squire and Evatt parted for the night in the upper hall, the former being, as usual, not tipsy, but in a jovial mood toward all things; and as this attitude is conducive to sleep, his snores were ere long reverberating to all waking ears. One pair of these were so keenly alive to every noise that not the chirp of a cricket escaped them, and from time to time their owner started at the smallest sound. Owing to this attention, they heard presently the creak of the stairs, the soft opening of the front door, and even the swish of feet on the grass. Then, though the ears fairly strained to catch the least noise, came a silence, save for the squire's trumpeting, for what seemed to the girl a period fairly interminable.

Finally the rustling of the grass told of the return of the prowler, and as the girl heard it she once more began trembling. "Oh!" she moaned. "If only I had n't—if only he 'd go away!" She rose from the bed, and stole to the window.

"Mr. Evatt, I 'm so frightened, I don't dare," she whispered to the figure standing below. "Wait till to-morrow night!"

"Nonsense!" said the man, so loudly that Janice was more scared than ever. "I told ye it must be to-night. Come down quickly."

"Oh, please!" moaned Janice.

"Dost want to be the wife of that gawk?" demanded Evatt, impatiently.

Though he did not know it, the girl vacillated. "At least I 'm not frightened of Phil," was her thought.

"Well," called the man more loudly, "art going to keep me here all night?"

"Hush!" whispered Janice. "Thee 'll wake —"

"Belike I will," he retorted irritably. "And if they ask me what 's in the wind, they shall have the truth. Odd's life! I 'm not a man to be fooled by a chit of a girl."

"Oh, hush!" again she begged, more frightened at the prospect of her parents knowing than by any other possibility. "I 'll come if you 'll only be quiet."

She took a small bundle, hurriedly stole downstairs, and passed out of the house.

"Now ye 've come to your senses," said the man. "Give me the bundle and your hand," he continued, and set out at a rapid pace across the lawn, having almost to drag the girl, her feet carried her so unwillingly. "Over with ye," he ordered, as they reached the stile at the corner, and when Janice descended she found two horses hitched to the fence and felt a little comforted by the mere presence of Daisy. She was quickly mounted, and they set off, the girl so helpless in her fright that Evatt had to hold her horse's bridle as well as his own.

"Burn it!" exclaimed Evatt, presently, "art never going to end thy weeping?"

"If you would only have waited till —" sobbed Janice.

"'Twas no time for shilly-shallying," interrupted the man. "Dost not see that we had to take to-night, when the groom was gone, for there 'd have been no getting the horses with him sleeping in the stable?"

"What if we meet him returning?" cried the girl, her voice shaking.

"'T would little matter. Think ye he could catch us afoot?"

"But he could tell dadda."

"And by that time we shall be two-thirds of the way to Amboy. 'T is but a twenty miles, and we should be there by three. Then if we meet no delay in getting a boat, we shall be on the 'Asia' near seven. By eight the chaplain will have made us twain one."

"Oh!" moaned the girl, "what ever will dadda say?"

As this was a question no one could answer, a silence ensued, which lasted until they rode into Brunswick. Guiding the horses upon the green, to reduce the beat of their hoofs to a minimum, Evatt turned off the grass at the river road and headed toward the bridge across the Raritan. As they approached, a noise of some kind arrested Evatt's attention, and he was just checking the horses when a voice cried: —

"Stand!"

Janice gave a startled cry which instantly set a dog barking.

"Keep silence!" again ordered the unseen man.

Evatt, after an oath below his breath, demanded, "By what right do ye stop us, whoever ye are?"

"By the right of powder and ball," remarked the voice, drily.

Again the dog barked, and both Evatt and the unseen man swore. "Curse the beast!" said the latter. "Hist, Charles! Call the dog, or he 'll wake the town."

Another voice from a little distance called, "Clarion!" in a guarded inflection; meantime the hound had discovered his mistress, and was jumping about her horse, giving little yelps of pleasure.

In another instant Charles came running up. "What 's wrong?" he questioned.

"'T is a couple of riders I 've halted," said the voice from the shadow.

"Out of the way!" ordered Evatt. "Ye 've no right to prevent us from going forward. I 've pistols in my holsters, and ye 'd best be careful how ye take the law into your own hands."

The groom gave an exclamation as he recognised the riders; and paying no attention to Evatt, he sprang to the side of the girl and rested his hand on the bridle, as if to prevent her horse from moving, while he asked in amazement: "What brings you here?"

Speechless and shamed, the girl hung her head.

"Let go that bridle, ye whelp!" blustered Evatt, throwing back the flap of his holster and pulling out a heavy horse pistol.

As he made the motion, the bondsman dropped the rein and seized the hand that held the weapon. For a moment there was a sharp struggle, in which the third man, who sprang from the shadow, joined. Nor did Evatt cease resistance until three men more came running up, when, overborne by numbers, he was dragged from his horse and held to the ground. In the whole contest both sides had maintained an almost absolute silence, as if each had reasons for not waking the villagers.

"Stuff a sod of grass in his mouth to keep him quiet," ordered Charles, panting, "and tie him hand and foot." Taking a lantern from one of the men, he walked back to the speechless and frightened girl and held the light to her face. "'T is not possible you — you — oh! I 'll never believe it of you."

With pride and mortification struggling for mastery, Janice replied: "What you think matters not to me."

"You were eloping with this man?"

Though the groom's thoughts were of no moment to the girl, she replied: "To escape marrying Philemon Hennion."

"What things women are!" he exclaimed contemptuously. "You deserve no better than to be his doll common, but — "

"We were to be married," cried Janice.

"In the reign of Queen Dick!"

"This very day on the 'Asia' frigate."

"A likely tale," jeered the man. "Bring that fellow down to the boat," he called, and catching hold of the bridle, he started walking.

"Whither are you taking me?" inquired Janice, in fright.

"The parson is down by the river, helping transfer the powder, and I'm going to leave you with him to take back to Greenwood."

"Oh, Charles," besought the girl, "you'll not be so cruel! I'd sooner die than — than — Think what mommy — and dadda — and the whole village — I did n't want to go with him — but — Please, oh, please! You'll not disgrace me? I'll promise never to go off with him — indeed — "

"Of that I'll be bound," sneered the servant, with a harsh laugh, "for I'm going to take him with me to Cambridge."

For a moment Janice was silent, then cried: "If you only knew how I hate you."

The man laughed bitterly. "I do — from the way I hate — ay, and despise you!"

Another moment brought them to the edge of a wharf, where a number of men were busying themselves in stowing barrels on board a small sloop. "Hold this horse," ordered the servant, while he joined one of the toilers and drew him apart in consultation.

"Powder aboard, cap'n," presently called some one.

"Take that man and stow him below decks along with it," ordered Charles. "Good-by, parson. I hope to send good news from Cambridge of this night's work. Boys, take Bagby out of the stocks before daylight, and tell him if the Invincibles want their powder to follow us, and they shall have fifty rounds of it a man, with plenty of fighting to boot. All aboard that are for the front!"

Half a dozen men followed, while those on the wharf cast off the fasts. But all at once stood still when the parson, with bowed head, began a prayer for the powder, for the adventurers who took it, and for the general and army it was designed to serve. Sternly yet eloquently he prayed until the boat had drifted with the tide out of hearing, and the creak of the blocks came across the water, showing that those on board were making sail. Then, as the men on the wharf dispersed, he mounted the horse Evatt had ridden.

"Janice Meredith," he said sternly, "I propose to occupy this ride with a discourse upon the doctrine of total depravity, from which downward path you have been saved this night, deducing therefrom an illustration of the workings of grace through foreordination, — the whole with a view to the saving of your soul and the admonishment of your sinful nature."

XXI

A SUDDEN SCARCITY OF BEAUX

IT was daylight when the parson and Janice rode through the gate of Greenwood, and the noise of hoofs brought both the girl's parents to the window of their bedroom in costumes as yet by no means completed. Yet when, in reply to the demand of the squire as to what was the meaning of this arrival, it was briefly explained to him that his daughter had attempted to elope with his guest, he descended to the porch without regard to scantiness of clothing.

A terrible ten minutes for Janice succeeded, while the squire thundered his anger at her, and she, overcome, sobbed her grief and mortification into Daisy's mane. Then, when her father had drained the vials of his wrath, her mother appeared more properly garbed, and in her turn heaped blame and scorn on the girl's bowed head. For a time the squire echoed his wife's indignation, but it is one thing to express wrath oneself and quite another to hear it fulminated by some one else; so presently the squire's heart began to soften for his lass, and he attempted at last to interpose in palliation of her conduct. This promptly resulted in Mrs. Meredith's ordering Janice off the horse and to her room. "Where I'll finish what I have to say," announced her mother; and the girl, helped down by Mr. Meredith, did as she was told, longing only for death.

The week which succeeded was a nightmare to Janice, her mother constantly recurring to her wickedness, the servants addressing her with a scared breathlessness which made her feel that she was indeed declassed for ever, while the people of the neighbourhood, when she ventured out-of-doors, either grinned broadly or looked dourly when they met her, showing the girl that her shame was town property.

Mrs. Meredith also took frequent occasion to insist on the girl's marriage with Mr. McClave, on the ground that he alone could properly chasten her; but to this the squire refused to listen, insisting that such a son-in-law he would never have, and that he was bound to Philemon. "We 'll keep close watch on her for the time he 's away, and then marry her out of hand the moment he 's returned," he said.

Had the parents attempted to carry out the system of espionage that they enforced during the first month they would have had their hands full far longer than they dreamed. Week after week sped by, summer ripened into fall, and fall faded into winter, but Philemon came not. Little by little Janice's misconduct ceased to be a general theme of village talk, and the life at Greenwood settled back into its accustomed groove. Even the mutter of cannon before Boston was but a matter of newspaper news, and the war, though now fairly inaugurated, affected the squire chiefly by the loss of the bondsman, for whom he advertised in vain.

One incident which happened shortly after the proposed elopement, and which cannot be passed over without mention, was a call from Squire Hennion on Mr. Meredith. The master of Boxely opened the interview by shaking his fist within a few inches of the rubicund countenance of the master of Greenwood, and, suiting his words to the motion, he roared: "May Belza take yer, yer old ——" and the particular epithet is best omitted, the eighteenth-century vocabulary being more expressive than refined — "fer sendin' my boy ter Boston, wheer, belike, he 'll never git away alive."

"Don't try to bully me!" snorted the squire, shaking his fist in turn, and much nearer to the hatchet-face of his antipathy. "Put that down or I 'll teach ye manners! Yes, damn ye, for the first time in your life ye shall be made to behave like a gentleman!"

"I defy yer ter make me!" retorted Hennion, with unconscious humour.

"Heyday!" said Mrs. Meredith, entering, "what 's the cause of all this hurly-burly?"

"Enuf cause, an' ter spare," howled Hennion. "Here this ——" once more the title is left blank for propriety's sake —

"hez beguiled poor Phil inter goin' on some fool errand ter Boston, an' the feller knew so well I would n't hev it thet all he dun wuz ter write me a line, tellin' how this —— insisted he should go, an' thet he 'd started. 'Twixt yer whiffet of a gal an' yer old —— of a husband, yer 've bewitched all the sense the feller ever hed in his noddle, durn yer!"

"Let him talk," jeered the squire. "'T will not bring Phil back. What s more, I 'll make him smile the other side of his teeth before I 've done with him. Harkee, man, I 've a rod in pickle that will make ye cry small." The squire took a bundle of papers from an iron box and flourished them under Hennion's nose "There are assignments of every mortgage ye owe, ye old fox, and pay day 's coming."

"Let it," sneered the owner of Boxely. "Yer think I did n't know, I s'pose? Waal, thet 's wheer yer aout. Phil, he looked so daown in the maouth just afore yer went ter York thet I knew theer must be somethin' ter make him act so pukish, an' I feels araound a bit, an' as he ain't the best hand at deceivin' I hez the fac's in no time. An' as I could n't hev them 'ere mortgages in better hands, I tell 'd him ter go ahead an' help yer all he could. 'T was I gave him the list of them I owed."

The squire, though taken aback, demanded: "And I suppose ye have the money ready to douse on pay day?"

Hennion sniggered. "Yer won't be hard, thet I know, squire. I reckon yer 'll go easy on me."

"If ye think I 'm going to spare ye on account of Phil ye are mightily out. I 'll foreclose the moment each falls due, that I warn ye."

"Haow kin yer foreclose whin theer ain't no courts?"

"Pish!" snapped the creditor. "'T is purely temporary; within a twelve-month there 'll be law enough. Think ye England is sleeping?"

"We 'll see, we 'll see," retorted Hennion. "In the meantime, squire, I hope yer won't worrit because I don't pay interest. Times is thet onsettled thet yer kain't sell craps naw nothin,' an' ready money 's pretty hard ter come by."

"Not I," rejoined the squire. "'T will enable me to foreclose all the quicker."

"When theer's courts ter foreclose," replied Hennion, grinning suggestively. With this parting shot, he left the house and rode away.

On the same day this interview occurred, another took place in the Craigie House in Cambridge, then occupied as the headquarters of General Washington. The commander-in-chief was sitting in his room, busily engaged in writing, when an orderly entered and announced that a man who claimed to have important business, which he refused to communicate except to the general, desired word with him. The stranger was promptly ushered in, and stood revealed as a fairly tall, well-shaped young fellow, clad in coarse clothing, with a well-made wig of much better quality, which fitted him so ill as to suggest that it was never made for his head.

"I understand your Excellency is in dire need of powder," he said as he saluted.

A stern look came upon Washington's face. "Who are you, and how heard you that?" he demanded.

"My name is John Brereton. How I heard of your want was in a manner that needs not to be told, as —"

"Tell you shall," exclaimed Washington, warmly. "The fact was known to none but the general officers and to the powder committee, and if there has been unguarded or unfaithful speech it shall be traced to its source."

"Your Excellency wrote a letter to the committee of Middlesex County in Jersey?"

"I did."

"The committee refused to part with the powder."

Washington rose. "Have they no public spirit, no consideration of our desperate plight?" he exclaimed.

"But your Excellency, though the committee would not part with the powder, some lads of spirit would not see you want for it, and — and by united effort we succeeded in getting and bringing to Cambridge twenty half-barrels of powder, which is now outside, subject to your orders."

With an exclamation mingling disbelief and hope, the commander sprang to the window. A glance took in the two carts loaded with kegs, and he turned, his face lighted with emotion.

"God only knows the grinding anxiety, the sleepless nights, I have suffered, knowing how defenceless the army committed to my charge actually was! You have done our cause a service impossible to measure or reward." He shook the man's hand warmly.

"And I ask in payment, your Excellency, permission to volunteer."

"In what capacity?"

"I have served in the British forces as an officer, but all I ask is leave to fight, without regard to rank."

"Tell me the facts of your life."

"As I said, my name is John Brereton. Nothing else about me will ever be known from me."

Washington scrutinised the man with an intent surprise. "You cannot expect us to trust you on such information."

"An hour ago it would have been possible for me to have sneaked by stealth into the British lines with this letter," said the man, taking from his pocket a sheet of paper and handing it to the general. "What think you would Sir William Howe have given me for news, over the signature of General Washington, that the Continental Army had less than ten rounds of powder per man?"

Washington studied the face of the young fellow steadily for twenty seconds. "Are you good at penmanship?" he asked.

"I am a deft hand at all smouting work," replied Brereton.

"Then, sir," said Washington, smiling slightly, "as I wish to keep an eye on you until you have proved yourself, I shall for the present find employment for you in my own family."

Thus a twelve-month passed without Philemon Hennion, John Evatt, Charles Fownes, Parson McClave, or any other lover so much as once darkening the doors of Greenwood.

"Janice," remarked her mother at the end of the year, "dost realise that in less than a twelve-month thou 'lt be a girl of eighteen and without a lover, much less a husband? I was wed before I was seventeen, and so are all respectably behaved females. See what elopements come to. 'T is evident thou 'rt to die an old maid."

XXII

THE OLIVE BRANCH

IF this year was bare of courtships, of affairs of interest it was far otherwise. Scarcely was 1776 ushered in than news came that the raw and ill-equipped force, which for nine months had held the British beleaguered in Boston, had at last obtained sufficient guns and powder to assume the offensive, and had, by seizing Dorchester Heights, compelled the evacuation of the city. Howe's army and the fleet sailed away without molestation to Halifax, leaving behind them a rumour, however, that great reinforcements were coming from Great Britain, and that upon their arrival, New York would be reduced and held as a strategic base from which all the middle colonies would be overrun and reduced to submission.

This probability turned military operations southward. General Lee, who early in the new year had been given command of the district around Manhattan Island, set about a system of fortifications, even while he protested that the water approaches made the city impossible to hold against such a naval force as Britain was certain to employ. At the same time that this protection was begun against an outward enemy, a second was put in train against the inward one, and this involved the household of Meredith.

One morning, while the squire stood superintending two of his laborers, as they were seeding a field, a rider stopped his horse at the wall dividing it from the road and hailed him loudly. Mr. Meredith, in response to the call, walked toward the man; but the moment he was near enough to recognise Captain Bagby, he came to a halt, indecisive as to what course to pursue toward his enemy.

"Can't do no talking at this distance, squire," sang out Bagby, calmly; "and as I 've got something important to say, and my nag prevents me from coming to you, I reckon you 'll have to do the travelling."

After a moment's hesitation, the master of Greenwood came to the stone wall. But it was with a bottled-up manner which served to indicate his inward feelings that he demanded crustily, "What want ye with me?"

"It 's this way," explained Joe. "If what 's said is true, Howe is coming to York with a bigger army than we can raise, to fight us, if we fights, but with power to offer us all we wants, if we won't. Now there 's a big party in Congress as is mortal afraid that there 'll be a reconciliation, and so they is battling tooth and nail to get independence declared before Howe can get here, so that there sha'n't be no possibility of making up."

"The vile Jesuits!" exclaimed the squire, wrathfully, "and but a three-month gone they were tricking their constituents with loud-voiced cries that the charge that they desired independence was one trumped up by the ministry to injure the American cause, and that they held the very thought in abhorrence."

"'T is n't possible to always think the same way in politics straight along," remarked the politician, "and that 's just what I come over to see you about. Now, if there 's going to be war, I guess I 'll be of some consequence, and if there 's going to be a peace, like as not you 'll be on top; and I 'll be concerned if I can tell which it is like to be."

"I can tell ye," announced Mr. Meredith. "'T is —"

"Perhaps you can, squire," broke in Bagby, "but your opinions have n't proved right so far, so just let me finish what I have to say first. Have you heard that the Committee of Safety has arrested the Governor?"

"No. Though 't is quite of a piece with your other lawless proceedings."

"Some of his letters was intercepted, and they was so toryish that 't was decided he should be put under guard. And at the same time it was voted to take precautionary proceedings against all the other enemies of the country."

"Then why are n't ye under arrest?" snapped the squire.

"'Cause there 's too many of us, and too few of you," explained Bagby, equably. "Now the Committee has sent orders to each county committee to make out a list of those we think ought to be arrested, and a meeting 's to be held this afternoon to act on it. Old Hennion he came to me last night and said he wanted your name put on, and he 'd vote to recommend that you be taken to Connecticut and held in prison there along with the Governor."

"Pox the old villain!" fumed Mr. Meredith. "For a six-months I 've sat quiet, as ye know, and 't is merely his way of paying the debts he owes me. A fine state ye 've brought the land to, when a man can settle private scores in such a manner."

"There is n't no denying that you 're no friend to the cause, and if any one 's to be took up hereabouts, it should be you. Still, I 'm a fair-play fellow, and so I thought, before I let him have his way, I 'd come over and have a talk with you, to see if we could n't fix things."

"How?"

"If the king 's come to his senses and intends to deal fair with us," remarked Bagby, with a preliminary glance around and a precautionary dropping of his voice, "that 's all I ask, and so I don't see no reason for attacking his friends until we are more certain of what 's coming. At the same time, if Hennion wants to jail you, I think you 'll own I have n't much reason to take your part. You 've always been as stuck up and abusive to me as you well could be. So 't is only natural I should n't stand up for you."

The lord of Greenwood swallowed before he said, "Perhaps I 've not been neighbourly, but what sort of revenge is it to force me from my home, and distress my wife and daughter?"

"That 's it," assented the Committeeman. "And so I came over to see what could be done. We have n't been the best of friends down to now, but that is n't saying that we could n't have been, if you 'd been as far-seeing as me, and known who to side in with. It seemed to me that if I stood by you in this scrape we might fix it up to act together. I take it that my brains and your money could run Middlesex County about as we pleased, if we quit fighting, and work together. Squire Hennion would have to take a back seat in politics, I guess."

The squire could not wholly keep the pleasure the thought gave him from his face. "'T would be a god-send to the county," he cried. "Ye know that as well as I."

"As to that, I'll say nothing," answered Joe. "But of course, if I'm going to throw my influence with you, I expect something in return."

"And what's that?" asked Mr. Meredith, still dwelling on his revenge.

"I need n't tell you, squire, that I'm a rising man, and I'm going to go on rising. 'T won't be long before I'm about what I please, especially if we make a deal. Now, though there has n't been much intercourse between us, yet I've had my eye on your daughter for a long spell, and if you'll give your consent to my keeping company with her, I'll be your friend through thick and thin."

For a moment Mr. Meredith stood with wide-open mouth, then he roared: "Damn your impudence! ye — ye — have my lass, ye — be off with ye — ye — " There all articulate speech ended, the speaker only sputtering in his wrath, but his two fists, shaken across the wall, spoke eloquently the words that choked him.

"I thought you'd play the fool, as usual," retorted the suitor, as he pulled his horse's head around. "You'll live to regret this day, see if you don't." And with this vague threat he trotted away toward Brunswick.

Whether Bagby had purposely magnified the danger with the object of frightening the squire into yielding to his wishes, or whether he and Hennion were outvoted by Parson McClave and the other members of the Committee, Mr. Meredith never learned. Of what was resolved he was not left long in doubt, for the morning following, the whole Committee, with a contingent of the Invincibles, invaded the privacy of Greenwood, and required of him that he surrender to them such arms as he was possessed of, and sign a parol that he would in no way give aid or comfort to the invaders. To these two requirements the squire yielded, at heart not a little comforted that the proceedings against him were no worse, though vocally he protested at such "robbery and coercion."

"Ye lord it high-handedly now," he told the party, "but ye 'll sing another song ere long."

"Yer 've been predictin' thet fer some time," chuckled Hennion, aggravatingly.

"'T will come all the surer that it comes tardily. 'Slow and sure doth make secure,' as ye 'll dearly learn. We 'll soon see how debtors who won't pay either principal or interest like the law!"

Hennion chuckled again. "Yer see, squire," he said, "it don't seem ter me ter be my interest ter pay principal, nor my principle ter pay interest. Ef I wuz yer, I would n't het myself over them mogiges; I ain't sweatin'."

"I 'll sweat ye yet, ye old rascal," predicted the creditor.

"When 'll thet be?" asked Hennion.

"When we are no longer tyrannised over by a pack of debtors, scoundrels, and Scotch Presbyterians," with which remark the squire stamped away.

It must be confessed, however, that bad as the master of Greenwood deemed the political situation, he gave far more thought to his private affairs. Every day conditions were becoming more unsettled. His overseer had left his employ to enlist, throwing all care of the farm on the squire's shoulders; a second bondsman, emboldened by Charles' successful levanting, had done the same, making labourers short-handed; while those who remained were more eager to find excuses taking them to Brunswick, that they might hear the latest news, and talk it over, than they were to give their undivided attention to reaping and hoeing. Finally, more and more tenants failed to appear at Greenwood on rent day, and so the landlord was called upon to ride the county over, dunning, none too successfully, the delinquent.

Engrossing as all this might be, Mr. Meredith was still too much concerned in public events not to occasionally find an excuse for riding into Brunswick and learning of their progress; and one evening as he approached the village, his eyes and ears both informed him that something unusual was in hand, for muskets were being discharged, great fires were blazing on the green, and camped upon it was a regiment of troops.

Riding up to the tavern, where a rushing business was being done, the squire halted the publican as he was hurrying past with a handful of mugs, by asking, "What does all this mean?"

"Living jingo, but things is on the bounce," cried the landlord, excitedly. "Here 's news come that the British fleet of mor 'n a hundred sail is arrived inside o' Sandy Hook, an' all the Jersey militia hez been ordered out, an' here 's a whole regiment o' Pennsylvania 'Sociators on theer way tew Amboy tew help us fight 'em, an' more comin'; an' as if everythin' was tew happen all tew once, here 's Congress gone an' took John Bull by the horns in real arnest." The cupbearer-to-man thrust a broadside, which he pulled from his pocket, into the squire's hand, and hastened away cellar-ward.

The squire unrumpled the sheet, which was headed in bold-faced type: —

In Congress, July 4, 1776,
A Declaration by the Representatives of the United States of America in General Congress assembled.

Ere he had more than seen the words, he was interrupted by Joe, who, glass in hand, left the bench and came to the rider, where, in a low voice, he said: —

"You see, squire, the independents has outsharped the other party, and got the thing passed before Howe got here. It was a durned smart trick, and don't leave either side nothing but to fight. I guess 't won't be long before you 'll be sorry enough you did n't take up with my offer."

Mr. Meredith, who had divided his attention between what his interlocutor was saying and the sentence, "When, in the course of human events, it becomes necessary for one people to dissolve the political bands which have connected them with another," concluded that human events could wait, and ceasing to read, he gave his attention to the speaker.

"If ye think to frighten or grieve me, ye are mightily out," he trumpeted loudly. "Hitherto Britain has dealt gently with ye, but now ye 'll feel the full force of her wrath. A six weeks will serve to bring the whole pack of ye to your knees, whining for pardon."

The prediction was greeted with a chorus of gibes and protests, and on the instant the squire was the centre of a struggling mass of militiamen and villagers, who roughly pulled him from his horse. But before they could do more, the colonel of the troops and the parson interfered, loudly commanding the mob to desist from all violence; and with ill grace and with muttered threats and angry noddings of heads, the crowd, one by one, went back to their glasses. That the interference was none too prompt was shown by the condition of the squire, for his hat, peruke, and ruffles were all lying on the ground in tatters, his coat was ripped down the back, and one sleeve hung by a mere shred.

"You do wrong to anger the people unnecessarily, sir," said Mr. McClave, sternly. "Dost court ducking or other violence? Common prudence should teach you to be wiser."

The squire hastily climbed into the saddle. From that vantage point he replied, "Ye need not think Lambert Meredith is to be frightened into dumbness. But there are some who will talk smaller ere long." Then, acting more prudently than he spoke, he shook his reins and started Joggles homeward.

It was little grief, as can be imagined, that the events of the next few weeks brought to Greenwood; and the day the news came that Washington's force had been outflanked and successfully driven from its position on the hills of Brooklyn, with a loss of two of its best brigades, the squire was so jubilant that nothing would do but to have up a bottle of his best Madeira,—a wine hitherto never served except to guests of distinction.

"Give a knave rope enough and he 'll hang himself," he said gloatingly. "Because the land favoured them at Boston, they got the idea they were invincible, and Congress would have it that New York must be defended, though a hundred thousand troops could not have done it against the fleet, let alone Howe's army. Ho! By this time the rogues have learned what fifteen thousand butchers and bakers and candlestick-makers can do 'gainst thirty thousand veterans. And they 've had but the first mouthful of the dose they 'll have to swallow."

The jubilation of the prophet was short-lived, for even as he spoke, and with decanter but half emptied, the tramp of feet sounded in the hallway, and the door was flung open to admit four men, armed with muskets.

"In the name of the Continental Congress, and by orders of General Washington, I arrests yer, Lambert Meredith," announced the spokesman.

"For what?" cried Janice.

"For treason."

XXIII

HEADQUARTERS IN 1776

ON September 15, a group of horsemen, occupying a slight eminence of ground on the island of Manhattan, were gazing eastward. Below and nearer the water were spread lines of soldiers behind intrenchments, while from three men-of-war lying in the river came a heavy cannonade that swept the shore line and spread over the water a pall of smoke which, as it drifted to leeward, obscured the Long Island shore from view.

"'T is evidently a feint, your Excellency," presently asserted one of the observers, "to cover a genuine attack elsewhere — most likely above the Haarlem."

The person addressed — a man with an anxious, care-worn face that made him look fifty at least — lowered his glass, but did not reply for some moments. "You may be right, sir," he remarked, "though to me it has the air of an intended attack. What think you, Reed?"

"I agree with Mifflin. The attack will be higher up. Hah! Look there!"

A rift had come in the smoke, and a column of boats, moving with well-timed oars, could for a moment be seen as it came forward.

"They intend a landing at Kip's Bay, as I surmised," exclaimed the general. "Gentlemen, we shall be needed below." He turned to Reed and gave him an order concerning reinforcements. then wheeled and, followed by the rest, trotted over the ploughed field. Once on the highway, he spurred his horse, putting him to a sharp canter.

"What troops hold the works on the bay, Mifflin?" asked one of the riders.

"Fellows' and Parsons' brigades, Brereton."

"If they are as good at fighting as at thieving, they 'll distinguish themselves."

"Ay," laughed Mifflin. "If the red coats were but chickens or cattle, the New England militia would have had them all captured ere now."

"They 'll be hearn from to-day," said a third officer. "They 've earthworks to git behind, and they 'll give the British anuther Bunker Hill."

"Then you ought to be quick, General Putnam," said Brereton, "for that 's the fighting you like."

The road lay in the hollow of the land, and not till the party reached a slight rise were they able once more to get a glimpse of the shores of the bay. Then it was to find the flotilla well in toward its intended landing-place, and the American troops retreating in great disorder from their breastworks.

Exclamations of surprise and dismay sprang from the lips of the riders, and their leader, turning his horse, jumped the fence and galloped across the fields to intercept the fugitives. Five minutes brought them up to the runaways, who, out of breath with the sharpness of their pace, had come to a halt, and were being formed by their officers into a little less disorder.

"General Fellows, what was the reason for this shameful retreat?" demanded the general, when within speaking distance.

"The men were seized with a panic on the approach of the boats, your Excellency, and could not be held in the lines."

Washington faced the regiments, his face blazing with scorn. "You ran before a shot had been fired! Before you lost a man, you deserted works that have taken weeks to build, and which could be held against any such force." He paused for a moment, and then, drawing his sword, he called with spirit: "Who 's for recovering them?"

A faint cheer passed down the lines; but almost as it sounded, the red coats of fifty or sixty light infantry came into view on the road, a skirmishing party thrown forward from the landing to reconnoitre. Had they been Howe's whole army, however, they could not have proved more effective, for instantly the two brigades broke and dissolved once more into squads of flying men.

At such cowardice, Washington lost all control of himself, and, dashing in among the fugitives, he passionately struck right and left with the flat of his sword, thundering curses at them; while Putnam and Mifflin, as well as the aides, followed his example. It was hopeless, however, to stay the rush; the men took the blows and the curses unheeding, while throwing away their guns and scattering in every direction.

Made frantic by such conduct, Washington wheeled his horse. "Charge!" he cried, and rode toward the enemy, waving his sword.

If the commander-in-chief had hoped to put some of his own courage into the troops by his example, he failed. Not a man of the runaways ceased fleeing. None the less, as if regardless of consequences in his desperation, Washington rode on, until one of the aides dashed his spurs into his horse and came up beside his general at a mad gallop.

"Your Excellency!" he cried, "'t is but hopeless and will but end in—" Then, as his superior did not heed him, he seized the left rein of his horse's bridle and, pulling on it, swung him about in a large circle, letting go his hold only when they were riding away from the enemy.

Washington offered no resistance, and rode the hundred yards to where the rest of his staff were standing, with bowed head. Nothing was said as he rejoined the group, and Blueskin, disappointed in the charge for which he had shown as much eagerness as his rider, let his mind recur to thoughts of oats; finding no control in the hand that held his bridle, he set out at an easy trot toward headquarters.

They had not ridden many yards ere Washington lifted his head, the expression of hopelessness, which had taken the place of that of animation, in turn succeeded by one of stern repose. He issued three orders to as many of the riders, showing that his mind had not been dwelling idly on the disaster, slipped his sword into its scabbard, and gathered up his reins again.

"There!" thought Blueskin, as a new direction was indicated by his bit, "I'm going to have another spell of it riding all ways of a Sunday, just as we did last night. And it's coming on to rain."

Rain it did very quickly; but from post to post the horsemen passed, the sternly silent commander speaking only when giving the necessary orders to remedy so far as possible the disaster of the afternoon. Not till eleven, and then in a thoroughly drenched condition, did they reach the Morris House on Haarlem Heights. It was to no rest, however, that the general arrived; for, as he dismounted, Major Gibbs of his life guards informed him that the council of war he had called was gathered and only awaited his attendance.

"Get you some supper, gentlemen," he ordered, to such of his aides as were still of the party, "for 't is likely that you will have more riding when the council have deliberated."

"'T is advice he might take himself to proper advantage," said one of the juniors, while they were stripping off their wet coverings in a side room.

"Ay," asserted Brereton. "The general uses us hard, Tilghman, but he uses himself harder." Then aloud he called, "Billy!"

"Yis, sah!"

"Make a glass of rum punch and take it in to his Excellency."

"Foh de Lord, sah, I doan dar go in, an' yar know marse neber drink no spirits till de day's work dun."

"Make a dish of tea, then, you old coward, and I'll take it to him so soon as I get these slops off me. 'Fore George! How small-clothes stick when they're wet!"

"You mean when a man's so foppish that he will have them made tight enough to display the goodness of his thighs," rejoined Gibbs, who, being dry, was enjoying the plight of the rest. "Make yourselves smart, gentlemen, there are ladies at quarters to-night."

"You don't puff that take-in on us, sirrah," retorted Tilghman.

"'Pon honour. They arrived a six hours ago, and have been waiting to see the general."

"You may be bound they are old and plain," prophesied

Brereton, "or Gibbs would be squiring them, 'stead of wasting time on us."

"There you 're cast," rejoined the major, "I caught but a glimpse, yet 't was enough to prove to me that all astronomers lie."

"How so?"

"In saying that but twice in a century is there a transit of Venus."

"Then why bide you here, man?"

"That 's the disgustful rub. They were with a man under suspicion, and orders were that none should hold converse with him before the general examined into it. A plague on't!"

Discussion of Venus was here broken by the announcement of supper, and the make-shift meal was still unfinished when the general's body-servant appeared with the tea. Taking it, Brereton marched boldly to the council door, and, giving a knock, he went in without awaiting a reply.

The group of anxious-faced men about the table looked up, and Washington, with a frown, demanded, "For what do you interrupt us, sir?"

The young officer put the tea down on the map lying in front of the general. "Billy didn't dare take this to your Excellency, so I made bold to e'en bring it myself."

"This is no time for tea, Colonel Brereton."

"'T is no time for the army to lose their general," replied the aide. "I pray you drink it, sir, for our sake if you won't for your own."

A kindly look supplanted the sternness of the previous moment on the general's face. "I thank you for your thoughtfulness, Brereton," he said, raising the cup and pouring some of the steaming drink into the saucer. Then as the officer started to go, he added, "Hold!" Picking up a small bundle of papers which lay on the table, he continued: "Harrison tells me that there is a prisoner under guard for my examination. I shall scarce be able to attend to it this evening, and to-morrow is like to be a busy day. Take charge of the matter, and report to me the moment the council breaks up. Here are the papers."

Standing in the dim light of the hallway, the aide opened the papers and read them hastily. Either the strain on the eyes, or some emotion, put a frown on his face, and it was still there as he walked to the door before which stood a sentry, and passed into a badly lighted room.

"Powerful proud ter meet yer Excellency," was his greeting from a man in civilian shorts and a military coat, who held out his hand. "Captain Bagby desired his compliments ter yer, an' ter say that legislative dooties pervented his attindin' ter the matter hisself."

Paying no heed to either outstretched hand or words, the officer looked first at a man standing beside the fireplace and then at the two women, who had risen as he entered. He waited a moment, glancing from one to the other, as if expecting each of them to speak; but when they did not, he asked gruffly of the guard, though still with his eyes on the prisoners: "And for what were the ladies brought?"

"Becuz they wud n't be left behind on no accaount. Yer see, yer Excellency, things hez been kinder onsettled in Middlesex Caounty, an' it hain't been a joyful time to them as wuz Tories; so when orders cum ter bring old Meredith ter York Island, his wife an' gal wuz so scar't nothin' would do but they must come along."

"Ay," spoke up the man by the fireplace, bitterly. "A nice pass ye 've brought things to, that women dare not tarry in their own homes for fear of insult."

"You may go," said the officer to the captor, pointing at the door.

"Ain't I ter hear the 'zamination, yer Excellency?" demanded the man, regretfully. "The hull caounty is sot on knowin' ther fac's." But as the hand still pointed to the entrance, the man passed reluctantly through it.

Taking a seat shadowed from the dim light of the solitary candle, the officer asked: "You are aware, Mr. Meredith, on what charge you are in military custody?"

"Not I," growled the master of Greenwood. "For more than a year gone I 've taken no part in affairs, but 't is all of a piece with ye Whigs that — to trump up a charge against —"

"This is no trumpery accusation," interrupted the officer. "I hold here a letter to Sir William Howe, found after our army took possession of Boston, signed by one Clowes, and conveying vastly important information as to our lack of powder, which he states he obtained through you."

"Now a pox on the villain!" cried the squire. "Has he not tried to do me enough harm in other ways, but he must add this to it? Janice, see the evil ye 've wrought."

"Oh, dadda," cried the girl, desperately, "I know I was — was a wicked creature, but I 've been sorry, and suffered for it, and I don't think 't is fair to blame me for this. 'T was not I who brought him — "

"Silence, miss!" interrupted her mother. "Wouldst sauce thy father in his trouble?"

"I presume you obtained the knowledge Clowes transmitted from your daughter?" surmised the officer.

"My daughter? Not I! How could a chit of a girl know aught of such things? Clowes got it from young Hennion, and devil a thing had I really to do with it, write what he pleases."

"Pray take chairs, ladies," suggested the aide, with more politeness. "Now, sir, unravel this matter, so far as 't is known to you."

When the squire's brief tale of how the information was obtained and forwarded to Boston was told, the officer was silent for some moments. Then he asked: "Hast had word of Clowes since then?"

"Not sight or word since the night the — "

"Oh, dadda," moaned Janice, "please don't!"

"Since he attempted to steal my girl from me. And if e'er I meet him I trust I 'll have my horsewhip handy."

"Is Hennion where we can lay hold upon him?"

"Not he. 'T was impossible for him to get out of Boston, try his best, and the last word we had of him — wrote to his rascally father — was that he 'd 'listed in Ruggles' loyalists."

"Then the only man we can bring to heel is this bond-servant of thine."

"Not even he. The scamp took French leave, and if ye want him ye must search your own army."

"Canst aid us to find him?"

"I know naught of him, or his doings, save that last June I received the price I paid for his bond, through Parson McClave, who perhaps can give ye word of him."

The officer rose, saying: "Mr. Meredith, I shall report on your case to the general, so soon as he is free, and have small doubt that you will be acquitted of blame and released. I fear me you will find headquarters' hospitality somewhat wanting in comfort, for we 're o'ercrowded, and you arrive in times of difficulty. But I 'll try to see that the ladies get a room, and, whatever comes, 't will be better than the guard-house." He went to the hall door and called, "Grayson!"

"Well?" shouted back some one.

"There are two ladies to be lodged here for the night. May I offer them our room?"

"Ay. And my compliments to them, and say they may have my company along with it, if they be youngish."

"Tut, man," answered Brereton, reprovingly. "None of your Virginian freeness, for they can hear you." He turned and said: "You must be content with a deal feather-bed on the floor here, Mr. Meredith, but if the ladies will follow me I will see that they are bestowed in more comfortable quarters;" and he led the way upstairs, where, lighting a candle, he showed them to a small room, very much cluttered by military clothes and weapons, thrown about in every direction. "I apologise, ladies," he remarked; "but for days it 's been ride and fight, till when sleeping hours came 't was bad enough to get one's clothes off, let alone put them tidy."

"And indeed, sir, there is no need of apology," responded Mrs. Meredith, warmly, "save for us, for robbing you of the little comfort you possess."

"'T is a pleasure amid all the strife we live in to be able to do a service," replied the officer, gallantly, as he bowed low over Mrs. Meredith's hand and then kissed it. He turned to the girl and did the same. "May you rest well," he added, and left the room.

"Oh, mommy!" exclaimed Janice, "didst ever see a more distinguished or finer-shaped man? And his dress and manners are —"

"Janice Meredith! Wilt never give thy thoughts to something else than men?"

"Well, Brereton," asked Tilghman as the aide joined his fellow-soldiers, "how did his Excellency take your boldness?"

"As punishment he sent me to examine Gibbs' Venus."

"Devil take your luck!" swore Gibbs. "I'll be bound ye made it none too short. Gaze at the smug look on the dandy's face."

Brereton laughed gleefully as he stripped off his coat and rolled it up into a pillow. "I've just kissed mamma's hand," he remarked.

"I can't say much for thy taste!"

"In order," coolly went on Brereton, as he stretched himself flat on the floor, "that I might then kiss that of Venus — and over hers I did not hurry, lads. Therefore, gentlemen, my present taste is, despite Gibbs' slur, most excellent, and I expect sweet dreams till his Excellency wants me. Silence in the ranks."

XXIV

THE VALUE OF A FRIEND

AS the sun rose on the following morning, Brereton came cantering up to headquarters.

"Is his Excellency gone?" he demanded of the sentry, and received reply that Washington had ridden away toward the south ten minutes before. Leaving his horse with the man, the aide ran into the house and returned in a moment with a great hunk of corn bread and two sausages in his hand. Springing into the saddle, he set off at a rapid trot, munching voraciously as he rode.

"Steady, dear lass," he remarked to the mare. "If you make me lose any of this cake, I 'll never forgive you, Janice."

Fifteen minutes served to bring the officer to a group of horsemen busy with field-glasses. Riding into their midst, he saluted, and said: "The Maryland regiments are in position, your Excellency." Then falling a little back, he looked out over the plain stretched before them. Barely had he taken in the two Continental regiments lying "at ease" half-way down the heights on which he was, and the line of their pickets on the level ground, when three companies of red-coated light infantry debouched from the woods that covered the corresponding heights to the southward. As the skirmishers fell back on their supports, the British winded their bugles triumphantly, sounding, not a military order, but the fox-hunting "stole away," — a blare intended to show their utter contempt for the Americans.

Washington's cheeks flushed as the derisive notes came floating up the hills, and he pressed his lips together in an attempt to hide the mortification the insult cost him. "They do not intend we shall forget yesterday," he said.

"We 'll pay them dear for the insult yet," cried Brereton, hotly.

"'T is a point gained that they think us beneath contempt," muttered Grayson; "for that is half-way to beating them."

"Colonel Reed, order three battalions of Weedon's and Knowlton's rangers to move along under cover of the woods, and endeavour to get in the rear of their main party," directed the commander-in-chief, after a moment's discussion with Generals Greene and Putnam. "As you know the ground, guide them yourself."

"Plague take his luck!" growled Brereton.

"Ha, ha!" laughed Tilghman, jeeringly. "Some of us have hands to kiss and some regiments to fight. Harkee, macaroni. The general thinks 't would be a pity to spot those modish buskins and gloves. So much for thy dandyism."

"Colonel Brereton," said the general, "order the two Maryland regiments to move up in support of Knowlton."

Brereton saluted, and, as he wheeled, touched his thumb to his nose at Tilghman. "You are dished," he whispered. "The general dresses too well himself to misjudge a man because he tries to keep neat and *à la mode*."

A quarter of an hour later, as battalions of Griffiths' and Richards' regiments advanced under guidance of Brereton, the sharpness of the volleys in their front showed that the fighting was begun; and in response to his order, they broke into double-quick time. Once out of the timber, it was to find the Connecticut rangers scattered in small groups wherever cover was to be had, but pouring in a hot fire at the enemy, who had been reinforced materially.

"Damn them!" cried Brereton. "Will they never fight except under cover?" Louder he shouted: "Forward! Charge them, boys!" The order given, he rode toward the rangers. "Where's your colonel?" he shouted.

"Dead," cried one, "and there's no one to tell us what to do."

"Do?" roared the aide. "Get out from behind that cover, and be damned to you. Show that Connecticut does n't always skulk. Come on!"

A cheer broke out, and, without even stopping to form, the men went forward, driving the enemy into the woods for shelter, and then forcing them through it. The fire of the

British slackened as they fell back, and when new Continental troops appeared on their right flank as well, the retreat became almost a rout.

"We 'll drive them the length of the island," yelled Brereton, frantic with excitement, as the men went clambering up the rocks after the flying enemy.

"Colonel Brereton, his Excellency directs you to call in the regiments to their former position," shouted Grayson, cantering up.

Brereton swore forcibly before he galloped among the men, and even after they, in obedience to his orders, had fallen back slowly and taken up their original position, he growled to the aide as they began the ascent, "I 'm sick of this over-caution, Grayson! What in —"

"The general was right," asserted Grayson. "Look there." He pointed over the treetops that they had now risen above to where columns of Royal Highlanders and Hessian Yagers were hastening forward at double-quick. "You would have had a sharp skimper-scamper hadst been allowed to go another half-mile."

"'T is too bad, though," sighed the young officer, "that when the men will fight they have to be checked."

"Be thankful you did your double-quick in the cool of the morning, and are done with it. Lord! it makes me sweat just to see the way they are hurrying those poor Yagers. 'T is evident we 've given them a real scare."

Upon reaching the top of the height Brereton rode forward to where Washington still stood. "I tried to have the 'stole away' sounded, your Excellency," he said exultingly, "but those who knew it were so out of breath chasing them that there was not a man to wind it."

Washington's eyes lighted up as he smiled at the enthusiasm of the young fellow. "At least you may be sure that they had less wind than you, for they ran farther. They 've had the best reply to their insult we could give them."

"Thet there fox they wuz gwine tu hunt did a bit of huntin' hisself," chuckled Putnam.

"They are still falling back on their supports," remarked Greene. "Evidently there is to be no more fighting to-day."

"They've had their bellyful, I guess," surmised Putnam.

"Then they're better off than I am," groaned Brereton. "I could eat an ox."

When the fact became obvious that the British had no intention of renewing their intended attack, a general move was made toward quarters, and as they rode Brereton pushed up beside Washington and talked with him for a moment.

The commander ended the interview by nodding his head. "Colonel Tilghman," he ordered, as Brereton dropped behind, "ride on to announce our coming; also present my compliments to Mr. Meredith and bespeak his company and that of his ladies to dinner."

Mrs. Meredith and Janice, not having gone to bed till after one the previous night, slept until they were wakened by the firing; and when they had dressed and descended it was to find headquarters practically deserted, save for the squire and a corporal's guard. At the suggestion of the servant who gave them breakfast, they climbed to the cupola of the house, but all they could see of the skirmish were the little clouds of smoke that rose above the trees and the distant advance of the British reinforcements. Presently even these ceased or passed from view, and then succeeded what Janice thought a very "mopish" two hours, terminated at last by the arrival of the aide with his invitation, which sent her to her room for a little extra prinking.

"If I had only worn my lutestring," she sighed. Her toilet finished, — and the process had been lengthened by the trembling of her hands,— Janice descended falteringly to go through the hall to the veranda. In the doorway she paused, really taken aback by the number of men grouped about on the grass; and she stood there, with fifty eyes turned upon her, the picture of embarrassment, hesitating whether to run away and hide.

"Come hither, child," called her mother; and Janice, with a burning face and down-turned eyes, sped to her side. "This is my daughter Janice, your Excellency," she told the tall man with whom she had been speaking.

"Indeed, madam," said Washington, bowing politely over the girl's hand, and then looking her in the face with pleasure. "My staff has had quite danger enough this morning without my subjecting them to this new menace. However, being lads of spirit, they will only blame me if I seek to spare them. Look at the eagerness of the blades for the engagement," he added with a laugh, as he turned to where the youngsters were idling about within call.

"Oh, your Excellency!" gasped Janice, "I—I—please may n't I talk to you?"

"Janice!" reproved her mother.

"Oh! I did n't mean that, of course," faltered the girl. "'T was monstrous bold, and I only wanted—"

"Nay, my child," corrected the general. "Let an old man think it was intended. Mrs. Meredith, if you 'll forgive the *pas*, I 'll glad General Greene with the privilege of your hand to the table, while the young lady honours me with hers. Never fear for me, Miss Janice," he added, smiling; "the young rascals will be in a killing mood, but they dare not challenge their commander. There, I 'll spare your blushes by joking you no more. I hope you were not greatly discomforted in your accommodation?" he asked, as they took their seats at the long table under the tent on the lawn.

"No, indeed, your Excellency. One of thy staff—I know not his name, but the one who questioned dadda—was vastly polite, and gave his room to us."

"That was Colonel Brereton,—the beau of my family. Look at him there! Wouldst think the coxcomb was in the charge this morning?"

Janice, for the first time, found courage to raise her eyes and glance along what to her seemed a sea of men's faces, till they settled on the person Washington indicated. Then she gave so loud an exclamation of surprise that every one looked at her. Conscious of this, she was once more seized with stage fright, and longed to slip from her chair and hide herself under the table.

"What startled thee, my child?" asked the general.

"Oh—he—nothing—" she gasped. "Who—what didst thou say was his name?"

"John Brereton."

"Oh!" was all Janice replied, as she drew a long breath.

"'T will ne'er do to let him know you 've honoured him by particular notice," remarked the commander; "for both at Boston and New York the ladies have pulled caps for him to such an extent that 't is like he 'll grow so fat with vanity that he 'll soon be unable to sit his horse."

"Is — is he a Virginian, your Excellency?"

"No. 'T is thought he 's English."

Janice longed to ask more questions, but did not dare, and as the bottle passed, the conversation became general, permitting her to become a listener. When the moment came for the ladies to withdraw, she followed her mother.

"Oh, mommy!" she said the instant she could, "didst recognise Charles?"

"Charles! What Charles?"

"Charles Fownes — our bond-servant — Colonel Brereton."

"Nonsense, child! What maggot idea hast thee got now?"

"'T is he truly — and I never thought he could be handsome. But his being clean-shaven and wearing a wig —"

"No more of thy silly clack!" ordered her mother. "A runaway bond-servant on his Excellency's staff, quotha! Though he does head the rebels, General Washington is a man of breeding and would never allow that."

Before the men rose from the table the ladies were joined by Washington and Mr. Meredith.

"I have already expressed my regrets to your husband, Mrs. Meredith," said the general, "that a suspicion against him should have put you all to such material discomfort, and I desire to repeat them to you. Yet however greatly I mourn the error for your sake, for my own it is somewhat balanced by the pleasure you have afforded me by your company. Indeed, 't is with a certain regret that I received Colonel Brereton's report, which, by completely exonerating Mr. Meredith, is like to deprive us of your presence."

"Your Excellency is over-kind," replied Mrs. Meredith, with an ease that excited the envy of her daughter.

"The general has ordered his barge for us, my dear," said the squire, "and 't is best that we get across the river while there 's daylight, if we hope to be back at Greenwood by to-morrow evening"

Farewells were promptly made, and, under the escort of Major Gibbs, they set out for the river. Once in the boat, Janice launched into an ecstatic eulogium on the commander-in-chief.

"Ay," assented Mr. Meredith; "the general 's a fine man in bad company. 'T is a mortal shame to think he 's like to come to the gallows."

"Dadda! No!"

"Yes. They put a bold face on 't, but after yesterday's defeat they can't hold the island another week; and when they lose it the rebellion is split, and that 's an end to 't. 'T will be all over in a month, mark me."

Janice pulled a very serious face for a moment, and then asked: "Didst notice Colonel Brereton, dadda?"

"Ay. And a polite man he is. He not merely had us released, but I have in my pocket a protection from the general he got for me."

"Didst not recognise him?"

"Recognise? Who? What?"

"Oh, nothing," replied Janice.

XXV

FREEDOM IN RETROGRADE

THE departure of the Merediths for headquarters under arrest had set Brunswick agog, and all sorts of surmises as to their probable guilt and fate had given the gossips much to talk of; their return, three days later, not merely unpunished, but with a protection from the commander-in-chief, set the village clacks still more industriously at work.

Events were moving so rapidly, however, that local affairs were quickly submerged. News of Washington's abandonment of the island of New York and retreat into Westchester, pursued by Howe's army, of the capture of Fort Washington and its garrison, of the evacuation of Fort Lee, of the steady dwindling of the Continental Army by the expiration of the terms of enlistment, and still more by wholesale desertions, reached the little community in various forms. But interesting though all this was for discussion at the tavern of an evening, or to fill in the vacant hour between the double service on a Sunday, it was still too distant to seem quite real, and so the stay-at-home farmers peacefully completed the getting in of their harvests, while the housewives baked and spun as of yore, both conscious of the conflict more through the gaps in the village society, caused by the absences of their more belligerently inclined neighbours, than from the actual clash of war.

The absent ones, it is needless to say, were the doughty warriors of the "Invincibles," who had been called into service along with the rest of the New Jersey militia when Howe's fleet had anchored in the bay of New York three months before, and who had since formed part of the troops defending the towns of Amboy and Elizabethport, but a few miles away, from the possible descent of the British forces lying on Staten Island. This arrangement not only spared them from all active service, thus saving the parents and wives of Brunswick from serious anxiety, but also permitted frequent home visits, with or without furlough, thus supplying the town with its chief means of news.

An end came, however, to this period of quiet. Early in November vague rumours, growing presently to specific statements, told the villagers that their day was approaching. The British troops on Staten Island were steadily reinforced; the small boats of the line-of-battle ships and frigates were gathered opposite Amboy and Paulus Hook; large supplies of forage and cattle were massed at various points. Everything betokened an intended descent of the royal army into New Jersey; that the new-made State was to be baptised with blood.

The successive defeats of the Continental army wonderfully cooled many of the townspeople who but a few months before had vigorously applauded and saluted the glowing lines of the Declaration of Independence, when it had been read aloud to them by the Rev. Mr. McClave. One of the first evidences of this alteration of outward manner, if not of inward faith, was shown in the sudden change adopted by the community toward the household of Greenwood. When the squire had departed in custody he apparently possessed not one friend in Brunswick, but within a month of his return the villagers, the parson excepted, were making bows to him, in the growing obsequiousness of which might be inferred the growing desperation of the Continental cause. Yet another indication was the appearance of certain of the "Invincibles," who came straggling sheepishly into town one by one — "Just ter see how all the folks wuz" — and who, for reasons they kept more private, failed to rejoin their company after having satisfied their curiosity. Most incriminating of all, however, was the return of Bagby from the session of the Legislature then being held in Princeton, and his failure to go to Amboy to take command of his once gloried-in company.

"'T would n't be right to take the ordering away from Zerubbabel just when there's a chance for fighting, after he's done the work all summer," was the captain's explanation of his conduct; and though his townsmen may have suspected another motive, they were all too bent on staying at home themselves, and were too busy taking in sail on the possibility of having to go about on another tack, to question his reasons.

If the mountain would not go, Mahomet would come; and one evening late in November, while the wind whistled and the rain beat outside the "Continental Tavern," as it was now termed, the occupants of the public room suddenly ceased from the plying of glasses and pipes, upon the hurried entrance of a man.

"The British is comin'!" he bellowed, bringing every man to his feet by the words.

"How does yer know?" demanded Squire Hennion.

"I wuz down ter the river ter see if my boat wuz tied fast enuf ter stand the blow an' I hearn the tramp of snogers comin' across the bridge."

"The bridge!" shouted Bagby. "Then they must be — Swamp it! there is n't more than time enough to run."

Clearly he spoke truly, for even as he ended his sentence the still unclosed door was filled by armed men. A cry of terror broke from the tavern frequenters, but in another moment this was exchanged for others of relief and welcome, when man after man entered and proved himself to be none other than an invincible.

"How, now, Leftenant Buntling?" demanded Bagby, in an attempt to regain his dignity. "What is the meaning of this return without orders?"

"The British landed a swipe o' men at Amboy this mornin', makin' us fall back mighty quick ter Bonumtown, an' there, arter the orficers confabulated, it wuz decided thet as the bloody-backs wuz too strong ter fight, the militia and the flyin' camp thereabouts hed better go home an' look ter their families. An' so we uns come off with the rest."

"You mean to say," asked Joe, "that you did n't strike one blow for freedom; did n't fire one shot at the tools of the tyrant?"

"Oh, cut it, Joe," growled one of the privates. "Thet 'ere

talk duz fer the tavern and fer election times, but 't ain't worth a darn when ye 've marched twenty miles on an empty stomick. Set the drinks up fer us, or keep quiet."

"That I will for you all," responded Bagby, "and what 's more, the whole room shall tipple at my expense."

No more drinks were ordered, however; for a second time the occupants of the room were startled by the door being thrown open quickly to give entrance to a man wrapped in a riding cloak, but whose hat and boots both bespoke the officer.

"Put your house in readiness for General Washington and his staff, landlord," the new-comer ordered sharply. "They will be here shortly, and will want supper and lodgings." He turned in the doorway and called: "Get firewood from where you can, Colonel Hand, and kindle beacon fires at both ends of the bridge, to light the waggons and the rest of the forces; throw out patrols on the river road both to north and south, and quarter your regiment in the village barns." Then he added in a lower voice to a soldier who stood holding a horse at the door: "Put Janice in the church shed, Spalding; rub her down, and see to it that she gets a measure of oats and a bunch of fodder." He turned and strode to the fire, his boots squelching as he walked, as if in complaint at their besoaked condition. Hanging his hat upon the candle hook on one side of the chimney breast and his cloak on the other, he stood revealed a well-dressed officer, in the uniform of a Continental colonel.

It had taken the roomful a moment to recover their equipoise after the fright, but now Squire Hennion spoke up:

"So yer retreatin' some more, hey?"

The officer, who had been facing the fire in an evident attempt to dry and warm himself, faced about sharply: "Retreat!" he answered bitterly. "Can you do anything else with troops who won't fight; who in the most critical moment desert by fifties, by hundreds, ay, by whole regiments? Six thousand men have left us since we crossed into Jersey. A brigade of your own troops — of the State we had come to fight for — left us yesterday morning, when news came that Cornwallis was advancing upon our position at Newark. What can we do but retreat?"

"Well, may I be dummed!" ejaculated Bagby, "if it is n't Squire Meredith's runaway bondsman, and dressed as fine as a fivepence!"

The officer laughed scornfully. "Ay," he assented. "'T is the fashion of the land to run away, so 't is only *à la mode* that bondsmen and slaves should imitate their betters."

"Yer need n't mount us Americans so hard, seein' as yer took mortal good care ter git in the front ranks of them as wuz retreatin'," asserted an Invincible.

"I undertook to guide the retreat, because I knew the roads of the region," retorted the officer, hotly, evidently stung by the remark; then he laughed savagely and continued: "And how comes it, gentlemen all, that you are not gloriously serving your country? Cornwallis, with nine thousand picked infantry, is but a twenty miles to the northward; Knyphausen and six thousand Hessians landed at Perth Amboy this morning, and would have got between us and Philadelphia but for our rapid retreat. Canst sit and booze yourself with flip and swizzle when there are such opportunities for valour? Hast forgotten the chorus you were for ever singing?" Brereton sang out with spirit:—

"'In Freedom we 're born, and, like Sons of the Brave,
We'll never surrender,
But swear to defend her,
And scorn to survive, if unable to save.'"

"'T ain't no good fighting when we hav n't a general," snarled Bagby.

"Now damn you for a pack of dirty, low-minded curs!" swore the officer, his face blazing with anger. "Here you 've a general who is risking life, and fortune, and station; and then you blame him because he cannot with a handful of raw troops defeat thirty thousand regulars. There 's not a general in Europe — not the great Frederick himself — who 'd so much as have tried to make head against such odds, much less have done so much with so little. After a whole summer's campaign what have the British to show? They 've gained the territory within gunshot of their fleet; but at White Plains, though they were four to one, they dared not attack us, and valiantly turned tail about, preferring to overrun undefended country to assaulting our position. I tell you General Washington is the honestest, bravest, most unselfish man in the world, and you are a pack of —"

"Are my quarters ready, Colonel Brereton?" asked a tall man, standing in the doorway.

"This way, yer Excellency," obsequiously cried the landlord, catching up a candle and coming out from behind the bar. "I 've set apart our settin'-room and our bestest room — thet 'ere with the tester bed — for yer honourable Excellency."

"Come with me, Colonel Brereton," ordered the general, as he followed the publican.

Motioning the tavern-keeper out of the room, Washington threw aside his wet cloak and hat, and taking from a pocket what looked like a piece of canvas, he unfolded and spread it out on the table, revealing a large folio map of New Jersey.

"You know the country," he said; "show me where the Raritan can be forded."

"Here, here, and here," replied Brereton, indicating with his finger the points. "But this rain to-night will probably so swell it that there 'll be no crossing for come a two days."

"Then if we destroy the bridge Cornwallis cannot cross for the present?"

"No, your Excellency. But if 't is their policy to again try to outflank us, they 'll send troops from Staten Island by boat to South Amboy; and by a forced march through Monmouth they can seize Princeton and Trenton, while Cornwallis holds us here."

"'T is evident, then, that we can make no stand except at the Delaware, should they seek to get in our rear. Orders must be sent to secure all the boats in that river, and to —"

A knock at the door interrupted him, and in reply to his "Come in," an officer entered, and, saluting, said hurriedly: "General Greene directs me to inform your Excellency that word has reached him that a brigade of the New Jersey militia have deserted and have seized and taken with them the larger part of the baggage train. The commissary reports that the stores saved will barely feed the forces one day more."

Washington stood silent for a moment. "I will send a message back to General Greene by you presently. In the meantime join my family, who are supping, Major Williams." Then, when the officer had left the room, the commander sat down at the table and rested his head on his hand, as if weary. "Such want of spirit and fortitude, such disaffection and treachery, show the game to be pretty well up," he muttered to himself.

Brereton who had fallen back at the entrance of the aide, once more came to the table. "Your Excellency," he said, "we are but losing the fair-weather men, who are really no help, and what is left will be tried troops and true."

"Left to starve!"

"'This is a region of plenty. But give me the word, and in one day I'll have beef and corn enough to keep the army for a three months."

"They refuse to sell for Continental money."

"Then impress."

"It must come to that, I fear. Yet it will make the farmers enemies to the cause."

"No more than they are now, I wot," sneered the aide. "And if you leave them their crops 't will be but for them to sell to the British. 'T is a war necessity."

Washington rose, the moment's discouragement already conquered and his face set determinedly. "Give orders to Hazlett and Hand to despatch foraging parties at dawn, to seize all cattle, pigs, corn, wheat, or flour they may find, save enough for the necessities of the people, and to impress horses and wagons in which to transport them. Then join us at supper."

Brereton saluted, and turned, but as he did so Washington again spoke: —

"I overheard what you were saying in the public room, Brereton," he said. "Some of my own aides are traducing me in secret, and making favour with other generals by praising them and criticising me, against the possibility that I may be superseded. But I learned that I have one faithful man."

"Ah, your Excellency," impulsively cried the young officer,

starting forward, "'t is a worthless life, — which brought disgrace to mother, to father, and to self; but what it is, is yours."

"Thank you, my boy," replied Washington, laying his hand affectionately on Brereton's shoulder. "As you say, 't is a time which winnows the chaff from the wheat. I thank God He has sent some wheat to me." And there were tears in the general's eyes as he spoke.

XXVI

NECESSITY KNOWS NO LAWS

WHILE the family of Greenwood were still at the breakfast-table on the following morning, they were startled by a shriek from the kitchen, and then by Peg and Sukey bursting into the room where they sat.

"Oh, marse," gasped the cook, "de British!"

Both the squire and Janice sprang to the windows, to see a file of soldiers, accompanied by a mounted officer, drawn up at the rear of the house. As they took this in, the line broke into squads, one of which marched toward the stable, a second toward the barn, while the third disappeared round the corner of the house. With an exclamation the squire hurried to the kitchen and intrenched himself in the door just as the party reached it.

"Who are ye, and by what right do ye trespass on my property?" he demanded.

"Git out of the way, ole man," ordered the sergeant. "We hev orders ter take a look at yer store-room and cellar, an' we ha'n't got no time to argify."

"Ye 'll not get into my cellar, that I can tell —" began the squire; but his remark ended in a howl of pain, as the officer dropped the butt of his musket heavily on the squire's toes. The agony was sufficient to make the owner of Greenwood collapse into a sitting position on the upper step and fall to nursing the injured member.

Janice, who had followed her father into the kitchen, sprang forward with a cry of sympathy and fright, just as the mounted officer, who had heard the squire's yell, came trotting round the corner.

"No violence, sergeant!" he called sternly.

"Not a bit, sir," replied the aggressor. "One of the boys happened ter drop his muskit on the old gentleman's corns, an' I was apologisin' fer his carelessness."

"You dreadful liar!" cried Janice, hotly, turning from her attempted comforting of the squire. "He did it on — oh!" She abruptly ended her speech as the mounted officer uncovered and bowed to her, and the "Oh!" was spoken as she recognised him. "Charles — Colonel Brereton!" the girl exclaimed.

"Charles!" exclaimed Mrs. Meredith, coming to the door. "Hoighty toighty, if it is n't!"

"I am very sorry that we are compelled to impress food, Mrs. Meredith," said the aide; "but as it is useless to resist I trust you will not make the necessity needlessly unpleasant."

"Ye 're a pack of ruffians and thieves!" cried the squire.

"Nay, Mr. Meredith," answered the aide, quietly; "we pay for it."

"In paper money that won't be worth a penny in the pound, come a month."

"That remains to be seen," responded the officer.

"'T is quite of a piece that a runaway redemptioner should return with other thieves and rob his master!" fumed the owner of Greenwood.

Brereton grew red, and retorted: "I am not in command of this force, and rode out with them at some sacrifice to save you from possible violence or unnecessary discomfort. Since you choose to insult me, I will not remain. Do your duty, sergeant," was the officer's parting injunction as he wheeled his horse and started toward the road.

"Stick him with yer bagonet, Pelatiah," ordered the sergeant, motioning toward the squire, who, still sitting in the doorway, very effectually blocked the way. Pelatiah, duly obedient, pricked the well-developed calf of the master of Greenwood, bringing that individual to his feet with another howl, which drew sympathetic shrieks from Mrs. Meredith and Janice.

Evidently the cries made it impossible for Colonel Brereton to hold to his intention, for he once again turned his horse and came riding back. By the time he reached the door the squire had been shoved to one side, and the men could be heard ransacking the larder and cellar none too quietly.

"Though you slight my services," the aide explained, "I 'll bide for the present."

Meanwhile the parties that had been detached to the other points could be seen harnessing oxen and horses to the hay cart, farm waggons, and even the big coach, and loading them from the corn-crib and barn. Presently the cortége started for the house, and here more stores of various kinds were loaded.

During the whole of this operation the squire kept busily expressing his opinions of the proceedings of the foragers, of the army to which they belonged, and of the Continental cause generally, which, but for the presence of the staff officer, would have probably led to his ducking in the horse trough, or to some other expression of the party's displeasure.

"I see ye take good care to steal all my horses, so that I shall not be able to ride to Brunswick and report ye to the commander," he railed, just as the last armful of hams and sides of bacon was thrown into the coach. "We heard tales of how ye robbed and plundered about York, unbeknownst to the general, and I 've no doubt ye are thieving now without his knowledge."

"If you want to get to Brunswick you shall have a lift," offered the aide. "We 'll drive you there, and I 'll see to it that you have a horse to bring you back."

"Ay. And leave my wife and daughter to be outraged by you villainous Whigs."

Again Brereton lost his temper. "I challenge you to prove one case of our army insulting a woman," he cried. "And hast heard of the doings of the last few days? Of the conduct of British soldiers to the women of Hackensack and Elizabethtown, or of the brutality of the Hessians at Rahway? At this very moment Mr. Collins is printing for us broadsides of the affidavits of the poor miserable victims, in the hopes that we can rouse the country by them."

"'T is nothing but a big Whig clanker, I 'll be bound!" snorted Mr. Meredith.

"I would for the sake of manhood they were!" said the

officer. "I was once proud to be a British soldier —" he checked himself sharply, and then went on: "If you fear for Mrs. Meredith and Miss Janice, take them with you. I 'll see to it that you all return in comfort."

Although the squire had no particular fear of the safety of his womankind, he did not choose to confess it after what he had said; and so, without more ado, his wife and daughter were ordered to don their calashes and cloaks. Then the odd-looking caravan, of five vehicles, nine cows, and four squealing pigs, started, — Mrs. Meredith and Janice and the squire seated on the box of the coach, while the driver bestrode one of the horses.

The excitement of the drive was delightful to Janice, and it was not lessened by what she heard. The aide rode beside the coach, and at first tried to engage her in conversation, but the girl was too shy and self-conscious to talk easily to him, and so it ended in chat between the officer and Mr. and Mrs. Meredith, in which he told of how he had secured his position on the staff of the general, and gave an outline history of the siege of Boston, the campaigning about New York, and the retreat to Brunswick.

"I knew the rake-hells 'ud never fight," asserted the squire, at one point.

"Like all green troops, they object to discipline, and have shown cowardice in the face of the enemy. But the British would not dare say as much as you say, after the lessons they 've had. The fault is mainly with the officers, who, by the system of election or appointment, are chiefly politicians and popularity-seekers not fit to black boots, much less command companies and regiments. Here in this town, the life was sapped out of the 'Invincibles' by their own officers; but the parson went among the men this morning, and the best of them formed a new company under him and enlisted for the year. And those who helped me take the powder to Cambridge volunteered, and have proved good men. All they need are good officers to make them good soldiers."

"What did ye with that rogue Evatt?" demanded the squire, his mind recalled to the subject by the allusion to the powder; and Janice hastily caught hold of the fore-string of her calash to pull the headgear forward so that her face should be hidden from the aide. Yet she listened to the reply with an attentive if red face.

"Our kidnapping of him not being easy to justify, I did not choose to take him to Cambridge and so, when we spoke a brig outside Newport, bound for Madeira, I e'en bargained his passage on her. 'T is naturally the last I ever heard of him."

Then poor Janice had to hear her father and mother express their thanks to the officer and berate the runaway pair; and the painful subject was abandoned only when they drove into Brunswick, where its interest could not compete with that of the masses of soldiers camped on the green, the batteries of artillery planted along the river front, and the general hurly-burly everywhere.

"You had best sit where you are, ladies," the aide remarked, "for the inn is full of men;" and the two accepted his suggestion, and from their coign of vantage surveyed the scene, while the squire, tumbling off the waggon, demanded word with the commander-in-chief.

"I 'll tell him you wish speech with him," said Brereton, dismounting and going into the tavern.

It is only human when one is in misery to take a certain satisfaction in finding that misfortune is not a personal monopoly. While the squire waited to pour out his complaint, he found farmer after farmer standing about with similar intent; and, greatly comforted by the grievances of his neighbors, he became almost joyous when Squire Hennion, following a long line of carts loaded with his year's harvest, added himself to the scene, and with oaths and wails sought in turn to express his anger and misery.

"Tew rob a genuine Son o' Liberty," he whined, "ez hez allus stood by the cause! The general shall hear o' 't. I 'm ruined. I 'll starve. I 'll—"

"Ho, ho!" laughed Mr. Meredith, heartily. "So sitting on both sides don't pay, eh? And a good serve out it is to ye, ye old trimmer. What! object to paper dollars, when ye are so warm a Whig? What if they are only worth two shillings in the pound, specie? Liberty for ever! Ho, ho! This is worth the trip to Brunswick alone."

Colonel Brereton came out of the tavern with a paper in his hand, and called the squire aside.

"Mr. Meredith," he said in a low voice, his face eager, yet worn with anxiety, "I find that since I left camp this morning the rest of the New Jersey and all of the Maryland flying camps have refused to stay, and have left us, though Cornwallis's advance is at Piscataway, and as he is pushing forward by forced marches he will reach the Raritan within two hours."

"No doubt, no doubt," assented the squire, gleefully. "Another week will put him in Philadelphia, and then ye rebels will dance for it. No wonder ye look frighted, man."

"I am not scared on my own account," replied the officer, bitterly. "A dozen bullets, whether in battle or standing blindfold against a white wall, are all the same to me. I'll take the gallows itself, if it comes, and say good quittance."

"Ay," grunted Mr. Meredith, "go on. Tip us a good touch of the heroics."

The aide smiled, but then went on anxiously: "But what I do fear, and why I tell you what I do, is for — for — for Mrs. Meredith and — The loss of this force leaves us barely three thousand men to fight Cornwallis's and Knyphausen's fifteen thousand. We shall burn the bridge within the hour, but that will scarce check them, and so we must retreat to the Delaware."

"And how does this affect me?"

"Every hour brings us word of the horrible excesses of the British soldiery. No woman seems safe from — For God's sake, Mr. Meredith, don't remain here! But go with our army, and I'll pledge you my word you shall be safe and as comfortable as it is in my power to make you."

"Tush! British officers never — "

"'T is not the officers, but the common soldiers who straggle from the lines for plunder and — while the pigs of Hessians and Waldeckers, sold by their princes at so much per head, cannot be controlled, even by their own officers. See, here, is the broadside of which I spoke. I have seen every affidavit, and swear to you that they are genuine. Don't — you can't risk such a fate for Mrs. Meredith or — " Brereton stopped, unable to say more, and thrust the paper he held in his hand into that of the squire.

"I'll have none of your Whig lies puffed on me!" persisted the squire, obstinately.

The officer started to argue; but as he did so the gallop of a horse's feet was heard, and Colonel Laurens came dashing up. Throwing himself from the saddle, he flung into the tavern; and that he brought important news was so evident that Brereton hurriedly left Mr. Meredith and followed. Barely a moment passed when aide after aide issued from the inn, and, mounting, spurred away in various directions. The results were immediate. The carts were hurriedly put in train and started southward on the Princeton post-road, smoke began to rise from the bridge, the batteries limbered up, and the regiments on the green fell in and then stood at ease.

While these obvious preparations for a retreat were in progress a coloured man appeared, leading so handsome and powerful a horse that Janice, who had much of her father's taste, gave a cry of pleasure and, jumping from her perch, went forward to stroke the beast's nose.

"What a beauty!" she cried.

"Yes, miss, dat Blueskin," replied the darky, grinning proudly. "He de finest horse from de Mount Vernon stud, but he great villain, jus' de same. He so obstropolus when he hear de guns dat the gin'l kian't use him, an' has tu ride ole Nelson when dyars gwine tu be any fightin'."

Janice leaned forward and kissed the "great villain" on his soft nose, and then turned to find the general standing in the doorway watching her.

"I have not time to attend to your complaints, gentlemen," he announced to the two esquires and the group of farmers, all of whom started forward at his appearance. "File your statements and claims with the commissary-general, and in due time they'll receive attention." Then he came toward his horse, and as he recognised the not easily forgotten face he uncovered. "I trust Miss Janice remembers me!" he said, a smile succeeding the careworn look of the previous moment, and added: "Had ye been kind, ye'd have kept that caress for the master."

Janice coloured, but replied with a mixture of assurance and shyness: "Blueskin could not ask for it, but your Excellency —" Then she paused and coloured still more.

Washington laughed, and, stooping, kissed her hand. "Being a married man, must limit the amount of his yielding to temptation," he said, finishing the sentence for the girl. "I would I were to have the honour of your company at dinner once more, but your friends, the British, will not give us the time. So I must mount and say farewell."

Janice turned an eager face up to the general, as he swung himself into the saddle. "Oh, your Excellency," she exclaimed below her breath, "dadda would think it very wicked of me, but I hope you'll beat them!"

Washington's face lighted up, and, leaning over, he once more kissed her hand. "Thank you for the wish, my child," he said, and, giving Blueskin the spur, rode toward the river.

"If Philemon was only like his Excellency!" thought the girl.

XXVII

A CHECK TO THE ENEMY

THERE followed a weary hour of waiting, while first the carts, then the artillery, and finally the few hundred ill-clad, weary men filed off on the post-road. Before the rear-guard had begun its march, British regiments could be discerned across the river, and presently a battery came trotting down to the opposite shore, and a moment later the guns were in position to protect a crossing. This accomplished, a squadron of light dragoons rode into the water and struck boldly across, a number of boats setting out at the same moment, each laden with redcoats. While they were yet in mid-stream the Continental bugles sounded the retreat, and the last American regiment marched across the green and disappeared from view.

Owing to the fact that the coach had not been parked with the waggons, but had been brought to the tavern door, the baggage-train had moved off without it, — a circumstance, needless to say, which did not sadden the squire. It so happened that the vehicle had stopped immediately under the composite portrait sign-board of the inn; and no sooner was the last American regiment lost to view than the publican appeared, equipped with a paint-pot and brush, and, muttering an apology to the owner of the coach, now seated beside his wife and daughter on the box, he climbed upon the roof and, by a few crude strokes, altered the lettering from "Gen. George the Good" into "King George the Good." But he did not attempt to change the firm chin and the strong forehead the bondsman had added to the face.

Barely was the operation finished when the British light horse came wading out of the water and cantered up the river road to the green, the uniforms and helmets flashing brilliantly, the harness jingling, and the swords clanking merrily.

"There are troops worth talking about," cried the squire, enthusiastically.

He spoke too quickly, for the moment the "dismount" sounded, twenty men were about the coach.

"Too good horses for a damned American!" shouted one, and a dozen hands were unharnessing them on the instant. "A load of prog, boys!" gleefully shouted a second, and both doors were flung open, and the soldiers were quickly crowding each other in their endeavours to get a share. "Egad!" announced another, "but I'll have a tousel and a buss from yon lass on the box." "Well said!" cried a fourth, and both sprang on the wheel, as a first step to the attainment of their wishes.

Mr. Meredith, from the box, had been shrieking affirmations of his loyalty to King George without the slightest heed being paid to him; but there is a limit to passivity, and as the two men on the wheel struggled which should first gain the desired prize, the squire kicked out twice with his foot in rapid succession, sending both disputants back into the crowd of troopers. Howls of rage arose on all sides; and it would have fared badly with the master of Greenwood had not the noise brought an officer up.

"Here, here!" he cried sharply, "what's all this pother about?"

"'T is a damned Whig, who is —"

"A lie!" roared the squire. "There is no better subject of King George living than Lambert Meredith."

The officer jeered. "That's what every rebel claims of late. Not one breathes in the land, if you'd but believe the words of you turncoats."

"'T is not a lie," spoke up Janice, her face blazing with temper and her fists clinched as if she intended to use them. "Dadda always —"

"Ho!" exclaimed the officer, "what a pretty wench! Art a rebel, too? for if so, I'll see to it that guard duty falls to me. Come, black eyes, one kiss, and I'll send the men to right about."

Janice caught the whip from its socket and raised it threateningly, just as another officer from a newly arrived company came spurring up and, without warning, began to strike right and left with the flat of his sword. "Off with you, you damned rapscallions!" he shouted. "Leftenant Bromhead, where are your manners?"

"And where are yours, Mr. Hennion, that ye dare speak so to your superior officer?" demanded the lieutenant.

There was no mistaking Philemon, changed though he was. He wore a fashionable wig, and his clothes fitted well a figure that, once shambling and loose-jointed, had now all the erectness of the soldier, but the face was unchanged.

"I'll not quarrel with you now," swaggered Philemon. "If you want ter fight later I'm your man, an' if you want ter go before Colonel Harcourt with a complaint I'll face you. But now I've other matters." He turned to the trio on the box, and exclaimed as he doffed his hat: "Well, squire, didst ever expect sight of me again? An' how do Mrs. Meredith and Janice? Strap my vitals, if I've seen such beauty since I left Brunswick," he added airily, and making Janice feel very much put out of countenance.

"Welcome, Philemon!" cried Mrs. Meredith, "and doubly welcome at such a moment."

"Ay," shouted the squire, heartily. "Ye arrived just in the nick o' time to save your bride, Phil." A remark which sent the whip rattling to the ground from the hands of Janice. "An' ye a king's officer!" he ended. "Bubble your story to us, lad."

"There ain't much ter tell as you don't know already. Sir William put no faith in the news I carried, thinkin' it but a Whig trick, and so they held me prisoner. But later, when 't was too late ter use it, they learned the word I brought them was true; so they set me free, and as there was no gettin' away from Boston, the general gave me a cornetcy, that I should not starve."

"I'll lay to it that there'll be no more starvation now that you're back home," cried the squire, "though betwixt your cheating old sire, who'll pay no interest on his mortgages, and the merchants gone bankrupt in York, and now this loss of harvest and stock, 't is like Greenwood will show but a lean larder for a time. But mayhaps now that ye 've gone up in the world, ye 'd like to cry off from the bargain?"

"But let me finish the campaign by capturin' Philadelphia, and dispersin' Washington's pack of peddlers and jail-birds, which won't take mor 'n a fortnight, and then you can't name a day too soon for me, an' I hope not for your daughter. You can't call me gawk any longer, I reckon, Janice?"

"Thou camst nigh to losing her, Phil," declared Mrs. Meredith.

"Ay," added the squire. "Hast heard of how that scoundrel Evatt schemed — "

"Oh, dadda!" moaned Janice, imploringly.

"No scoundrel is he, squire, nor farmer neither; he bein' Lord Clowes," asserted Phil. "He joined our army at New York, and is Sir William's commissary-general an' right-hand man."

A more effectual interruption than that of the girl's prevented Mr. Meredith from enlarging upon the theme, for the bugle sounded in quick succession the "assembly" and "boots and saddles."

"That calls me," announced Phil, with an air of importance. "We ain't goin' ter give the runaways no rest, you see."

"But Phil," cried the squire, "ye 'll not leave us to be again — And they 've stole Joggles and Jumper, and all my hams and sides. Ye must — "

"I can't bide now," called back the cornet, hurriedly taking his position just as the bugle called the marching order, and the squadron moved off after the retreating Continentals.

Helpless to move, the Merediths sat on their coach while an officer, accompanied by a file of soldiers and half a dozen drummers, took station at the Town Hall. First a broadside was posted on the bulletin-board, and the drums beat the "parley" long and loudly. Then the drummers and the file split into two parties, and marching down the village street in opposite directions, the non-commissioned officers, to the beat of drum, shouted summons to all the population to assemble at the hall to take the oath of allegiance to "King George the Third, by the grace of God, of Great Britain, France, and Ireland, King, Defender of the Faith, and so forth."

The first man to step forward to take the oath, sign the submission, and receive his pardon was the Hon. Joseph Bagby, erstwhile member of the Assembly of New Jersey, but now loudly declaring his loyalty to the crown, and his joy that "things were to be put in order again." The second signer was the publican; the third was Esquire Hennion; and after him came all the townsmen, save those who had thrown in their lot along with the parson that morning by marching off with Washington.

Mr. Meredith descended from his seat and waited his turn to go through what was to him a form, and during this time the ladies watched the troops being ferried across the river. Presently an officer rode up the river road, issuing orders to the regiments, which promptly fell in, while the rider halted at the tavern, announced the soon-to-be-expected arrival of Generals Howe and Cornwallis, and bade the landlord prepare his best cheer. While he spoke a large barge landed its burden of men and horses on the shore, and a moment later a dozen officers came trotting up to the tavern between lines of men with their guns at "present arms."

"What ho! Well met, friend Meredith," cried one of the new-comers, as the group halted at the tavern. "I was but just telling Sir William that the king had one good friend in Brunswick town, and now here he is!" Evatt, or Clowes, swung out of the saddle and extended his hand.

Although the squire had just recovered the whip dropped by Janice, he did not keep to his intention of laying it across the shoulders of the would-be abductor, but instead grasped the hand offered.

"Well met, indeed," he assented cordially. "'T is a glad sight to us to see our good king's colours and troops."

"Sir William," called the baron, "thou must know Mr. Lambert Meredith, first, because he 's the one friend our king has in this town, and next, because, as thy commissary, I forbid thee to dine at the tavern on the vile fried pork or bubble and squeak, and the stinking whiskey or rum thou 'lt be served with, and, in Mr. Meredith's name, invite thee and his Lordship to eat a dinner at Greenwood, where thou 'lt have the best of victuals, washed down with Madeira fit for Bacchus."

"Ay," cried Mr. Meredith, "the rebels have done their best to bring famine to Greenwood, but it shall spread its best to any of his Majesty's servants."

"Here 's loyalty indeed," said Sir William, heartily, as he leaned in his saddle to shake the squire's hand. "Damn your rebel submissions and oaths, not worth the paper they 're writ on; but good Madeira, — that smacks loyal and true on a parched tongue and cannot swear false. Lead the way, Mr. Meredith, and we 'll do as much justice to your wine as later we 'll do to Mr. Washington, if we can ever come up with him. Eh, Charles?"

The officer addressed, who was frowning, gave an impatient movement in the saddle that seemed to convey dissent. "Of what use was our forced march," he demanded, "if not to come up with the fox before he finds cover?"

"Nay, the rebels are so little hampered by baggage that they can outstrip all save our light horse. And because they have the legs of us is no reason for our starving ourselves; the further they run, the more exhausted they 'll be."

"Well argued," chimed in Clowes. "And your Excellency will find more at Greenwood than mere meat and drink. Come, squire, name your dame and Miss Janice to Sir William. In playing quadrille to win, man, we never hold back the queens."

All the horsemen uncovered to the ladies, as they were introduced, and Howe uttered an admiring epithet as his eyes fixed on the girl. "The Queen of Hearts scores, and the game is won," he cried, bowing low to Janice. "Ho, Charles, art as hot for the rebels as thou wert a moment since?"

"I still think the light horse had best be pushed, and should be properly supported by the grenadiers."

"Nay, wait till Knyphausen comes up, and then we 'll —"

"'T is no time to play a waiting game."

"Tush! Lord Cornwallis," replied Sir William, irritably. "The infantry have done their twenty miles to-day. I 'll not jade my troops into the runaway state of the rebels. What use to kill our men, when the rebellion is collapsing of itself?" During all his argument the commander-in-chief kept his eyes fixed on Janice.

"I can't but think —" began the earl.

"Come, come, man," interjected Howe, "we must n't let the Whigs beat us by starvation. Must we, eh, Mr. Meredith?"

"'T would be a sad end to all our hopes," assented the squire. "And while we have to do with the rebels, let me point out to ye the two most malignant in this town. There stand the precious pair who have done more to foment disloyalty than any other two men in the county." It is needless to say that Mr. Meredith was pointing at Squire Hennion and Bagby, who, more curiously than wisely, had lingered at the tavern.

"He lies!" and "'T ain't so! shrieked Bagby and Hennion in unison, and each began protestations of loyalty, which were cut short by Sir William, who turned to Cornwallis and ordered the two under arrest, pending further information.

"Now we'll see justice," chuckled the master of Greenwood, gleefully. "If ye'll not pay interest on your debts, I'll pay interest on mine — ay, and with a hangman's cord belike."

"But I signed a submission and oath, and here's my pardon," protested Bagby, producing the paper, an example that Hennion imitated.

"Damn Campbell's carelessness!" swore Howe. "He deals pardons as he would cards at piquet, by twos, without so much as a look at their faces. A glance at either would have shown both to be rapscallion Whigs. However, 't is done, and not to be undone. Release them, but keep eye on each, and if they give the slightest cause, to the guardhouse with them. Now, Mr. Meredith."

"I must ask your Excellency's assistance to horse my coach, and his Majesty owes me a pair not easy to match, stole by your troops this very morning."

"Make note of it, Mr. Commissary, and see to it that Mr. Meredith has the two returned, with proper compensation. And, Charles, if the theft can be fixed, let the men have a hundred stripes apiece. Unless a stop can be put to this plundering and raping, we'll have a second rebellion on our hands."

Cornwallis shrugged his shoulders and issued the necessary orders. Then horses being secured for the carriage, the squire and dames, accompanied by the generals, set out for Greenwood.

It was long past the customary dining hour when the house was reached, and though Mrs. Meredith and Janice joined Sukey and Peg in the hurried preparation of the meal, it was not till after three that it could be announced. As a consequence, before the men had tired of the Madeira, dark had come. One unfortunate of the staff was therefore despatched to order the regiments to bivouac for the night.

"Tell the commissaries to issue an extra ration of rum," directed Sir William, made generously minded by the generous use of the wine. "And now, friend Lambert, let 's have in the spirits, and if it but equal thy Madeira in quality we 'll sing a Te Deum and make a night of it."

Janice, at a call from the host, brought in the squat decanters; and the general insisted, with a look which told his admiration, that his first glass should be mixed by the girl.

"Nay, nay," he cried, checking her as she reached for the loaf sugar." "Put it to thy lips, and 'twill be sweeter than any sugar can make it. Take but a sip and give us a toast along with it." And the general caught at the girl's free hand and tried to put his other arm about her waist.

"Oh, fie, Sir William!" called Clowes, too flushed with wine to guard his tongue. "What will Mrs. Loring think of such talk?"

"Think! Let her think what she may," retorted the general, with a laugh. "Dost thou not know that woman is never sweeter than when she is doubtful of her empire?"

Janice, with heightened colour and angry eyes, eluded Howe's familiarities by a backward step, and, raising the glass, defiantly gave, "Success to Washington!" Then, scared at her own temerity, she darted from the room, in her fright carrying away the tumbler of spirits. But she need not have fled, for her toast only called forth an uproarious burst of laughter.

"I always said 'twas a rebellion of petticoats," chuckled Sir William. "And small blame to them when they sought to tax their only drink. 'Fore George, I 'd rebel myself if they went to taxing good spirits unfairly. Ah, gentlemen, after we have finished with Mr. Washington next week, what sweet work 't will be to bring the caps to a proper submission! No wonder Cornwallis is hot to push on and have done with the men."

The morrow found Sir William no less inclined to tarry than he had been the day before, and, using the plea that they would await the arrival of Knyphausen's force, he sent orders to the advance to remain bivouacked at Brunswick, much to the disgust of Cornwallis, who was little mollified by the consent he finally wrung from his superior to push forward the Light Horse on a reconnoissance, — a task on which he at once departed.

Thus rid of his disagreeable spur, the general settled down before the parlour fire to a game of piquet with Clowes, not a little to the scandalising of card-hating Mrs. Meredith. Worse still to the mother, nothing would do Sir William but for Janice to come and score for him, and it is to be confessed that his attention was more devoted to the black of her eyes and the red of her cheeks than it was to the same colours on the cards. Three times he unguarded a king in the minor hand, and twice he was capoted unnecessarily. As a result, the baron won easily; but the gain in purse did not seem to cheer him, for he looked discontented even as he pocketed his winnings. And as every gallant speech his commander made the girl had deepened this look, the cause for the feeling was not far to seek.

Dinner eaten, the general, without leaving the table, lapsed into gentle, if somewhat noisy, slumber; and his superior thus disposed of for the moment, Clowes sought Janice, only to find that two young fellows of the staff, having abandoned the bottle before him, had the longer been enjoying her society. He joined the group, but, as on the preceding evening, Janice chose to ignore his presence. What he did not know was something said before his entrance, which had much to do with the girl's determination to punish him.

"Who is this person who is so intimate with Sir William?" she had asked the staff secretary.

McKenzie gave his fellow-staffsman a quick glance which, manlike, he thought the girl would not perceive. "He 's commissary-general of the forces," he then replied.

Janice shrugged her shoulders. "Thank you for enlightening my ignorance," she said ironically. "Let me add in payment for the information that this is a spinet."

Again McKenzie exchanged a look with Balfour. The latter, however, after a glance at the door, said, in a low voice: "He's no favourite with us; that you may be sure."

"He — Is he — Is Baron Clowes his true name?" Janice questioned.

"More true than most things about him," muttered McKenzie.

"Then he has another name?" persisted the girl.

"A half-dozen, no doubt," assented Balfour. "There are dirty things to be done in every kind of work, Miss Meredith, and there are always dirty men ready to do them. I'd not waste thought on him. Knaves go to make up a complete pack as much as kings, you know," he finished, as Lord Clowes entered the room.

Cornwallis returned at nightfall, with word of the junction of reinforcements; but, despite the news, it required all the urgence of himself and Clowes to induce the commander-in-chief to give the marching order for the next morning. Nor, when the hour of departure came, was Howe less reluctant, lingering over his adieux with his host and hostess, and especially with their daughter, to an extent which set the earl stamping with impatience and put a scowl on Clowes' face. Even when the general was in the saddle, nothing would do him but he must have a stirrup cup; and when this had been secured, he demanded another toast of the girl.

"You gave Mr. Washington your good wishes last time, Miss Janice, runaway though he was. Canst not give a toast for the troops that don't run?" he pleaded.

Janice, with a roguish look in her eyes that boded no good to the British, took the glass, and, touching it to her lips, said: "Here's to the army which never runs away, and which never —" Then she paused, and caught her breath as if wanting courage.

"Out with it! Complete the toast!" cried the general, eagerly.

"And which never runs after!" ended Janice.

XXVIII

THE EBB-TIDE

CLOWES lingered behind for a brief moment after the departure of Howe, in pretended desire to advise Mr. Meredith concerning the British policy about provisions and forage, but in truth to say a word of warning which proved that he already regretted having secured for his commander-in-chief the *entrée* of Greenwood.

"I heard Sir William say he 'd bide with ye on his return from Philadelphia," the commissary told the squire in parting. "Have an eye to your girl, if he does. Though a married man, his Excellency is led off by every lacing-string that comes within reach."

The master of Greenwood privately thought that the precautionary advice as to his daughter might come with better grace from some other source; but both guest and host, for reasons best known to each, had tacitly agreed to ignore the past, and so the squire thanked his counsellor.

"Ye 'll not forget to seek out my horses!" he added, when the commissary picked up his bridle.

"Assuredly not," promised Clowes. "How many didst say ye lost?"

"Two. All the Whig thieves left to me of the nine I had."

"Fudge, man! Say nothing of the Whig thieves, but lay them all to our account. We 've plunderers in plenty in our own force, let alone the dirty pigs of Hessians, and King George shall pay for the whole nine."

"Nay, Lord Clowes, because I 've been robbed, I 'll not turn —" began the squire.

"What is more," went on the benevolently-inclined officer, "I will tell ye something that will be worth many a pound. 'T was decided betwixt Sir William and myself that we should seize all provisions and fodder throughout the province. But I need scarce say — "

"Surely, man, thou wilt do nothing as crazy as that," burst out Mr. Meredith. "Dost not see that it will make an enemy of every man, from one end — "

"Which they are already," interrupted the baron, in turn. "'T is our method of bringing punishment home to the scamps. We 'll teach them what rebellion comes to ere we have finished with them. But, of course, such order does not extend to my personal friends, and if ye have any fodder or corn, or anything else ye can spare, I will see to it that his Majesty buys it at prices that will more than make good to ye what ye lost through the rebels."

The squire made a motion of dissent. "The Whig rascals have swept my barn and storehouses so clean that I 'll have to buy for my own needs, and — "

"Then buy what ye can hereabout before we begin seizing, and see to it that ye buy a good surplus which ye can sell to us at a handsome advance. Our good king is a good paymaster, and I 'll show ye what it is to have a friend in the commissariat." With this Clowes put spurs to his horse, confident that he had more than offset any prejudice against him that might still exist in Mr. Meredith's mind. None the less, that individual stood for some moments on the porch with knitted brows, gazing after the departing horseman; and when he finally turned to go into the house he gave a shake to his head that seemed to express dissatisfaction.

Although Mr. Meredith did not act upon the commissary's suggestion in securing a supply of provisions, there was quickly no lack of food or forage at Greenwood. From the moment that Brunswick was occupied by the British, every one of Mr. Meredith's tenants, who for varying periods had refused to pay rent, adopted a different course and wholly or in part settled up the arrears owing. Most of them first endeavoured to liquidate the claim in the Continental currency, now depreciated through the desperation of the American cause to a point that made it scarcely worth the paper on which its pseudo-value was stamped. The squire, however, with many a jeer and flout at each would-be payer for his folly in having taken the money, and his still greater foolishness in expecting to pay rent on leaseholds with it, declined to accept it. His refusal of each tender, which indeed had been expected, was usually followed by a second offer of payment in the form of fodder or provisions, or "in kind," as the leases then expressed it; and the moment the rumour went through the community that the British were forcibly seizing provisions, every farmer hastened to save his entire surplus by paying it to his landlord.

Nothing better proved the hopeless outlook of the American cause than the conduct of Esquire Hennion, for that worthy rode to Greenwood, and after a vain attempt, like that of the tenants, to pay in the worthless paper money the arrears of interest on his mortgages, with a like refusal by Mr. Meredith, he completely broke down, and with snivels and wails besought his "dear ole friend" to be lenient and forbearing. "I made a mistake, squire," he pleaded; "but I allus liked yer, an' Phil he likes yer, an' naow yer 're too ginerous ter push things too far, I knows."

"Huh!" grunted the creditor. "I said I 'd make ye cry small, ye old trimmer. So it 's no longer to your interest to pay principal, or your principle to pay interest, eh? No, I won't push ye too far! I 'll only turn ye out of Boxely and let ye be farmed on the town as a pauper. If I had the dealing with ye, ye 'd be in the provost prison at York awaiting trial as a traitor. And my generosity would run to just six feet of rope."

Of the tide of war only vague rumours came back to the non-combatants, until at noon, a week later, Sir William, accompanied by two aides and an escort of dragoons, came cantering up.

"In the king's name, dinner!" he cried cheerily, as he shook the welcoming hand of the squire. "You see, Mr. Meredith, we 've forgot neither your loyalty nor your Madeira. No, nor your dainty lass, either; and so we are here again to levy taxation without representation on them all. 'T is to be hoped, Mrs. Meredith, that 't will be met more kindly than our Parliamentary attempt at the same game. Ah, Miss Janice, your face is a pleasant sight to look at after the bleak banks of the Delaware, at which we 've been staring and cursing for the last five days."

"We hoped to hear of ye as in Philadelphia before this, Sir William," said the squire, so soon as they were seated at the table.

"Ay, and so did we all; but Mr. Washington was too quick and sharp for us. By the time we had reached Trenton, he had got safely across the river, and had taken with him or destroyed all the boats."

"Could ye not have forded the river higher up?"

"Cornwallis was hot for attempting something of the sort, but sight of the ice-floes in the river served to cool him, so he is going into winter quarters and will not stir from his cantonments until spring, unless the river freeze strong enough for him to cross on the ice."

"And what of the rebels?"

"'T is sudden gone so out of fashion there is scarce one left. Washington has a few ragged troops watching us from across the river; but, except for these, there 's not a man in the land who will own himself one. How many pardons have we issued in the Jerseys alone, Henry?" demanded the general, appealing to his secretary.

"Nigh four thousand; and at Trenton and Burlington, Mr. Meredith, the people are flocking in in such numbers that over four hundred took the king's oath yesterday," responded McKenzie.

"That shows how the wind holds, and what a summer's squall the whole thing has been," answered the host, gleefully; "I always said 't was a big windy bubble, that needed but the prick of British bayonets to collapse."

"There 'll be little left of it by spring, I doubt not," asserted Howe. "In faith, we may take it as a providence that we could not cross the Delaware, for a three-months will probably put an end to all armed opposition, and we may march into Pennsylvania with beating drums and flying colours. Even Cornwallis himself confesses that time is playing our game."

"Miss Meredith will be put to 't to find a new toast," suggested Balfour.

"Well spoke," laughed his superior. "What will it be, fair rebel?"

"However," asserted Janice.

"Bravo!" vociferated the general. "Now indeed rebellion is on its last legs. You make me regret I can tarry but the meal, for when submission is so near 't is a pity not to stay and complete it."

"Was that why you left the Delaware, your Excellency?" asked Janice, archly.

The colour came flushing into Howe's cheeks, while both father and mother spoke sharply to the girl for her boldness and impertinence. But in a moment the general's good-nature was once more in the ascendant, and he interfered to save her from the scolding.

"Nay, nay," he interjected. "'T was but a proper retort to my teasing. I left the Delaware, Miss Janice, because the 'Brune' frigate sails for England in three days, and there are despatches to be writ and sent by her. And for the same reason I can tarry here but another hour, much as I should like to stay. Mr. Meredith, 't is a man's duty to aid a creditor to pay his debts. May I not hope to see you and Mrs. Meredith and Miss Janice at headquarters ere long? For if you come not willingly, I 'll put Miss Janice under arrest as an arrant and avowed rebel, and have her brought to York under guard."

The departure of these guests gave but a brief quiet to the household, for two days later, at dusk, Clowes rode up, and his coming was welcomed all the more warmly that his escort of half a dozen dragoons led with them Joggles and Jumper.

"Have in, have in, man," cried the host, genially, "to where there 's a fire and something to warm your vitals."

"Curse thy climate!" ejaculated the new-comer, as he stamped and shook himself in the hallway, to rid his shoulders and boots of their burden of snow. "The storm came on after we started; and six hours it 's took us to ride from Princeton, while the wind blew so I feared the cattle would founder. But here 's warmth enough to make up for the weather," he added, as he entered the parlour, all aglow with the light of the great blazing logs, and of the brushwood and corn-cobs which Janice had thrown on their top when the horses had first been heard at the door. He shook Mrs. Meredith's hand, and then extended his own to Janice, only to have it ignored by her. In spite of this, and of an erect attitude, meant to express both distance and haughtiness, her flushed cheeks, and eyes that looked everywhere except into those of the visitor, proved that the girl was not as unmoved as she wished to appear.

"Where are thy manners, Jan?" reproved the father, who, having declared an amnesty as regarded the past, forgot that his daughter might not be equally forgiving.

"Give Mr. — Lord Clowes thy hand, child," commanded her mother, sternly, "and place a seat for him by the fire."

Janice pulled one of the chairs nearer to the chimney breast, and then returned to the quilting-frame, at which she had been working when the interruption came.

"Didst hear me?" demanded Mrs. Meredith.

Janice turned and faced the three bravely, though her voice trembled a little as she replied: "I will not shake his hand."

"Yoicks! Here 's a kettle of fish!" ejaculated the commissary. "What 's wrong?"

"Janice, do as thou art told, or go to thy room," ordered the mother.

The girl opened her lips as if about to protest, but courage failed her, and she hurriedly left the parlour, and flying to her room, she threw herself on the bed and wept out her sense of wrong on her pillow.

"I never would have, if he had n't — and it was n't I asked him to the house — and he took a mean advantage — and he was n't scolded for it, nor shamed to all the people — and now they show him every honour, though he — though for a year it was held up to me."

Presently the girl became conscious of the clatter of knives and forks on plates in the room beneath her, and of an accompaniment of cheerful voices and laughter. Far from lessening her woe, they only served to intensify it, till finally she rose in a kind of desperation, wishing only to escape from the merry sounds. "I 'll go and see Clarion and Joggles and Jumper," she thought. "They love me, and — and they don't punish me when others are to blame."

Not choosing to pass through the kitchen, where the dragoons would probably be sitting, she stole out of the front door, without wrap or calash, and in an instant was almost swept off her feet and nearly blinded by the rush of wind and snow. Heeding neither, nor the instant wetting of her slippered feet, she struggled on through the waxing drifts to the stable door. With a sigh of relief that the goal was attained, she passed through the partly open doorway and paused at last, breathless from her exertion.

On the instant she caught her breath, however, and then demanded, "Who 's there?" A whinny from Joggles was the only response. Taking no heed of the horse's greeting, Janice stood, listening intently for a repetition of the sound that had alarmed her. "I heard you," she continued, after a moment. Then she gave a little cry of fright, which was scarcely uttered when it was succeeded by a half-sob and half-exclamation of mingled joy and relief. "Oh, Clarion!" she exclaimed, "you gave me such a turn, with your cold nose. And what was mommy's darling doing with the harness? I thought some one was here."

Again Joggles whinnied, and, her fright entirely gone, Janice walked to his stall. "Was my precious glad to get back?" she asked, patting him on the back as she went into the stall. "Why, my poor dear! Did they go to their supper without even taking his saddle off? Well, he should — and his bridle, too, so that he could n't eat his hay! 'T was a shame, and — " Once again, Janice uttered an exclamation of fright, as her fingers, moving blindly forward in search of the buckle, came in contact with some cloth, under which she felt a man's arm. Nor was her fright lessened, though she did not scream, when instantly her arm in turn was seized firmly. The unknown peril is always the most terrifying.

"I did not want to frighten you, Miss Janice — " began the interloper.

"Charles!" ejaculated the girl. "I mean, Colonel Brereton."

"I thought you 'd scarcely come into the stall, and hoped to get away undiscovered."

"But what are you — I thought you were across — How did you get here?"

"I had business to the northward," explained the officer, "and meant to have been in Bound Brook by this time. But the cursed snow came on, and, not having travelled the westerly roads, I thought best to keep to those with which I was familiar, though knowing full well that I ran the risk of landing in the arms of the British. Fortunately their troops are no fonder of facing our American weather than our American riflemen, and tucked themselves within doors, leaving it to us —" There the aide checked his flow of words.

"But why did you come here?"

Brereton laughed. "Does not a runaway servant always turn horse thief? My mare has covered near forty miles today, the last ten of it in the face of this storm, and so I left her at the Van Meter barn, and thought to borrow Joggles to ride on to Morristown to do the rest." Colonel Brereton's hand, which had continued on the girl's arm, relaxed its firm hold, and slipped down till it held her fingers. "And then, I — I wanted word of you, for the stories of Hessian doings that come to us are enough to make any man anxious." Janice felt his lips on her hand. "All is well with you?" he asked eagerly, after the caress.

Janice, forgetful of her recent woe, answered in the affirmative, as she tried to draw herself away. Her attempt only led to the man's hand on hers tightening its grip. "I can't let you go, Miss Janice, till you give me your word not to speak of this meeting. They could scarce catch me such a night, but my mission is too vital to take any risks."

"I promise," acceded Janice, readily.

Brereton let go her hand at once, and his fingers rattled the bit, as he hastily completed the buckling the girl's entrance had interrupted. "If I never return, you will claim your namesake, my mare, Miss Janice," he suggested as he backed Joggles out of the stall. "And treat her well, I beg you. She 's the one thing that has any love for me. God knows if I ever see her again."

Forgetting that Brereton could not see her, Janice nodded her head. "You are going for good?" she asked.

"I fear for anything but that! For good or bad, however, I must ride my thirty miles to-night."

"Thirty miles!" cried Janice, with a shiver. "And your hands are dreadfully cold, and your teeth chatter."

"'T is only the chill of inaction after hard and hungry riding. Ten minutes of cantering will set the blood jumping again."

"Can't you wait a moment while I get something for you to eat?" besought the girl.

"Bless you for the thought," replied the aide, with a little husk in his voice. "But my mission is too important to risk delay, much more the nearness of yon dragoons."

"For what are you going?" questioned Janice.

"To order — to get the dice for a last desperate main."

"General Washington is going to try — ?"

"Ay. Ah, Miss Janice, they have beaten our troops, but they 've still to beat our general, and if I can but make Lee — I must not linger. Wilt give me a good-by and God-speed to warm me on the ride?"

"Both," answered Janice, holding out her hand, which the officer once again stooped and kissed. "And to-night I'll pray for his Excellency."

Brereton shoved open the door wide enough for the horse to pass through. "And not for his Excellency's aide?" he asked.

Janice laughed a little shyly as she replied: "Does not the greater always include the lesser?"

Barely were the words spoken, when a sound from the outside reached them, making both start and listen intently. It needed but an instant's attention to resolve the approaching noise into the jingle of bits and sabres.

"Hist!" whispered the officer, warningly. "Cavalry." He threw back the holster-flap of the saddle to free a pistol, and, grasping his scabbard to prevent it from clanking, he stepped through the doorway, leading Joggles by the bridle.

"Ho, there!" came a voice out of the driving snow. "We 've lost sight and road. Which way is 't to Greenwood?"

Brereton put foot in the stirrup and swung into the saddle.

"Away to the right," he responded, as he softly drew his sabre, and slipped the empty scabbard between his thigh and the saddle. Gathering up the reins, he wheeled Joggles to the left.

"Can't ye give us some guidance, whoever ye be?" asked the voice, now much nearer, while the sound of horses' breathing and the murmur of men's voices proved that a considerable party were struggling through the deepening snow. "Where are you, anyway?"

Brereton touched Joggles with the spur gently, and the steed moved forward. Not five steps had been taken before the horse shied slightly to avoid collision with another, and, in doing so, he gave a neigh.

"Here 's the fellow, Hennion," spoke up a rider. "Now we 'll be stabled quick enough." He reached out and caught at the bridle.

There was a swishing sound, as Brereton swung his sword aloft and brought it down on the extended arm. Using what remained of the momentum of the stroke, the aide let the flat of the weapon fall sharply on Joggles' flank; the horse bounded forward, and, in a dozen strides, had passed through the disordered troop.

A shrill cry of pain came from the officer, followed by a dozen exclamations and oaths from the troopers, and then a sharp order, "Catch or kill him!"

"Ha, Joggles, old boy," chuckled his rider, "there 's not much chance of our being cold yet a while. But we know the roads, and we 'll show them a trick or two if they 'll but stick to us long enough."

Bang! bang! bang! went some horse-pistols.

"Shoot away!" jeered the aide, softly, though he leaned low in the saddle as he wheeled through the small opening in the hedge and galloped over the garden beds. "'T is only British dragoons who 'd blindly waste lead on a northeaster. 'T is lucky the snow took no offence at my curses of it an hour ago."

XXIX

ON CONTINENTAL SERVICE

ONCE across the garden, the aide rode boldly, trusting to the snow overhead to hide his doings and the snow underfoot to keep them silent. Turning northward, he kept Joggles galloping for five minutes, then confident that his pursuers had been distanced, or misled, he varied the pace, letting the horse walk where the snow was drifted, but forcing him to his best speed where the road was blown clear.

"We know the route up to Middlebrook, Joggles; but after that we get into the hills, and blindman's work 't will be for the two of us. So 't is now we must make our time, if we are to be in Morristown by morning."

The rider spoke truly, for it was already six o'clock when he reached the cross-roads at Baskinridge. Halting his horse at the guide-post, he drew his sword and struck the crosspiece a blow, to clear it of its burden of snow.

"Morristown, eight miles," he read in the dark grayness of approaching day. "Hast go enough in thee left to do it, old fellow? Damn Lee for his tardiness and folly, which forces man and beast to journey in such cold." Pulling a flask from his pocket, he uncorked it. "There 's scarce a drop left, but thou shouldst have half, if it would serve thee," he said, as he put it to his lips and drained it dry. "'T is the last I have, and eight miles of Lee way still to do!" He laughed at his own pun, and pricked up the horse. Just as the weary animal broke into a trot, the rider pulled rein once more and looked up at a signboard which had attracted his notice by giving a discordant creak as the now dying storm swung it.

"A tavern! Here 's luck, for at least we can get some more

rum." Spurring the horse up to the door, he pulled a pistol from its holster and pounded the panel noisily.

It required more than one repetition of the blows to rouse an indweller, but finally a window was enough raised to permit the thrusting out of a becapped head.

"Who's below, and what do yez want?" it challenged gruffly.

"Never mind who I am. I want a pint of the best spirits you have, and a chance to warm myself for a ten minutes, if you've a spark of fire within."

"Oi've nothin' for anny wan who comes routin' me out av bed at such an hour, an' may the devil fly off wid yez for that same," growled the man. "Go away wid yez, an' niver let me see yez more."

The head was already drawn in, when Brereton, with quick readiness, called lustily: "Do as I order, or I'll have my troopers break in the door, and then look to yourself."

"Just wan minute, colonel," cried the man, in a very different tone; and in less than the time asked for the bolts were slipped back and the door was opened by a figure wrapped in a quilt, which one hand drew about him, while the other held a tallow dip aloft.

In the brief moment it took to do this, the officer not so much dismounted as tumbled from his horse, and he now walked stiffly into the public room, stamping his feet to lessen their numbness.

"Where's thim troopers yez was talkin' av?" questioned the landlord, peering out into the night.

"Throw some wood on those embers, and give me a drink of something, quickly," ordered Brereton, paying no heed to the inquiry.

"Bad 'cess to yez lies," retorted the man, shutting the door. "It's not wan bit av firing or drink yez get this night from — Oh, mother in hivin, don't shoot, an' yez honour shall have the best in the house, an' a blessin' along wid it! Only just point it somewheer else, darlin', for thim horse-pistols is cruel fond av goin' off widout bein' fired. Thank yez, sir, it's my wife in bed will bless the day yez was born." The man hastily raked open the bed of ashes and threw chips and billets on the embers. Then he unlocked a corner cupboard. "Oi 've New England rum, corn whiskey, an' home-made apple-jack, sir."

"Give me the latter, and if you 've any food, let me have it. Brrrew! From nigh Brunswick I 've rid since nine last night and thought to perish a dozen times with the cold, dismount and run beside my horse as I would."

"Drop that pistol, or I shoot!" came a sharp order, spoken from the gloom of a doorway across the room. "You are a prisoner."

Brereton had been stooping over the fire, as it gained fresh life, but with one spring he was behind the chimney breast.

"'T is idle to resist," persisted the hidden speaker. "The way is barred in both directions, and there are three of us."

Brereton laughed recklessly. "Come on, most courageous three. I 've a bullet for one, and a sword for two."

"Howly hivin! just let me out first off," besought the publican.

"If I had lead to spare, you should have the first of it for letting me into this trap," Brereton told him viciously. "Why did you not warn me there were British hereabout?"

"Hold!" came the distant voice. "If you think us British, who are you?"

The officer hesitated, pondering on the possibility of being tricked, or of possibly tricking. "If you were a gentleman," he said, after a pause, "you 'd give me a hint as to which side you belong."

The unseen man laughed heartily at Jack's reply. "Set me an example, then."

"That I will," said Jack, "though I don't guarantee the truth of it. I am an aide of General Washington, riding on public service."

"Time enough it took you to know it. And if so, what were you doing near Brunswick?"

"I took the route I knew best."

"Thy name is?"

"Jack Brereton."

"Art thou a green-eyed, carrot-faced put, who frights all the women with his ill looks?" cried the man, entering.

Brereton laughed as he stepped out from the sheltering projection. "Switch you, whoever you are, for keeping me from the fire when I am chilled to the marrow. Why, Eustace, this is luck beyond belief! But hast swallowed a frog? You croak so that I knew you not."

"Not I," responded the new-comer, shaking his fellow-officer's hand, "but I swallowed enough of yesterday's storm to spoil my voice, let-alone this creeping out of bed in shirt only, to catch some malignant Tory or spy of King George."

"Where art thy comrades?" inquired Brereton, peering past the major.

Eustace laughed. "They're making acquaintance with thy troop of horse."

"But what art thou doing here in this lonely hostel, with a British force no further away than Springfield? Dost court capture?"

"Just what I told the general when he said he'd bide here till — "

"The general!" interrupted Brereton. "Is Lee here — in this tavern?"

"Ay. And sleeping through all the rout you made as sound — "

"'T is madness! However, I'll not throw blame, for it has saved me eight miles of weary riding. Wake him at once, as I must have word with him. And you, landlord, stable my horse, and see to it that he has both hay and oats in plenty."

There was some delay before Eustace returned with the word that the major-general would see the aide, and with what ill grace the interview was granted was shown by the reception, for on Brereton being ushered into the room, it was to find Lee still in bed, and so far under the counterpane that only the end of a high-coloured but very much soiled nightcap was in view, while on the top of the covering lay two dogs, who rose with the entrance of the interloper.

"Who the devil are ye; why the devil did ye have me waked; and what the devil do ye want?" was the greeting, grumbled from the bedclothes.

Brereton flushed as he answered sharply: "Eustace has no

doubt told you who I am, and letters from his Excellency must have already broke the purport of my mission. Finding you paid no heed to his written orders, he has sent me with verbal ones, trusting your hearing may not be as seriously defective as your eyesight."

The head of the general appeared, as he sat up in bed. "Is this a message from General Washington?" he vociferated.

"No. 'T is my own soft speaking, in recognition of your complaisant welcome. But I bear a message of his Excellency. He directs that you march the entire force under you, without delay, by way of Bethlehem and Easton, and effect a junction with him."

"To what end?"

"The British think us so bad beat, and are so desirous to hold a big territory, for purposes of forage and plunder, that they have scattered their troops beyond supporting distance. Can we but get a force together sufficient to attack Burlington, Trenton, or Princeton, 't will be possible to beat them in detail."

"I have a better project than that," asserted Lee. "Let Washington but make a show of activity on the Delaware, and he shall hear of my doings shortly."

"But what better can be done than to drive them back from a country rich with food supplies, relieve the dread of their advancing upon Philadelphia, and give the people a chance to rally to us?" protested the aide.

"Pooh!" scoffed Lee. "'T is pretty to talk of, but 't is another thing to bring it off, and I make small doubt that 't will be no more successful than the damned ingenious manœuvres of Brooklyn and Fort Washington, which have unhinged the goodly fabric we had been building. I tell you we shall be in a declension till a tobacco-hoeing Virginian, who was put into power by a trick, and who has been puffed up to the people as a great man ever since, is shown to be most damnably weak and deficient. He 's had his chance and failed; now 't is for me to repair the damage he 's done."

Brereton clinched his fist and scowled. "Do I understand that you refuse to obey the positive orders of his Excellency?"

"'T is necessary in detachment to allow some discretion to the commanding officer. However, I 'll think on it after I 've finished the sleep you 've tried to steal." The general dropped back on the pillows, and drew up the bedclothes so as to cover his nose.

The aide, muttering an oath, stamped noisily out of the room, slamming the door with a bang that rattled every window in the house.

"I read failure in your face," remarked Eustace, still crouched before the fire.

"Failure!" snapped the scowling man, as he, too, stooped over the blaze. "Nothing but failure. Here, when the people have been driven frantic by the outraging of their women and the plundering of their property, and want but the smallest encouragement to rise, one man dishes all our hopes by his cursed ambition and disobedience."

"How so?"

Too angry to control himself, even to Lee's aide, Jack continued his tirade. "Ever since the general was put into office his subordinates have been scheming to break him down, and in Congress there has always been a party against him, who, through dislike or incapacity, clog all he advises or asks. With the recent defeats, the plotters have gained courage to speak out their thoughts, and your general goes so far as to refuse to obey orders that would make possible a brilliant stroke, because he knows that 't would stop this clack against his Excellency. Instead, he would have Washington sit passive and freezing on the Delaware while he steals the honours by some attempted action. And all the while he is writing to his Excellency letters signed, 'Yours most affectionately,' or 'God bless you,' — cheap substitutes for the three thousand troops he owes us." The aide went to the cupboard and helped himself to the apple-jack. "Canst get me a place to sleep, for God knows I 'm tired?"

"Thou shalt have my bed, and welcome to thee," offered Eustace, leading the way upstairs. "Thou 'lt not mind my getting into my clothes, for 't is not shirt-tail weather."

"Sixty miles and upward I 've come since five o'clock yesterday morning, and I 'd agree to sleep under a field-piece in full action." Brereton took off his cap and wig to toss both on the floor, unbuckled his belt, and let his sabre fall noisily; then sitting on the bed, he begged, "Give me a hand with my boots, will you?" Those pulled off, without rising he rolled over, and, bundling the disarranged bedclothes about him, he was instantly asleep.

It was noon before consciousness returned to the tired body, and only then because the clatter of horses' feet outside waked the sleeper and startled him so that he sprang from the bed to the window. Relieved by the sight of Continental uniforms, Brereton stretched himself as if still weary, and felt certain muscles, to test their various degrees of soreness, muttering complaints as he did so. Throwing aside his jacket, waistcoat, and shirt, he took his sword and pried out the crust of ice on the water in the tin milk-pail which stood on the washstand. Swashing the ice-cold water over his face and shoulders, he groaned a curse or two as the chill sent a shiver through him. But as he rubbed himself into a glow, he became less discontented, and when resuming the flannel shirt, he laughed. "Thank a kind God that it's as cold to the British as 't is to us, and there are more of them to suffer." Another moment served to don his outer clothing and boots, and to fit on his wig and sword. His toilet made, he went downstairs, humming cheerily. He turned first to the kitchen door, drawn thither by the smell that greeted his nostrils.

"Canst give a bestarved man a big breakfast and quickly?" he asked the woman.

"Shure, Oi 've all Oi can do now," was the surly response, "wid the general an' his staff, an' his escort, an' thim as is comin' an' goin', an'—"

Brereton came forward. "Ye 'd niver let an Oirishman go hungry," he appealed, putting a brogue on his tongue. "Arrah, me darlin', no maid wid such lips but has a kind heart." The officer boldly put his hand under the woman's chin and made as if he would kiss her. Then, as she eluded the threatened blandishment, he continued, "Sure, and do ye call yeself a woman, that ye starve a man all ways to wanst?"

"Ah, go long wid yez freeness and yez blarney," retorted the woman, giving him a shove, though smiling.

"An', darlin'," persisted the unabashed officer, "it 's owin' me somethin' ye do, for it was meself saved yez father's life this very morning."

"My father — shure, it 's dead he 's been this — It 's my husband yez must be afther spakin' av."

"He 's too old to be that same," flattered Brereton.

"'T is he, Oi make shure," acknowledged the woman, as she nevertheless set her apron straight and smoothed her hair. "An' how did yez save his loife?"

"Arrah, by not shooting him, as I was sore tempted to do."

The landlady melted completely and laughed. "An' what would yez loike for breakfast?" she asked.

Brereton looked at the provisions spread about. "Just give me four fried eggs wid bacon, an' two av thim sausages, an' corn bread, wid something hot to drink, an' if that 's buckwheat batter in the pan beyant, just cook a dozen cakes or so, for I 've a long ride to take an' they do be so staying. Also, if ye can make me up something — ay, cold sausages an' hard-boiled eggs, if ye 've nothing else, to take wid me; an' then a kiss, to keep the heart warm inside av me, 't is wan man ye 'll have given a glimpse av hivin."

"Bless us all!" marvelled Eustace, when twenty minutes later he entered the kitchen, to learn what delayed the general's lunch. "How came you by such a spread, when it 's all any of us can do to get enough to keep life in us? Is 't sorcery, man?"

"No, witchery," laughed the aide. "If thy chief were but a woman, Eustace, I 'd have Washington reinforced within a two days."

His breakfast finished, the aide secured pen and paper, and wrote a formal order for Lee to march. This done, he sought the general, and, interrupting a consultation he was holding with General Sullivan, he delivered the paper into his hands.

"I ask General Sullivan to witness that I deliver you positive instructions to march your force, to effect a junction with General Washington."

"I 've already writ him a letter that will convince him I act for the best," answered Lee, holding out the missive.

The aide took it without a word, saluted, and left the room.

Going to the front door, where Joggles already awaited him, he put a Continental bill into the hands of the publican, bade adieu to Eustace, and rode away.

"'T is as bright a day as 't was dark a night, old man," he said to the horse, "but it never looked blacker for the cause, and I've had my long ride for nothing. Perhaps, though, there may be pay day coming. She knows that I'm to be at Van Meter's barn to-night. What say you, Joggles? Think you will she be there?"

XXX

SOME DOINGS BY STEALTH

THE sound of shots outside put a sudden termination to the supper in both the dining-room and kitchen of Greenwood, and served to bring inmates and candles to the front and back doors. Beyond the moment's rush of a body of horsemen past the house, no light on the interruption was obtained, until some of the escort of Clowes were despatched to the stable to learn if all was well with their horses. There they found the wounded man stretched on the snow, and just within the doorway lay Janice in a swoon, with Clarion licking her face. Both were carried to the house, and while Mrs. Meredith and the sergeant endeavoured to save the officer by a rude tourniquet, the squire held Janice's head over some feathers which Peg burned in a bed-warmer.

"Did they kill him?" was the first question the girl asked, when the combined stench and suffocation had revived consciousness.

"He 's just expiring," her father replied. "His arm was struck off above the elbow, and he bleeds like a stuck pig."

Janice staggered up, though somewhat languidly. "May — "Did he ask to see me?"

"Not he," she was told. "Come, lass, sit quiet for a bit till thy head is steady, and tell us what 't was all about."

Janice sank into the chair her father set beside the fire. "He was on some mission for his Excellency," she gasped, "and stopped here to get a fresh horse — that was how I came to know it — and while we were talking we heard the dragoons coming, so he mounted, to escape. Then I heard a cry — oh! such a cry — and the pistols — and — and — that 's all I remember."

"Why went he to the stable rather than to the house in the first case?" demanded her father.

Janice looked surprised. "He knew the troopers were here," she explained.

The squire was about to speak, when Clowes' hand on his shoulder checked him. "There's more here than we understand," the latter whispered. "Let me ask the questions." He came to the fire and said: —

"Why did he take this route, if he was bearing despatches?"

The first sign of colour came creeping back into the pale cheeks of the girl, as she recalled the double motive the aide had given. "Colonel Brereton said he did not know the westerly roads, and so —"

"Colonel Brereton!" rapped out her father. "And what was he doing hereabout? Plague take the scamp that he must be forever returning to worry us!"

"How much of a force had he with him?" asked the commissary.

"He was alone," replied Janice.

"Alone!" exclaimed the baron, incredulously; then his face lost its look of surprise. "He came by stealth to see you, eh?"

There was enough truth in the supposition to destroy the last visible signs of the girl's swoon, and she responded over-eagerly: "I told you he was on a mission for his Excellency, and but stopped here to get a fresh horse."

"Ay," growled the squire, "he steals himself, then steals my crop, and now turns horse thief."

"He was not stealing, dadda," denied Janice. "His own horse was tired, so he left her and said he'd return Joggles some time to-morrow evening."

Clowes whistled softly, as he and the squire exchanged glances. Just as the former was about to resume his questioning, the sound of the front door being violently thrown open gave him pause, and the next instant Phil hurriedly entered the room.

"The troopers at the stable say ye found Captain Boyde. Is he bad hurt?" he demanded.

"To the death," spoke up the squire, for once missing the commissary's attempt to keep him silent. "Hast caught Brereton?"

Janice had sprung to her feet and now stood listening, with a half-eager, half-frightened look.

"Brereton!" cried Philemon. "Did he head the party?"

The growing complexity was too much for the patience of the simple-minded owner of Greenwood. "May Belza have us all," he fumed, "if I can see the bottom or even the sides of this criss-cross business. Just tell us a straight tale, lad, if we are not to have the jingle brains."

"'T is a swingeing bad business," groaned Phil. "Our troop rode over from Princeton ter-day, an' the houses at Brunswick bein' full of soldiers, I tells 'em that we could find quarters here. We was gropin' our way when the enemy set upon us, an' in the surprise cuts down the captain, an' captures three of our men."

"Dost mean to say ye let one man kill your captain and take three of ye prisoners?" scoffed the squire.

"One man!" protested the dragoon. "Think you one man could do that?"

"Janice insists that there was but Brereton — but Charles Fownes, now a rebel colonel."

"You may lay ter it there was mor 'n —" Then Philemon wavered, for the sight of the flushed, guilty look on the girl's face gave a new bent to his thoughts. "What was he here for?" he vociferated, growing angrily red as he spoke and striding to the fire. "So he 's doin' the Jerry Sneak about you yet, is he? I tell you, squire, I won't have it."

"Keep thy blustering and bullying for the mess-room and the tavern, sir," rebuked Clowes, sharply, also showing temper. "What camp manners are these to bring into gentlemen's houses and exhibit in the presence of ladies?"

"'S death, sir," retorted Phil, hotly, "I take my manners from no man, nor —"

"Hoighty, toighty!" chided Mrs. Meredith, entering. "Is there not wind enough outside but ye must bellow like mad bulls within?"

"Ay," assented the squire, "no quarrelling, gentlemen, for we 've other things to set to. Phil, there is no occasion to go off like touchwood; 't is not as thee thinks. What is true, however, is that we 've a chance to catch this same rogue of a Brereton, if we but lay heads together."

"Oh, dadda!" expostulated Janice. "You 'll not — for I promised him to tell nothing — and never would have spoken had I not been dazed — and thinking him dead. I should die of —"

"Fudge, child!" retorted Mr. Meredith. "We 'll have no heroics over a runaway redemptioner who is fighting against our good king. Furthermore, we must know all else he told ye."

"I passed him my promise to keep secret —"

"And of that I am to be judge," admonished the parent. "Dost think thyself of an age to act for thyself? Come: out with it; every word he spake."

"I 'll not break my faith," rejoined Janice, proudly, her eyes meeting her father's bravely, though the little hands trembled as she spoke, half in fright and half in excitement.

"Nay, Miss Janice, ye scruple foolishly," advised Lord Clowes. "Remember the old adage, that 'A bad promise, like a good cake, is better broken than kept.'"

"'Children, obey thy parents in the Lord, for this is right,'" quoted Mrs. Meredith, sternly.

"God never meant for me to lie — and that 's what you would have me do."

The squire stepped into the hall, and returned with his riding-whip. "Thou 'rt a great girl to be whipped, Janice," he announced; "but if thou 'rt not old enough to obey, thou 'rt not too old for a trouncing. Quickly, now, which wilt thou have?"

"You can kill me, but I 'll keep my word," panted the maiden, while shaking with fear at her resistance, at the threatened punishment, and still more at the shame of its publicity.

Forgetful of everything in his anger, the squire strode toward his daughter to carry out his threat. Ere he had crossed the room, however, to where she stood, his way was barred by Philemon.

"Look a-here, squire," the officer remonstrated, "I ain't a-goin' ter stand by and see Janice hit, no ways, so if there 's any thrashin' ter be done, you 've got ter begin on me."

"Out of my way!" roared Mr. Meredith.

Phil folded his arms. "I 've said my say," he affirmed, shaking his head obstinately; "and if that ain't enough, I 'll quit talkin' and do something."

"The boy 's right, Meredith," assented Clowes. "Nor do we need more of her. Send the girl to bed, and then I 'll have something to say."

Reluctantly the squire yielded; and Janice, with glad tears in her eyes, turned and thanked Philemon by a glance that meant far more than any words. Then she went to her room, only to lie for hours staringly awake, listening to the wild whirring and whistling of the wind as she bemoaned her unintentional treachery to the aide, and sought for some method of warning him.

"I must steal away to-morrow to the Van Meters' barn at nightfall," was her conclusion, "and wait his coming, to tell him of my — of my mistake, for otherwise he may bring Joggles back and be captured. If I can only do it without being discovered, for dadda —" and the anxious, overwrought, tired girl wept the rest of the sentence into her pillow.

Meantime, in the room below, Lord Clowes unfolded his plan and explained why he had wished the maiden away.

"'T is obvious thy girl has an interest in this fellow," he surmised, "and so 't is likely she will try to-morrow evening to see him, or get word to him. Our scheme must therefore be to let her go free, but to see to 't that we know what she 's about, and be prepared to advantage ourselves by whatever comes to pass."

The storm ceased before the winter daylight, and with the stir of morning came information concerning the missing dragoons: the body of one was found close to the stable, with a bullet in his back, presumably a chance shot from one of his comrades; a second rode up and reported himself, having in the storm lost his way, and wellnigh his life, which he owed only to the lucky stumbling upon the house of one of the tenants; and Clarion discovered the third, less fortunate than his fellow, frozen stiff within a quarter of a mile of Greenwood.

"'T is most like that rebel colonel and horse-thief shared the same fate, for 't was a wild night," remarked Clowes at the breakfast table. "Howbeit, 't will be best to have some troops hid in your stable against this evening, for he may have weathered the storm."

The morning meal despatched, Philemon rode over to Brunswick to report the death of his superior to the colonel, as well as to unfold the trap they hoped to spring, and Harcourt considered the news so material that he and Major Tarleton accompanied Philemon on his return. After a plentiful justice to the dinner and to the decanters, the men, as the early winter darkness came on, settled down to cards, while Mrs. Meredith, in mute protest against the use of the devil's pictures, left the room, summoned Peg, and in the garret devoted herself to the mysteries of setting up a quilting-frame. As for the dragoons, they sprawled and lounged about the kitchen, playing cards or toss, and grumbling at the quantity and quality of the Greenwood brew of small beer, till Sukey was wellnigh desperate.

Had Janice been older and more experienced, the very unguardedness would have aroused her suspicions. To her it seemed, however, but the arrangement of a kind destiny, and not daring to risk a delay till after tea, when conditions might not again so favour her, she left the work she had sat down to in the parlour after dinner, and tiptoeing through the hall, lest she should disturb the card-players in the squire's office, she secured her warmest wrap. Returning to the parlour, she softly raised a window, and, slipping out, in another moment was within the concealing hedge-row of box.

Speeding across the garden, the girl crept through a break in the hedge, then, stooping low, she followed a stone wall till the road was reached. No longer in sight of the house, she hurried on boldly, till within sight of the Van Meter farm. She skirted the house at a discreet distance and stole into the barn. With a glance to assure herself that the mare was still there, and a kindly pat as she passed, she mounted into the mow, where for both prudence and warmth she buried herself deep in the hay. Then it seemed to Janice that hours elapsed, the sole sounds being the contented munching of horses and cattle, varied by the occasional stamp of a hoof.

Suddenly the girl sat up, with a realising sense that she had been asleep, and with no idea for how long. A sound below explained her waking, and as she listened, she made out the noise to be that of harnessing or unharnessing. Creeping as near the edge of the mow as she dared, she peered over, but all was blackness.

"Colonel Brereton?" she finally said.

A moment's silence ensued before she had an answer, though it was eager enough when it came. "Is 't you, Miss Janice, and where are you?"

The girl came down the ladder and moved blindly toward the stalls. As she did so, somebody came in contact with her; instantly she was enfolded by a pair of arms, and before she could speak she felt a man's eager lips first on her cheek, and next on her chin.

"Heaven bless you for coming, my darling," whispered Brereton.

Janice struggled to free herself as Brereton tried to caress her the third time. "Don't," she protested. "You — I — How dare you?"

"A pretty question to ask an ardent lover and a desperate man, whose beloved confesses her passion by coming to him!"

"I did n't!" expostulated the girl, as, desperate with mortification, she broke away from the embrace by sheer strength and fled to the other side of the barn. "How dare you think such things of me?"

"Then for what came you?" inquired Jack.

"To warn you."

"Of what?"

"That you must not bring Joggles back, for they — the soldiers — are watching the stable."

"You told them?"

The girl faltered, hating to acknowledge her mistake, now that it was remedied. "If I had, why should I take the risk and the shame of coming here?" she replied.

"Forgive me, Miss Janice, for doubting you, and for my freedom just now. I did — for the moment I thought you like other women. I wanted to think you came to me, even though it cheapened you. And being desperate, I — "

"Why?" questioned the girl.

"I have failed in my mission, thanks to Lee's folly and selfishness. Would to God the troopers who lie in wait for me would go after him! A quick raid would do it, for he lies eight miles from his army, and with no guard worth a thought. There 'd be a fine prize, if the British did but know it."

"Thanks for the suggestion," spoke up a deep voice, and at the first word blankets were tossed off two lanterns, followed by a rush of men. For a moment there was a wild hurly-burly, and then Brereton's voice cried, "I yield!"

As the confusion ended as suddenly as it had begun, he added scornfully: —

"To treachery!"

XXXI

AN EXCHANGE OF PRISONERS

THE prisoner's arms were hurriedly tied and he was mounted behind one of the troopers. Janice, meanwhile, who had been seized by Philemon and drawn to one side out of the struggle, besought permission of her special captor to speak to Brereton, her fright over the surprise and her dread of what was to come both forgotten in the horror and misery the last words of the aide caused her. The jealousy of the lover, united to the strictness of the soldier, made Philemon heedless of her prayers and tears, and finally, when the cavalcade was ready to start, she was forced to mount her namesake, and, with such seat as she could keep in the man's saddle, ride between Colonel Harcourt and Hennion.

No better fortune awaited her at Greenwood, the captive being taken to the kitchen, while the culprit was escorted to the parlour, to stand, shivering, frightened, and tearful, as her father and mother berated her for most of the sins of the Decalogue.

Fortunately for the maid, other hearts were not so sternly disapproving; and Lord Clowes, after waiting till the girl's distress was finding expression in breathless sobs, in order that she might be the more properly grateful, at last interfered.

"Come, come, squire," he interjected, crossing to the bowed form, and taking one of Janice's hands consolingly, "the lass has been giddy, but 't is an ill wind, truly, for through it we have one fine bird secured yonder, to say nothing of an even bigger prize in prospect. Cry a truce, therefore, and let the child go to bed."

"Ay, go to thy room, miss," commanded Mrs. Meredith, who had in truth exhausted her vocabulary, if not her wrath. "A pretty hour 't is for thee to be out of bed, indeed!"

Janice, conscious at the moment of but one partisan, turned to the baron. "Oh, please," she besought, "may n't I say just one word to Colonel Brereton — just to tell him that I did n't — "

"Hast not shamed us enough for one night with thy stolen interviews?" ejaculated her mother. "To thy room this instant!"

Made fairly desperate, Janice was actually raising her head to protest, when Harcourt and Philemon entered.

"One moment, madam," intervened the colonel. "I have been plying our prisoner with questions, and have some to ask of your daughter. Now, Miss Meredith, Lee's letter, that we found on the prisoner, has told us all we need, but we want to test the prisoner's statements by yours. Look to it that you speak us truly, for if we find any false swearing or quibbling, 't will fare ill with you." Then for three or four minutes the officer examined the girl concerning her first interview with the rebel officer, seeking to gain additional information as to Lee's whereabout. Finding that Janice really knew nothing more than had been overheard in the Van Meter barn, he ended the examination by turning to Philemon and saying: —

"Sound boots and saddles, Lieutenant Hennion. You can guide us, I take it, to this tavern from which General Lee writes?"

"That I kin," asserted Phil, "though 't will be a stiff ride ter git there afore morning."

As the two officers went toward the door Janice made her petition anew. "Colonel Harcourt, may I have word with Colonel — with the prisoner, that he shall not think 't was my treachery?" she pleaded.

"I advise agin it, Colonel Harcourt," interjected Philemon, his face red with some emotion. "That prisoner 's a sly, sneaky tyke, and — "

"Get the troop mounted, Mr. Hennion," commanded his superior. "Mr. Meredith, I leave our captive in charge of a sergeant and two troopers, with orders that if I am not back within twenty-four hours he be taken to Brunswick. Whether we succeed or fail in our foray, Sir William shall hear of the service you have been to us." Unheeding Janice's plea, the colonel left the room, and a moment later the bugle sounded in quick succession, "To horse," "The march," and "By fours, forward."

Interest in the departing cavalry drew the elders to the windows, and in this preoccupation Janice saw her opportunity to gain by stealth what had been denied her. Slipping silently from the parlour, she sped through hall and dining-room, pausing only when the kitchen doorway was attained, her courage wellnigh gone at the thought that the aide might refuse to believe her protestations of innocence. Certainty that she had but a moment in which to explain prevented hesitancy, and she entered the kitchen.

The two troopers were already stretched at full length on the floor, their feet to the fire, while the sergeant sat by the table, with a pitcher of small beer and a pipe to solace his particular hours of guard mount over the prisoner. The latter was seated near the fire, his arms drawn behind him by a rope which passed through the slats of the chair back. So far as these fetters would permit, Brereton was slouched forward, with his chin resting on his chest in a most break-neck attitude, sound asleep. There could be no doubt about it, beyond credence though it was to the girl! While she had been miserably conceiving the officer as ablaze with wrath at her, he, with the philosophy of the experienced soldier, had lost not a moment in getting what rest he could after his forty-eight hours of hard riding.

Such callousness was to Janice a source of indignation, and as she debated whether she should wake the slumberer and make her explanation, or punish his apathy by letting him sleep, Mrs. Meredith's voice calling her name in a not-to-be-misunderstood tone turned the balance, and, flying up the servants' stairway, Janice was able to answer her mother's third call from her own room. Worn out by excitement, worry, and physical fatigue, the girl, like the soldier, soon found oblivion from both past and future.

It was well toward morning when a finish was made to the night's doings, and the early habits of the household were for once neglected to such an extent that the dragoons at last lost patience and roused Peg and Sukey with loudly shouted demands for breakfast, — a racket which served to set all astir once more.

With the conclusion of the morning meal, Janice rose from the table and went toward the kitchen, — an action which at once caused Mrs. Meredith to demand: "Whither art thou going, child?"

Facing about, the girl replied with some show of firmness: "'T is but fair that Colonel Brereton should know I had no hand in his captivation; and I have a right to tell him so."

"Thou shalt do nothing of the sort," denied Mrs. Meredith. "Was not thy conduct last evening indelicate enough, but thou must seek to repeat it?"

Janice, with her hand on the knob, began to sob. "'T is dreadful," she moaned, "after his doing what he did for us at York, and later, that he should think I had a hand in his capture."

"Tush, Jan!" ejaculated the squire, fretfully, the more that his conscience had already secretly blamed him. "No gratitude I owe the rogue, if both sides of the ledger be balanced. 'T is he brought about the scrape that led to my arrest."

"Ay," went on Mrs. Meredith, delighted to be thus supported, "I have small doubt thy indelicacy with him will land us all in prison. Such folly is beyond belief, and came not from my family, Mr. Meredith," she added, turning on her husband.

"Well, well, wife; all the folly in the lass scarce comes from my side, for 't is to be remembered that ye were foolish enough to marry me," suggested the squire, placably, his anger at his daughter already melted by the sight of her distress. "Don't be too stern with the child; she is yet but a filly."

"Thee means but a silly," snapped Mrs. Meredith, made the more angry by his defence of the girl. "Men are all of a piece, and cannot hold anger if the eyes be bright, or the waist be slim," she thought to herself wrathfully, quite forgetful of the time when that very tendency in masculine kind had been to her one of its merits. "Set to on the quilt, girl, and see to it that there 's no sneaking to the kitchen."

Scarcely had Janice, obedient to her mother's behest, seated herself at the big quilting-frame, when Lord Clowes joined her.

"They treat ye harsh, Miss Janice," he remarked sympathetically; "but 't is an unforgiving world, as I have good cause to wot."

Janice, who had stooped lower over the patches when first he spoke, flashed her eyes up for an instant, and then dropped them again.

"And one is blamed and punished for much that deserves it not. I' faith, I know one man who stands disgraced to the woman he loves best, for no better cause than that the depth of his passion was so boundless that he went to every length to gain her."

The quilter fitted a red calimanco patch in place, and studied the effect with intense interest.

"Wouldst like me to carry a message to the prisoner, Miss Janice?"

"Oh, will you?" murmured the girl, gratefully and eagerly. "Wilt tell him that I knew nothing of the plan to capture him, and was only trying to aid his escape? That, after all his kindness, I would never —"

Here the eager flow of words received a check by the re-entrance of Mrs. Meredith. Dropping his hand upon the quilting-frame so that it covered one of the girl's, the commissary conveyed by a slight pressure a pledge of fulfilment of her wish, and, after a few moments' passing chat, left the room. Before a lapse of ten minutes he returned, and took a chair near the girl.

Glancing at her mother, to see if her eyes wandered from the sock she was resoling, Janice raised her eyebrows with furtive inquiry. In answer the baron shook his head.

"'T is a curious commentary on man," he observed thoughtfully, "that he always looks on the black side of his fellow-creatures, and will not believe that they can be honest and truthful."

"Man is born in sin," responded Mrs. Meredith. "Janice, that last patch is misplaced; pay heed to thy work."

"I lately had occasion to justify an action to a man," went on Clowes, "but, no, the scurvy fellow would put no faith in my words, insisting that the person I sought to clear was covinous and tricky, and wholly unworthy of trust."

"The thoughts of a man who prefers to think such things," broke in Janice, hotly, "are of no moment."

"Ye are quite right, Miss Janice," assented the emissary, "and I would I'd had the wit to tell him so. 'T is my intention some day to call him to account for his words."

Further communion on this topic was interrupted by the incoming of Mr. Meredith, and during the whole day the two were never alone. His forgiveness partly won by his service, the commissary ventured to take a seat beside the quilter, and sought to increase his favour with her by all the arts of tongue and manner he had at command. As these were manifold, he saw no reason, as dusk set in, to be dissatisfied with the day's results. Inexperienced as Janice was, she could not know that the cooler and less ardent the man, the better he plays the lover's part; and while she never quite forgot his previous deceit, nor the trouble into which he had persuaded her, yet she was thoroughly entertained by what he had to tell her, the more that under all his words he managed to convey an admiration and devotion which did not fail to flatter the girl, even though it stirred in her no response. Entertained as she might be, her thoughts were not so occupied by the charm and honey of Lord Clowes's attentions as to pretermit all dwelling on the aide's opinion of her, and this was shown when finally an interruption set her free from observation.

It was after nightfall ere there was any variation of the monotonous quiet; and indeed the tall clock had just announced the usual bedtime of the family when Clarion's bark made the squire sit up from his drowse before the fire, and set all listening. Presently came the now familiar sound of hoof-beat and sabre-clank; springing to his feet and seizing a candle, Mr. Meredith was at the front door as a troop trotted in from the road.

"What cheer?" called the master of Greenwood.

"'T was played to a nicety," answered the voice of Harcourt, as he threw himself from the saddle. "Sound the stable call, bugler. Dismount your prisoner, sergeant, and bring him in," he ordered; and then continued to the host: "We had the tavern surrounded, Mr. Meredith, ere they so much as knew, bagged our game, and here we are."

The words served to carry the two to the parlour, and closely following came a sergeant and trooper, while between them, clothed in a very soiled dressing-gown and a still dirtier shirt, in slippers, his queue still undressed, and with hands tied behind his back, walked the general who but a few hours before had been boasting of how he was to save the Continental cause.

"If you have pity in you," besought the prisoner, "let me warm myself. What method of waging war is it which forces a man to ride thirty miles in such weather in such clothes? For the sake of former humanity, Mr. Meredith, give me something hot to drink."

In the excitement and confusion of the new arrivals, Janice had seen her chance, and, intent upon making her own statement of justification, she once again stole from the parlour and into the kitchen, so softly that the occupants of neither room were aware of escape or advent. She found the prisoner still tied to his chair, his body and head hanging forward in an attitude denoting weariness, Sukey engaged in cutting slices of bacon in probable expectation of demands from the newcomers, while the single trooper on guard had just opened the entry door, and was shouting inquiries concerning the success of the raid to his fellow-dragoons as they passed to the stable.

Acting on a sudden impulse which gave her no time for consideration, Janice caught the knife from the hand of Sukey, and, with two hasty strokes, cut the cord where it was passed through the slats of the chair-back, setting the prisoner free.

"Fo' de good Lord in hebin —" began the cook, in amazement; but, as the import of her young mistress's act dawned upon her, she ran to the fireplace and, catching up a log of wood, held it out to Brereton.

Owing to his stooping posture, the release of the cords had caused the aide to fall forward out of the chair; but he instantly scrambled to his feet, and without so much as a glance behind him, seized the billet from the hands of the cook and sprang toward the doorway, reaching it at the moment the dragoon turned about to learn the cause of the sudden commotion. Bringing the log down with crushing force on the man's head, Jack stooped as the man plunged forward, possessed himself of his sabre, caught one of the long cavalry capotes from its hook in the entry, and, banging to the door, vanished in the outer darkness. There he stood for a moment, listening intently, apparently in doubt as to his next step; then electing the bolder course, he threw the coat about his shoulders, fastened the sabre to his side, and ran to the stable, where the tired troopers, in the dim light furnished by a solitary lantern, were now dismounting from their horses. Without hesitation the aide walked among them, and in a disguised voice announced: "Colonel Harcourt orders me to look to his horse."

"Here," called a man, and the fugitive stepped forward and caught the bridle the trooper threw to him. He stood quietly while the dragoons one by one led their horses into the stable, then pulling gently on the reins, he slowly walked the colonel's horse forward as if to follow their example, but, turning a little to the left, he passed softly around the side of the building. Letting down the bars into the next field, he quickened his pace until the road was reached; swinging himself into the saddle, he once more spurred northward.

"Poor brute," he remarked, "spent as thou art, we must make a push for it until beyond Middle-Brook, if I am to save my bacon. 'T is a hard fate that makes thee serve both sides by turn, until there is no go left in thee. Luckily, the other horses are as tired as thou, or my escape would be very questionable, even though I had wit enough about me to see to it that I got the officer's mount. Egad, a queer shift it is that ends with Lee in their hands and me spurring northward to repeat the general's orders to Sullivan. Who knows but Mrs. Meredith and the parson may be right in their holding to foreordination?"

XXXII

UNDER DURANCE

As Brereton slammed the kitchen door behind him, the girl ran to the assistance of the injured trooper, only to recoil at sight of the blood flowing from his mouth and nose, and in uncontrollable horror and fright she fled to her own room. Here, cowering and shivering, she crouched on the floor behind her bed, her breath coming fast and short, as she waited for the sword of vengeance to fall. Ere many seconds the sounds below told her that the escape had been discovered, bangings of doors, shouts, bugle calls, and the clatter of horses' feet each in succession giving her fresh terror. Yet minute after minute passed without any one coming to find her, and at last the suspense became so intolerable that the girl rose and went to the head of the stairs to listen. From that point of vantage she could hear in the dining-room the voice of Harcourt sternly asking questions, the replies to which were so inarticulate and so intermixed with sobs and wails that Janice could do no more than realise that the cook was under examination. Harcourt's inquiries, however, served to reveal that the faithful Sukey was endeavouring to conceal her young mistress's part in the prisoner's escape; and as Janice gathered this, the figure which but a moment before had expressed such fear suddenly straightened, and without hesitation she ran down the stairs and entered the dining-room just in time to hear Sukey affirm: —

"I dun it, I tells youse, I dun it, and dat 's all I will tells youse."

"Colonel Harcourt," announced the girl, steadily, "Sukey did n't do it. I took the knife from her and cut the prisoner loose before she knew what I had in mind."

"Doan youse believe one word dat chile says," protested Sukey.

"It is true," urged Janice, as eager to assume the guilt as five minutes before she had been anxious to escape it; "and if you want proof, you will find the knife on my bed upstairs."

"Oh, missy, missy!" cried Sukey, "wha' fo' youse tell dat? Now dey kill youse an' not ole Sukey;" and the sobs of the slave redoubled as she threw herself on the floor in the intensity of her grief.

It took but few interrogations on the part of Harcourt to wring all the truth from the culprit, and ordering her to follow him to the parlour, he angrily denounced the girl to her parents. Much to her surprise, she found that this latest enormity called forth less of an outburst than her previous misconduct, her father being quite staggered by its daring and seriousness; while Mrs. Meredith, with a sudden display of maternal tenderness that Janice had not seen for years, took the girl in her arms, and tried to soothe and comfort her.

One more friend in need proved to be Clowes, who, when Harcourt declared that the girl should be carried to Princeton in the morning, along with Lee, that Lord Cornwallis might decide as to her punishment, sought to make the officer take less summary measures, but vainly, except to win the concession that if Hennion recaptured the prisoner he would take a less drastic course. The morrow brought a return of the pursuing party, empty-handed, and in a hasty consultation it was agreed that the squire should accompany Janice, leaving Mrs. Meredith under the protection of Philemon, — an arrangement by no means pleasing to the young lieutenant, and made the less palatable by the commissary's announcement that he should retrace his own steps to Princeton in the hope of being of service to his friends. Philemon's protests were ineffectual, however, to secure any amendment; and the sleigh, with Brereton's mare and Joggles to pull it, received the three, and, together with Lee and the escort, set out for headquarters about noon.

With the arrival at Nassau Hall, then serving as barracks for the force centred there, a fresh complication arose, for Colonel Harcourt learned that Lord Cornwallis, having seen his force safely in winter quarters at Princeton, Trenton, and Burlington, had departed the day previous for New York, while General

Grant, who succeeded him, was still at Trenton. Taking the night to consider what was best to be done, Harcourt made up his mind to carry his prisoners to New York, a decision which called forth most energetic protests from the squire, who had contrived in the doings of the last two days to take cold, and now asserted that an attack of the gout was beginning. His pleadings were well seconded by the baron, and not to harass too much one known to be friendly both to the cause and to the commander-in-chief, the colonel finally consented that the fate of Janice should be left to the general in command. This decided, Lee was once more mounted, and captive and captors set about retracing their steps, while the sleigh carried the squire and Janice, under guard, on to Trenton, Mr. Meredith having elected to make the short trip to that town rather than await the indefinite return of Grant.

It was dusk when they reached Trenton, and once more they were doomed to a disappointment, for the major-general had departed to Mount Holly. Mr. Meredith's condition, as well as nightfall, put further travel out of the question, and an appeal was made to Rahl, the Hessian colonel commanding the brigade which held the town, to permit them to remain, which, thanks to the influence of the commissary, was readily granted, on condition that they could find quarters for themselves.

"No fear," averred the squire, cheerily. "I 'll never want for sup or bed in Trenton while Thomas Drinker lives."

"Ach!" exclaimed the colonel. "Dod iss mein blace ver I sleeps und eats und drinks. Und all bessitzen you will it find."

Notwithstanding the warning, the sleigh was driven to the Drinkers' door, now flanked by a battery of field-pieces, and in front of which paced sentries, who refused to let them pass. Their protests served to attract the attention of the inmates, and brought the trio of Drinkers running to the door; in another moment the two girls were locked in each other's arms, while Mr. Meredith put his question concerning possible hospitality.

"Ay, in with thee all, Friend Lambert," cried Mr. Drinker, leading the way. "Thou 'lt find us pushed into the garret, and forced to eat at second table, while our masters take our best, but of what they leave us thou shalt have thy share."

"Is 't so bad as that?" marvelled Mr. Meredith, as, passing by the parlour, he was shown into the kitchen, and a chair set for him before the fire.

"Thee knows the tenets of our faith, and that I accept them," replied the Quaker. "Yet the last few days have made me feel that non-resistance —"

"Thomas!" reproved his sister. "Say it not, for when the curse is o'er, 't will grieve thee to have even thought it."

If the tempered spirit of the elders spoke thus, it was more than the warm blood of youth could do, and Tabitha gave a loose to her woes.

"'T is past endurance!" she cried, "to come and treat us all as if we were enemies who had no right even to breathe. They take possession of our houses and turn them into pig-sties with their filthy German ways; they eat our best and make us slave for them day and night; they plunder as they please, not merely our cattle and corn, so that we are forced to beg back from them the very food we eat, but take as well our horses, our silver, our clothes, and whatever else happens to please their fancy. The regiment of Lossberg has at this moment nine waggon-loads of plunder in the Fremantle barn. No woman is safe on the streets after sundown, and scarcely so in the day-time, while night after night the town rings with their drunken carousals. I told Friend Penrhyn the other night that if he had the spunk of a house cat he would get something to fight with, if 't were nothing better than a toasting-fork tied to a stick, and cross the river to Washington; and so I say to every man who stays in Trenton. I only wish I were not a female!"

"Hush, Tabitha!" chided Miss Drinker, "'t is God's will that we suffer as we do, and thee shouldst bow to it."

"I don't believe it 's God's will that we should be turned out of our rooms and made to live in the garret, or even in the barns, as some are forced to do; I don't believe it 's God's will that they should have taken our silver tea-service and spoons. If God is just, He must want Washington to beat them, and so every man would be doing God's work who went to help him."

Evidently with whatever strength her father and aunt held to the tenets of their sect, Tabitha's was not sufficiently ingrained to stand the test of the Hessian occupation.

"Dost think it is God's work to kill fellow-mortals?" expostulated Miss Drinker. "No more of such talk, child; it is time we were making ready for supper."

There was, however, very much more talk of this kind over the hastily improvised meal, and small wonder for it. In a town of less than a thousand inhabitants, nearly thirteen hundred troops, with their inevitable camp followers, were forcibly quartered, filling every house and every barn, to the dire discomfort of the people. As if this in itself were not enough, the Hessian soldiery, habituated to the plundering of European warfare, and who had been sold at so much per head by their royal rulers to fight another country's battles, brought with them to America ideas of warfare which might serve to conquer, but would never serve to pacify, England's colonies. Open and violent seizure had been made, without regard to the political tenets of the owner, of every kind of provision; and this had generally been accompanied with stealthy plundering of much else by the common soldiery, and, indeed, by some of the officers. Thus, in every way, despite their submissions and oaths of allegiance to King George, the Jerseymen were being treated as if they were enemies.

Of this treatment the Drinker family was a fair example. Without so much as "by your leave," Colonel Rahl had taken possession of the first two floors of their house for himself and the six or seven officers whom he made his boon companions. Moreover, Mr. Drinker was called upon to furnish food, firewood, and even forage for them; while his servants were compelled to labour from morning till night in the service of the new over lords.

When the squire, after his fatiguing day, was compelled, along with his host and hostess and the girls, to climb two flights of stairs to an ice-cold garret, his loyalty was little warmer than the atmosphere; and when the five were further forced to make the best they could of two narrow trundle-beds, but a brief time before deemed none too good for the coloured servitors, with a scanty supply of bedclothes to eke the discomfort, he became quite of the same mind with Tabitha. Even the most flaming love of royalty and realm serves not to keep warm toes extended beyond short blankets at Christmas-tide. It is not strange that late in December, 1776, all Jersey was mined with discontent, and needed but the spark of Continental success to explode.

Clowes had left his friends, after the interview with Rahl, to quarter himself upon an army acquaintance, and thus knew nothing of the hardships to which they were subjected. When he heard in the morning how they had fared, he at once sought the commander, and by a shrewd exaggeration of the Merediths' relations with Howe, supplemented by some guineas, secured the banishment of enough officers from the house to restore to the Drinkers two of their rooms.

To contribute to their entertainment, as well as to their comfort, he brought them word that Colonel Rahl, by his favour, bid them all to a Christmas festival the following day; and when Mr. and Miss Drinker refused to have aught to do with an unknown German, and possibly Papistical, if not devilish orgy, he obtained the rescinding of this veto by pointing out how unwise it would be to offend a man on whom their comfort for the winter so much depended.

It was, as it proved, a very novel and wonderful experience to the girls. After the two o'clock dinner which the invading force had compelled the town to adopt, the three regiments of Anspach, Lossberg, and Rahl, and the detachments of the Yagers and light horse, with beating drums and flying colours, paraded from one end of the town to the other, ending with a review immediately in front of the Drinkers' house. Following this the regimental bands of hautboys played a series of German airs which the now disbanded rank and file joined in vocally. Then, as night and snow set in, a general move was made indoors, at Rahl's quarters, to the parlour, where a tall spruce tree, brilliant with lighted tallow dips, and decorated with bits of coloured paper, red-tinted eggs, and not a little of the recent plunder, drew forth cries of admiration from both Janice and Tabitha, neither of whom had ever seen the like.

After a due enjoyment of the tree's beauty, the gifts were distributed; and then the company went to the dining-room, where the table sagged with the best that barnyard and pantry could be made to produce, plus a perfect forest of bottles,—tall, squat, and bulbous. The sight of such goodly plenty was irresistible, and the cheer and merriment grew apace. The girls, eagerly served and all the time surrounded by a host of such officers as could speak English, and in fact by some who, for want of that language, could only show their admiration by ardent glances, were vastly set up by the unaccustomed attentions; the squire felt a new warmth of loyalty creep through his blood with the draining of each glass; and even Miss Drinker's sallow and belined spinster face took on a rosy hue and a cheerful smile as the evening advanced.

A crescendo of enjoyment secured by means of wine is apt to lack restraint, and presently, as the fun grew, it began to verge on the riotous. The officers pressed about the girls until the two were separated, and Janice found herself in a corner surrounded by flushed-faced men who elbowed and almost wrestled with one another as to which should stand closest to her. Suddenly one man so far forgot himself as to catch her about the waist; and but for a prompt ducking of her head as she struggled to free herself, she would have been forcibly kissed. Her cries rose above the sounds of conviviality; but even before the first was uttered, Clowes, who had kept close to her the whole evening, struck the officer, and the whole room was instantly in a turmoil, the women screaming, the combatants locked, others struggling to separate them, and Rahl shouting half-drunken orders and curses. Just as the uproar was at its greatest came a loud thundering at the door; and when it was opened a becloaked dragoon, white with snow, entered and gave Rahl a despatch. Both the dispute and the conviviality ceased, as every one paused to learn what the despatch portended.

The commander was by this time so fuddled with drink that he could not so much as break the seal, much less read the contents; and the commissary, who for personal reasons had been drinking lightly, came to his assistance, and read aloud as follows:—

BURLINGTON, *Dec. 25, 1776.*

SIR,—*By a spy just come in I have word that Mr. Washington, being informed of our troops having marched into winter quarters, and having been reinforced by the arrival of a column under the command of Sullivan, meditates an attack on some of our posts. I do not believe that in the present state of the river a crossing is possible, but be assured my information is undoubtedly true, and in case the ice clears, I advise you to be upon your guard against an unexpected attack at Trenton.*

I am, sir, your most obed't h'ble serv't,

JAMES GRANT, *Major-General.*

"Nein, nein," grunted Rahl, tipsily, "I mineself has vort dat Vashington's mens hass neider shoes nor blankets, und die mit cold und hunger. Dey vill not cross to dis side, mooch ice or no ice, but if dey do, ve prisoners of dem make."

And once more the toasting and merry-making was resumed.

With not a little foresight the three ladies had availed themselves of the lull to escape from the festival to their own room, where, not content with locks and bolts, nothing would do Miss Drinker, as the sounds below swelled in volume and laxity, but the heavy bureau should be moved against the door as an additional barrier.

"Our peril is dire," she admonished the girls; "and if to-morrow's sun finds me escaped unharmed I shall thank Heaven indeed." Then she proceeded to lecture Janice. "Be assured thee must have given the lewd creatures some encouragement, or they would never have dared a familiarity. Not a one of them showed me the slightest disrespect!"

"Oh, Jan," whispered Tibbie, once they were in bed and snuggled close together, "if thee hadst been kissed!"

"What then?" questioned the maiden.

"It would be so horrible to be kissed by a man!" declared the friend.

"Wilt promise to never, *never* tell?" asked Janice, with bated breath.

"Cross my heart," vowed Tabitha.

"It — well — I — It isn't as terrible as you'd think, Tibbie!"

XXXIII

ANOTHER CHRISTMAS PARTY

AT the same hour that the Hessians were parading through the village streets a horseman was speeding along the river road on the opposite side of the Delaware. As he came opposite the town, the blare of the hautboys sounded faintly across the water, and he checked his horse to listen for a moment, and then spurred on.

"Ay, prick up your ears," he muttered to his steed. "Your friends are holding high carnival, and I wonder not that you long to be with them, 'stead of carrying vain messages in a lost cause. But for this damned floe of ice you'd have had your wish this very night."

A hundred rods brought the rider within sight of the cross-road at Yardley's Ferry, just as a second horseman issued from it. The first hastily unbuckled and threw back his holster flap, even while he pressed his horse to come up with the new arrival; while the latter, hearing the sound of hoofs, halted and twisted about in his saddle.

"Well met, Brereton," he called when the space between had lessened. "I am seeking his Excellency, who, I was told at Newtown, was to be found at Mackonkey's Ferry. Canst give me a guidance?"

"You could find your way, Wilkinson, by following the track of Mercer's brigade. For the last three miles I could have kept the route, even if I knew not the road, by the bloody footprints. Look at the stains on the snow."

"Poor fellows!" responded Wilkinson, feelingly.

"Seven miles they've marched to-day, with scarce a sound boot to a company, and now they'll be marched back with not so much as a sight of the enemy."

"You think the attack impossible?"

"Impossible!" ejaculated Brereton. "Look at the rush of ice, man. 'T would be absolute madness to attempt a crossing. The plan was for Cadwallader's brigade to attack Burlington at the same time we made our attempt, but I bring word from there that the river is impassable and the plan abandoned. His Excellency cannot fight both the British and such weather."

"I thought the game up when my general refused the command and set out for Philadelphia," remarked Wilkinson.

"Gates is too good a politician and too little of a fighter to like forlorn hopes," sneered Brereton. "He leaves Washington to bear the risk, and, Lee being out of the way, sets off at once to make favour with Congress, hoping, I have little doubt, that another discomfiture or miscarriage will serve to put him in the saddle. If we are finally conquered, 't will not be by defeat in the field, but by the dirty politics with which this nation is riddled, and which makes a man general because he comes from the right State, and knows how to wire-pull and intrigue. Faugh!"

A half-hour served to bring them to their destination, a rude wooden pier, employed to conduct teams to the ferry-boat. Now, however, the ice was drifted and wedged in layers and hummocks some feet beyond its end, and outside this rushed the river, black and silent, save for the dull crunch of the ice-floes as they ground against one another in their race down the stream. On the end of the dock stood a solitary figure watching a number of men, who, with pick and axe, were cutting away the lodged ice that blocked the pier, while already a motley variety of boats being filled with men could be seen at each point of the shore where the ground ice made embarkation possible. Along the banks groups of soldiers were clustered about fires of fence-rails wherever timber or wall offered the slightest shelter.

Dismounting, the two aides walked to the dock and delivered their letters to the commander. Taking the papers, Washington gave a final exhortation to the sappers and miners: "Look alive there, men. Every minute now is worth an hour to-morrow," and, followed by Brereton, walked to the ferry-house that he might find light with which to read the despatches. By the aid of the besmoked hall lantern, he glanced hastily through the two letters. "General Gates leaves to us all the honour to be gained to-night. Colonel Cadwallader declares it impossible to get his guns across," he told his aide, without a trace of emotion in his voice, as he refolded the despatches and handed them to him. Then his eye flashed with a sudden exultation as he continued: "It seems there are some in our own force, as well as the enemy, who need a lesson in winter campaigning."

"Then your Excellency intends to attempt a crossing?" deprecated Brereton.

"We shall attack Trenton before daybreak, Brereton; and as we are like to have a cold and wet march, stay you within doors and warm yourself after your ride. You are not needed, and there is a good fire in the kitchen."

Brereton, with a disapproving shake of his head, stepped from the hallway into the kitchen. Only one man was in the room, and he, seated at the table, was occupied in rolling cartridges.

"Ho, parson, this is new work for you," greeted Brereton, giving him a hearty slap on the shoulder. "You are putting your sulphur and brimstone in concrete form."

"Ay," assented McClave, "and, as befits my calling, properly combining them with religion."

"How so?" demanded Brereton, taking his position before the fire.

"You see, man," explained the presbyter, "it occurred to me that, on so wet a night, 't would be almost impossible for the troops to keep their cartridges dry, since scarce a one in ten has a proper cartouch-box; so I set to making some new ones, and, having no paper, I 'm e'en using the leaves of my own copy of Watts' Hymns."

"A good thought," said Brereton; "and if you will give them to me I will see to it that they be kept dry and ready for use. Not that they will need much care; there is small danger that Watts will ever be anything but dry."

"Tut, tut, man," reproved the clergyman. "Dry or not dry, he has done God's work in the past, and, with the aid of Heaven, he 'll do it again to-night."

The rumble of artillery at this point warned the aide that the embarkation was actually beginning, and, hastily catching up the cartridges already made, he unbuttoned the flannel shirt he wore and stuffed them in. Throwing his cloak about him, he hurried out.

The ice had finally been removed, and a hay barge dragged up to the pier. Without delay two 12-pounders were rolled upon it, with their complement of men and horses; and, leaving further superintendence of the embarkation to Greene and Knox, Washington and his staff took their places between the guns. Two row galleys having been made fast to the front, the men in them bent to their oars, and the barge moved slowly from the shore, its start being the signal to all the other craft to put off.

The instant the shelter of the land was lost, the struggle with the elements began. The wind, blowing savagely from the northeast, swept upon them, and, churning the river into foam, drove the bitterly cold spray against man and beast. Masses of ice, impelled by the current and blast, were only kept from colliding with the boat by the artillerymen, who, with the rammers and sponges of the guns, thrust them back, while the bowsmen in the tractive boats had much ado to keep a space clear for the oars to swing. To make the stress the greater, before a fifty yards had been compassed the air was filled with snow, sweeping now one way and now another, quite shutting out all sight of the shores, and making the rushing current of the black, sullen river the sole means by which direction could be judged.

"Damn this weather!" swore Brereton, as an especially biting sweep of wind and water made him crouch the lower behind his shivering horse.

"Nothing short of that would serve to put warmth into it," asserted Colonel Webb. "You 're not like to obtain your wish, Jack, though your cursing may put you where you 'll long for a touch of it."

"Thou canst not fright me with threat of hell-fire damnation on such a night as this, Sam," retorted Brereton.

"Gentlemen," interposed Washington, drily, "let me call your attention to the General Order of last August, relative to profane language."

"Can your Excellency suggest any more moderate terms to apply to such a night?" asked Brereton, with a laugh.

"Be thankful you've something between you and the river, my boy. Twenty-four years ago this very week I was returning from a mission to the Ohio, and to cross a river we made a raft of logs. The ice surged against us so forcibly that I set out my pole to prevent our being swept down the stream; but the rapidity of the current threw the raft with so much violence against the pole that it jerked me out into ten feet of water, and I was like to have drowned. This wind and sleet seem warm when I remember that; and had Gates and Cadwallader been there, the storm and ice of to-night would not have seemed to them such obstacles. 'T was my first public service," he added after a slight pause. "Who knows that to-night may not be my last?"

"'T is ever a possibility," spoke up Webb, "since your Excellency is so reckless in exposing yourself to the enemy's fire."

Washington shrugged his shoulders. "I am in more danger from the rear than from the enemy," he said equably.

"Ay," agreed Jack, "but we fight both to-night. Give us victory at Trenton, and we need not spend thought on Baltimore."

"Congress is too frightened itself—" began Baylor, but a touch on his arm from the commander-in-chief checked the indiscreet speech.

Departure had been taken from the Pennsylvania shore before ten; but ice, wind, and current made the crossing so laborious and slow that a landing of the first detachment was not effected till nearly twelve. Then the boats were sent back for their second load, the advance meanwhile huddling together wherever there was the slightest shelter from the blast and the hail that was now cutting mercilessly. Not till three o'clock did the second division land, and another hour was lost in the formation of the column. At last, however, the order to march could be given, and the twenty-four hundred weary, besoaked, and well-nigh frozen men set off through the blinding storm on the nine-mile march to Trenton.

At Yardley's Ferry the force divided, Sullivan's division keeping to the river turnpike, intending to enter Trenton from the south, while the main division took the cross-road, so as to come out to the north of the town, the plan being to place the enemy thus betwixt two fires.

Owing to the delay in crossing the river, it was daylight when the outskirts of the town were reached, but the falling snow veiled the advance, and here the column was halted temporarily to permit of a reconnoissance. While the troops stood at ease an aide from Sullivan's detachment reported that it had arrived on the other side of the village, and was ready for the attack, save that their cartridges were too damp to use.

"Very well, sir," ordered Washington. "Return and tell General Sullivan he must rely on the bayonet."

"Your Excellency," said Colonel Hand, stepping up, "my regiment is in the same plight, and our rifles carry no bayonets."

"We kin club both them and the Hessians all the same," spoke up a voice from the ranks.

"Here are some dry cartridges," broke in Brereton.

"Let your men draw their charges and reload, Colonel Hand," commanded Washington.

In a moment the order to advance was issued, and the column debouched upon the post road leading toward Princeton. The first sign of life was a man in a front yard, engaged in cutting wood; the commander-in-chief, who was leading the advance, called to him: —

"Which way is the Hessian picket?"

"Find out for yourself," retorted the chopper.

"Speak out, man," roared Webb, hotly, "this 's General Washington."

"God bless and prosper you, sir!" shouted the man. "Follow me, and I 'll show you," he added, starting down the road at a run. As he came to the house, without a pause, he swung his axe and burst open the door with a single blow. "Come on," he shrieked, and darted in, followed by some of the riflemen.

Leaving them to secure the picket, the regiments went forward, just as a desultory firing from the front showed that the alarm had been given by Sullivan's attack. Pushing on, a sight of the enemy was gained, — a confused mass of men some three hundred yards away, but in front of them two guns were already being wheeled into position by artillerists, with the obvious purpose of checking the advance till the regiments had time to form.

"Capture the battery!" came the stern voice of the commander.

"Forward, double quick!" shouted Colonel Hand.

Brereton, putting spurs to his horse, joined in the rush of men as the regiment broke into a run. "Look out, Hand!" he yelled. "They 'll be ready to fire before we can get there, and in this narrow road we 'll be cut to pieces. Give them a dose of Watts."

"Halt!" roared Hand, and then in quick succession came the orders, "Deploy! Take aim! Fire!"

"Hurrah for the Hymns!" cheered Brereton, as a number of the gunners and matross men dropped, and the remainder, deserting the cannon, fell back on the infantry. "Come on!" he roared, as the Virginia light horse, taking advantage of the open order, raced the riflemen to the guns. Barely were they reached, when a mounted officer rode up to the Hessian regiments and cried: "Forwärts!" waving his sword toward the cannon.

"We can't hold the guns against them!" yelled Brereton. "Over with them, men!"

In an instant the soldiers with rifles and the cavalry with the rammers that had been dropped were clustered about the cannon, some prying, some lifting, some pulling, and before the foe could reach them the two pieces of artillery were tipped over and rolled into the side ditches, the Americans scattering the moment the guns were made useless to the British.

This gave the Continental infantry in the rear their opportunity, and they poured in a scathing volley, quickly followed by the roar of Colonel Forrest's battery, which unlimbered and opened fire. A wild confusion followed, the enemy advancing, until the American regiments charged them in face of their volleys. Upon this they broke, and falling back in disorder, endeavoured to escape to the east road through an orchard. Checking the charge, Washington threw Stevens' brigade and Hand's riflemen, now re-formed, out through the fields, heading them off. Flight in this direction made impossible, the enemy retreated toward the town, but the column under Sullivan now blocked this outlet. Forrest's fieldpieces were pushed forward, Washington riding with them, utterly unheeding of both the enemy's fire, though the bullets were burying themselves in the snow all about him, and of the expostulations of his staff. Indicating the new position for the guns, he ordered them loaded with canister.

Colonel Forrest himself stooped to sight one of the 12-pounders, then cried: "Sir, they have struck."

"Struck!" exclaimed Washington.

"Yes," averred Forrest, exultingly. "Their colours are down, and they have grounded their arms."

Washington cantered toward the enemy.

"Your Excellency," shouted Baylor, who with the infantry had been well forward, "the Hessians have surrendered. Here is Colonel Rahl."

Washington rode to where, supported by two sergeants, the officer stood, his brilliant uniform already darkened by the blood flowing from two wounds, and took from his hand the sword the Hessian commander, with bowed head, due to both shame and faintness, held out to him.

"Let his wounds receive instant attention," the general ordered. Wheeling his horse, he looked at the three regiments of Hessians. "'T is a glorious day for our country, Baylor!" he said, the personal triumph already forgotten in the greater one.

XXXIV

HOLIDAY WEEK AT TRENTON

THE Christmas revel of the Hessians had held far into morning hours; and though the ladies so prudently retired, it was not to sleep, as it proved, for the uproar put that out of the question. At last, however, the merry-making ceased by degrees, as man after man staggered off to his quarters, or succumbing to drink, merely took a horizontal position in the room of the festivity, and quiet, quickly succeeded by slumber, descended upon the household.

To the women it seemed as if the turmoil had but just ended, ere it began anew. The first alarm was a thundering on the front door, so violent that the intent seemed to be to break it down rather than to gain admission from the inside. Then came a rush of heavy boots pounding upstairs, followed by a renewal of the ponderous blows on every door, accompanied now by the stentorian shouting of hasty sentences in German.

As if the din were not sufficient, Miss Drinker, in her fright at the assault directed against the barrier to which she had pinned her own reliance of safety, promptly gave vent to a series of shrieks, intermixed, when breath failed, with gasping predictions to the girls as to the fate that awaited them, scaring the maidens most direfully. Their terror was not lessened by the growing volume of shouts outside the house, and by the rub-a-dub-dub of the drums, and the tantara of the bugles, as the "To arms" was sounded along the village street. Barely had they heard Rahl and the other officers go plunging downstairs, when the scattering crack of muskets began to be heard, swelling quickly into volleys and then into the unmistakable platoon firing, which bespoke an attack in force. Finally, and as a last touch to their alarm, came the roar of artillery, as Forrest's and Knox's batteries opened fire.

The whole conflict took not over thirty-five minutes, but to the three bedfellows it seemed to last for hours. The silence that then fell so suddenly proved even more awful, however, and became quickly so insupportable that Janice was for getting out of bed to learn its cause, a project that Miss Drinker prohibited. "I know not what is transpiring," she avowed, "but whatever the disturbance, our danger is yet to come."

The event verified her opinion, for presently heavy and hurried footsteps of many men sounded below stairs, terminating the brief silence. With little delay the tramp of boots came upstairs, and a loud rap on the door drew a stifled cry from the spinster as she buried her head under the bedclothes, and made the two girls clutch each other with fright.

"Open!" called a commanding voice. "Open, I say!" it repeated, as no answer came. "Batter it in, then!" and at the order the stocks of two muskets shattered the door panels; the bureau was tipped over on its face with a crash, and Brereton, sword in hand, jumped through the breach.

It was an apparently empty room into which the aide entered, but a mound under the bedclothes told a different tale.

"Here are other Hessian pigs who've drunk more than they've bled," he sneered, as he tossed back the counterpane and blankets with his sword-point, thus uncovering three becapped heads, from each of which issued a scream, while three pairs of hands wildly clutched the covering.

The nightcaps so effectually disguised the faces that not a one did the officer recognise in his first hasty glance.

"Ho!" he jeered. "Small wonder the fellow lay abed. Come, up with you, my Don Juan," he added, prodding Miss Drinker through the bedclothes with his sword. "'T is no time for bearded men to lie abed."

"Help, help!" shrieked Janice, and "'T is my aunt!" cried Tabitha, in unison, but the spinster's fear was quite forgot in the insulting allusion to the somewhat noticeable hirsute adornment on her face; sitting up in bed, she pointed at the door, and sternly ordered, "Cease from insulting gentlewomen, brute, and leave this chamber!"

"Zounds!" burst out Jack, in his amazement; then he turned and roared to the gaping and snickering soldiers, "Get out of here, every doodle of you, and be —— to you!" Keeping his back to the bed, he said, "I pray your pardon, ma'am, for disturbing you; our spies assured us that only Hessian officers slept here."

"Go!" commanded the offended and unrelenting old maid.

The officer took a step toward the door, halted, and remarked savagely, "Our positions are somewhat reversed, Miss Meredith. 'T is poetic justice, indeed, which threatens you a taste of the captivity you schemed in my behalf; 'he cries best who cries last.'"

"I had naught to do with thy captivation!" protested Janice, indignantly, "though thou wouldst not believe me; and but for me thou 'dst still be a prisoner."

"A well-dressed-up tale, but told too late to gain credence," sneered the officer. "You made a cully of me once. I defy you to ever again."

"A man who thinks such vile thoughts is welcome to them," retorted the girl, proudly.

"Dost intend to put a finish to thy intrusion upon the privacy of females?" objurgated Miss Drinker; and at the question Brereton flung out of the room without more words.

The ladies made a hasty toilet, and descended to the kitchen, to find the maids deep in the preparation of breakfast, while standing near the fire was a coloured man in a brown livery who ducked low to Janice as he grinned a recognition.

"Oh!" exclaimed the girl, and then, "How 's Blueskin?"

"Lor' bless de chile, she doan forget ole Willium nor dat horse," chuckled the darkey. "Dat steed, miss, hardly git a good feed now once a week, but he knows dat he carries his Excellency, an' dat de army 's watchin' him, an' he make believe he chock full of oats all de time. He jus' went offen his head when Ku'nel Forrest's guns wuz a-bustin' de Hessians all to pieces dis mornin', an' de way he dun arch his neck an' swish his tail when Gin'l Howe give up his sword made de enemy stare."

"You 'll purvey my compliments to his Highness, Mr. Lee," requested the cook, "an' 'spress to him de mortification we 'speriences at being necessitated to tender him his tea outen de elegantest ob best Japan. 'Splain to him dat we 'se a real quality family, an' regularly accustomed to de finest ob plate, till de Hessians depredated it."

"Is this for General Washington?" questioned Janice, with sudden interest in the tray upon which the cook had placed a china tea-service, some hot corn bread, and a rasher of bacon.

"Yes, miss," explained William. "His Excellency 's in de parlour, a-lookin' over de papers of de dead gin'l, an' he say see if I kian't git him some breakfast."

"Oh," begged the girl, eagerly, "may n't I take it to him?"

"Dat yo' may, honey," acceded the black, yielding to the spell of the lass. "Massa allus radder see a pooty face dan black ole Billy's. Jus' yo' run along with it, chile, an' s'prise him."

Catching up the waiter, the maiden carried it to the parlour, which she entered after knocking, in response to Washington's behest. The general looked up from the paper he was conning and instantly smiled a recognition to the girl.

"You are not rid of us yet, you see, Miss Janice," he said.

"Nor wish to be, your Excellency," vouched the girl, as she set the tray on the table.

"I remember thy wish for our cause when last we met," went on the commander, "and who knows but it has served us in good stead this very morning? I had the vanity that day to think thy interest was for the general, but I have just unravelled it to its true source."

"Indeed," protested Janice, sorely puzzled by his words, "'t was only thy —"

"Nay, nay, my dear," chided Washington, smiling pleasantly; "'t is nothing to be ashamed of, and I ought to have suspected that thy interest was due to some newer and brighter blade than an old one like myself. He is a lucky fellow to have won so charming a maid, and one brave enough to take such risk for him."

"La, your Excellency," stammered the girl, completely mystified, "I know not what you mean!"

Still smiling, Washington set down the tea he was now drinking and selected a paper from a pile on the table. "I have just been perusing Colonel Harcourt's report to General Grant, in reference to the traitorous conduct of one Janice Meredith, spinster, and it has informed me of much that Colonel Brereton chose to withhold, though he pretended to make me a full narration. The sly beau said 't was the *cook* cut him loose, Miss Janice."

"Oh, prithee, General Washington," beseeched a very blushing young lady, "wilt please favour me by letting Colonel Brereton — who is less than nothing to me — read the report?"

"Thou takest strange ways to prove thy lack of interest," rejoined the general, his eyes merry at the seeming contradiction.

"'T is indeed not as thou surmisest," protested Janice, redder than ever; "but Colonel Brereton thought I was concerned in his captivation, and would not believe a message I sent to him, and but just since he has cruelly insulted me, and so I want him to learn how shamefully he has misjudged me, so that he shall feel properly mean and low."

"That he shall," Washington assented, "and every man should be made to feel the same who lacks faith in your face, Miss Janice. The rascal distinguished himself in this morning's affair, so I let him bear my despatches and the Hessian standard to Congress; however, as soon as he returns he shall smart for his sins, be assured. But, my dear," and here the eyes of the speaker twinkled, "when due punishment has been meted out, remember that forgiveness is one of your sex's greatest excellences." Washington took the hand of the girl and bent over it. "Now leave me, for we have much to attend to before we can set to getting our prisoners across the river, out of the reach of their friends."

Twenty-four hours later the village which had been so overburdened with soldiers was stripped as clear of them as if there were not one in the land. It took a day to get the thousand prisoners safely beyond the Delaware, and three more were spent in giving the Continentals a much-needed rest from the terrible exposure and fatigue they had undergone; but this done, Washington once more crossed the river and reoccupied Trenton, induced to take the risk by the word brought to him that the militia of New Jersey, driven to desperation by the British occupation, and heartened by the success of Trenton, were ready to rise if they had but a fighting point about which to rally.

The expectation proved erroneous, for the presence of the little force at Trenton was more than offset by the prompt mobilisation of all the British troops in the State at Princeton, and the hurrying of Cornwallis, with reinforcements, from New York, to resume the command. As Washington's army mustered less than five thousand, one-third of whom were raw Pennsylvania militia, while that of the British general when concentrated exceeded eight thousand, the prudent elected to stay safely within doors and await the result of the coming conflict before deciding whether they should forget their recently signed oaths of allegiance and cast in their lot with the Continental cause.

Yet another difficulty, too, beset the commander-in-chief. The terms of the New England regiments expired on the last day of the year, and though the approach of the enemy made a speedy action certain, the men refused to re-enlist, or even to serve for a fortnight longer. Such was the desperate plight of the general that he finally offered them a bounty if they would but remain for six weeks, and, after much persuasion, more than half of them consented to stay the brief time. The army chest being wholly without funds, Washington pledged his personal fortune to the payment of the bounty, though in private he spoke scornfully of the regiments' "noble example" and "extraordinary attachment to their country," the fighting spirit too strong within him to enable him to understand desertion of the cause at such an hour. Quite a number, even, who took the bounty, deserted the moment the money was received.

Cornwallis lost not a moment, once his troops were gathered, in seeking vengeance for Trenton; and on January 2 spies brought word to Washington that the British were approaching in force by the Princeton post-road. A detachment was at once thrown forward to meet their advance, and for several hours every inch of ground was hotly contested. Then, the main body of the enemy having come up, the Americans fell back on their reserves, and the whole Continental army retreated through the village and across the bridge over Assanpink Creek, — a tributary stream emptying into the Delaware just east of Trenton. Here the troops were ranged along the steep banks to renew the contest, the batteries being massed at the bridge and at the two fords, and some desultory firing occurred. But it was now dark, and Cornwallis's troops having marched fifteen miles, the commander postponed the attack till the morrow, and the two armies bivouacked for the night on opposite sides of the brook, within a hundred and fifty yards of each other.

"My Lord," protested Sir William Erskine, when the order to encamp was given, "may not the enemy escape under cover of the night?"

"Where to?" demanded Cornwallis. "This time there will be no crossing of the Delaware, for we are too close on their heels; and if they retreat down the river, we can fight them when we please. A little success has undone Mr. Washington, and the fox is at last run to cover."

While at supper, the British commander was informed by an orderly that two civilians desired word with him, and without leaving the table he granted an audience.

"A petticoat, eh?" he muttered, as a man and woman entered the room; and then as the lady pushed back her calash, he ordered: "A chair for Miss Meredith, sergeant." The girl seated, he went on: "Sir William spoke of you to me just as I was leaving New York, and instructed me, if you were findable, to send you to New York. I' faith, the general had more to say of your coming than he had of my teaching Mr. Washington a lesson. He told me to put you under charge of Lord Clowes without delay."

"But he was captivated," announced Mr. Drinker.

"So I learned at Princeton; therefore the matter must await my return."

"I have come with the young lady, my Lord," spoke up Mr.

Drinker, "to ask thy indulgence in behalf of herself and her father."

"Yes, Lord Cornwallis," said Janice, finding her tongue and eager to use it. "We came here to see General Grant, but he was away, and dadda had a slight attack of the gout, from a cold he took, and then he very rashly drank too much at Colonel Rahl's party, and that swelled his foot so that he 's lain abed ever since, till to-day, when we thought to set out for Brunswick; but the snow having melted, our sleigh could not travel, and every one expecting a battle wanted to get out of town themselves, so we could get no carriage, nor even a cart." Here Miss Meredith paused for breath with which to go on.

"Friend Meredith," said Mr. Drinker, taking up the explanation, "though not able to set foot to the ground, conceives that he can travel on horseback by easy riding; and rather than risk remaining in a town that is like to be the scene of to-morrow's unrighteous slaughter, he hopes thee will grant him permission and a pass to return to Brunswick."

"There will be no fight in the town to-morrow," asserted Cornwallis; "but there may be some artillery firing before we can carry their position, so 't is no place for non-combatants, much less women. You can't do better than get back to Greenwood, where later I'll arrange to fulfil Sir William's orders. Make out a pass for two, Erskine. When do you wish to start, Miss Meredith?"

"Dadda said we 'd get away before daylight, so as to be well out of town before the battle began."

"Wisely thought. The second brigade lies at Maidenhead and the fourth at Princeton; and as both have orders to join me, you 'll meet them on the road. This paper, however, will make all easy."

"Thank you," said the girl, gratefully, as she took the pass.

"Didst see Mr. Washington when he was in town?" inquired the earl of Mr. Drinker.

"Not I," replied the Quaker; "but friend Janice had word with him."

"You seem to play your cards to stand well with both commanders, Miss Meredith," intimated the officer, a little ironically. "Did the rebel general seem triumphant over his easy victory?"

"He said naught about it to me," answered Janice.

"Within a few hours he'll learn the difference between British regulars and half-drunk Hessians." Cornwallis glanced out of the window to where, a quarter of a mile away, could be seen the camp-fires of the Continental force burning brightly. "He'd best have done his bragging while he could."

CHAPTER XXXV

THE "STOLE AWAY"

IT was barely four o'clock the following morning when, after a breakfast by candle-light, the squire and Janice, the former only with much assistance and many groans, mounted Joggles and Brereton's mare. Mr. Drinker rode with them through the village, on his way to join the Misses Drinker, who, two days before, on the first warning of a conflict, had been sent away to a friend's, as would Janice have been also, had she not insisted on staying with her father. At the crossroads, therefore, after a due examination of their passes by the picket, adieux were made, and the guests, with many thanks, turned north on the Princeton post-road, while the host trotted off on the Pennington turnpike.

It was still dark when, an hour later, the riders reached Maidenhead, to find the second brigade of the British clustered about their camp-fires; but in the moment's delay, while the officer of the day was scrutinising the safe-conduct, the drums beat the reveille, and the village street was alive with breakfast preparations as father and daughter were permitted to resume their journey. It was a clear, cold morning, and as the twilight slowly brightened into sunshine, the whole landscape glistened radiantly with a heavy hoar-frost that for the moment gleamed and shimmered as if the face of the country had been rubbed with some phosphorescent substance, or as if the riders were viewing it through prism glasses.

"Oh, dadda, isn't it beautiful?" exclaimed Janice, delightedly, as they rode down the hill to the bridge over Stony Creek.

"What? Where?" demanded that worthy, looking about in all directions.

"The fields, and the trees, and —"

"Can't ye keep your thoughts from gadding off on such nonsense, Jan?" cavilled her father, fretfully, his gouty foot putting him in anything but a sweet mood. "One would think ye had never seen pasture or woodland be — Ho!" he ejaculated, interrupting his reproof, "what 's that sound?"

The words were but spoken when the front files of a regiment just topping the hill across the brook came in view and descended the road at quick step to the bridge, their gay scarlet uniforms, flying colours, and shining gun barrels adding still more to the brilliancy.

"Halt!" was the order to the troops as they came up to the riders, and the officer took the pass that the squire held out to him. "What hour left you Trenton?" he demanded.

"Four o'clock."

"And heard you any firing after leaving?" asked Colonel Mawhood, eagerly.

"Not a sound."

"I fear none the less that the fighting will be all over ere the Seventeenth can get there, much more the Fortieth and Fifty-fifth," he grumbled, as he returned the paper. "Attention! Sections, break off! Forward — march!"

The order, narrowing the column, allowed the squire and Janice to ride on and cross the bridge. On the other side of the stream a by-road joined the turnpike, and as Janice glanced along it, she gave a cry of surprise. "Look, dadda," she prompted, "there are more troops!"

"Ay," acceded Mr. Meredith, "'t is the rest of the brigade just coming in view."

"But that leads not from Princeton," observed Janice. "'T is the roundabout way to Trenton that joins the river road on the other side of Assanpink Creek. And, oh, dadda, look at the uniforms! Is 't not the hunting shirt of the Continental riflemen?"

"Gadsbodikins, if the lass is not right!" grunted the squire, when he had got on his glasses. "What the deuce do they here?"

An equal curiosity apparently took possession of the British colonel, for when the Seventeenth had breasted the hill to a point where the American advance could be seen, the regiment was hastily halted, and in another moment, reversing direction, returned on its route at double quick, its commander supposing the force in sight a mere detachment which he could capture or cut to pieces, and little recking that Washington's whole army, save for a guard to keep their camp-fires burning, had stolen away in the night from the superior force of British at Trenton, with the object of attacking the fourth brigade at Princeton.

"By heavens!" snorted the squire, in alarm. "Quicken thy pace, Jan. We are out of the frying-pan and into the fire with a vengeance." Then as the horses were put to a trot, he howled with the pain the motion caused his swathed foot. "Spur on to Princeton, Jan. The pace is more than I can bear, and I'll turn off into this orchard for safety," he moaned, as he indicated a slope to the right of the road.

"I'll not leave thee, dadda," protested the girl, as she guided the mare over the let-down bars of the fence, through which her father put Joggles, and in a moment both horses were climbing the declivity under the bare apple-trees.

The squire's knowledge of warfare was never likely to win him honour, for with vast circumspection he had selected the strongest strategic position of the region; and though his back to the British and the rising land in his front prevented him from realising it, both commanders, with the quick decision of trained officers, put their forces to a run, in the endeavour to occupy the hill. The Continental riflemen, having the advantage of light accoutrements and little baggage, were successful; and just as the two riders reached the crest, it was covered by green and brown shirted men.

"Get to the rear!" stormed an officer at the pair; while, without stopping to form, the men poured in a volley at the charging British, who, halting, returned the fire, the bullets hurtling and whistling about the non-combatants in a way that made the squire forget the agonies of his gout in the danger of his position.

Ere the riflemen could reload, the Seventeenth, with fixed bayonets, were upon them, and the two American regiments, having no defensive weapon, broke and fled in every direction.

A mounted officer rode forward and attempted to stay the flight of the riflemen, then fell wounded from his horse. As he came to the ground, Janice and her father found themselves once more on the other side of the conflict, as the charging British swept by them; and the girl screamed as she saw two of the soldiers rush to where the wounded man lay, and repeatedly thrust their bayonets into him, though she was ignorant that it was Washington's old companion in arms, General Mercer.

As the riflemen fell back down the hill, Washington in person headed two regiments of Pennsylvania militia, supported by a couple of pieces of artillery from the right flank to cover the fugitives. Although conscious by now that he had no mere detachment to fight, Colonel Mawhood, with admirable coolness, ordered the recall sounded, and re-forming his regiment, led a charge against the new foe. Seeing the Seventeenth advancing at double quick, in the face of the guns, so fearlessly and steadily, the militia wavered, and were on the point of deserting the battery, when Washington spurred forward, thus placing himself between the two lines of soldiers. His splendid and reckless courage steadied the raw militia; they gave a cheer and levelled their muskets just as the Seventeenth halted and did the same. Within thirty yards of the enemy, and well in advance of his own men, Washington stood exposed to both volleys as the two lines fired, and for a moment he was lost to view in the smoke which, blown about him, united in one dense cloud. Slowly the mass lifted, revealing both general and horse unhurt, and at the sight the Pennsylvania regiments cheered once more.

The time lost by the British in halting and firing proved fatal to the capture of the guns. Hand's riflemen, advancing, threw in a deadly, scattering fire of trained sharpshooters, while two regiments under Hitchcock came forward at a run. One moment the Seventeenth held its ground, then broke and fled toward the road, leaving behind them two brass cannon. For four miles the fugitives were pursued, and many prisoners were taken.

Musketry on the right showed the day not yet won, however, the Fifty-fifth having pressed forward upon hearing the fusillade, and but for the check it met from a New England brigade would have come to the aid of its friends. The flight of the Seventeenth enabled Washington to mass his force against the new arrival; and it was driven in upon the Fortieth, and then both fell back into the town, taking possession of the college building, with the evident hope of finding in its walls protection sufficient to make a successful stand. But when the Continental artillery was brought up and wheeled into position, at the first shot the British abandoned the stronghold and fled in disorder along the road leading to Brunswick, hotly pursued by a force which Washington joined.

"It 's a fine fox chase, my boys!" he shouted to the men, in the excitement of the moment.

Brereton, who was riding within hearing, called something to a bugler; and the man, halting in the race, put his trumpet to his lips and blew a fanfare.

"There are others can sound the 'Stole Away,' your Excellency," shouted Jack, triumphantly. "That insult is paid in kind."

The Continental soldiers were too exhausted by their long night march and their morning fight to follow the fugitives far, the more that the English, by throwing away their guns, knapsacks, and other accoutrements, and by being far less fatigued, were easily able to outstrip their pursuers. Perceiving this, the general ordered the bugles to sound the recall, and the men fell back on Princeton village.

"With five hundred fresh troops, or a proper force of light horse, we could have captured every man of them," groaned Brereton, "and probably have seized Brunswick, with all its stores."

Washington nodded his head in assent. "'T is idle to repine," he said calmly, "because the measure of our success might have been greater. The troops have marched well and fought well."

"What is more," declared Webb, "a twelve hours ago, the enemy thought us in a cul-de-sac. We have not merely escaped, but turned our flight into a conquest. How they will grit their teeth when they find themselves outgeneralled!"

"Less a couple of hundred prisoners to boot," chimed in

Brereton, pointing at the village green, where the captives were being collected.

"Your Excellency," reported General Greene, as Washington came up to the college building, "we have found a store of shoes and blankets in the college, and all of the papers of the Lord Cornwallis and General Grant."

"Look to them, Brereton, and report to me at once if there is anything needing instant attention," directed Washington.

Jack, tossing his reins to a soldier, followed Greene into Nassau Hall, and was quickly running over the bundles of papers which the British, with more prudence than prescience, had for safety left behind. Presently he came upon a great package of signed oaths of allegiance, which he was shoving to one side as of no immediate importance, when the name signed at the bottom of the uppermost one caught his eye.

"Oh, Joe, Joe!" he laughed, taking up the paper, "is this thy much-vaunted love of freedom?" Glancing at the second, he added, "And Esquire Hennion! Well, they deserve it not; but I'll do the pair a harmless service all the same, merely for old-time days," he muttered, as he folded up the two broadsides and stuffed them into his pocket.

While the aide was thus engaged, Washington rode over to inspect the prisoners. Here it was to discover the squire and Janice, the former having been made a prize of by a more zealous than sagacious militiaman. Giving directions to march the prisoners at once under guard to Morristown, the commander turned to the girl.

"Thou 'rt not content to give us thy good wishes, Miss Janice," he said, motioning to the guard to let the two go free, "but addest the aid of thy presence as well."

"And were within an ace of getting shot thereby," complained the squire, still not entirely over his fright. "Egad, general, we were right between the shooting at one minute, and heard the bullets shrieking all about us."

"But so was his Excellency, dadda," protested Janice. "Oh, General Washington," she added, "when you rode up so close to the British, and I saw them level their guns, I was like to have fell off my horse with fear for you."

"Ay," remarked the squire, for once unprecedentedly diplomatic. "The lass stood her own peril as steadily as ever I did, but she turned white as a feather when the infantry fired at you, and, woman-like, burst into tears the moment the smoke had lifted enough to show you still unhurt."

"And now has tears in her eyes because I was not shot, I suppose," Washington responded, with a smiling glance at the maiden.

"No, your Excellency," denied the girl, in turn smiling through the tears. "But dadda is quite wrong: 't was not anxiety for you that made me weep, but fear that they might have killed Blueskin!"

Washington laughed at the girl's quip. "It seems my vanity is so great that I am doomed ever to mistake the source of your interest. Come," he added, "the last time we met I was beholden to you for a breakfast. Let me repay the kindness by giving you a meal. One of my family reports that the lunch of the officers' mess of the Fortieth was just on the table at the provost's house when our movements gave them other occupation. 'T is fair plunder, and I bid you to share in it."

During the repast the father and daughter told how they had come to be mixed in the conflict, and the squire grumbled over the prospect before him.

"I 've no place to go but Greenwood, and now they threat to take my lass to New York over this harebrain scrape she 's got us all into."

"'T would be gross ingratitude," asserted Washington, "if we let Miss Meredith suffer for her service to us, and 't is a simple matter to save her. Get me pen, ink, and a blank parole, Baylor."

The paper brought, Washington filled in a few words in his flowing script, and then placed it before the girl. "Sign here," he told her, and when it was done he took back the document. "You are now a prisoner of war, released on parole, Miss Janice," he explained, "and pledged not to go more than ten miles from Greenwood without first applying to me for permission. Furthermore, upon due notice, you are again to render yourself my captive."

Janice, with a shy glance, which had yet the touch of impertinence that was ingrain in her, replied, "I was that the first time I met your Excellency, and have been so ever since."

An end was put to the almost finished meal at this point by the clatter of hoofs, followed by the hurried entrance of Brereton. "General St. Clair sends word, sir, that a column of British is advanced as far as Stony Brook, and is —" There the aide caught sight of Janice, and stopped speaking in his surprise.

"Go on, sir!" ordered Washington, sternly.

"And is driving in our skirmishes. He has report that 't is the first of the whole English army, which is pressing on by forced marches."

"'T is time, then, that we were on the wing," asserted the general, rising. "Colonel Webb, tell General St. Clair to hold the enemy in check as long as he can. You, Baylor, direct Colonel Forrest to plant his guns on the green, to cover the rearguard. General Greene, let the army file off on the road to Somerset Court-house."

The orders given, he turned to make his farewell to Janice. "This time Lord Cornwallis did not cheat us of our meal, though he prevents our lingering long at table. You should know best, sir," he said to the esquire, "what course to pursue, but I advise you to start for Greenwood without delay, for there will be some skirmishing through the town, and the British commander is not likely to be in the best of moods."

"We 'll be off at once," assented Mr. Meredith.

"Then Miss Janice will allow me the office of mounting her," solicited the general, as they all went to the door. "Is not that Colonel Brereton's mare?" he continued, as the orderly brought up the horses.

"Yes, your Excellency," stammered Janice. "'T was by a strange chance —"

"No doubt, no doubt —" interrupted Washington, smiling.

"Belike he wants her back," intimated the squire, glancing anxiously at the aide, who stood, with folded arms, watching the scene.

"I think he 'll not grudge the loan, in consideration of the rider," insinuated Washington. "The more that Congress has just voted him a sword and horse for his conduct at Trenton. How is it, Brereton?"

With a shrug of the shoulders Jack muttered, "'T is no time to demand her back, got though she was by a trick," and walked away.

"You have not shown him the paper?" questioned Janice, as she settled herself in the saddle.

"No, my child," replied Washington. "He returned from Baltimore only last evening, and there has been no time since. But rest easy, he shall see it. Keep good wishes for us, and fare thee well."

Two hours later the British marched into Princeton. But the Continental forces had made good their retreat, and all that was left to their pursuers was to march on wearily to Brunswick to save the broken regiments and the magazines that had been lost in spite of them, had Washington possessed but a few fresh troops. The English general had been outmanœuvred, his best brigade cut to pieces, and the army he had thought to annihilate was safe among the hills of New Jersey.

"Confound the fox!" stormed Cornwallis. "Can I never come up with him?"

"He 's got safe off twice, my lord; the third time is proverbial, and the odds must turn," urged Erskine.

"Pray Heaven that some day we may catch him in a cul-de-sac from which there can be no retreat."

XXXVI

BETWIXT MILLSTONES

THE reunion of the Merediths was so joyful a one that little thought was taken of the course of public events. Nor were they now in a position easily to learn of them. Philemon and his troop had hastened to rejoin at the first news of the British reverses, the remaining farm servants had one by one taken advantage of the anarchy of the last eight months secretly to desert, or boldly enlist, the squire's gout prevented his going abroad, and the quiet was too great a boon to both Mrs. Meredith and Janice to make them wish for anything but its continuance.

If there was peace at Greenwood, it was more than could be said for the rest of the land. The Continental success at Princeton, small though it was in degree, worked as a leaven, and excited a ferment throughout the State. Every Whig whom the British successes had for a moment made faint-hearted, every farmer whose crops or stock had been seized, every householder on whom troops had been quartered, even Joe Bagby and the Invincibles took guns from their hiding-places and, forming themselves into parties, joined Washington's army in the Jersey hills about Morristown, or, acting on their own account, boldly engaged the British detachments and stragglers wherever they were encountered. Withdrawn as the Merediths might be, the principal achievements were too important not to finally reach them, and by infinite filtration they heard of how the Waldeckers had been attacked at Springfield and put to flight, how the British had abandoned Hackensack and Newark without waiting for the assaults, and how at Elizabethtown they had been surprised and captured. Less than a month from the time that the royal army had practically held the Jerseys, it was reduced to the mere possession of Brunswick, Amboy, and Paulus Hook, and every picket or foraging party sent out from these points was almost certain of a skirmish.

It was this state of semi-blockade which gave the Merediths their next taste of war's alarums. Late in February a company of foot and a half troop of horse, with a few waggons, made their appearance on the river road, and halted opposite the gate of Greenwood. Painful as was the squire's foot, this sight was sufficient to make him bear the agony of putting it to the ground, and bring him limping to the door.

"How now! For what are ye come?" he shouted at a detachment which was already filing through the gate.

At the call, two officers who had been seemingly engaged in a discussion, rode toward the porch, and the moment they were within speaking distance one of them began an explanation.

"I was just a-tellin' Captain Plunkett that we 'd done a mighty bad stroke this mornin', but that this 'ud be a worse one, for —"

"Why, it 's Phil!" cheerfully exclaimed Mr. Meredith. "Welcome, lad, and all the more that I feared 't was another call the thieving Whigs were about to pay my cribs and barn. Where have ye been, lad? But, rather, in with ye and your friend," he said, interrupting his own question, as the other officer approached, "and tell your errand over a bottle where there 's more warmth."

"It 's such a mighty sorry errand, squire," replied Philemon, with evident reluctance, and reddening, "that it won't take many words ter tell. We was sent out yestere'en toward Somerset Court-house, a-foragin', and this mornin' as we was returnin', we was set upon by the rebels."

"Devil burn it!" muttered the captain, "what do you call such mode of warfare? At Millstone Ford, where they attacked us, they scattered like sheep as we deployed for a charge. But the moment we were on the march in column, ping, ping, ping from every bit of cover, front, flank, and rear, and each bullet with a billet at that, no matter what the distance. Not till we reached Middle Brook did their stinging fire cease."

"And 'stead of bringin' into Brunswick forty carts of food and forage, and a swipe of cattle," groaned Philemon, "we has only four waggon-loads of wounded ter show for our raid."

"With the post nigh to short commons," went on Plunkett. "Therefore, Mr. Meredith, we are put to the necessity of taking a look at your barn and granaries."

"What!" roared the squire, incredulously, yet with a wrath in his voice that went far to show that conviction rather than disbelief was his true state of mind. "'T is impossible that British regulars will thieve like the rebels."

Both the officers flushed, and Philemon began a faltering explanation and self-exculpation, but he was cut short by his superior saying sharply: "Tush, sir, such language will not make us deal the more gently with your cribs; so if you'd save something, mend your speech."

"I done my best, squire," groaned Philemon, "ter dissuade Captain Plunkett, but General Grant's orders was not ter come back without a train."

"Then at least ye'll have the grace to pay for what ye take? Ye'll be no worse than the rebel, that I'll lay to."

"Ay, and so we should, could we pay in the same worthless brown paper. In truth, sir, 't was General Howe's and the commissary's orders that nothing that we seize was to be paid for, so if thou hast a quarrel 't is with those whom Mr. Hennion says are thy good friends. Here's a chance, therefore, to exhibit the loyalty which the lieutenant has been dinging into my ears for the last half-mile."

"Belza burn the lot of ye!" was the squire's prompt expression of his loyalty.

Neither protests nor curses served, however, to turn the marauders from their purpose. Once again the outbuildings and store-rooms of Greenwood were ransacked and swept clear of their goodly plenty, and once again, as if to deepen the sense of injury, the stable was made to furnish the means with which the robbery was to be completed.

While the troops were still scattered and occupied in piling the loot upon the sleighs and sledges, a volley of something more potent than the squire's oaths and objurgations interrupted them. From behind the garden hedgerow of box came a discharge of guns, and a dozen of the foraging party, including both the captain and the lieutenant of foot, fell. A moment of wild confusion followed, some of the British rushing to where the troopers' steeds were standing, and, throwing themselves into the saddles, found safety in flight, while the rest sought shelter in the big barn. Here Lieutenant Hennion succeeded in rallying them into some order, but it was to find that numbers of the infantry had left their muskets, and that many of the light horse were without their sabres, both having been laid aside to expedite the work.

Not daring offensive operations with such a force, the young officer, aided by the one subaltern, made the best disposition possible for defence, trusting to hold the building until the fugitives should return with aid from Brunswick. Those who had their muskets were stationed at the few windows, while the dragoons with drawn swords were grouped about the door, ready to resist an attack.

The Jersey militia had too often experienced the effectiveness of British bayonets and sabres to care to face them, and so they continued behind the hedge, and coolly reloaded their guns. Yet they, as well as their opponents, understood that time was fighting against them, and as soon as it became obvious that those in the barn intended no sortie they assumed the initiative.

The first warning of this to the besieged was another volley, which sent bullets through the windows and the crack in the door, without doing the slightest injury. At the same moment four men trailing their rifles appeared from behind the hedge, and, scattering and dodging as they ran, made for the cow yard. Two of the infantry who guarded the window that overlooked this movement, thrust out their muskets and fired; but neither of their shots told, for the moment they appeared five flashes came from the hedge, and one of the defenders, as his hand pressed the trigger, was struck in the forehead by a rifle ball, and, staggering sidewise, he clutched his comrade's gun, so that it sent its bullet skyward. Before new men could take their places, the four runners had leaped the low fence and dashed across the yard to the shelter under the barn.

Knowing that they must be dislodged, the lieutenant commanded that the manure trap should be raised and a number of the dragoons drop down it; but no sooner had one started to swing himself through the opening than a gun cracked below, and the man, relaxing his hold, fell lifeless on his face. Another, not pausing to drop, jumped. He landed in a heap, but was on his feet in a flash, only to fall backward with a bullet through his lung. The rest hung back, unwilling to face such certain death, though their officers struck them with the flat of their swords.

Another moment developed the object of the attack, for through the trap-door suddenly shone a red light, and with it came the sound of crackling faggots. A cry of terror broke from the British, and there was a wild rush for the door, which many hands joined in throwing open. As it rolled back a dozen guns spoke, and the seven exposed men fell in a confused heap at the opening,—a lesson sharp enough to turn the rest to right about.

All pretence of discipline disappeared at once, the men ceasing to pay the slightest heed to their officers; and one, panic-stricken with fear, threw off his coat and, fairly tearing his shirt from his back, tied it to his bayonet and waved it through the door. Hennion, with an oath, sprang forwards, caught the gun and wrenched it out of the fellow's hands, at the same moment stretching him flat with a blow in the neck; but as he did so one of the troopers behind him cut the officer down with his sabre. The subaltern of foot who rushed to help his superior was caught and held by two of the men, and the officers thus disposed of, the white flag was once more held through the doorway.

At the very instant that this was accomplished, the fire below found some crevice in the flooring under the hay, and in a trice the mow burst into spitting and crackling flame. With the holder of the white flag at their head, the men dashed through the doorway, those with arms tossing them away, and most of them throwing themselves flat upon the ground, with the double purpose of signalling their surrender and of escaping the bullets that might greet their exit.

In a moment they were the centre of a hundred men, who,

but for their guns, might have been taken for a lot of farmers and field hands. One alone wore a military hat with a cockade, and it was he who demanded in a voice of self-importance: —

"Have you surrendered, and where is your commanding officer?"

"Yes," shouted a dozen of the British, while the three men still holding the subaltern dragged him forward, without releasing their hold on his arms.

"Give up your sword, then," demanded the wearer of the cockade.

"I'll die first!" protested the young fellow, — a lad of not over seventeen at most, — still struggling with his soldiers. "You'll not see an officer coerced by his own men, sir," he sobbed, as another of the soldiers caught him by the wrist and twisted his sword from his hand.

"A mighty good lesson it is for your stinking British pride," was the retort of the militia officer, as he accepted the sword. "I guess you're the kind of man we've been looking for to make an example of. We'll teach you what murdering our generals and plundering our houses come to — eh, men?"

"Hooray fer Joe Bagby!" shouted one of the conquerors.

"Some of you tie the prisoners, except him, two and two, and start them down the road at double quick," ordered Captain Bagby. "Collect all the guns and sabres and throw them on the sledges. Look alive there, for we've no time to lose. Well, squire, what do you want?" he demanded, as he turned and found the latter's hand on his sleeve.

"I've to thank ye for arriving in the nick o' time to save me from being plundered," said Mr. Meredith, speaking as if he were taking a dose of medicine. "Now can't ye set to and save my outbuildings from taking fire?"

"Harkee, squire," replied Joe, dropping his voice to a confidential pitch, while at the same time leading his interlocutor aside out of hearing. "The sledges and what they hold is our prize, captivated from the British in a fair fight, yet we'll get around that if you'll say the right word."

"And what's that?" queried the squire.

"You know as well as I what 't is. The sledges are yours, and we 'll do our prettiest to prevent the stables and cribs from catching, if you 'll but say what I want said as to Miss Janice."

"I 'd see her in her grave first."

"Some of you fellows start those sleighs and sledges up the road!" shouted Bagby. "Now then, have you got that officer ready?"

"He ain't ready, but we is, cap," answered one of the little group about the prisoner.

"Up with him, then!" ordered Bagby. "See-saw 's the word: down goes Mercer, up goes a bloody-back."

At the command, half a dozen men pulled on a rope which had been passed over the bough of a tree, and the young subaltern was swung clear of the ground. He struggled so fiercely for a moment that the cords which bound his wrists parted and he was able to clutch the rope above his head in a desperate attempt to save himself. It was useless, for instantly two rifles were levelled and two bullets sent through him; his hands relaxing, he hung limply, save for a slight muscular quiver.

"If your friends, the British, come back, you can tell them that 's only the beginning," Bagby told the squire. "And look out for yourself, or it 's what will come to you. Now then, fellows, fall in," he called. "The line of retreat is to Somerset Court-house, and you are to guard the prisoners and the provisions if you can, but scatter if attacked in force. March!"

The motley company, without pretence of order, set off on their long, weary night tramp through the snow. Behind them the flame of the barn, now towering sixty feet in the air, made the whole scene bright with colour, save where the swinging body of the lad threw a shifting shadow across a stretch of untrampled snow.

XXXVII

BLUES AND REDS

AS the squire still stood gloomily staring, now at the departing Whigs, now at the blazing barn, and now at his stable and other buildings, Clarion, who had taken a great interest in the last hour's doings, suddenly pricked up his ears and then ran forward to a snow-drift within a few yards of the burning building. Here he halted and gave vent to a series of loud yelps. Limping forward, the squire heard his name called in a faint voice, and the next instant discovered Philemon hidden in the snow.

"I 'm bad hurt, squire," he groaned; "but I made out to crawl from the barn."

"Gadsbodikins!" exclaimed Mr. Meredith. "Why, Phil, I e'en forgot ye for the moment. Here 's a pass, indeed. And none but women and a one-legged man to help ye, now ye 're found."

It took the whole household to carry Philemon indoors, and as it was impossible, in the squire's legless and horseless condition, to send for aid, Mrs. Meredith became the surgeon. The wound proved to be a shoulder cut, serious only from the loss of blood it had entailed, and after it was washed and bandaged the patient was put to bed. Daylight had come by the time this had been accomplished, and the squire was a little cheered to find that the snow on the roofs of his farm buildings had prevented the sparks of the barn from igniting them.

Twenty-four hours elapsed before help came to the household, and then it was in the form of Harcourt's dragoons. From Tarleton it was learned that the fugitives, on their arrival at Brunswick, asserted that Washington's whole army had attacked them, and was in full advance upon the post,—

news which had kept the whole force under arms for hours, and prevented any attempt to come to the assistance of the detachment. When the major learned that eighty picked troops had been killed or captured by a hundred raw militia, his language was more picturesque than quotable. There was nothing to be done, however; and after they had vowed retaliation for the subaltern, buried the dead, and the surgeon had looked at Phil's wound and approved of Mrs. Meredith's treatment, the squadron rode back to Brunswick.

This and other like experiences served to teach the English that it was not safe to send out foraging parties, and for a time active warfare practically ceased. The Continental forces, reduced at times to less than a thousand men, were not strong enough to attack the enemy's posts, and the British, however much they might grumble over a fare of salt food, preferred it to fresher victuals when too highly seasoned with rifle bullets.

The Merediths were somewhat better provided, Sukey's store-rooms proving to have many an unransacked cupboard, while the farmers in the vicinity, however bare they had apparently been stripped, were able, when money was offered, to supply poultry, eggs, milk, and many other comforts, which through lack of stock and labour Greenwood could no longer furnish.

His wound was therefore far from an ill to the lieutenant of horse, since it not merely relieved him from the stigma of the surrender, but saved him from the privation of the poor food and cramped quarters his fellow troopers were enduring at Brunswick. Nor did he count as the least advantage the tendance that Janice, half by volition and half by compulsion, gave him. When at last he was able to come downstairs, the days were none too long as he sat and watched her nimble fingers sew, or embroider, or work at some other of her tasks.

One drawback there was to this joy. In spite of strict orders against straggling, many a red-coated officer risked punishment for disobedience, and capture by the enemy, by sneaking through the pickets and spending long hours at Greenwood. Though Phil's service had given him much more tongue and assurance than of yore, he was still unable to cope with them; and, conscious that he cut but a poor figure to the girl when they were present, he was at times jealous and quarrelsome.

Twice he laid his anxieties and desires before the squire and begged for an immediate wedding, but that worthy was by no means as ready as once he had been; for while convinced of the eventual success of the British, he foresaw unsettled times in the immediate future, and knew that the marriage of his girl to an officer of the English army was a serious if not decisive step. Yet delay was all he wished, being too honest a man to even think of breaking faith with the young fellow; and finally one evening, when he had become genial over a due, or rather undue, amount of Madeira and punch, he was won over by Philemon's earnest persuasions, and declared that the wedding should take place before the British broke up their winter quarters and marched to Philadelphia.

The next morning the squire had no remembrance of his evening's pledge, but he did not seek to cry off from it when reminded by Philemon. Mrs. Meredith was called into conclave, and then Janice was summoned and told of the edict.

"And now, lass, thou hast got thyself and us into more than one scrape," ended the father, "so come and give thy dad a kiss to show that thou 'rt cured of thy wrong-headedness and will do as thy mother and I wish."

Without a word Janice went to her father and kissed him; then she flung her arms about his neck, buried her head in his shoulder, and burst into tears.

The squire had been quite prepared for the conduct of two years previous and had steeled himself to enforce obedience, but this contrary behaviour took him very much aback.

"Why, Jan," he expostulated, "this is no way to carry on when a likely young officer bespeaks ye in marriage. Many 's the maid would give her left hand to —"

"But I don't love him," sobbed the girl.

"And who asked if thou didst, miss?" inquired her mother, who by dint of nursing Phil had become his strong partisan. "Dost mean to put thy silly whims above thy parents' judgments?"

"But you would n't do as your father wished, and married dadda," moaned Janice.

"A giddy, perverse child I was," retorted Mrs. Meredith; "and another art thou, to fling the misbehaviour in thy mother's face."

"Nay, nay, Patty—" began the squire; but whether he was stepping forward in defence of his wife or his daughter he was not permitted to say, for Mrs. Meredith continued:—

"We 'll set the wedding for next Thursday, if that suits thee, Philemon?"

"You can't name a day too soon for me, marm," assented Philemon, eagerly; "and as I just hearn the sound of hoofs outside, 't is likely some officers has arrived, and I 'll speak ter them so 's ter get word ter the chaplain, and ter my regiment. You need n't be afraid, Miss Janice, that 't won't be done in high style. Like as not, General Grant will put the whole post under arms." In truth, the lover was not at his ease, and was glad enough for an excuse which took him from the room. Nor was he less eager to announce his success to his comrades, hoping it would put an end to their attentions to his bride.

"Then ye 'll do as I bid ye, Jan?" questioned her father.

"Yes, dadda," Janice assented dutifully, while striving to stifle her sobs. "I—I 've been a—a—wicked creature, I know, and now I 'll do as you and mommy tell me."

If Philemon had been made uneasy by the girl's tears, her manner during the balance of the day did not tend to make him happier. Her sudden gravity and silence were so marked that his fellow-officers who had come to supper, and who did not know the true situation, rallied them both on Miss Meredith's loss of spirits.

"I' faith," declared Sir Frederick Mobray, moved perhaps by twinges of the little green monster, "but for the lieutenant's word I 'd take oath 't was a funeral we were to attend, and issue orders for the casing of colours and muffling of drums. In the name of good humour, Mr. Meredith, have in the spirits, and I 'll brew a punch that shall liquidate the gloom."

After one glass of the steaming drink, the ladies, as was the custom, rose to leave the room. At the door Janice was intercepted by Peg, with word that Sukey wished to advise with her anent some matter, so the maid did not follow her mother, but turned and entered the kitchen.

The cook was not in view; but as the girl realised the fact, a cloaked man suddenly stepped from behind the chimney breast, and before the scream that rose to Janice's lips could escape, a firm hand was laid on them. Yet, even in the moment of surprise, the girl was conscious that, press as the fingers might, there was still an element of caress in their touch.

"I seem doomed to fright you, Miss Meredith," said Brereton, "but, indeed, 't is not intentional. Twice in the last week I've tried to gain speech of you without success, and so to-night have taken desperate means." He took his hand from her mouth. "This time I know myself safe in your hands. Ah, Miss Janice, wilt not forgive me the suspicion? for not one easy hour have I had since I knew how I had wronged you. I was sent to eastward with despatches to the New England governors, or nothing would have kept me from earlier seeking you to crave a pardon."

"Yet thou wouldst not believe me, sir, when I sent thee word."

"Sent me word, when?"

"By Lord Clowes."

"Clowes?"

"Yes. The morning after you were captivated."

"Not one word did he speak to me from the moment I was trapped until — until you, like a good angel, as now I know, came to my rescue." He bowed his head and pressed his lips upon the palm of her hand.

The girl was beginning an explanation when a loud laugh from the dining-room recalled to her the danger. "You must not stay," she protested, as she caught away her hand, which the aide had continued holding. "There are five —"

"I know it," interrupted Jack; "and if you'd not come to me, I'd have burst in on them rather than have my third ride futile."

"Oh, go; please go!" begged the girl, his reckless manner adding yet more to her alarm.

"Say that you forgive me," pleaded the officer, catching her hands.

"Yes, yes, anything; only go!" besought Janice, as a second laugh from the dining-room warned her anew of the peril.

Jack stooped and kissed each hand in turn, but even as he did so one of the officers in the next room bawled: —

"Here's a toast to Leftenant Hennion and his bride, — hip, hip, hip, bumpers!"

Janice felt herself caught by both shoulders, with all the tenderness gone from the touch.

"What does that mean?" the aide demanded, his face very close to her own.

The girl, with bowed head, partly in shame, and partly to escape the blazing eyes which fairly burned her own, replied: "I am to marry Mr. Hennion next Thursday."

"Willingly?" burst from her questioner, as if the word were shot from a bomb.

"No."

"Then you'll do nothing of the kind," denied Brereton, with a sudden gaiety of voice. "My horse is hid in the woods by the river; but say the word, and you shall be under Lady Washington's protection at Morristown before daylight."

"And what then?" questioned the girl.

"Then? Why, a marriage with me the moment you'll give me ay."

"But I care no more for you than I do for Mr. Hennion; and even — "

"But I'll make you care for me," interrupted Jack, ardently.

"And even if I did," concluded Janice, "you yourself helped to teach me what the world thinks of elopements."

"Ah, don't let — don't deny — "

"No, once for all; and release me, sir, I beg."

"Not till you swear to me that this accursed wedding is not to take place till Thursday."

"Of course not."

"And where is it to be?"

"At the church in Brunswick."

"And is the looby with his regiment or staying here?"

"Here."

Brereton laughed gaily, and more loudly than was prudent. "A bet and a marvel," he bantered: "a barley-corn to Miss Janice Meredith, that the sweetest, most bewitching creature in the world lacks a groom on her wedding day! I must not tarry, for 't is thirty miles to Morristown, and three days is none too much time for what I would do. Farewell," Jack ended, once more catching her hands and kissing them. He hurriedly crossed the room, but as he laid hold of the latch he as suddenly turned and strode back to the maid. "Has he ever kissed you?" he demanded, with a savage scowl on his face.

"Never!" impulsively cried the girl, while the colour flooded into her cheeks.

"Bless him for a cold-blooded icicle!" joyfully exclaimed the officer; and before Janice could realise his intention she was caught in his arms and fervently kissed. The next moment a door slammed, and he was gone, leaving the girl leaning for very want of breath against the chimney side, with redder cheeks than ever.

The colour still lingered the next morning to such an extent that it was commented upon by both her parents, who found in it proof that she was now reconciled to their wishes. Had they been closer observers, they would have noticed that several times in the course of the day it waxed or waned without apparent reason, that their daughter was singularly restless, and that any sound out of doors caused her to start and listen. Not even the getting out and trying on of her wedding gown seemed to interest her. Yet nothing occurred to break the usual monotony of the life.

Her state of nervous expectancy on the second day was shown when the inevitable contingent of English officers arrived a little before dinner; for as they appeared without previous warning in the parlour door, Janice gave a scream, which startled Philemon, who was relying upon but two legs of his chair, into a pitch over backward, and brought the squire's gouty foot to the floor with a bump and a wail of pain.

"Body o' me!" ejaculated one of the new-comers. "Dost take us for Satan himself, that ye greet us so?"

"Tush, man!" corrected Mobray. "Miss Meredith could not see under our cloaks, and so, no doubt, thought us rebels. Who would n't scream at the prospect of an attack of the Continental blue devils — eh, Miss Janice?"

"Better the blue devils," retorted Janice, "than a scarlet fever."

"Hah, hah!" laughed a fellow-officer. "'T was you got us into that, Sir Frederick. Lieutenant Hennion, your first task after to-morrow's ceremony is plain and clear.

"Would that I had the suppression of this rebellion!" groaned the baronet, "'stead of one which fights us with direst cold and hunger, to say nothing of the scurvy and the putrid fever."

For the next few hours cold and hunger and disease were not in evidence, however; and it took little persuasion from the squire, who dearly loved jovial company, to induce the visitors to stay on to tea, and then to supper.

While they were enjoying the latter, the interruption Janice had expected came at last. In the midst of the cheer, the hall door was swung back so quietly that no one observed it, and only when he who opened it spoke did those at table realise the new arrival. Then the sight of the blue uniform with buff facings brought every officer to his feet and set them glancing cornerward, to where their side arms were stood.

"I grieve to intrude upon so mirthful a company," apologised the new arrival, bowing. "But knowing of the unstinted hospitality of Greenwood, I made bold, Mrs. Meredith, to tell a friend that we could scarce fail of a welcome." Brereton turned to say, "This way, Harry, after thou 'st disposed thy cloak and hat," and entered the room.

"Odds my life!" burst out the baronet, as the second interloper, garbed in Continental dragoon uniform, entered and bowed respectfully to the company. "What 's to pay here?"

"But nay," went on Brereton, "I see your table is already filled, so we 'll not inconvenience you by our intrusion. Perhaps, however, Miss Janice will fill us each a glass from yon bowl of punch. 'T is a long ride to Morristown, and a stirrup cup will not be amiss. Yet stay again. Let me first puff off my friend to you. Ladies and gentleman, Captain Henry Lee, better known as Light Horse Harry."

"May I perish, but this impudence passes belief!" gasped one of the officers. "Dost think thou 'rt not prisoners?"

"Ho, Jack! I told thee thy harebrainedness and love of adventure would get us into the suds yet," spoke up Lee. "Then the ninety light horse whom we left surrounding the house are thy troops?" he questioned laughingly, of the four officers.

"Devil pick your bones, the two of you!" swore Mobray. "Wast not enough that we should be so confoundedly gapped, but you must come with the bowl but half emptied. Hast thou no bowels for gentlemen and fellow-officers?"

"Fooh!" quizzed Brereton. "Pick up the bowl and down with it at a gulp, man. Never let it be said that an officer of the Welsh Fusileers made bones of a half-full —" There the speaker caught himself short, and suddenly turned his back on the table.

"Whom have we here?" demanded the baronet. "By Heavens, Charlie, who'd think— Does Sir William know of —?"

"'Sdeath!" cried Jack, facing about, and meeting the questioner eye to eye. "Canst not hold thy tongue, man?" Then he went on less excitedly: "I am Leftenant-Colonel John Brereton, aide-de-camp to his Excellency General Washington."

For a moment Sir Frederick stood speechless, then he held out his hand, saying: "And a good fellow, I doubt not, despite a bad trade. Fair lady," he continued after the handshake, "since we are doomed for the moment to be captives of some one other than thee, help to cheer us in the exchange by filling us each a parting glass. Come, Charlie, canst give us one of thy old-time toasts?"

Brereton laughed, as he took a glass from the girl. "'Tis hardly possible, with ladies present, to fit thy taste, Fred. However, here goes: Honour, fame, love, and wealth may desert us, but thirst is eternal."

"Even in captivity, thank a kind Providence," ejaculated one of the officers, as he set down his drained tumbler.

"Now, gentlemen, boots and saddles, an' it please you," suggested Lee, politely.

"Thee'll not force a wounded man to take such exposure," protested Mrs. Meredith. "Lieutenant Hennion —"

Brereton carried on the speech: "Can drink punch and study *divinity*. I'll warrant he's not so near to death's door but he can bear one-half the ride of our poor starved troopers and beasts."

"Farewell, Miss Janice," groaned the baronet; "'t was thy beauty baited this trap."

Jack lingered a moment after Lee and the prisoners had passed into the hallway.

"Can I have a moment's word with you apart, Miss Meredith?" he asked.

"Most certainly not," spoke up the squire, recovering from the dumbness into which the rapid occurrences of the last three minutes had reduced him. "If ye have aught to say to my lass, out with it here."

"'T is — 't is just a word of farewell."

"I like not thy farewells," answered the girl, colouring.

"For once we agree, Miss Janice," replied the officer, boldly; "and did it rest with me, there should never be another." He bowed, and went to the door. "Mr. Meredith," he said, "I've stolen a husband from your daughter. 'T is a debt I am ready to pay on demand."

XXXVIII

BLACK AND WHITE

HOW much the squire would have grieved over the capture of his almost son-in-law was never known, for events gave him no opportunity. Spring was now come, and with it the breaking up of winter quarters. The moment the roads were passable, the garrison of Brunswick, under the command of Cornwallis, marched up the Raritan to Middle Brook, driving back into the Jersey hills a detachment of the Continental army. In turn Washington's whole force was moved to the support of his advance, but the British had fallen back once more to their old position. Early in June, Howe himself arrived at Brunswick, bringing with him heavy reinforcements, and first threatened a movement toward the Delaware, hoping to draw Washington from his position; but the latter, surmising that his opponent would never dare to jeopardise his communications, was not to be deceived. Disappointed in this, the British faced about quickly, and tried to surprise the Americans by a quick march upon their encampment, only to find them posted along a strong piece of ground, fully prepared for a conflict. Although the British outnumbered the Continentals almost twice over, the deadly shooting of the latter had been so often experienced that Howe dared not assault their position, and after a few days of futile waiting, his army once more fell back on Brunswick, crossed the Raritan to Amboy, and then was ferried across to Staten Island. Washington, by holding his force in a menacing position, without either marching or attacking, had saved not merely his troops, but Philadelphia as well; and Howe learned that if the capital was to be captured, it could not be by the direct march of his command across the Jerseys, but must be by the far slower way of conveying it by ships to the southward.

Before the campaign opened, Mr. Meredith had been loud and frequent in complaints over his lack of stock and labour with which to cultivate his farm. Had he been better situated, however, it is probable that his groans would have been multiplied fivefold, for he would have seen whatever he did rendered useless by this march and counter-march of belligerents. Thrice the tide of war rolled over Greenwood; and though there was not so much as a skirmish within hearing of the homestead, the effects were almost as serious to him and to his tenantry. When the British finally evacuated the Jerseys, scarce a fence was to be found standing in Middlesex County, having in the two months' manœuvring been taken for camp-fires, and the frames of many an outbuilding had been used for similar purposes.

The depleted larders of Greenwood, together with the small prospect of replenishing them from his own farm, drove the squire to the necessity of pressing his tenants for the half-yearly rentals. Whatever his needs, the attempt to collect them was thoroughly unwise; Mr. Meredith, as a fact, being in better fortune than many of his tenants, for they had seen their young crops ridden over, or used as pasture, by the cavalry of both sides, and were therefore not merely without means of paying rent, but were faced by actual want for their own families. The surliness or threats with which the squire's demands were met should have proven to him their impolicy; but if to the simple-minded landlord a debt was a debt and only a debt, he was quickly to learn that there are various ways of payment. No sooner had the Continental army followed Howe across the Raritan, and thus left the country-side to the government, or lack of government, of its own people, than the tenants united in a movement designed to secure what might legally be termed a stay of proceedings, and which possessed the unlegal advantage of being at once speedy and effective.

One night in July the deep sleep of the master of Greenwood was interrupted by a heavy hand being laid on his shoulder, and ere he could blink himself into effective eyesight, he was none too politely informed by the spokesman of four masked men who had intruded into his conjugal chamber, that he was wanted below. While still dazed, the squire was pulled, rather than helped, out of bed, and Mrs. Meredith, who tried to help him resist, was knocked senseless on the floor. Down the stairs and out of the house he was dragged, his progress being encouraged by such cheering remarks as, "We 'll teach you what Toryism comes ter." "Where 's them tools of old George you 've been a-feeding, now?" "Want your rents, do you? Well, pay day's come."

On the lawn were a number of men similarly masked, grouped about a fire over which was already suspended the tell-tale pot. To this the squire was carried, his night-shirt roughly torn from his back; and while two held him, a coating of the hot tar was generously applied with a broom, amid screams of pain from the unfortunate, echoed in no minor key by Janice and the slave servants, all of whom had been wakened by the hubbub. Meantime, one of the law-breakers had returned to the house, and now reappeared with Mrs. Meredith's best feather-bed, which was hastily slashed open with knives, and the squire ignominiously rolled in the feathers, transforming that worthy at once to an appearance akin to an ill-plucked fowl of mammoth proportions.

Although, as already noted, the fences had disappeared from the face of the land, with the same timeliness which had been shown in the production of the mattress, a rail was now introduced upon the scene, and the miserable object having been hoisted thereon, four men lifted it to their shoulders. A slight delay ensued while the squire's ankles were tied together, and then, with the warning to him that, "If yer don't sit right and hold tight, ye 'll enjoy yer ride with yer head down and yer toes up," the men started off at a trot down the road. Sharing the burden by turns, the squire was carried to Brunswick, where, daylight having come, he was borne triumphantly twice round the green, amid hoots and yells from a steadily growing procession, and then was finally ferried across the river and dumped on the opposite bank with the warning from the spokesman that worse would come to him if he so much as dared show his face again within the county.

Lack of apparel and an endeavour to revive Mrs. Meredith had kept Janice within doors during the actual tarring and feathering; but so soon as the persecutors set off for Brunswick, the girl left her now conscious though still dizzy mother, hastily dressed, and started in pursuit, the alarm for her father quite overcoming her dread of the masked rioters. Try her best, they had too long a start to be overtaken, and when she reached the village, it was to learn from a woman to whom she appealed for information what Mr. Meredith's fate had been. Still suffering the keenest anxiety, the girl went to the ferryman's house, and begged to be rowed across the river, but he shook his head.

"Cap' Bagby 's assoomed command, ontil we gits resottled, an' his orders wuz thet no one wuz ter be ferried onless they hez a pass; so, ef yer set on followin' yer dad, it 's him yer must see. I guess he ain't far from the tavern."

This proved a correct inference, for Joe, glass in hand, was sitting on a bench near the doorway, watching and quizzing the publican as that weather-cock laboured to unscrew the rings which suspended his sign in the air.

"Who 's name are you going to paint in this time, Si?" he questioned, as the girl came within hearing.

The tavern-keeper, having freed the sign-board from the support, descended with it. "This 'ere tavern 's got tew git along without no sign," he said, as he mopped his brow. "I 'm jus' wore out talkin' first on one side o' my mouth, an' next on t' other."

"You ain't tired, I guess, of lining first one pocket and then the other?" surmised Bagby.

"'T ain't fer yer tew throw that in my teeth," retorted the publican. "It 's little money o' yours has got intew my pocket, Joe, often as yer treat yerself an' the rest."

Janice went up to the captain. "Mr. Bagby, I want to go across the river to my father, and —" so far she spoke steadily, her head held proudly erect; but then, worn out with the anxiety, the fatigue, and the heat, her self-control suddenly deserted her, and she collapsed on the bench and began to sob.

"Now, miss," expostulated Bagby, "there is n't any call to take on so." He took the girl's hand in his own. "Here, take some of my swizzle. 'T will set you right up."

Before the words had passed his lips, Janice had jerked her hand away and was on her feet. "Don't you dare touch me," she said, her eyes flashing.

"I was only trying to comfort you," asserted Joe, while the tavern loungers gave vent to various degrees of laughter.

"Then let me go to my father."

"Can't for a moment," answered Bagby, angrily. "He 's shown himself inimical to his country, and we must n't on no account allow communications with the enemy. That 's the rule as laid down in the general orders, and in a Congress resolution."

Bagby's voice, quite as much as his words, told the girl that argument was useless, and without further parley she walked away. She had not gone ten paces when the publican overtook her and asked: —

"Say, miss, where be yer a-goin'?"

"Home," answered Janice.

"Then come yer back an' rest a bit in the settin'-room, an' I 'll have my boy hitch up an' take yer thar. 'T is a mortal warm day, an' I calkerlate yer 've walked your stent." He put his hand kindly on her arm, and the girl obediently turned about and entered the tavern.

"You are very kind," she said huskily.

"That 's all right," he replied. "The squire 's done me a turn now an' agin, an' then quality 's quality, though 't ain't fer the moment havin' its way."

While she awaited the harnessing, Bagby came into the room.

"I wanted to say something to you, miss, but I guessed it might fluster you with all the boys about," he said. "Has the squire ever told you anything concerning a scheme I proposed to him?"

"No," Janice replied, coldly.

"Well, perhaps he would have, if he could have seen forward a little further. It 's being far-seeing that wins, miss." The speaker paused, as if he expected a response, but getting none, he continued, "Would you like to see him home, and everything quiet and easy again?"

"Oh!" said the girl, starting to her feet. "I'd give anything if—"

"Now we're talking," interjected the captain, quite as eagerly. "Only say that you'll be Mrs. Bagby, and back he is before sundown, and I'll see to it that he isn't troubled no more."

Janice had stepped forward impulsively, but she shrank back at his words as if he had struck her; then without a word she walked from the room, went to where the cart was being got ready, and rested a trembling hand upon it, as if in need of support, while her swift breathing bespoke the intensity of her emotion.

At Greenwood she found her mother still suffering from the fright and the blow too much to allow the girl to tell her own troubles, or to ask counsel for the future, and the occupation of trying to make the sufferer more comfortable was in fact a good diversion, exhausted though she was with her fruitless journey.

Before Mrs. Meredith was entirely recovered, or any news of the squire had reached the household, fresh trouble was upon them. Captain Bagby and two other men drove up the third morning after the incursion, and, without going through the form of knocking, came into the parlour.

"You'll get ready straight off to go to Philadelphia," the officer announced.

"For what?" demanded Mrs. Meredith.

"The Congress's orders is that any one guilty of seeking to communicate with the enemy is to be put under arrest, and sent to Philadelphia to be examined."

"But we haven't made the slightest attempt, nor so much as thought of it," protested the matron.

"Oh, no!" sneered Joe; "but, all the same, we intercepted a letter last night written to you by your old Tory husband, and—"

"Oh, prithee," broke in Janice, without a thought of anything but her father, "was he well, and where is he?"

"He was smarting a bit when he wrote," Bagby remarked

with evident enjoyment, "but he 's got safe to his friends on Staten Island, so we are n't going to let you stay where you can be sneaking news to the British through him. I 'll give you just half an hour to pack, and if you are n't done then, off you goes."

Protests and pleadings were wholly useless, though Joe yielded so far as to suggestively remark in an aside to the girl, that "there was one way that you know of, for fixing this thing." Getting together what they could in the brief time accorded to them, and with vague directions to Peg and Sukey as to the care of all they were forced to leave behind, the two women took their places in the waggon, and with only one man to drive them, set out for their enforced destination.

How little of public welfare and how much of private spite there was in their arrest was proven upon their arrival the following day in the city of brotherly love. The escort, or captor, first took them to the headquarters of the general in command of the Continental forces of the town, only to find that he was inspecting the forts down the Delaware. Leaving the papers, he took his charges to the Indian King Tavern, and after telling them that they 'd hear from the general "like as not to-morrow," he departed on his return to Brunswick.

Whether the papers were mislaid by the orderly to whom they had been delivered, or were examined and deemed too trivial for attention, or, as is most probable, were prevented consideration by greater events, no word came from headquarters the next day, or for many following ones. Nor could the initiative come from the captives, for Mrs. Meredith sickened the second day after their arrival, and developed a high fever on the third, which the physician who was called in declared to be what was then termed putrid fever, — a disease to which some three hundred of the English and Hessian soldiery at Brunswick had fallen victims during the winter. Under his advice, and without hindrance from the innkeeper, who took good care to forget that he was to "keep tight hold on the prisoners till the general sends for 'em," she was removed to quieter lodgings on Chestnut Street.

The nursing, the anxiety, and the isolation all served to make public events of no moment to Janice, though from the doctor or her loquacious landlady she heard of how Burgoyne's force, advancing from Canada, had captured Ticonderoga, and of how Sir William had put the flower of his army on board of transports and gone to sea, his destination thus becoming a sort of national conundrum affording infinite opportunity for the wiseacres of the taverns.

Mrs. Meredith, for the sake of the quiet, had been put in the back room, the daughter taking that on the street, and this arrangement, as it proved, was a fortunate one. Late in August, after a hard all-night's tendance of her mother, Janice was relieved, once the sun was up, by the daughter of the lodging-house keeper, and wearily sought her chamber, with nothing but sleep in her thoughts, if thoughts she had at all, for, too exhausted to undress, she threw herself upon the bed. Scarcely was her head resting on the pillow when there came from down the street the riffle of drums and the squeaks of fifes, and half in fright, and half in curiosity, the girl sprang up and pushed open her blinds.

Toward the river she could see what looked like an approaching mob, but behind them could be distinguished horsemen. As she stood, the rabble ran, or pattered, or, keeping step to the music, marched by, followed by a drum-and-fife corps. After them came the horsemen, and the girl's tired eyes suddenly sparkled and her pale face glowed, as she recognised, pre-eminent among them, the tall, soldierly figure of Washington, sitting Blueskin with such ease, grace, and dignity. He was talking to an odd, foreign-looking officer of extremely youthful appearance — whom, if Janice had been better in touch with the gossip of the day, she would have known to be the Marquis de Lafayette, just appointed by Congress a major-general; and while the commander-in-chief bowed and removed his hat in response to the cheers of the people, this absorption prevented him from seeing the girl, though she leaned far out of the window in the hope that he would do so. To the lonely, worried maid it seemed as if one glance of the kindly blue eyes, and one sympathetic grasp of the large, firm hand, would have cut her troubles in half.

After the group of officers came the rank and file, — lines of men no two of whom were dressed alike, many of them without coats, and some without shoes; old uniforms faded or soiled to a scarcely recognisable point, civilian clothing of all types, but with the hunting-shirt of linen or leather as the predominant garb; and equipped with every kind of gun, from the old Queen Anne musket which had seen service in Marlborough's day to the pea rifle of the frontiersman. A faint attempt to give an appearance of uniformity had been made by each man sticking a sprig of green leaves in his hat, yet had it not been for the guns, cartouch boxes, powder horns, and an occasional bayonet and canteen, only the regimental order, none too well maintained, differentiated the army from the mob which had preceded them.

While yet the girl gazed wistfully after the familiar figure, her ears were greeted with a still more familiar voice.

"Close up there and dress your lines, Captain Balch. If this is your 'Column in parade,' what, in Heaven's name, is your 'March at ease'?" shouted Brereton, cantering along the column from the rear.

He caught sight of Janice as he rode up, and an exclamation of mingled surprise and pleasure burst from him. Throwing his bridle over a post, he sprang up the three steps, lustily hammered with the knocker, and in another moment was in the girl's presence.

"This is luck beyond belief," he exclaimed, as he seized her hand. "Your father wrote me from New York, begging that I see or send you word that he was well, and asking that you be permitted to join him. At Brunswick I learned you were here, but, seek you as I might, I could not get wind of your whereabout. And now I cannot bide to aid you, for we are in full march to meet the British."

"Where?"

"They have landed at the head of the Chesapeake, so we are hastening to get between them and Philadelphia, and only diverged from our route to parade through the streets this morning, that the people might have a chance to see us, so 't is given out, but in fact to overawe them; for the city is none too loyal to us, as will be shown in a few days, when they hear of our defeat."

"You mean?" questioned the girl.

"General Washington, generous as he always is, has sent some of his best regiments to Gates, and so we are marching eleven thousand ill-armed and worse officered men, mostly new levies, to face on open ground nineteen thousand picked troops. What can come but defeat in the field? If it depended on us, the cause would be as good as ended, but they are beaten, thanks to their dirty politics, before they even face us."

"I don't understand."

"'T is simple enough when one knows the undercurrents. Germaine was against appointing the Howes, and has always hated them. So he schemes this silly side movement of Burgoyne's from Canada, and plans that the army at New York shall be but an assistant to that enterprise, with no share in its glory. Sir William, however, sloth though he be, saw through it, and, declining to be made a cat's-paw, he gets aboard ship, to seek laurels for himself, leaving Burgoyne to march and fight through his wilderness alone. Mark me, the British may capture Philadelphia, but if we can but keep them busy till it is too late to succour Burgoyne, the winter will see them the losers and not the gainers by the campaign. But there," he added, "I forget that all this can have but small interest to you."

"Oh," cried Janice, "you would n't say that if you knew how good it is just to hear a friend's voice." And then she poured out the tale of her mother's illness and of her own ordeal.

"Would that I could tarry here and serve and save you!" groaned Brereton, when she had ended; "but perhaps luck will attend us, and I may be able to hurry back. Have you money in plenty?"

The girl faltered, for in truth there had been little cash at Greenwood when they were called upon to come away, and much of that little was already parted with for lodgings and medicines. Yet she managed to nod her head.

Her pretence did not deceive Jack, and in an instant his purse was being forced into her unwilling fingers. "The fall in our paper money gives a leftenant-colonel a lean scrip in these days, but what little I have is yours," he said.

"I can't take it," protested Janice, trying to return the wallet.

Brereton was at the door ere her hand was outstretched. "Thy father's letters to me are in the purse, so thou must keep it," he urged. "It's a toss whether I ever need money again, but if I weather this campaign, we'll consider it but a loan, and if I don't, 't is the use of all others to which I should wish it put." This he said seriously, and then more lightly went on: "And besides, Miss Janice, I owe you far more than I can ever pay. We Whigs may forcibly impress, but at least we tender what we can in payment. Keep it, then, as a beggar's poor thanks for the two happiest moments of his life." The aide passed through the doorway, and the next moment a horse's feet clattered in the street.

Janice stood listening till the sound had died out of hearing, then, overcome by this first kindness after such long weeks of harshness and trial, she kissed the purse. And if Brereton could have seen the flush of emotion that swept over her face with the impulsive act, it is likely that something else would have been kissed as well.

XXXIX

SHORT COMMONS

THE moment's cheer that the brief dialogue with Brereton brought Janice was added to by the reading of the two letters from her father to him, which reaffirmed and amplified the little the aide had told her, and ended that source of misery. And, as if his advent in fact marked the turn of the tide, the doctor announced the next day that Mrs. Meredith's typhoid had passed its crisis, and only good nursing was now needed to insure a safe recovery. The girl's prayers suddenly changed from ones of supplication to ones of thanksgiving; and she found herself breaking into song even when at her mother's bedside, quite forgetful of the need for quiet. This she was especially prone to do while she helped the long hours of watching pass by knitting on a silken purse of the most complicated pattern.

The materials for this trifle were purchased on the afternoon following the march of the Continental army, and for some days the progress was very rapid. Public events then interfered and checked both song and purse. On September 11 the low boom of guns was heard, and that very evening word came that the Continental army had been defeated at Brandywine. The moment the news reached Philadelphia an exodus of the timid began, which swelled in volume as the probability of the capture of the city grew. The streets were filled with waggons carting away the possessions of the people; the Continental Congress, which had been urging Washington to fight at all hazard, took to its heels and fled to Lancaster; and all others who had made themselves prominent in the Whig cause deserted the city. Among those who thought it necessary to go was the lodging-house keeper; for, her husband being an officer of one of the row galleys in the river, she looked for nothing less than instant death at the hands of the British. With a plea to Janice, therefore, that she would care for the house and do what she could to save it from British plundering, the woman and her daughter departed. Her example was followed by the doctor, not from motives of fear, but from a purpose to join Washington's army as a volunteer. This threw upon the girl's shoulders the entire charge of her mother, and the cooking and providing as well; the latter by far the most difficult of all, for the farmers about Philadelphia were as much panic-stricken as the townspeople, and for a time suspended all attempts to bring their produce to market.

The two weeks of this chaos were succeeded by a third of unwonted calm, and then one morning as she opened the front door on her way to make her daily purchases, Janice's ears were greeted with the sound of military music. Turning up Second Street, curiosity hastening her steps, she became part of the crowd of women and children running toward the market, and arrived there just in time to see Harcourt's dragoons, followed by six battalions of grenadiers, march past to the tune of "God Save the King." Following these came Lord Cornwallis, and then four batteries of heavy artillery; and the crowd cheered the conquerors as enthusiastically and joyfully as they had Washington's ragged regiments so short a time before.

The advent of the British did not lessen the difficulties of Janice, as they not only promptly seized all the provisions of the town, but their main army, camped outside the city at Germantown, intercepted the few fresh supplies which the farmers successfully smuggled through Washington's lines above the city. Fresh beef rose to nine shillings the pound, bread to six shillings the quartern loaf, and everything else in like ratio. Though Brereton's loan furnished her with the wherewithal for the moment, each day's purchases made such inroads into it that the girl could not but worry over the future.

The stress she had foreseen came far sooner than even she had feared, or had reason to expect. Without warning, the tradespeople united in refusing to sell for Continental money;

and Janice, when she went to make her usual purchases one day, found that she could buy nothing, and had but stinted and pinched herself only to husband what in a moment had become valueless.

At first the girl's distress was so great that she could think of no means of relief; but after hours of miserable and tearful worrying over her helplessness, her face suddenly brightened, and the cause of the change was revealed by her thrusting her hand into her neckerchief, to draw out the miniature of herself. With her knitting needle she pried up the glass and, removing the slip of ivory, laid it carefully in her housewife, heaving, let it be confessed, a little sigh, for it was hard to part with the one trinket she had ever owned. Unconscious of how many hours she had been dwelling on her troubles, she caught up her calash, and with the miniature frame in her hand, hurried to the front door; but the moment she had opened it, she was reminded that it was long after the closing of the markets, and so postponed whatever she had in mind for another day.

On the following morning she sallied forth, so engrossed in her difficulties, or her project, that she paid no heed to the distant sound of cannon, nor to the groups of townspeople who stood about on corners or stoops, evidently discussing something of interest; and it was only when she turned into the market-place, and found it empty alike of buyers and sellers that she was made to realise that something unusual was occurring.

"Why are all the stands closed this morning?" she asked of an urchin.

"'Cause nawthing 's come ter town along of the fightin'."

"Fighting?"

"Guess you 're a deefy," contemptuously suggested the youngster. "Don't you hear them guns? The grenadiers went out lickety split this mornin' and folks says they 've got Washington surrounded, an 'll have him captured by night. All the other boys hez gone out on the Germantown road ter see the fun, but daddy said he 'd lick me if I went, so I did n't dare," he added dejectedly. "Hurrah! There come some more wounded!" he cried, with sudden cheerfulness and breaking into a run as an army van came in sight down Second Street.

The girl turned away and went into one of the few shops which had opened its shutters.

"You would not take Continental money yesterday," she said to the proprietor; "but perhaps you — you will — I thought — I have no other kind of money, but perhaps you will accept this in payment?" Janice, with a flushed, anxious face, unwrapped from her handkerchief and laid down on the counter the miniature frame.

The man took it up and eyed it for a moment, then raised it to his mouth and pressed his teeth on the edge; satisfied by the experiment, he scrutinised the brilliants. "How d' ye come by this?" he demanded suspiciously.

"Oh, indeed, sir," explained Janice, growing yet redder, "it is mine, I assure you, given me by — that is, he said I might keep it."

"'Tain't for me to say it ain't yourn," responded the shop-keeper; "but the times is bad times and there 's roguery of all sorts going on in the city." He looked it over again, and demanded, "Who does 'W. H. J. B.' mean?"

"I don't — I never knew," faltered Janice.

"Then where 's the picture that was in it?"

"I — I took it out," explained the girl, "not wishing to part with that."

"That 's just what ye would have done if ye 'd not come by it by rights," replied the man.

"Then I 'll put it back," hastily offered Janice, very much alarmed and flustered. "I — I never dreamed that — that the picture would make it worth any more."

"'T would have made it look more regular. How much d' ye want for it?"

"I thought — Would five pounds be too much?"

The shop-keeper laid the frame down on the counter and shoved it toward Janice. "No, I don't want it," he said.

"Would three pounds — ?"

"I don't want it at no such price," interrupted the man.

"Oh," bewailed the girl, "what am I to do? The doctor said she was to have nourishing food; and I have nothing but a little corn meal left. Would you give me one pound for it?"

"I tell ye, I won't buy it at any price. And I don't even want it in the shop, so take it away. And if you want to keep out of jail, I would n't be offering it about; I 've most a mind to call the watch myself, as 't is."

The threat was enough to make Janice catch up the bijou and leave the shop almost at a run; nor did her pace lessen as she hurried homeward, and, safely there, she fast bolted the door. This done, with hands which trembled not a little, she replaced her portrait in the frame, hoping dimly from what the shopkeeper had said, that this would help to prove her ownership. Yet all that day and the succeeding one she stayed within doors, dreading what might come; and any unusual noise outside set her heart beating with fear that it might portend the approach of a danger all the more terrible that it was indefinite. As if her suffering were not great enough, an added horror was the army vans loaded with groaning wounded, which rumbled by her door during the sleepless night she spent.

As time lessened her fright, her necessities grew more pressing, and finally became so desperate, that, braving everything, she went boldly to headquarters, and asked for Lord Cornwallis.

She was referred by the sentry at the stoop to a room on the ground floor, her entrance being accompanied by the man shouting down the hallway: "Here 's wan more av thim townsfolks, sir." Entering, Janice discovered two men seated at a table, each with a little pile of money at his elbow, passing the time with cards.

"Well," growled the one with his back to the door, "I suppose 't is the usual tale: No bread, no meat, no firewood; sick wife, sick baby, sick mother, sick anything that can be whined about. Body o' me, must we not merely die by bullets or starvation, but suffer a thousand deaths meantime with endless whimpering!"

"Slowly, slowly, Mobray," advised he who faced Janice. "This is no nasal-voiced and putty-faced cowardly old Quaker. 'T is a damned pretty maid, with eyes and a waist and an ankle fit to be a toast. Ay, and she can mantle divinely, when she 's admired!"

"Ye don't foist that take-in on me, John André! I score six to my suit, and a quint is twenty-one, and a card played is twenty-two. — Well, graycoat, say your say, and don't stand behind me as a kill-joy."

"I wish to see Lord Cornwallis, Sir Frederick," faltered Janice, nerved only by thought of her mother, and ready to sink through the floor in her mortification.

At the sound of a woman's voice the officer turned his head sharply, and with the first glance he was on his feet. "Miss Meredith," he cried, "a thousand pardons! Who 'd have thought to find you here? How can I serve you?"

"I wish to see Lord Cornwallis," repeated Janice.

"'T is evident you pay little heed to what has been occurring," replied Mobray, as he placed a chair for her. "We thought we had all the spirit beat out of Mr. Washington's pack o' ragamuffins; but, egad, day before yesterday, quite contrary to all the rules of polite warfare, and in a most ungentlemanly manner, they set upon us as we lay encamped at Germantown, and wellnigh gave us a drubbing. Lord Cornwallis went to Sir William's assistance, running his grenadiers at double quick the whole distance, and he has not yet returned."

"We deemed rebellion well under our heel when we gained possession of its capital," chimed in Captain André; "but Mr. Washington seems in truth to make a fourth with 'a dog, a woman, and a chestnut-tree, the more they are beat the better they be.' Our very successes are teaching his army how to fight, and I fear me the day will come when we shall have thrashed them into a victory."

"But all this is not helping Miss Meredith," spoke up Mobray. "Lord Cornwallis being beyond reach, can I not be of aid?"

In a few words the girl poured out the tale of her mother's sickness, and then with less glibness, and with reddened cheeks, of her moneyless and foodless condition.

Before she had well finished, the baronet swept up his pile of money on the table and held out the handful of coins to the girl.

"Oh, no," cried Janice, shrinking back. "I — Oh, I thank you, but I can't take your — "

"Ah, Miss Meredith," pleaded Sir Frederick, "I was less proud last winter when we were half starving in scurvy-plagued and fever-stricken Brunswick."

"But food was nothing," exclaimed Janice, "and that is all I want; just enough for my mother. I thought Lord Cornwallis might — "

"In truth, Miss Meredith, you ask for what is far scarcer than guineas in these days," said André. "The rebels hold the forts in the lower Delaware so tenaciously that our supply ships have not yet been able to get up to us, and as Washington's army is between us and the back country, we are as near in a state of siege as nineteen thousand men were ever put by an inferior force."

"Our men are on quarter rations, and we officers fare but little better," grumbled Mobray.

"Then what am I to do?" cried Janice, despairingly.

"Come, Fred," said André, "can't something be done?"

Mobray shook his head gloomily. "I did my best yesterday to get the wounded rebels given some soup and wine, or at least beef and biscuit that was n't rotten or full of worms, but 't was not to be done; there 's too much profit in buying the worst and charging for the best."

"Damn the commissary! say I," growled André, "and let his fate be to starve ever after on the stuff he palms on us as fit to eat."

"Amen," remarked a voice outside, and Lord Clowes stepped into the room. "I 'll take hell and army rations, Captain André, rather than lose the pleasure of your society," he added ironically.

"Small doubt I shall be found there," retorted André, derisively; "but I fear me we shall be no better friends, Baron Clowes, than we are here. There is a special furnace for *paroled prisoners!*"

"Blast thy tongue, but that insult shall cost thee dear!" returned the commissary, white with rage. "To whom shall I send my friend, sir?"

"Hold, André," broke in Mobray, "let me answer, not for you, but for the army." He faced Clowes and went on.

"When you have surrendered yourself into the hands of the rebels, and have been properly exchanged, sir, you may be able to find a British officer to carry a challenge on your behalf; until then no man of honour would lower himself by fighting you."

"I make Sir Frederick's answer mine, my Lord," said André, "and I suggest, as a lady is present, that we put a finish to our war of words, which can come to nothing."

The commissary gave a quick glance about the room, and as he became aware of the presence of Janice, he uttered an exclamation and started forward with outstretched hand. "Miss Meredith!" he ejaculated. "By all that 's wonderful!"

Mobray made an impulsive movement as Clowes stooped and kissed the girl's hand, almost as if intending to strike the baron; but checking himself, he sarcastically remarked, with a frowning face: "If you enjoy the favour of his Lordship, Miss Meredith, you need not look further for help. We fellows who fight for our country barely get enough to keep life in us, but the commissariat knows not short commons. Mr. Commissary-General, you have an opportunity to aid Miss Meredith that you should not have were it in my power to forestall you."

"Come to my office, Miss Janice," requested Clowes, perhaps glad to get away from the presence of the young officers. He led the way across the hallway to another room, and, after the two were seated, would have taken the girl's hand again had she not avoided his attempt.

In the fewest possible words Janice retold her plight, broken only by interjections of sympathy from her listener, and by two futile endeavours to gain possession of her hand.

"Have no fear of any want in the future," he exclaimed heartily. "In truth, Miss Meredith, on our entrance we seized much that was unfit for the troops, while since then the military necessities have compelled the destruction of many of the finest houses about Germantown, and I took good care that what store of delicacies and wines they might hold should not be destroyed along with them. But give me thy number, and thy mother shall have all that she needs." Clowes caught the maiden's hand, and though she rose with the action, and slightly shrank away from him, this time he had his will and kissed it hotly.

Janice gave the address and thanked him with warm words of gratitude, somewhat neutralised by her trying to free her hand.

Instead of yielding to her wish, the commissary only tightened his grasp. "Ye have owed me something for long," he said, drawing her toward him in spite of her striving. "Surely I have earned it to-day."

"Lord Clowes, I beg —" began Janice; but there she ended the plea, and, throwing her free arm as a shield before her face, she screamed.

Instantly there was a sound of a falling chair, and both the card-players burst into the room.

Quick as they were, Clowes had already dropped his hold, and at a respectful distance was saying: "The wine and food shall reach ye within the hour, Miss Meredith."

Janice silently curtseyed her thanks, and darted past the young officers, alike anxious to escape explanation to them, or further colloquy with her persecutor.

In this latter desire the girl secured but a brief postponement, for she was not long returned when the knocker summoned her to the front door, and on the steps stood the commissary and two soldiers laden with a basket apiece.

"Ye see I'm true to my word, Miss Meredith," said Lord Clowes. "Give me the whiskets, and be off with ye," he ordered to the men; and then to the girl continued: "Where will ye have them bestowed?"

"Oh, I'll not trouble thee," protested Janice, blocking the entrance, "just hand them to me."

"Nay, 't is no trouble," the officer assured her, setting one foot over the sill. "And, besides, I have word of your father to tell ye."

Reluctantly the maiden gave him passage, and pointed out a place of deposit in the entry for his burden. Then she fell back to the staircase, and went up a few steps. Yet she eagerly questioned: "What of my father?"

Clowes came to the foot of the ascent. "He is on one of the transports in the lower Delaware, and as soon as we can reduce the rebel works, and break through their cursed *chevaux-de-frise*, he will come up to Philadelphia."

"Oh," almost carolled Janice, "what joyous news!"

"And does the bringer deserve no reward?"

"For that, and for the food, I thank you deeply, Lord Clowes," said the girl, warmly.

"I'm not the man to take my pay in mere lip music," answered the commissary. "Harkee, Miss Meredith, there is a limit to my forbearance of thy skittishness. Thou wast ready enough to wed me once, and I have never released thee from the bargain. Henceforth I expect a lover's privileges until they can be made those of a husband." Clowes took two steps, upward.

"I think, Lord Clowes, that 't is hardly kind of you to remind me of my shame," replied Janice, with a gentle dignity very close to tears. "Deceitful I was and disobedient, and no one can blame me more than I have come to blame myself. But you are not the one to speak of it nor to pretend that my giddy conduct was any pledge."

"Then am I to understand that I was lover enough when thy needs required it, but that now I am to be jilted?" demanded the man, harshly.

"Your version is a cruel one that I am sure you cannot think just."

"Ye hold to it that ye are not bound to me?"

"Yes."

The commissary fell back to where he had set the baskets. "In your necessity ye felt otherwise, and I advise ye to remember that ye still require my aid. I am not one of those who lavish favours and expect no return, though a good friend to those who make it worth my while. If I am to have naught from ye, ye shall have naught from me." He picked up the baskets. "Here is milk, bread, meat, jellies, and wines, to be had for a price, and only for a price."

"Oh, prithee, Lord Clowes," begged Janice, despairingly, "you cannot seek to advantage yourself of my desperate plight. All I had to give my mother this morning was some water gruel, and I have not tasted food myself for a twenty-four hours."

"Your anxiety for your mother cannot be over great. I only ask ye to avow that ye consented to become my wife, and should have done so, had we been left free."

The girl wavered; then buried her face in her hands, and in a scarcely audible voice said: "I did intend — for a brief space — did think to — to marry you."

"And ye 've never given a promise to another man?"

"Never."

Clowes set down the baskets. "That is all I wished acknowledged," he said. "I 'll ask no more till ye have decided whether ye will be true to the troth ye have just confessed, Janice." He opened the front door, and added as he passed out: "When these supplies are exhausted, ye know where more is to be had."

XL

THE BATTLE FOR FOOD AND FORAGE

WHEN Janice came to examine the contents of the baskets, she was somewhat disappointed at the mess of pottage for which she had half bartered herself. Though every article the commissary had enumerated was to be found, it was in meagre quantities, and the girl was shrewd-witted enough to divine the giver's intention, — that she should be quickly forced again to appeal to him. Her mother's requirements and her own hunger, however, prevented dwelling on the future, and scarcely had these been attended to, when Mobray and André appeared, to inquire if her immediate needs were supplied, and with a plan of assistance.

"Miss Meredith," said Mobray, "Captain André and I have had assigned to us for quarters the Franklin house down on Second Street; and he and I have agreed that, if Mrs. Meredith can be moved, you are to come and share it with us."

"We ask it as a favour, which, if granted, will make us the envy of the army," remarked André. "And it will, I trust, not be an entirely one-sided benefit. The old fox's den is more than comfortable, Mobray and I have a couple of rankers as servants, one of whom has more or less attached to him a woman who cooks well enough to make even the present ration eatable, and, lastly, though our presence may be something of a handicap, yet in such unsettled times one must tolerate the dogs if they but keep out the wolves. Hang and whip as we may, the men will plunder, and some in high office are little better. Alone here, you are scarcely safe, but with us you need have no fear."

Janice attempted some objections, but her previous helplessness and loneliness, as well as her recent fright from the commissary, made them faint-hearted, and it needed little urgence to win her consent to the plan. Her mother approving, a surgeon and an ambulance were secured, and before nightfall the removal was safely accomplished.

When, after the first good night's sleep she had enjoyed since her mother sickened, the girl was summoned to breakfast, she found that others had been more wakeful. In the middle of the table was a pail of milk, a pile of eggs, four unplucked fowls, and two sucking pigs, arranged with some pretence of ornament, with two officer's sword-knots to better the attempt at decoration, and the whole surmounted by a placard reading: "Only the brave deserve the fare."

"Gaze, Miss Meredith!" cried André, jubilantly. "See the results of a valour of which you were the inspiration! Marathon, Cressy, Fontenoy, and Quebec pale before the march, the conflict, and the retreat of last night, the glories of which would ne'er be credited, even alas! were it not necessary that they should ne'er be told."

"We held counsel concerning our larder," Sir Frederick explained, as the girl looked questioningly from man to man, "and agreed that since you had honoured us, we could not dare to starve you and Mrs. Meredith on salt pork and sea biscuit. So, last night, André and I, with our two servants, laid hold of a boat, crossed the Delaware, levied tribute on a fat Jersey farm, and returned ere day had come. Item. — To disobeying the general orders by stealing through the lines: one hundred lashes on the bare back. Item. — For ordering a soldier to break the rules of war: ten days in the guardhouse. Item. — For plundering, contrary to proclamation: death by shooting. Wilt drop a tear o'er my grave, fair lady?"

"Oh, sirs!" exclaimed Janice, "you should not — to take such risk —"

"Not since I went birds-nesting in Kent have I had such a night's sport," declared André, gleefully. "And the thought that we were checkmating that scoundrel Clowes did not bate the pleasure. If he were fit company for gentlemen we'd have him to dinner to-day, just to spoil his appetite with sight of our cates."

"You do not like — Why do you call Lord Clowes scoundrel?" asked Janice.

Mobray shrugged his shoulders as he made answer: "On enough grounds and to boot. But 't is sufficient that he gave his parole to the rebels, and then broke it by escaping to our lines. He is a living daily disgrace to the uniform we all wear, and yet his influence is so powerful with Sir William that we can do nothing against him. Pray Heaven that some day he 'll not be able to keep in the rear, and that the rebels recapture and give him the rope he merits."

In contrast to the past, the next few days were very happy ones to Janice. Her mother mended steadily, and was soon able to come to meals and to stay downstairs. The servants relieved the girl of all the household drudgery, and spared her from all dwelling on her empty purse. As for the young officers, they could not do enough to entertain her, and, it is to be suspected, themselves. Piquet was quite abandoned, and in place of it nothing would do André but he must teach Janice to paint. Not to be thrown in the background, Mobray produced his flute, and, thanks to a fine harpsichord Franklin had imported for his daughter, was able to have numberless duets with the maiden. Then they took short rides to the south of the city, where the Delaware and Schuylkill safeguarded a restricted territory from rebel intrusion, and daily walks along the river-front or in the State House Gardens, where one of the bands of a few regiments garrisoning the city played every afternoon for the amusement of the officers and townspeople, and where Janice was made acquainted with many a young macaroni officer or feminine toast. Save for the high price of provisions, and the constant war talk, Philadelphia bore little semblance to being in a state of semi-siege, and the prize which two armies were striving to hold or win, not by actual conflict, but by a strategy which aimed to keep closed or to open sources of supplies.

Late in October Howe's army fell back from Germantown and took position just outside the city, where it was set to work throwing up lines of fortifications. And a startling rumour which seemed to come from nowhere, but which, in spite of denials from headquarters, spread like wildfire, supplied a reason for both the retrograde movement and the construction of blockhouses and redoubts.

"The rebels have the effrontery to give it out that they have captured General Burgoyne's whole force," sneeringly announced Mobray, as he returned from guard mount. "There seems no limit to the size of their lies."

"La! Sir Frederick," exclaimed Janice, "'t is just what Colonel — what somebody predicted. He said that if General Washington could but keep Sir William busy until it would be too late for him to go General Burgoyne's aid, all would be well at the end of the campaign."

"And having conceived the hope, they seek to bolster their cause by spreading the tale abroad," scoffed the baronet.

"'Facile est inventis addere,'" laughed André. "They are merely settling the moot point as to who is the father of invention."

"What rebel was it bubbled the conceit to you, Miss Meredith?" inquired Mobray.

"'T was Colonel Brereton," replied the girl, with a faint hesitation. Then she added, as if a new idea occurred to her, "So you see the American is not the father of invention, Colonel Brereton being an Englishman." Though spoken as an assertion, the statement had a definite question in it.

"Who is this fellow, who, like Charles Lee, fights against his own country?" asked André.

"No one you ever knew, John," replied Mobray; "but I, who do, have it not in my heart to blame him."

"Wilt not tell us his history?" begged Janice, eagerly. "Once he said his great-grandfather was King of England, and since then I've so longed to know it!"

"'T is truth he spoke, poor fellow, but he was an old-time friend of mine, which would be enough to seal my lips respecting his sorry tale, since he wishes oblivion for it. But I am his debtor as well, for he it was who helped me to a prompt exchange when I was taken prisoner last spring."

"Of course I would not have thee tell me anything that is secret," remarked Janice. Then, after a moment, she went on, "There is, however, something of which you may be able to inform me?"

"But name your desire."

"I must get it," announced the girl, and she left the room

and went upstairs. But once in the upper hallway, she did not go to her room, merely pausing long enough to take the miniature from its abiding spot, and then returned. "Wilt tell me if the diamonds are false?" she requested, placing the ornament in André's hand.

"No, for a certainty," replied the captain.

"Then is it not worth five pounds?" exclaimed Janice.

"Five pounds," laughed André, derisively. "'T is easily worth five hundred!"

"Oh, never!" cried the girl.

"Ay. Am I not right, Mobray?"

"Beyond question. And then 't is not worth the portrait it encircles," asserted Mobray, gallantly.

"And yet I could not get one pound for it," marvelled Janice, and told the two officers how she had sought to barter it.

"'T is evident you asked too little, Miss Meredith," surmised André, "and so made him suspect your title."

"Would that you might offer it to me at a hundred times five pounds!" bemoaned the baronet. "To think of such a pearl being cast before such swine!"

"Who painted it, Miss Meredith?" asked André.

"'T was Colonel Brereton."

Mobray looked up quickly at her, then once more at the miniature. He turned it over, and as the initials on the back caught his eye, he frowned, but more with intentness than anger. For a moment he held it, then handed it to Janice with the remark, "Know you the frame's history?"

"Only that it once held another portrait, and that of a most beautiful girl."

"Whom he forgot, it appears, once you were seen, for which small blame to him, Miss Meredith," replied Mobray, as he rose and left the room, his face set sternly, as if he were fighting some emotion.

For two days the young officers continued to get infinite amusement out of the rebel news, but on the third their gibes and flouts ceased, and a sudden gravity ensued, the cause of which was explained to the women that evening when the time had come for "good-night."

"Ladies," said André, "the route is ordered before daybreak to-morrow, so we must say a farewell to you now, and leave you for a time to the sole charge of Mrs. O'Flaherty. She has orders from us, and from her putative spouse, to take the greatest care of you both, and we have endeavoured to arrange that you shall want for nothing during what we fervently hope will be but a brief absence."

"For what are you leaving us?" asked Mrs. Meredith.

"In truth, 't is a sorry business," growled Mobray. "Confirmation came last night of Burgoyne's capitulation, and this means that General Gates's army will at once effect a juncture with Washington's, and the combined force will give us more than we bargained to fight. Burgoyne's fiasco makes it all the more necessary that we hold Philadelphia, and so, as our one chance, we must, ere the union is effected, capture the forts on the Delaware, that our warships and supplies may come to us, lest, when the moment arrives for our desperate struggle, we be handicapped by short commons and no line of retreat."

"Wilt pray for our success, Miss Meredith?"

"Ay," urged the baronet, "for whatever your sympathies, remember that we fight this time to reunite you with your father."

And that night Janice made her first plea in behalf of the British arms.

The absence of Mobray and André brought the commissary once again to the fore. Previous to their departure he had dropped in upon the Merediths, only to receive a cool greeting from Janice, and such cold ones from the two captains as discouraged repetition. Now, relieved of their supercilious taunts and affronts, the baron became a daily visitor. He always brought gifts of delicacies, paid open court to Mrs. Meredith, and never once recurred to the words he had wrung from Janice, for the time making himself both useful and entertaining. From his calls the ladies learned the course of the war and of what the distant cannonading meant: of the bloody repulse of Donop's Hessians at Red Bank, of the burning of the Augusta 64, of the bombardment of the forts on Mud Island, and of the other desperate fighting by which the British struggled to free their jugular vein, the river, from the clutch of Washington's forces.

It was Clowes who brought them the best proof of the final triumph of the royal army, for one November morning he broke in upon their breakfast, unannounced, and with him came Mr. Meredith.

Had the squire ever doubted the affection of his wife and daughter, the next few minutes of inarticulate but ecstatic delight would have convinced him once for all. Mrs. Meredith, who, since her fever, had been unwontedly gentle and affectionate, welcomed him as he had not been greeted in years; and Janice, shifting from tears to laughter and back again, wellnigh choked him in her delight. Breakfast was forgotten, while the exile was made to tell all his adventures, and of how finally he had escaped from the ship on which perforce he had been for three months.

"'T was desperate fighting on both sides, but we were too many for them, and the river is free at last. The transport 'Surrey' was third to come up to the city, and the moment I was ashore I sought out Lord Clowes, hoping to get word of ye, and was not disappointed. Pox me! but I'd begun to think that never again should I see ye!"

There was so much to tell and to listen to in the next few days that the reunited family gave little heed to public events, though warm salutations and thanks were lavished on Mobray and André upon the return of the regiments which had operated against the forts.

An enforced change speedily brought them back to the present. The mustering of all the royal army, now swelled by reinforcements of three thousand troops hurriedly summoned from New York, compelled a rebilleting of the troops, and nine more officers were assigned by the quartermaster-general to the Franklin house, overcrowding it to such an extent as to end the possibility that it should longer shelter the Merediths. The squire went to Sir William Erskine, only to be told that as he was a civilian, the Quartermaster's Department could, or at least would, do nothing for him. An appeal to Clowes resulted better, for that officer offered to share his own lodgings with his friends, — a generosity which delighted Mr. Meredith, but which put an anxious look on his daughter's face and a scowl on that of Mobray.

"I make no doubt 't was a well-hatched scheme from the start," he asserted. "Lord Clowes and Erskine are but Tom Tickle and Tom Scratch."

With the same thought in her own mind, Janice took the first opportunity to beg her father to seek further rather than accept the commissary's hospitality.

"Nay, lass," replied Mr. Meredith. "Beggars cannot be choosers, and that is what we are. Remember that I am without money, and have been so ever since those rascals hounded me from home. Had not Lord Clowes generously stepped forward as he has, we should be put to it to get through the winter without being frozen or starved. And your mother's health is not such as could stand either, that ye know."

"You are quite right, dadda," assented the girl, as she stooped and kissed him. "I — I had a reason — which now I will not trouble you with — and selfishly forgot both mommy and our poverty." Then flinging her arms about his neck, she hid her head against his shoulder and said: "I am promised — you have given Philemon your word, and you'll not go back on it, will you, dadda?" almost as if she were making a prayer.

"Odds my life! what scatter-brains women are born with!" marvelled Mr. Meredith. "No wonder the adage runs that 'a woman's mind and a winter's wind oft change'! In the name of evil, Jan, what started ye off on that tangent?"

"You will keep faith with him, dadda?" pleaded the daughter.

"Of course I will," affirmed the squire. "And glad I am, lass, to find that ye 've come to see that I knew not merely what was best for ye, but what would make ye happiest. If the poor lad is ever exchanged, 't will be glad news for him."

The removal to the commissary's quarters might have been for a time postponed, for barely had the new arrangement been achieved when another manœuvre well-nigh emptied the city of the British troops. Massing fourteen thousand soldiers, Howe sallied forth to attack the Continental army in its camp at Whitemarsh.

"We have word," Lord Clowes explained, "that Gates is playing his own game, and, instead of bringing his army to Mr. Washington's aid, he keeps tight hold of it, and has, after needless delay, sent him but a bare four thousand men. So, in place of waiting for an attack, Sir William intends to drive the rebels back into the hills, that we may obtain fresh provisions and forage as we need them."

The movement proved but a march up a hill to march down again, and four days later saw the British troops back in Philadelphia with only a little skirmishing and some badly frosted toes and ears to show for the sally, the young officers tingling and raging with shame at not having been allowed to fight the inferior Continental army.

The commissary, however, took it philosophically. "Their position was too strong, and they shoot too straight," he told his guests. "It will all turn for the best, since no army can keep the field in such weather, and Washington will be forced to go into winter quarters. He must then fall back on Lancaster and Reading, out of striking distance, leaving us free to forage on the country at will."

Once again his prediction was wrong. "That marplot of a rebel general has schemed a new method of troubling us," he grumbled angrily a week later. "Instead of wintering his troops in a town, as any other commander would, our spies bring us word that he has marched them to a strong position on Valley Creek, a bare twenty miles from here, and has them all as busy as beavers throwing up earthworks and building huts. If God does n't kindly freeze the devil's brood, they 'll tie us into our lines just as they did last winter, and give us an ounce of lead for every pound of forage we seek. No sooner do we beat them, and take possession of a town, than they close in and put us in a state of siege, just as if they were the superior force. Small wonder that Sir William has written the Ministry that America can't be conquered, and asking his Majesty's permission to resign. A curse on the man who conceived such a mode of warfare!"

XLI

WINTER QUARTERS

NO sooner had the British returned from their brief sally than they settled into winter quarters, and gave themselves up to such amusements as the city afforded or they could create.

The commissary had taken good heed to have one of the finest of the deserted Whig houses in the city assigned to him, and whatever it had once lacked had been supplied. A coach, a chair, and four saddle-horses were at his beck and call; a dozen servants, some military and some slave, performed the household and stable work; a larder and a cellar, filled to repletion, satisfied every creature need, and their contents were served on plate and china of the richest.

"I' faith," explained the officer, when Mr. Meredith commented on the completeness and elegance of the establishment, "'t is something to be commissary-general in these times; and since the houses about Germantown were to be destroyed, 't was contrary to nature not to take from them what would serve to make me comfortable. Their owners, be they friends or foes, are none the poorer, for they think it all perished in the flames, as it would have done but for my forethought."

However lavish the hospitality of Lord Clowes could be under these circumstances, it was not popular with the army, and such officers as came to eat and drink at his table were more remarkable for their gastronomic abilities than for their wits and manners. In his civilian guests the quality was better, the man being so powerful through his office that the best of the townsfolk only too gladly gathered about his table when they were bidden, — an eagerness at which the commissary jeered even while he invited them.

"They are all to be bought," he sneered. "There is Tom Willing, who made the most part of his money importing

Guinea niggers, and now is in a mortal funk lest some of it, like them, shall run away. Two years ago he was a member of the rebel Congress and a partner of that desperate speculator Morris, with a hand thrust deep in the Continental treasury rag-bag. Now he has trimmed ship better than any of his slavers ever did, gone about on the opposite tack, and is so loyal to British rule that his greatest ambition is to get his other hand in some government contracts. He and his pretty wife will dine here every time they are asked, and so will all the rest, ye 'll see."

During the first days in their new domiciliary, Janice showed the utmost nervousness, seldom leaving her mother's or father's side, and never venturing into the hallways without a previous peep to see that they were empty. As the weeks wore on without any attempt on the commissary's part to surprise her into a *tête-à-tête*, to recur to the words he had forced her to utter, or to be anything but a polite, entertaining, and thoughtful host, the girl gained courage, and little by little took life more equably. She would have been been less easy, though better able to understand his conduct, had she overheard or had repeated to her a conversation between Lord Clowes and her father on the day that they first took up their new abode.

"A beggar's thanks are lean ones, Clowes," the squire had said, over the wine; "but if ever the dice cease from throwing me blanks, ye shall find that Lambert Meredith has not forgot your loans of home and money."

"Talk not to me in such strain, Meredith," replied the host, with the frank, hearty manner he could so well command. "I ask no better payment than your company, but 'tis in your power to shift the debt onto my shoulders at any time, and by a single word at that."

"How so?"

"It has scarce slipped thy memory that in a moment's mistrust of thee — which I now concede was both unfriendly and unjustifiable — I sought to run off with thy beautiful maid. She was ready to marry me out of hand; but give thy consent as well, and I shall be thy debtor for life."

"Ye know — " began Mr. Meredith.

"And what is more," went on the suitor, "though 't is not for me to make boast, I can assure ye that Lord Clowes is no bad match. In the last two years I 've salted down nigh sixty thousand pounds in the funds and bank stock."

"Adzooks!" aspirated the squire. "How did ye that?"

"Hah, hah!" laughed the commissary, triumphantly. "That is what it is to play the cards aright. 'T was all from being carried on that cursed silly voyage to the Madeiras which at that moment I deemed the work of the Evil One himself. I could get but a passage to Halifax, and by luck I arrived there just as Sir William put in with the fleet from Boston. We had done a stroke or two of business in former times, and so I was able to gain his ear, and unfold a big scheme to him."

"And what was that?"

"Hah! a great scheme," reiterated Clowes, smacking his lips, after a long swallow of spirits. "Says I, make me commissary-general, and I'll make our fortunes. We'll impress food and forage, and the government shall pay us for every pound of—"

"'T was madness," broke in Mr. Meredith. "Dost not know that nothing has so stirred the people as the taking their crops without payment?"

"Like as not," assented the commissary; "but 't is also the way to subdue them. They began a war, and they must pay the usual penalty until they are sickened of it. And since the seizures were to be made, 't was too good a chance not to turn an honest penny. Pray Heaven they don't lay down their arms too soon, for I ambition to be wealthier still. Canst hope better for your daughter than that she be made Lady Clowes, and rich to boot?"

"She 's promised —" began the squire, but once again the suitor cut him off.

"She herself told me she is pledged to no one but me."

"Nay, I 've passed my word to Leftenant Hennion."

"Chut! A subaltern who'll bless his stars if he ever is allowed to starve on a captain's pay. Thou canst not really mean to do thy daughter such an injury?"

"My word is passed; and Lambert Meredith breaks not

that. The lad 's a good boy, too, who 'll make her a good husband, with a fine estate, if peace ever comes again in the land."

The officer thrummed a moment on the table. "Then 't is only thy word to this fellow, and no want of friendliness that leads thee to give me nay?" he asked.

"Of that ye may be sure," assented Mr. Meredith, eagerly availing himself of the easy escape from the quandary that his host made for him.

"And but for the promise ye 'd give her to me?"

The father hesitated and swallowed before he made reply, and when the words came, it was with an observable reluctance that he said: "Ye should know that."

"That is all I ask," cried the commissary. "I knew ye were not the man to eat another's bread and not do what ye could for him. We 'll not hope for harm to the lad, but if the camp fever or small-pox or aught else should come to him, I 'll remind ye of the promise ye 've just spoken, sure that the man who won't break his word to one won't to t' other."

"That ye may tie to," acceded Mr. Meredith, though with a dubious manner, as if something perplexed him. And in his own room that evening he paused for a moment after removing his wig and remarked to himself: "Promise I suppose I did, though I ne'er intended it. Well, let 's hope that Phil gets her; and if some miscarriage prevents, 't is something that she should be made great and rich, though I wish the money had come in some more honest way to a more honest man."

As for the commissary, once retired to his own room, he wrote a letter which he superscribed "To David Sproat, Deputy Commissary of Prisoners at New York." But this done, he tore it up, and tossed the fragments into the fire, with the remark: "Why should I put my name to it, when Loring or Cunningham can give the order just as well? I 'll see one or t' other to-morrow, and so prevent all chance of its being traced to me." Then he sat looking for a time at the embers reflectively. "'T is folly to want her," he said finally, as he rose and began the removal of his coat, "now that ye need not her money; but she 's enough to tempt any man with blood in his veins, and I can afford the whim. Keep that blood in check, however, till ye have her fast; and do not frighten her as ye have done. To think of Lord Clowes, cool enough to match any man, losing his head over a whiffling bit of woman-flesh! What devil's baits they are!"

Put at ease by the commissary's conduct toward her, Janice entered eagerly into the gaiety with which the army beguiled the tedium of winter quarters. Dislike of Clowes precluded André and Mobray from coming to the house, but they saw much of the maiden elsewhere. She and Peggy Chew had been made known to each other by André early in the British occupation, and they promptly established the warm friendship that girls of their age so easily form, and spent many hours together. The two captains were quick to discover that the Chew house was a pleasant one, and became almost as constant visitors there as Janice herself. At André's suggestion the painting lessons were resumed, with Miss Chew as an additional pupil, and he undertook to teach them French as well; the music, too, was revived for Mobray's benefit, though now more often as a trio or quartette; and many other pleasures were shared in common. Both young officers were deeply concerned in the series of plays for which the theatre was being made ready; and the girls not merely heard them rehearse their respective parts, but with scissors and needles helped to make costumes for the amateur actors.

"Oh!" sighed Janice one day, after hearing Mobray through his lines in "The Deuce is in Him," "I'd give a finger but to see it played."

"See it!" exclaimed the baronet. "Of course you'll see it."

"They say there's a great demand for places," demurred Peggy.

"Have no fear as to that," said André. "Do you think I've risked my neck painting the curtain and scenery, and worked myself thin over it generally, not to get what I deserve in return. My name was next down after Sir William's for a box, and in it such beauty shall be exhibited that 't is likely we poor Thespians will get not so much as a look from the exquisites of the pit."

"Lack-a-day!" grieved Janice, "mommy will never hear of my going to see a play. I 've not so much as dared to tell her that I 'm helping you."

"Devil seize me, but you shall attend, if it takes a provost guard to do it," predicted Mobray.

Neither the protests nor prayers of the baronet, however, served to gain Mrs. Meredith's consent that her daughter should enter what she called "The Devil's Pit," but what he could not bring to pass the commissary did.

"I have bespoke a box for the first performance at the theatre," Lord Clowes announced at dinner one evening, "and bid ye all as my guests."

"'T is a sinful place, to which I will never lend my countenance," said Mrs. Meredith, with such promptness as to suggest a forestalling of her husband and daughter.

The commissary bowed his head in apparent acquiescence, but when he and the squire were left to their wine he recurred to the matter.

"I look to ye, Meredith," he said, "to overcome your wife's absurd whimsey."

"'T is useless to argue with Matilda when her mind 's made up," answered the husband, dejectedly. "That I have learned time and again."

"And so 't is with all women, if a man 's so foolish as to argue. Didst ever hear of ignorance paying heed to reason? There 's but one way to deal with the sex: 'Do this, do that; ye shall, ye sha'n't,' is all the vocabulary a man needs to make matrimony agreeable. Put your foot down, and, mark me, she 'll come to heel like a spaniel. But go ye must, for Sir William makes it a positive point that all of prominence attend the theatre and assembly, that the public may learn that the gentry are with us."

"They brought no clothes for such occasions," objected the squire, falling back on a new line of defence.

"Take fifty pounds more from me; 't will be money well spent."

"I like not to increase my borrowings, and especially for female fallals and furbelows."

"Nonsense, man; don't shy at a few hundred pounds. Ye

know one year of order and rents will pay all ye owe me twice over. Ye must not displeasure Sir William for such a sum."

So it came to pass that the squire, when they rejoined the ladies, emboldened by his wine, promptly let fall the observation that he had decided they were all to go to the theatre.

"Thou heardst me say that I am principled against it," dissented Mrs. Meredith.

"Tush, Matilda! I gave in to your Presbyterian swaddling clothes and lacing-strings at Greenwood, but now ye must do as I say. So get ye to a mercer's to-morrow, and set to on proper clothes."

"Dost wish to see thy wife and daughter damned, Lambert?"

"Ay, if that 's to be my fate, and so should ye. Go I shall to the theatre, and so shall Janice. If ye prefer salvation to our company, stay at home."

"Oh, mommy, please, please go," eagerly implored Janice. "Captain André assures me that 't is not in the least evil."

With tears in her eyes, Mrs. Meredith rose. "'T is not right; but if sin thou must, I too will eat of the fruit, rather than be parted from thee." She kissed both Mr. Meredith and Janice with an almost savage tenderness, and passed hurriedly from the room, leaving a very astounded husband and a very delighted daughter.

The girl's delight was not lessened the next day when they went a-shopping, and with the purchases a sudden end was put to her help of the theatricals, and even, temporarily, to the French and painting lessons. If ever maid was grateful for the weary hours of training in fine sewing and embroidery, Janice was, as she toiled, with cheeks made hectic by excitement, over the frock in which her waking thoughts were centred. When finally the day came for the trying on, and it fulfilled her highest expectation, her ecstasy, unable to contain itself, was forced to find expression, and she poured the rapture out in a letter to Tabitha, though knowing full well that only by the luckiest chance could it ever be sent.

"Only to think of it, Tibbie!" she wrote. "We are to have plays given by the officers, and weekly dancing assemblies, and

darling dadda says I am to go to both; and all my gowns being monstrous nugging and frumpish, he told mommy to see that I had a new one, though where the money came from (for though I did every stitch myself, it cost a pretty penny — no less than seventeen pounds and eight shillings, Tibbie!) I have puzzled not a little to fancy. I fear me I cannot describe it justly to you, but I will do my endeavour. 'Tis a black velvet, with pink satin sleeves and stomacher, and a pink satin petticoat, over which is a fall of white crape; the sides open in front, spotted all over with gray embroidery, and the edge of the coat and skirt trimmed with gray fur. Oh, Tibbie, 't is the most elegant and dashy robing that ever was! Pray Heaven I don't dirt it, for it is to serve for the whole winter! Peggy has three new frocks, and Margaret Shippen four, but mine is the prettiest, and by tight lacing (though no tighter than theirs) I make my waist an ell smaller than either. In addition, I have a nabob of gray tabby silk trimmed with the same fur, which has such a sweet and modish air that I could cry at having to remove it but for what it would conceal. I intend to ask Peggy if 't would be citified and à la mode *to keep it on for a little while after entering the box by the plea that the playhouse is cold. The high mode now is to dress the hair enormous tall — a good eight inches, Tibbie — over a steel frame, powdered mighty white, and to stick a mouchet or two on the face. It seems to me I cannot wait for the night, yet my teeth rattle and my hands tremble and I am all in a shake whenever I think of it; if I can but keep from being mute as a stock-fish, and gawkish, for I am all alive with fear that I shall be both, and shame us all! Peggy has taught me the minuet glide and curtsey and languish, and I am to step it at the first Assembly with Captain André, — such a pretty, engaging fellow, Tibbie, who will never swing for want of tongue; and Lord Rawdon has bespoke my hand for the quadrille, — a stern, frowning man, who frights me greatly, but 't is a monstrous distinction I need scarce say to be asked by one who will some day be an earl, Tibbie — and I dance the Sir Roger de Coverley with Sir Frederick Mobray, who is delightsome, too, by his rallying, performs most entrancingly on the flute, and is one of the best bowlers in the weekly cricket matches, but who is said to play very deep at Pharaoh in the club the officers have established, and to keep a great number of fighting cocks on which he wagers vast sums — if rumour speaks true, as high as a hundred guineas on a single main, Tibbie — at the cock-pit they have set up. A great crowd assembled yesterday to see him and Major Tarleton ride their chargers from Sixth Street to the river on a bet, and he lost because a little girl toddled out from the sidewalk and he pulled up, while the major, who is a wonderful horseman, spurred and leaped over her. But he was blamed for taking the risk, for his horse might not have risen, so Colonel Harcourt told Nancy Bond. 'T was Major Tarleton, I daresay you recollect, who was at our house when General Lee was captivated, and P. Hennion then told me he was considered the most reckless and dare-devil officer in the cavalry, but a cruel man. 'Mr. Lee,' as they all term him, here, — for they will not give the Whigs any titles, — has just been brought to Philadelphia and is at large on parole, pending an exchange, which has been delayed because 't is feared by the British that any convention may be taken as a recognition of the rebels, and be so considered by France and Spain.*

"So much has happened," the letter-writer continued a week later, "I scarce know where to begin, Tibbie, nor how to convey to you the wondrous occurrences. Oh, Tibbie, Tibbie, plays are the most amazing and marvellous things in the world! Not a one of the officers could I recognise, so changed they were, and they did us females to the life. 'T was so enchanting that at times I found myself gasping through very forgetfulness to breathe, and I was dreadfully rallied and quizzed because I burst into tears when the poor minor seemed to have lost both his love and his property. But how can I touch off my feelings, when, in the fourth act, the villain was detected, and all ended as it should! And, oh! Tibbie, mommy enjoyed it nearly as much as I, though the farce at the end vastly shocked her — and, indeed, Tibbie, 't was most indelicate, and made me blush a scarlet, and all the more that Sir William whispered that he enjoyed the broad parts through my cheeks — and she says if dadda insists, we'll go again, though not to stay to the farce. We had to sit in Lord Clowes' box — which sadly affronted Captain André — and Sir William, who has hitherto kept himself much se-

cluded, made his first appearance in public, and, as you will have inferred, visited our box during a part of the performance, drawing all eyes upon us, which agitated me greatly. Dadda told him I was learning to sketch, and nothing would do but I must give him an example, so on the back of the play-bill I made a caricature of General Lee, which was extravagantly praised, and was passed from hand to hand all over the house, and excited a titter wherever it went, for the general was in attendance; but judge of my feelings, Tibbie, when an officer passed it to Lee himself! He fell into a mighty rage, and demanded aloud to know who had thus insulted him, and but for Lord Clowes and Sir William preventing me, I'd have fled from the place, I was in such a panic. Pray Heaven he never learn! I dare not repeat to thee half the civil things which were said of this 'sweet creature,' as they styled me, for fear thou'lt think me vain. 'As thee is, I doubt not,' I hear thee say. Saucy Tibbie Drinker!"

At the very time that this account was being penned, some twenty miles away, a man was also writing, and a paragraph in his letter read: —

"*Our going into winter quarters, instead of keeping the field, can have been reprobated only by those gentlemen who think soldiers are made of stocks and stones and equally insensible to frost and snow; and, moreover, who conceived it easily practicable for an inferior army, under the disadvantages we are known to labour under, to confine a superior one, in all respects well appointed and provided for a winter's campaign, within the city of Philadelphia, and to cover from depredation and waste the States of Pennsylvania and Jersey. But what makes this matter still more extraordinary in my eye is that those very gentlemen — who well know that the path of this army from Whitemarsh to Valley Forge might have been tracked by the blood of footprints, and that not a boot or shoe had since been issued by the commissaries: who are well apprised of the nakedness of the troops from ocular demonstration; whom I myself informed of the fact that some brigades had been four days without meat, and were unsupplied with the very straw to save them from sleeping on the bare earth floors of the huts, so that one-third of this army should be in hospitals, if hospitals there were, and that even the common soldiers had been forced to come to my quarters to make known their wants and suffering — should think a winter's campaign and the covering of these States from the invasion of an enemy so easy and practical a business. I can assure those gentlemen that it is a much easier and less distressing thing to draw remonstrances in a comfortable room by a good fireside than to keep a cold, bleak hill and sleep under frost and snow without clothes or blankets. However, although they seem to have little feeling for the naked and distressed soldiers, I feel superabundantly for them, and from my soul I pity those miseries which it is neither in my power to relieve nor prevent.*

"It is for these reasons that I dwelt upon the subject to Congress; and it adds not a little to my other difficulties and distress to find that much more is expected of me than it is possible to perform, the more that upon the ground of safety and policy I am obliged to conceal the true state of this army from public view, and thereby expose myself to detraction and calumny."

The letter completed, the man took up the tallow dip, and passed from the cramped, chilly room in which he had sat to a still more cold and contracted hallway. Tiptoeing up a stairway, he paused a moment to listen at a door, then entered.

"I heard your voice, Brereton, so knew you were waking. Well, Billy, how does the patient?"

"Pohly, massa, pohly. De doctor say de ku'nel 'ud do fus-class ef he only would n't wherrit so, but he do nothin' but toss an' act rambunctious, an' dat keep de wound fretted an' him feverish."

"And fret I will," came a voice from the bed, "till I 've done with this feather-bed coddling and am allowed to take my share of the work and privation."

"Nay, my boy," said Washington, coming to the bedside and laying his hand kindly on Jack's shoulder; "there is naught to be done, and you are well out of it. Give the wound its chance to heal."

Brereton gave a flounce. "Do, in the name of mercy, Billy,

get me a glass of water," he begged querulously. Then, after the black had departed, he asked: "What has Congress done?"

"They have voted Gates president of the Board of War, with almost plenary powers."

"A fit reward for his holding back until too late the troops that would have put us, and not the British, in Philadelphia this winter. You won't let their ill-treatment force you into a resignation, sir?"

"I have put my hand to the plough and shall ne'er turn back. If I leave the cause, it will be by their act and not mine."

"Congress may hamper and slight you, sir, but will not dare to supersede you, for very fear of their own constituents. The people trust you, if the politicians don't."

"Set your mind on more quieting things, Brereton," advised Washington, taking the young fellow's hand affectionately. "May you have a restful night."

"One favour before you go, your Excellency," exclaimed Jack, as the general turned. "I — Could n't — Does McLane still get his spies into the city?"

"Almost daily."

"Could he — Wilt ask him — to — to make inquiry — if possible — of one — concerning Miss Janice Meredith, and let me know how she fares?"

The general pressed the aide's hand, and was opening his lips, when a figure, covered by a *négligée* night-gown of green silk, appeared at the door.

"I 've heard thee exciting John for the last half-hour, Mr. Washington," she said upbraidingly. "I am amazed at thy thoughtlessness."

"Nay, Patsy, I but stopped in to ask how he did and to bid him a good-night," replied Washington, gently.

"A half-hour," reiterated Mrs. Washington, sternly, "and now you still tarry."

"Only because you block the doorway, my dear," said the husband, equably. "If I delayed at all, 't was because Brereton wished to set in train an inquiry concerning his sweetheart."

"His what?" exclaimed the dame. "Let me pass in, Mr. Washington. John must tell me all about her this moment."

"You said he should sleep, Patsy," replied the general, smiling. "Come to our room, my dear, and I'll tell you somewhat of her."

But however much may have been told in the privacy of the connubial chamber, one fact was not stated: That far back in the bottom drawer of the bureau in which Janice kept her clothes lay a half-finished silk purse, to which not a stitch had been added since the day that the muttering of the guns of Brandywine had sounded through the streets of Philadelphia.

XLII

BARTER AND SALE

THE first check to Janice's full enjoyment of the novel and delightful world into which she had plunged so eagerly came early in March.

"I have ill news for thee, my child," Mr. Meredith apprised her, as he entered the room where she was sitting. "I just parted from Mr. Loring, the Commissary of Prisoners, and he asked if Philemon Hennion were not a friend of ours, and then told me that the deputy-commissary at Morristown writ him last week that the lad had died of the putrid fever."

"I am very sorry," the girl said, with a genuine regret in her voice. "He — I wish — I can't but feel that 't is something for which I am to blame."

"Nay, don't lay reproach on yeself, Jan," advised the father, little recking of what was in his daughter's mind. "If we go to blaming ourselves for the results of well-considered conduct, there is no end to sorrow. But I fear me his death will bring us a fresh difficulty. We 'll say nothing of the news to Lord Clowes, and trust that he hear not of it; for once known, he 'll probably begin teasing us to let him wed ye."

"Dadda!" cried Janice, "you never would — would give him encouragement? Oh, no, you — you love me too much."

"Ye know I love ye, Jan, and that whatever I do, I try to do my best for ye. But —"

"Then don't give him any hope. Oh, dadda, if you knew how I —"

"He 's not the man I 'd pick for ye, Jan, that I grant. Clowes is —"

"He beguiled me shamefully — and he broke his parole — and he takes mean advantage whene'er he can — and he crawls half the time and bullies the rest — and when he 's polite he makes me shudder or grow cold — and when he 's — "

"Now, don't fly into a flounce or a ferment till ye 've listened to what I have to say, child. 'T is — "

"Oh, dadda, no! Don't — "

"Hark to me, Janice, and then ye shall have all the speech ye wish. By this time, lass, ye are old enough to know that life is not made up of doing what one wishes, but doing what one can or must. The future for us is far blacker than I have chosen to paint to ye. Many of the British officers themselves now concede that the subduing of the rebels will be a matter of years, and that ere it is accomplished, the English people may tire of it; and though I 'll ne'er believe that our good king will abandon to the rule and vengeance of the Whigs those who have remained loyal to him, yet the outlook for the moment is darkened by the probability that France will come to the assistance of the rebels. The Pennsylvania Assembly has before it an act of attainder and forfeiture which will drive from the colony all those who have held by the king, and take from them their lands; and as soon as the Jersey Assembly meets, it will no doubt do the same, and vote us into exile and poverty. Even if my having taken no active part should save me from this fate, the future is scarce bettered, for 't will take years for the country to recover from this war, and rents will remain unpaid. Nor is this the depth of our difficulties. Already I am a debtor to the tune of nigh four hundred pounds to Lord Clowes — "

"Dadda, no!" cried the girl. "Don't say it!"

"Ay. Where didst thou suppose the money came from on which I lived in New York and all of us here? Didst think thy gown came from heaven?"

"I 'd have died sooner than owe it to him," moaned Janice. "How could you let me go to the expense?"

"'T was not to be avoided, Jan. As Sir William's wish was that we should lend our countenance to the festivities, 't would not have done to displeasure him, and since I was to be debtor to Lord Clowes, another fifty pounds was not worth balking at. More still I 'll have to ask from him, I fear, ere we are safe out of this wretched coil."

"Oh, prithee, dadda," implored the girl, "do not take another shilling. I 'll work my fingers to the bone — do anything — rather than be indebted to him!"

"'T is not to be helped, child. Think ye work is to be obtained at such a time, with hundreds in the city out of employment and at the point of starvation? Thank your stars, rather, that we have a friend who not merely gives us a shelter and food, but advances us cash enough to make us easy. Dost think I have not tried for employment myself? I 've been to merchant after merchant to beg even smouting work, and done the same to the quartermaster's and commissary's departments, but nothing wage-earning is to be had."

"'T is horrible!" despairingly wailed Janice.

"That it might be blacker can at least be said, and that is why I wish thee not to let thy feelings set too strongly against Lord Clowes. Here 's a peer of England, Jan, with wealth as well, eager to wed thee. He is not what I would have him, but it would be a load off my mind and off thy mother's to feel that thy future at least is made safe and —"

"I 'd die sooner than live such a future," cried the girl. "I could not live with him!"

"Yet ye ran off with this man."

"But then I did not know him as I know him now. You won't force me, will you, dadda?"

"That I 'll not; but act not impulsively, lass. Talk with thy mother, and view it from all sides. And meantime, we 'll hope he 'll not hear of the poor lad's death."

Left alone by her father to digest this advice, Janice lapsed into a despondent attitude, while remarking: "'T is horrible, and never could I bring myself to it. Starvation would be easier." She sat a little time pondering; then, getting her cloak, calash, and pattens, she set forth, the look of thought displaced by one of determination. A hurried walk of a few squares brought her to the Franklin house, where she asked for André.

"Miss Meredith," cried the captain, as he appeared at the door, "this is indeed an honour! But why tarry you outside?"

"I fear me, Captain André, that I am doing a monstrous

bold thing, and therefore will not enter, but beg of you instead that you walk with me a little distance, for I am in a real difficulty and would ask your help."

The officer caught up his hat and sword, and in a moment they were walking down Second Street. Several times Janice unsuccessfully sought to begin her tale, but André finally had to come to her assistance.

"You surely do not fear to trust me, Miss Meredith, and you cannot doubt the surety of assistance, if it be within my power?"

For a moment the girl's lips trembled; then she said, "Dost truly think the miniature frame I showed thee is worth as much as five hundred pounds?"

"I think 't is, beyond doubt."

"And dost thou think that thee couldst obtain four hundred pounds for it?"

"Of that I can scarce give assurance, for 't is a question whether a purchaser can be found for it. Yet I make small doubt, Miss Meredith," he added, "that if you will leave your portrait in it, one man there is in Philadelphia will gladly buy it at that price, though he run in debt to do it. If you desire to sell it, why do you not offer it to Mobray?"

The girl had coloured with André's first remark, and ere he had completed his speech, her cheeks were all aglow. "I — I could not offer it to him. Surely you can understand that 't would be impossible?" she stammered.

"I suppose I am dull-witted not to know it," said André, hurriedly, in evident desire to lessen her embarrassment. "However, 't was but a suggestion, and if you desire to sell, I will gladly undertake to negotiate it for you."

"Oh, will you?" cried the girl, eagerly. "'T will so greatly service me."

Without more ado, she held out her hand, which contained the miniature, and after a second outburst of thanks, quite unconscious of the fact that she was leaving him abruptly, she hurried away, not homeward, but in a direction which presently brought her to a house before which a sentry paced, where she stopped.

"Is Sir William within?" she asked of the uniformed

servant who answered her knock; and when told that he was, added: "Wilt say that Miss Meredith begs speech with him?"

The servant showed her into the parlour, then passed into the room back of it, and Janice heard the murmur of his words as he delivered her message.

"Miss Meredith," cried a woman's voice. "What does that puss want with you, Sir William?"

The bass of a masculine reply came to the visitor's ears, though pitched too low for her to distinguish words.

"I know better than to take any man's oath concerning that," retorted the feminine speaker; and on the last word the door was flung wider open, and a woman of full figure and of very pronounced beauty burst into the room where the girl sat, closely followed, if not in fact pursued, by the British commander-in-chief. "What do you want with Sir William?" she demanded.

Janice had risen, half in fright and half in courtesy; but the cry she uttered, even as the inquiry was put, was significant of something more than either.

"Well," went on the questioner, "art struck with a syncope that thou dost nothing but gape and stare at me?"

"I beg your pardon," faltered the girl. "I recognised — that is — I mean, 't was thy painting that — "

"Malapert!" shrieked the woman. "How dare you say I paint! Dost have the vanity to think thou 'rt the only one with a red and white skin?"

"Oh, indeed, madam," gasped Janice, "I alluded not to thy painting and powdering, but to the miniature that — "

"Sir William," screamed the dame, too furious even to heed the attempted explanation, "how can you stand there and hear this hussy thus insult me?"

"Then in Heaven's name get back to the room from which you should ne'er have come," muttered Howe, crossly.

"And leave you to the *tête-à-tête* you wish with this bold minx."

"Ay, leave me to learn why Miss Meredith honours me with this visit."

"You need not my absence, if that is all you wish to know. 'T would be highly wrong to leave a miss, however artful, unmatronised. Here I stay till I see cause to change my mind."

Sir William said something below his breath with a manner suggestive of an oath, shrugged his shoulders, and turned to Janice. "Old friends are not to be controlled, Miss Meredith," he said, "and since we are to have a third for our interview, let me make you known to each other. Mrs. Loring, Miss Meredith."

"I pray you, madam, to believe," entreated Janice, even as she made her curtsey, "that you entirely misinterpreted — "

"I care not what you meant," broke in Mrs. Loring, without the pretence of returning the obeisance. "Say your say to Sir William, and be gone."

"Damn you, Jane!" swore the general, bursting into a rage. "If you cannot behave yourself I will call in the servants and have you put from the room. Please be seated, Miss Meredith, and tell me in what manner I can serve you."

"I came, Sir William, to beg that you would give my father some position by which he could earn a living. We are totally without money, and getting daily deeper in debt."

"Your wish is a command," replied Sir William, gallantly, "but are you sure 't is best? Remember that the moment your father takes position from me he commits himself far more in the cause than he has hitherto, and the rebels are making it plain they intend to punish with the utmost severity all who take sides with us."

"But even that is better than — than — than living on charity," exclaimed Janice. "I assure you that anything is better — "

"Enough!" declared the general, as the girl hesitated. "Your father shall be gazetted one of the wardens of abandoned property at once. 'T will give him a salary and fees as well."

"Ah, Sir William, how can I ever thank you enough?" murmured the girl, feeling, indeed, as if an end had come to her troubles. She made a deep curtsey to Mrs. Loring, a second to the general, and then took the hand he offered her to the front door. "I beg, Sir William," she said at parting, "that you will assure Mrs. Loring that I really did not — "

The general interrupted her with a laugh. "A man with

an evil smell takes offence at every wrinkled nose," he asserted, "and you hit upon a subject on which my friend has perhaps cause to be sensitive."

Janice ran rather than walked the whole way home, and, not stopping when she reached the house to tell her father of her successful mission, or even to remove her cloak and calash, she tripped upstairs to her room, went straight to her bureau, and, pulling open the bottom drawer, took from it the unset miniature, and scrutinised it closely for a moment. "'T is she beyond question!" the girl ejaculated. "And I always thought of her as a young female, never suspecting it might have been some time painted. Why, she is a good ten years older than Colonel Brereton, or at least eight, let alone that she paints and powders! If that is the ill-mannered creature he gave his love to, I have little pity for him."

This decided, the maiden sought out her father and informed him of her mission and its successful result.

"Why, Jan," exclaimed her father, "thou 'rt indeed a wonderful lass to have schemed and carried it through. I 'd have spoken to Sir William myself, but he keeps himself so secluded that never a chance have I had to speak to him save in public. It is for the best, however, for I doubt not he paid more heed to thy young lips than ever he would to mine. Hadst thou told me, however, I would have gone with thee, for it must have been a tax on thy courage to have ventured alone."

"I did n't even let myself think of it," replied the daughter, "and, indeed, 't was so much easier than the thought of your further increasing your debt to Lord Clowes that 't was nothing." Then, after a slight pause, she asked: "Dadda, who is the Mrs. Loring I found at Sir William's?"

"Humph!" grunted the squire, with obvious annoyance. "'T is the wife of Joshua Loring, commissary of prisoners."

"Has she been long married to him?" asked Janice.

"That I know not; and the less ye concern yourself, Jan, with her, the better."

Despite this recommendation, Janice once again repeated her question, this time making it to André at the Assembly that evening.

"I know not," the captain told her, pursing up his lips and raising his eyebrows. Then he called to his opposite in the quadrille: "Cathcart, can you tell me how long Mrs. Loring has rejoiced in that title of honour?"

The earl laughed as if André had said something witty, and made reply: "Since ever I can remember, and that is a full five years."

When later the dancers adjourned to the supper-room, Lord Cathcart tossed a billet across the table to André, and he in turn passed it to Mobray, who was squiring Janice. The baronet held it so that she could see the message as well, and inscribed on the paper were the lines: —

"Your question don't think me a moment ignoring:
'How long has she *honoured* the surname of Loring?'
Wiseacre, first tell, how a man without *honour*
Could ever confer that fair jewel upon her?"

Sir Frederick, before handing it back, took Janice's pencil from her dancing-card, and scribbled on the back of the quip: —

"The answer is plain, for by means of her face,
The lady secured him an *honourable* place.
In return for the favour, by clergy and vow,
She made sure of her *honour*, but who knows when or Howe?"

And from that interchange of epigrams Janice asked no further questions relative to Mrs. Loring, unless it might be of herself.

XLIII

A CHOICE OF EVILS

AT this ball Janice was gladdened by word from André that he had effected the sale of the miniature, though he maintained absolute silence as to who the purchaser was, nor did she choose to inquire. The next morning brought a packet from him containing a rouleau of guineas, and so soon as they were counted, the girl hurried to the room on the ground floor which the commissary had taken as a half office, and, after an apology for the unannounced intrusion, said, —

"You have been good enough, Lord Clowes, to favour us with sundry loans, for which we can never be grateful enough, but 't is now in our power to repay them."

"Pay me!" cried the baron, incredulously.

"Yes," replied Janice, laying down the pile of gold on the desk. "Wilt tell me the exact amount?"

The guineas were too indisputable for Clowes to question the girl's ability to carry out her intention, but he demanded, "How came you by such a sum of gold?"

"'T is — That concerns thee not," replied the girl, with spirit.

"And does thy father know?"

"I ask you, Lord Clowes," Janice responded, "to tell me the amount we owe you."

For a moment the officer sat with a scowl on his face, then suddenly he threw it off, and with a hearty, friendly manner said: "Nay, Miss Meredith, think naught of it. You 're welcome ten times over to the money, and what more ye shall ever need." He rose as he spoke, and held out his hand toward the girl. "Generosity is not the monopoly of razorless youngsters of twenty."

Janice, ignoring the hand, said: "Once again, Lord Clowes, I ask you to inform me of the amount of our debt, which if you will not tell me, you will force me to leave all the money."

The angry frown returned to the commissary's face, and all the reply he made was to touch a bell. "Tell Mr. Meredith I would have word with him in my office," he said to the servant. Then he turned to Janice and remarked, "If ye insist on knowing the amount, 't is as well that your father give it to ye, since clearly ye trust me in nothing."

"Oh, Lord Clowes," begged Janice, "wilt thou not let me pay this without calling in dadda? I — I acted without first speaking to him, and I fear me — " There her words were cut short by the entrance of the squire.

"I sent for ye, man, to help us unsnarl a coil. Your daughter insists on repaying the money I have loaned ye, and I thought it best ye should be witness to the transaction." As he ended he pointed to the pile of coin.

"Odds bodikins!" exclaimed Mr. Meredith, as his eye followed the motion. "And where got ye such a sum, Jan?"

"Oh, dadda," faltered the girl, "'t is a long story, of which I promise to make you a full narration, once we are alone, though I fear me you will think that I have done wrong. But, meantime, will you not tell me how much you owe Lord Clowes, and let me pay him? Believe me, the money is honestly come by."

"No doubt, no doubt," said the commissary, with a rough laugh. "Young macaronis are oft known to give girls hundreds of pounds and get nothing in return."

All the reply Janice made was to go to the door. "Whenever you will come to the parlour, dadda, you shall know all, but I will not stay here to endure such speeches."

Without thought of the gold, Mr. Meredith was hurrying after his daughter, when Clowes interrupted him.

"The explanation is simple enough, Meredith," he said, "and I cannot but take it in bad part that your maid should borrow of Mobray in order to repay my loan to you."

"I cannot believe that that is the explanation, Clowes,"

protested Mr. Meredith. "But if it is, be assured that the money shall be returned him, and we will still stand your debtors." Then he sought his daughter, and she poured out to him the whole story of the miniature.

"Wrong I may have been, dadda, to have taken it to begin with, but Colonel Brereton refused to receive it from me, and when he himself placed it about my picture, I could not but feel that it had truly become mine, and that I could dispose of it."

"But who bought it of ye, Jan?" inquired the parent.

"That I know not," said the girl, though hesitating and colouring at the question in her own mind whether she were not prevaricating, for André's face and her own suspicions had really convinced her who was the nameless buyer. "Captain André assured me that the frame was fully worth five hundred pounds."

"That I will not gainsay, lass," replied the squire, "and the only blame I will lay on ye is that ye did not consult me before acting, for I could have negotiated it as well, and should have so managed as not to have offended Clowes. However, I make no doubt he'll not hold rancour when he knows that the money came by the sale of a piece of jewelry, and was not merely borrowed. Did ye take your picture from the frame?"

"No, dadda. I did so once before, only to bring suspicion on myself; so this time I let it remain."

"Ye might as well have removed it," said Mr. Meredith, "for it could have added no money value to it." Yet the squire had once been a lover, and should have known otherwise. This said, he returned to Clowes, and sought to mollify him by a statement of how the money had been obtained.

"Humph!" grunted the baron. "She'd better have brought the trinket to me, for I'd gladly have been the purchaser, for more even than she got by it."

"I told the lass she should have left the sale of it to me," answered the squire, "but ye know what women are."

"Egad, I sometimes think, shallow as the sex is, no man fully knows that. However, we will waste no further parley on the matter. Put the money in your purse, man, for your future needs, and think naught about the debt to me."

"Nay, Clowes. Since the money is here, 't is as well to pay up." And protest and argue as the commissary would, nothing would do the squire but to count out the amount on the spot from the heap of guineas, and to pocket, not without some satisfaction, the small surplus that remained. Then he left the room in great good cheer; but for some time after he was gone, the baron, leaving the gold piled on the table, paced the room in an evident fit of temper, while muttering to himself and occasionally shaking his head threateningly.

The gazetting of Mr. Meredith served only to increase this half-stifled anger, and on the very evening his appointment was announced in the "Pennsylvania Ledger," the commissary recurred to his proposal.

"I heard by chance to-day that young Hennion had fallen a victim to the camp fever," he told the squire, "and only held my tongue before the ladies through not wishing to be the reporter of bad tidings — though, as I understood it, neither Mrs. Meredith nor Miss Janice really wished the match."

The father took time over a swallow of Madeira, then said: "'T is a grievous end for the good lad."

"Ay, though I am not hypocrite enough to pretend that it affects me save for its freeing of your daughter, and so removing the one objection ye made to my taking her to wife."

Once more the squire gained a moment's breathing space over his wine before he replied: "Ye know, Clowes, that I'd willingly give ye the girl, but I find that she will have none of it, and 't is a matter on which I choose not to force her inclination."

"Well said; and I am the last man to wish an unwilling spouse," responded the aspirant. "But ye know women's ways enough not to be their dupes. In truth, having no stability of mind, the sex resemble a ship without a rudder, veering with every shift of the wind, and never sailing two days alike. But put a man at the helm, and they steer as straight a course as could be wished. Janice was hot to wed me once, and though she took affront later because she held me responsible for her punishment, yet she herself owned, but a few weeks ago, that she was still bound to me, which shows how little her moods mean. Having your consent secured, it will take me but a brief wooing to gain hers, that ye shall see."

"Well," rejoined Mr. Meredith, "she 's now old enough to know her own mind, and if ye can win her assent to your suit, mine shall not be lacking. But 't is for ye to do that."

"Spoken like a true friend, and here 's my hand on it," declared the commissary. "But there is one matter in which I wish ye to put an interfering finger, not so much to aid me as to save the maid from hazard. That fopling Mobray is buzzing about her and pilfering all the sweets that can be had short of matrimony — "

"Nay, Clowes, he 's no intriguer against my lass, that I am bound to say. 'T was only this morning, the moment he had news of Hennion's death, he came to me like a man, to ask permission to address her."

"Ho, he 's deeper bitten by her charms than I thought!" retorted the suitor. "Or, on second thought, more like 't is a last desperate leap to save himself from ruin. Let me warn ye that he has enough paper out to beggar him thrice over, and 't is only a question of time ere his creditors come down on him and force him to sell his commission; after which he must sink into beggary."

"I sorrow to hear it. He 's a likely lad, and has kindly stood us in stead more than once."

"And just because of his taking parts, he is likely to keep your girl's heart in a state of incertitude, for 't is only mortal for eighteen to fancy twenty more than forty-four. Therefore, unless ye want a gambling bankrupt for a son-in-law, give him his marching orders."

"I 'll not do that after his kindness to my wife and child; but I 'll take good care to warn Janice."

"Look that ye don't only make him the more interesting to her. Girls of her age think little of where the next meal is to come from, and dote on the young prodigal."

"Have no fear on that score," replied the father.

On the morning following this conversation Janice was stopped by the commissary as she was passing his office. "Will ye give me the honour of your presence within for a moment?" he requested. "I have something of import to say to ye."

With a little trepidation the girl entered, and took the seat he placed for her.

Taking a standing position at a respectful distance, Lord Clowes without circumlocution plunged at once into the object of the interview. "That I have long wished ye for my wife, Miss Meredith," he said with frank bluffness, "is scarce worth repeating. That in one or two instances I have given ye cause to blame or doubt me, I am full conscious; 't is not in man, I fear, to love such beauty, grace, and elegance, and keep his blood ever within bounds. 'T was this led me to suggest our elopement, and to my effort to bind ye to the troth. In both of these I erred, and now crave a pardon. Ye can scarce hold me guilty that my love made me hot for the quickest marriage I could compass, or that, believing ye in honour pledged to me, I should seek to assure myself of the plight from your own lips, ungenerous though it was at the moment. It has since been my endeavour to show that I regretted my impulsive persecution, and I trust that my long forbearance and self-effacement have proved to ye that your comfort and happiness are the first object of my heart."

"You have been very good to us all," answered Janice, "and I would that I were able to repay in full measure all we owe to you. But— "

"Ye can, and by one word," interjected the suitor.

"But, Lord Clowes," she continued, with a voice that trembled a little, "I cannot yield to thy wish. Censurable I know myself to be — and no one can upbraid me more than I upbraid myself — yet between the two wrongs I must choose, and 't is better for both of us that I break the implied promise, entered into at a moment when I was scarce myself, than to make a new one which I know to be false from the beginning, and impossible to fulfil."

"Of the old promise we will say naught, Miss Meredith," replied the baron. "If your sense of right and wrong absolve ye, Baron Clowes is not the man to insist upon it. But there is still a future that ye must not overlook. 'T will be years, if ever, ere ye once again enjoy your property, and though this appointment — which is like to prove dear-bought — for the moment enables ye to face the world, it is but a short-lived dependence. To ye I will confide what is as yet known to but a half-dozen: his Majesty has accepted Sir William's resignation, and he leaves us so soon as Sir Henry Clinton arrives. The new commander will have his own set of hungry hangers-on to provide with places, and your father's days will be numbered. In my own help I shall be as unstinting as in the past, but it is quite on the cards that I, too, lose my appointment, in which case I shall return to England. Would not a marriage with me make — "

"But I love you not," broke in Janice.

"Ye have fallen in love with that — "

"I love no one, Lord Clowes; and indeed begin to fear that I was born without a heart."

"Then your objection is that of a very young girl who knows nothing of the world. Miss Meredith, the women who marry for love are rare indeed, and but few of them fail of a bitter disappointment. I cannot hope that my arguments will convince ye of this, but counsel with your parents, and ye 'll find they bear me out. On the one side stands eventual penury and perhaps violence for ye all; on the other, marriage with a man who, whatever his faults, loves ye hotly, who will give ye a title and wealth, and who will see to it that your parents want for nothing. 'T is an alternative that few women would hesitate over, but I ask no answer now, and would rather that ye give none till ye have taken consideration upon it."

Janice rose. "I — I will talk with dadda and mommy," she said, "and learn their wishes." But even as she spoke the words a slight shiver unsteadied her voice.

XLIV

A CARTEL OF EXCHANGE

AFTER Janice left him the commissary-general mounted a horse, and, riding to the Franklin house, asked for Captain Mobray.

"I have called, sir," he announced, as the baronet entered the room, "on two matters —"

"Have they to do with the service, my Lord?" interrupted Mobray; "for otherwise I must decline —"

"First," the caller went on unheedingly, "a number of past-due bills of yours have come into my possession in exchange for special victuals or stores, and I wish to learn your intention concerning them."

"I — In truth — I —" haltingly began Sir Frederick, his face losing colour as he spoke. "I have had the devil's turn of luck of late, and — and I am not in a position to take them up at the moment. I trust that you'll give me time, and not press me too harshly."

With a smile that expressed irony qualified by enjoyment, the creditor replied: "'T is a pleasure to aid a man to whom I am indebted for so much courtesy."

Sir Frederick's ashen hue changed to a ruddy one, as he said: "Lord Clowes, 't is a bitter mouthful for a man to eat, but I ask your clemency till my luck changes, for change it must, since cards and dice cannot always run against one. I know I deserve it not at your hands, after what has passed —"

"Cease your stuttering, man," ordered the commissary. "Had I revenge in my heart I'd have sent the bailiff, not come myself. The bills shall wait your convenience, and all I ask for the lenience is that ye dine with me and do me one service. Ye did me a bad stroke with Miss Meredith; now

I ask ye to offset it by telling her what my vengeance has been."

Mobray hesitated. "Lord Clowes, I will do nothing to trick Miss Meredith, desperately placed as I am."

"Chut! Who talks of trickery? Ye told her the facts of my parole; therefore ye owe it to me, even though it may not serve your own suit, to tell her as well what is in my favour."

"And so help you to win her. I cannot do her that wrong, my Lord."

"Is it worse to tell her only the truth about me than to seek to persuade her into a marriage with a bankrupt?"

"You state it unsparingly."

"Not more so, I doubt not, than ye did the matter of my parole — which some day I shall be able to justify, and the gentlemen of the army will then sing a very altered tune — with this difference, that I say it to your face and ye did not."

With bowed head Sir Frederick answered: "You are right, my Lord, and I will say what I can in your favour to Miss Meredith."

"Spoke like an honest man. Fare ye well till next Wednesday, when I shall look for ye to a three-o'clock dinner."

Whatever pain and shame the words cost him, honourably the baronet fulfilled his promise by going to the commissary's quarters the following day and telling Janice the facts. The girl listened to his explanation with a face grave almost to sadness. "I — What you have told me, Sir Frederick," she said gently at the end, "is of much importance to me just at this time, and I thank you."

"I know, I know," groaned the young officer, miserably, "and 't is only part of my horrible run of luck that I should — that — ah — Take him, Miss Meredith, and end my torture."

"Can you advise me to marry Lord Clowes?"

"After his generosity to me, in honour I must say nothing against him, but 't is asking too much of human nature for me to aid his suit."

"I — oh, I know not what to do!" despairingly wailed the girl. "Mommy says 't is for me to decide, and dadda thinks

I cannot do better, and to the ear it seems indeed the only thing to do. Yet I shudder every time I think of it, and twice, when I have dreamed that I was his wife, I have waked the whole house with my screams to be saved from him."

"Miss Meredith," burst out the baronet, "give me the right to save you. You know I love you to desperation; that I would live to make you —"

"Ah, pray, Sir Frederick," begged Janice, "do not add to my pain and difficulty. What you wish —"

"I crave a pardon for my words. 'T was a moment's selfish forgetfulness of you and of my own position, that shall not occur again." Mobray stooped and kissed a loose end of the handkerchief the girl held, and hurried from the room.

As he was catching up his cloak and sabre in the hallway, the door of the office opened. "Come in here a moment, Sir Frederick," requested the commissary.

"I have done as I promised, and that is all I can do at the moment," almost sobbed the young fellow. "Nor will I dine here Wednesday, though you do your worst."

"Tush! Do as ye please as to that, but come in here now, for I have a thing to say that concerns Miss Meredith's happiness."

"And what is that?" demanded the baronet, as he entered.

"I see by the G. O. that ye are named one of the commissioners to arrange a cartel of exchange with the rebels at Germantown to-day."

"Would to God it were to arrange a battle in which I might fall!"

"'T is likely lists of prisoners will be shown, and should ye chance to see the name of Leftenant Hennion on any of those handed in by the rebels I recommend that ye do not advertise the fact when ye return to Philadelphia."

"But the fellow 's dead."

"Ye have been long enough in the service to know that some die whose names never get on any return, and so some are reported dead who decline to be buried. Let us not beat about the bush as to what I mean. We are each doing our best to obtain possession of this lovely creature, but the father holds to his promise to the long-legged noodle, and, if he is alive, our suits are hopeless. So let them continue to suppose him — "

"Mine is so already," groaned Mobray. "But if 't were not, I would not filch a woman's love by means of a deceit. Nor — "

"Fudge! Hear me through. The girl has always hated the match, which was one of her old fool of a father's conceiving, and will thank any one who saves her from the fellow. Let her say nay to us both, and it please her, but don't force her to a marriage of compulsion by needless blabbing."

"I will hold my peace, if that seems best for Miss Meredith; not otherwise, my Lord," answered Mobray, flinging from the room.

The baronet mounted his horse, and, stabbing his spurs into him, galloped madly down Market Street, and then up Second Street to where it forked into two country roads. Here the lines of British fortifications intersected it, and a picket of cavalry forced the rider to draw rein and show his pass. This done, he rode on, though at a more easy pace, and an hour later entered the village of Germantown. In front of the Roebuck Inn a guidon, from which depended a white flag, had been thrust into the ground, and grouped about the door of the tavern was a small party of Continental light horse. Trotting up to them, Mobray dismounted, and, after an inquiry and a request to one of them to take his horse, he entered the public room. To its one occupant, who was seated before the fire, he said: "The dragoons outside told me the reb — the Continental commissioners were here. Canst tell me where they are to be found, fellow?"

The person addressed rose from his seat, revealing clothes so soiled and tattered, and a pair of long boots of such shabby appearance, as to give him the semblance of some runaway prentice or bond-servant, but over his shoulder passed a green ribbon and sword sash which marked their wearer as a field officer; and as the baronet realised this he removed his hat and bowed.

"Since when did you take to calling your superior officers 'fellows,' Sir Frederick?" asked the other, laughing.

With a cry of recognition, Mobray sprang forward, his hand outstretched. "Charlie!" he exclaimed. "Heavens, man, we have made a joke in the army of the appearance of thy troops, but I never thought to see the exquisite of the Mall in clothes not fit for a tinker."

"My name, Fred, is John Brereton," corrected the officer, "which is a change for the better, I think you will own. As for my clothes, I 'll better them, too, if Congress ever gives us enough pay to do more than keep life in us. Owing to depreciation, a leftenant-colonel is allowed to starve at present on the equivalent of twenty-five dollars, specie, a month."

"And yet you go on serving such masters," burst out Mobray. "Come over to us, Charl — John. Sir William would give you — "

"Enough," interrupted Brereton, angrily. "For how long, Sir Frederick, have you deemed me capable of treachery?"

"'T is no treachery to leave this unnatural rebellion and take sides with our good king."

"Such talk is idle, and you should know it, Mobray. A word with you ere Grayson and Boudinot — who have gone to look at that marplot house of Cliveden which frustrated all our hopes four months since — return and interrupt us. I last saw you at the Merediths'; can you give me word of them?"

"Only ill ones, alas!" answered the captain. "Their necessities are such that I fear me they are on the point of giving their daughter to that unutterable scoundrel, Clowes."

Jack started as if he had been stung. "You cannot mean that, man! We sent you word he had broke his parole."

"Ay," replied the baronet, flushing. "And let me tell you, John, that scarce an officer failed to go to Sir William and beg him to send the cur back to you."

"And you mean that Mr. Meredith can seriously intend to give Miss Janice to such a creature?"

"I fear 't is as good as decided. You know the man, and how he gets his way, curse him!"

"I 'd do more than that, could I but get into Philadelphia," declared Jack, hotly. "By heavens, Fred — "

But here the entrance of other officers interrupted them,

and Colonel Brereton was set to introducing Boudinot and Grayson to the British officer.

Scarcely had they been made known to each other when Mobray's fellow-commissioners, Colonel O'Hara and Colonel Stevens, with a detail of dragoons, came trotting up; and so soon as credentials were exchanged the six sat down about a table in a private room to discuss the matter which had brought them together. One of the first acts of Mobray was to ask for a look at the Continental lists of prisoners; and after a hurried glance through them, he turned and said to Brereton in a low voice: "We had word in Philadelphia that Leftenant Hennion died of a fever."

"'T is a false rumour," replied Brereton. "If I could I 'd see that he failed of an exchange till the end of the war; and I would that one of our officers in your hands could be kept by you for an equal term."

"Who is that?" asked Mobray.

"That rascal, Charles Lee," muttered Brereton. "But, though he openly schemed against General Washington, and sought to supersede him, his Excellency is above resentment, and has instructed us to obtain his exchange among the first."

In the arrangement of details of the cartel Brereton showed himself curiously variable, at times sitting completely abstracted from what was being discussed, and then suddenly entering into the discussions, only to compel an entire going over of points already deemed settled, and raising difficulties which involved much waste of time.

"Confound it!" said O'Hara presently, after a glance at his watch. "At this rate we shall have to take a second day to it."

"Beyond question," assented Jack, with a suggestion of eagerness. "Gentlemen, I invite you to dinner, and there are good sleeping-rooms above."

"'T is out of the question," replied Stevens. "We officers give a masked ball in the city to-night, and I am one of the managers."

"Well, then," urged Brereton, "at least stay and dine with me at three, and you shall be free to leave by six. 'T is not much over an hour's ride to the city."

"That we 'll do with pleasure," assented O'Hara.

"Go on with the discussion, then, while I speak to the landlord," remarked Jack, rising and passing to the kitchen. "We wish a dinner for six," he informed the publican, "by three o'clock." Then in a low voice he continued: "And hark you! One thing I wish done that is peculiar. Give us such whiskey as we call for of thy best, with lemons and sugar, but in place of hot water in the kettle, see to it that as often as it is replenished, it be filled with thy newest and palest rum. Understand?"

"Jerusalem!" ejaculated mine host. "You gentlemen of the army must have swingeing strong heads to dilute whiskey with raw rum."

"I trust not," replied the aide, drily.

When dinner was announced Brereton drew Grayson aside for a moment and whispered: "'T is a matter of life and death to me that these fellows be made too drunk to ride, Will, yet to keep sober myself. You 've got the head and stomach of a ditcher; wilt make a sacrifice of yourself for my sake?"

"And but deem it sport," replied Grayson, with a laugh; and as he took his place at the table he remarked: "Gentlemen, we have tested British valour, we have tested British courtesy, and found them not wanting, but we understand that, though you turn not your backs to either our soldiery or our ladies, there is one thing which can make you tremble, and that is our good corn whiskey."

"Odds life!" cried O'Hara, "who has so libelled us? Man, we 'd start three glasses ahead of you, and then drink you under the table, on a challenge, but for this ball that we are due at."

"A pretty brag," scoffed Brereton, "since you have an excuse to avoid its test. But come, we have three good hours; but drink Grayson even in that time, and I will warrant you 'll not be able to sit your horses. Come, fill up your glasses from decanter and kettle, and I will give you a toast to begin, to which you must drink bumpers. Here 's to the soldier who fights and loves, and may he never lack for either."

Four hours later, when Brereton rose from the table, Stevens and O'Hara were lying on the floor, Boudinot was fallen forward, his head resting among the dishes on the table, fast asleep, and Mobray and Grayson, clasped in each other's arms, were reeling forth different ditties under the impression that they were singing the same song. Tiptoeing from the room, the aide went to the kitchen door and said to the publican, "Order one of the dragoons to make ready Captain Mobray's horse, as he wishes to ride back to Philadelphia." In the passageway he took from the hook the hat, cloak, and sword of the young officer, and, removing his own sash and sabre, donned the three. Stealing back to the scene of the revel, he found Mobray and Grayson now lying on the floor as well, unconscious, though still affectionately holding each other. Kneeling gently, he searched the pockets of the unconscious man until the passport was lighted upon. Thrusting it into his belt, he stole from the room.

"What are the orders for us, sir?" asked the dragoon who held Mobray's horse, as the aide mounted.

With an almost perfect imitation of the baronet's voice, Brereton answered, "Colonel O'Hara will issue directions later," and then as he cantered down the road he added gleefully: "Considerably later. What luck that it should be Fred, whose voice I know so well that I can do it to the life whenever I choose!" Then he laughed with a note of deviltry. "I am popping my head into a noose," he said; "but whether 't is that of hangman or matrimony, time only will show."

XLV

IN THE JAWS OF THE LION

THE ball had been in full progress for an hour when a masker, who from his entrance had stood leaning against the wall, suddenly left his isolated position and walked up to one of the ladies.

"Conceal your face and figure as you will, Miss Meredith, you cannot conceal your grace. Wilt honour me with this quadrille?"

"La, Sir Frederick! That you should know me, and I never dream it was you!" exclaimed the girl, as she gave her hand and let him lead her to where the figures were being formed. "There have been many guesses among the caps as to the identity of him who has held himself so aloof, but not a one suggested you. The disguise makes you look a good three inches taller."

As they took position a feminine domino came boldly across the room to them. "Is this the way you keep your word, Sir William?" she demanded in a low voice, made harsh and grating by the fury it expressed.

"You mistake me, madam," answered the dancer, "though I would such a rapid promotion were a possibility."

The interloper made a startled step backward. "I have watched you for a quarter hour," she exclaimed, as she turned away, "and would have sworn to your figure."

"'Tis wonderful," remarked Janice, "how deceiving a domino can be."

The dance ended, her partner said: "Miss Meredith, I have something to say to you of deepest consequence. Will you not come away from this crowd?"

"Ah, Sir Frederick," pleaded the girl, "do not recur to it again. Though you importune me for a day, I could but make the same reply."

"Sir Frederick passes his word that he will not tease you on that subject to-night; but speak I must concerning this match with Lord Clowes."

"'T is in vain, sir," replied Janice; "for every moment convinces me the more that I must wed him, and so you will but make my duty the harder."

"I beg you to give me a word apart, for I have a message to you from Colonel Brereton."

Janice's hand dropped from the officer's arm. "What is it?" she asked.

"'T is not to be given here," urged the man. "I pray you to let me order your equipage and take you away. Another dance will be beginning on the moment, and some one will claim you."

The girl raised her hand and once more placed it on her partner's arm; taking the motion as a consent to his wishes, the officer led her to the doorway.

"Call Miss Meredith's chair," he ordered of the guard grouped about the outer door, and in a moment was able to hand her into the vehicle.

"Where to?" he asked. "I mean — Home!" he cried, in a far louder voice, as if to drown the slip, at the same moment jumping in and taking his seat beside her.

As he did so, the girl shrank away from him toward her corner of the gig. "Who are you?" she cried in a frightened voice.

"Who should I be but John Brereton?"

"Are you mad," cried the girl, "to thus venture within the lines?"

"The news which brought me was enough to make me so," answered Jack. "You cannot know what you are doing that you so much as think of marrying that scum. For years he has been nothing but a spy and mackerel, willing to do the dirtiest work, and the scorn of every decent man in London, as here. Are you, are your father and mother, are your friends, all Bedlam-crazed that you even consider it?"

"'T is as horrible to me as it is to you," moaned Janice; "but it seems the only thing possible. Oh, Colonel Brereton, if you but knew our straits, — dependent for all we have, and with a future still more desperate, — you would not blame me for anything I am doing." The girl broke into sobs as she ended, and turning from him leaned her head against the leathern curtain, where she wept, regardless of the fact that the aide possessed himself of her hand, and tried to comfort her, until the chaise drew up at its destination. Lifting rather than helping her from the carriage, Jack supported the maiden up the steps and into the hallway; but no sooner were they there than she freed herself from his supporting arm and exclaimed, "You must not stay here. Any instant you might be discovered."

"Then take me to a room where we can be safe for a moment. I shall not leave you till I have said my say."

"Ah, please!" begged the girl. "Some one is like to enter even now."

Jack's only reply was to turn to the first door and throw it open. Finding that all was dark within, he caught Miss Meredith's fingers, and drew her in after him, saying, as he did so, "Here we are safe, and you can tell me truly of your difficulties."

With her hand held in both of the aide's, Janice began a disconnected outpouring of the tale of her difficulties intermixed by an occasional sob, caused quite as much by the officer's exclamations of sympathy as by the misery of her position. Before a half of it had been spoken one of the hands grasping hers loosened itself, and she was gently drawn by an encircling arm till her head could find support on his shoulder; not resenting and indeed, scarcely conscious of the clasp, she rested it there with a strange sense of comfort and security.

"Alas!" grieved Brereton, when all had been told, "I am as deep, if not deeper, in poverty than you, and so I can give you no aid in money. Bad as things are, however, there is better possible than selling yourself to that worm, if you will but take it."

"What?"

"The French have come to our aid at last, and are sending us a fleet. If Howe will but be as slow as usual, and the States but hasten their levies, we shall catch him between the fleet and army and Burgoyne him. Even if he act quickly, he can save himself only by abandoning Philadelphia and consolidating his forces at New York. They may then fight on, for both the strength and the weakness of the British is a natural stupidity which prevents them from knowing when they are beaten, but all doubt as to the outcome will be over. Once more it will be possible for you to dwell at Greenwood, if you will but — "

"But dadda says they will take it away and exile us," broke in Janice.

"I have no doubt the rag-tag politicians, if not too busy scheming how to cripple General Washington, will set to on some such piece of folly, for by their persecutions and acts of outlawry and escheatage they have driven into Toryism enough to almost offset the Whigs the British plundering has made. But from this you can be saved if you will but let me." As the officer ended, the clasp of his arm tightened, though it lost no element of the caress.

"How?"

"I stand well in the cause; and though I could not, I fear, save your property to you, they would never take it once it were in Whig hands, and so by a marriage to me you can secure it. Ah, Miss Meredith, you have said you do not love me, and I stand here to-night a beggar, save for the sword I wear; but I love you as never man loved woman before, and my life shall be given to tenderness and care for you. Surely your own home with me is better than exile with that cur! And I'll make you love me! I'll woo you till I win you, my sweet, if it take a life to do it." Raising the hand he held, the aide kissed it fondly. "I know I've given you reason to think me disrespectful and rough; I know I have the devil's own temper; but if I've caused you pain at moments, I've suffered tenfold in the recollection. Can you not forgive me?" Once again he eagerly caressed her hand; and finding that she offered no resistance to the endearments, Jack, with an inarticulate cry of delight, stooped and pressed his lips to her cheek.

On the instant Janice felt a hand laid on her shoulders, then on her head, as if some one were feeling of her.

"Who is this?" demanded Jack, lifting his head with a start.

The question was scarce uttered when the sound of a blow came to the girl's ears, and the arm which had been supporting her relaxed its hold, as the lover sank rather than fell to the floor. With loud screams the girl staggered backward, groping her way blindly in the dark. There came the sound of feet hurrying down the hallway, and the door was thrown open by one of the men servants, revealing, by the shaft of light which came through it, the figure of Jack stretched on the floor, with the commissary kneeling upon him, engaged in binding his wrists with a handkerchief.

"Out to the stables, and get me a guard!" ordered Lord Clowes. "I have a spy captured here. No; first light those candles from the lamp in the hall. I advise ye, Miss Meredith," he said scoffingly, "that next time ye arrange an assignation with a lover that ye take the precaution to assure yourself that the room is unoccupied."

"Oh, Lord Clowes," implored the girl, "won't you let him go for my sake?"

"That plea is the least likely of any to gain your wish," responded the baron, derisively.

"I will promise that I will never wed him, will never see him again," offered Janice.

"Of that I can give ye assurance," retorted the commissary, rising and picking up from where he had dropped it the horse pistol with which he had stunned the unconscious man. "A drum-head court-martial will sit not later than to-morrow morning, Miss Meredith, and there will be one less rebel in the world ere nightfall. Your promise is a fairly safe one to make. Here," he continued, as the soldiers came running into the room, "fetch a pail of water and douse it over this fellow, for I want to carry him before Sir William. Ye were wise not to remove your wraps, Miss Meredith, for I shall have to ask your company as well."

When the aide was sufficiently conscious to be able to stand, he was put between two of the soldiers, and ten minutes later the whole party reached the house of the commander-in-chief. Given entrance, without waiting to have their arrival announced, the commissary led the way through the parlour into the back room, where, about a supper table, the British commander, Mrs. Loring, and two officers were sitting.

"Ye must pardon this intrusion, Sir William," explained Lord Clowes, as Howe, in surprise, faced about, "but we have just caught a spy red-handed, and an important one at that, being none less than Colonel Brereton, an aide of Mr. Washington. Bring him forward, sergeant."

As Jack was led into the strong light, Mrs. Loring started to her feet with a scream, echoed by an exclamation of "By God!" from one of the officers, while the three or four glasses at Howe's place were noisily swept into a jumble by the impulsive swing of the general's arm as he threw himself backward and rested against the table.

"Charlie, Charlie!" cried Mrs. Loring. "You here?"

Standing rigidly erect, the aide said coldly, "My name is John Brereton; nor have I the honour of your acquaintance."

"What 's to do here?" ejaculated Lord Clowes. "I know the man to be what he says, and that he has come in disguise within our lines to spy."

Without looking at the commissary, Jack answered: "I wore no disguise when I passed through your lines, nor have I for a moment laid aside my uniform."

"Call ye those rags a uniform?" jeered the commissary.

Howe gave a hearty laugh. "Why, yes, baron," he answered. "Know you not the rebel colours by this time?"

"And how about the domino he wears over them, and the mask I hold in my hand?" contended Lord Clowes.

"I procured them this evening at the Franklin house in Second Street, as you will learn by sending some one to inquire, merely to attend the ball."

A second exclamation broke from Mrs. Loring: "Then 't was you I mistook for — Sir William, I thought 't was you from his figure."

Again the general laughed. "Ho, Loring," said he to one of the officers. "What say you to that?"

"Take and hang me, or send me to the pest hole you kill your prisoners in, but let me get away from here," raged Jack, white with passion, as he gave a futile wrench in an attempt to free his hands.

"Art so anxious to be hanged, boy?"

"'T is a fit end to a life begun as mine was!" answered the aide.

"Oh, Sir William," spoke up Janice, "he did not come to spy, but only to see me. You will not hang him for that, surely?"

"Yoicks! Must you snare, even into the hangman's noose, every one that looks but at you, Miss Janice? If the day ever comes when the innocent no longer swing for the guilty, 't is you will be hung."

"We lose time over this badinage, Sir William," complained the commissary, angrily. "The fellow is a spy without question."

"He is not," cried Mrs. Loring; "and he shall not even be a prisoner. You will not hold him, Sir William, when he came but to see the maid he loves?"

"Come, sir," said the general. "Wilt ask thy life of me?"

"No. And be damned to you!"

"You see, Jane."

"I care not what he says; you shall let him go free."

"Are ye all mad?" fumed the commissary.

"He ever had the art of getting the women on his side, Clowes," laughed Sir William, good-naturedly. "How the dear creatures love a man of fire! Look you, boy, with such a friend as Mrs. Loring — to say nothing of others — no limit can be set to your advancement, if you will but put foolish pride in your pocket, and throw in your lot with us."

"I 'd sooner starve with Washington than feast with you."

"That 's easily done!" remarked Loring, jeeringly.

"Not so easily as in your prisons," retorted Jack.

"Don't be foolish and stick to your tantrums, lad," persuaded Howe.

"Is a man foolish who elects to stick to the winning side? For you are beaten, Sir William, and none know it better than you."

"Damn thy tongue!" roared Howe, springing up.

"Don't blame him for it, William," cried Mrs. Loring. "How can he be other than a lad of spirit?"

Howe fell back into his seat. "There 't is again. Ah, gentlemen, the sex beat us in the end! Well, Jane, since thou 't commander-in-chief, please issue thy orders."

"Set him free at once."

"We can scarce do that, though we 'll not hang him as a spy, lest all the caps go into mourning. Commissary Loring, he is yours; we will hold him as a prisoner of war."

"Do that and you must answer for it," said Jack. "You can hang me as a spy, if you choose, but yesterday I rode into Germantown under a flag of truce, and on your own pass, as one of the commissioners of exchange. What word will you send to General Washington if you attempt to hold me prisoner?"

"Well done!" exclaimed Howe. "One would almost think it had been prearranged. Release his arms, sergeant. Loring, let the boy have a horse and a pass to Germantown. I rely on your honour, sir, that you take no advantage of what you have seen or heard within our lines."

Jack bowed assent without a word.

"And now, sir, that you are free," went on Sir William, "have you no thanks for us?"

"Not one."

"Ah, Charlie," begged Mrs. Loring, "just a single word of forgiveness."

Without a sign to show he heard her, Jack went to Janice and took her hand. "Don't forget my pledge. Save you I can, if you will but let me." He stooped his head slightly and hesitated for a moment, his eyes fixed on her lips, then he kissed her hand.

And as he did so, Mrs. Loring burst into tears. "You are killing me by your cruelty," she cried.

"Ah, Colonel Brereton, say something kind to her!" begged the girl, impulsively.

Wheeling about, Jack strode forward, till he stood beside the woman. "This scoundrel," he began, indicating Clowes with a contemptuous gesture, "is seeking to force Miss Meredith into a marriage: save her from that, and the wrong you did me is atoned."

"I will; I will!" replied Mrs. Loring, lifting her head

eagerly. "I 'll — Ah, Charlie, one kiss — just one to show that I am forgiven — No, not for that," she hurriedly added, as the aide drew back — "to show — for what I will do for her. Everything I can I will — Just one."

For an instant Brereton hesitated, then bent his head; and the woman, with a cry of joy, threw her arms about his neck, and kissed him not once, but five or six times, and would have continued but for his removing her hands and stepping backward.

"Come, sir," said Loring, irritably, "if the whole army is not to have wind of this, follow me. Daybreak is not far away, and you should be in the saddle."

The aide once more went to Janice, and would have again taken her hand; but the girl shrank away, and turned her back upon him.

"One farewell," pleaded Jack.

"You have had it," replied Janice, without turning.

"Ay. Be off with you," seconded Howe, and without a a word Brereton followed Loring from the room.

As the front door banged, and ere any one had spoken, the thunder of a cannon sounded loud and clear, and at short intervals other booms succeeded, as if the first was echoing repeatedly. But the trained ear of the general was not deceived.

"'T is the water battery saluting," he said, rising. "So Sir Henry Clinton has evidently arrived. Come, gentlemen, 't is only courteous that we meet him at the landing."

XLVI

THE FAREWELL TO HOWE

IN the movement that ensued, Janice slipped into the hallway, and in a moment she was scurrying along the street, so busy with her thoughts that she forgot the satin slippers which had hitherto been so carefully saved from the pavements. She had not gone a square when the sound of footsteps behind her made the girl quicken her pace; but instantly the pursuer accelerated his, and, really alarmed, Janice broke into a run which ended only as she darted up the steps of her home, where she seized the knocker and banged wildly. Before any one had been roused within, the man stood beside her, and with his first word the fugitive recognised Lord Clowes.

"I meant not to frighten ye," he said; "but ye should not have come away alone, for there are pretty desperate knaves stealing about, and had ye encountered the patrol, ye would have been taken to the provost-marshal for carrying no lantern."

Relieved to know who it was, but too breathless to make reply, Janice leaned against the lintel until a sleepy soldier gave them entrance. There was a further delay while Lord Clowes ignited a dip from the lamp and lighted her to the stairway. Here he handed it to her, but retaining his own hold, so as to prevent her departing, he said: —

"I lost my temper at hearing that young scamp make such ardent love, and so I spoke harshly to ye. Canst not make allowance for a lover's jealousy?"

"Please let me have the light."

"Whether ye pardon me or no, of one thing I am sure," went on Clowes, still holding the candle, "ye are not so love-sick of this rogue as to overlook his seeking the aid of his discarded mistress in his suit of ye. I noted your look as she kissed him."

"'T is not a subject I choose to discuss with you, nor is it one for any gentlewoman," said Janice, dropping her hold on the candle and starting upstairs. At the top she paused long enough to say, "Nor do I trust your version," and then hurried to her room and bolted the door.

Here, dark as it was, she went straight to the bureau, and pulling open the bottom drawer fumbled about in it. Her hands presently encountered the unfinished purse, and for a moment they closed on it, while something resembling a sob escaped her. But with one hand she continued searching; and so soon as her groping put her fingers on the miniature of Mrs. Loring she rose, and feeling the way to a window, she opened it and threw out the slip of ivory. The girl made a motion as if to send the purse after it, but checked the impulse, and forgetting to close the window, and without a thought of her once treasured gown, she threw herself on the bed, and began to sob miserably. Before many minutes, worn out with excitement, fatigue, and the lateness, she fell asleep, but it was only to dream uneasily over the night's doings, in which all was a confused jumble, save for the eager tones of her lover's voice as he pleaded his suit, the sight of him as he lay on the floor after the candles had been lighted, and, finally, the look in his eyes as he made his farewell. Yet no sooner did these recur than they were succeeded by that of Mrs. Loring's eager and passionate kissing of Brereton, and each time this served to bring Janice back into a half-awake condition.

After breakfast the next morning, as she was pretendedly reading Racine's "Iphigénie," lest her mother should find her doing nothing and order her to some task, a letter was handed her by one of the servants, with word that it had been brought by a soldier; and breaking the seal, Janice read:

My deer child

pleas do forgiv al i spoke to yu a bout the furst time i see yu for i did not understan it at al i was dredful up set bi last nite and feel mitey pukish this mawning, but i hope yu will cum to see me soon for i want much to tawk with yu a bout how i can help yu and to kiss and hugg yu for yu ar so prity that i shud lov just to tuch yu lik sum one else did yu see how his eys lovd yu when he was going a way he yused to look that way at me and i cried mitey hard al nite at his krulty pleas cum soon to unhapy

JANE LORING.

ps. i shal cum to yu if yu dont cum quick

"There is no answer," the maiden told the servant; then, as he went to the door she added, "And should a Mrs. Loring wish to see me, you will refuse me to her."

Left alone, Janice went to the fireplace, in which the advance of spring no longer made a fire necessary, and, taking from its niche the tinder box, she struck flint on steel, and in a moment had a blaze started. Not waiting to let it gain headway, she laid the letter upon the flame, and held it there with the tongs till it ignited. "I knew without your telling me," she said, "that he no longer loved you, and great wonder it is, considering your age, that he ever could."

"Hast turned fire-worshipper?" demanded André's voice, merrily, as she still knelt, "for if so, 't will be glad news for the sparks."

The girl sprang to her feet. "I — I was just burning a — a — some rubbish," she answered.

"Here I am, not in the lion's den, but in the jackal's, and my stay must be brief. Canst detect that I am big with news?"

"Of what?'"

"This morning Sir Henry Clinton arrived, and for the first time the army learns that Sir William has resigned his command, and is leaving us. The field officers wish to mark his departure by a farewell *fête* in his honour, and as it would be a mockery without the ladies, we are appealing to them to aid us. We plan to have a tourney of knights, each of whom is to have a damsel who shall reward him with a favour at the end of the contest. I have bespoken fair Peggy for mine, and I am sure Mobray, who is not yet returned, will ask you. Wilt help us?"

"Gladly," assented Janice, eagerly, "if dadda will let me."

"I met him in High Street on my way here, made my plea, and, though at first he pulled a negative look, when I reminded him he owed Sir William for a good place, he relented and said you could."

"And what am I to do?"

"You are to be gowned in a Turkish costume, in the —"

"Nay, Captain André," replied Janice, shaking her head, "we are too poor to spend any money in such manner."

"Think you the knights are so lacking in chivalry that we could permit our guests to pay? The subscription is large enough to cover all expenses, the stuffs are already purchased, and all you will have to do is to make them up in the manner of this sketch."

"Then I accept with pleasure and thanks."

"'T is we owe the thanks. And now farewell, for I have much to do."

"Captain André," said the girl, as he opened the door, "I have a question — Wilt answer me something?"

"Need you ask?"

"I suppose 't is a peculiar one, and so — Do you — is it generally thought by — Do the gentlemen of the army deem Mrs. Loring beautiful?"

"Too handsome for the good of our — of the army."

"Even though she paints and powders?"

"But in London and Paris 't is the mode."

"I think 't is a horrid custom."

"And so would every woman had she but thy cheeks. Ah, Miss Meredith, 't is easy for the maid whose tints are a daily toast at the messes to blame those to whom nature has not given a transparent skin and mantling blood."

When Mobray returned from Germantown, he at once sought out Janice and confirmed André's action. Though he found her working on the costume, it was with so melancholy a countenance that he demanded the cause.

"'T is what you know already," moaned the girl, miserably. "Lord Clowes is pressing me for an answer, and now dadda is urgent that I give him ay."

"Why?"

"He went to see Sir Henry, and had so cold a reception that he thinks 't is certain he is to lose his place, let alone the report that General Clinton was heard to say Sir William's friends were to be got rid of. What can we do?"

"But Char — Brereton assured me he had spoked the fellow's wheel by securing the aid of — "

"'T is naught to me what he has done," interrupted Janice, proudly; "nor did I give him the right to intervene."

"You must not give yourself to Clowes. 'T is — ah — rather than see that I 'll speak out."

"About what?"

"Leftenant Hennion is not dead! 'T was but another of Clowes' lies, and your father shall know it, let him do his worst." Without giving his courage time to cool, the young fellow dashed across the hallway to the office where the commissary and squire were sitting, and announced: "News, Mr. Meredith. Leftenant Hennion is alive, for his name was on the rebel lists of prisoners to be exchanged."

"Oddsbodikins!" ejaculated the squire. "Here 's an upset, Clowes, to all our talk."

"Ye 'll not be fool enough to let it make any difference," growled the baron, his eyes resting on Mobray with a look that boded no good. "Ye 'll only increase your difficulties by holding to that old folly."

"Nay, Clowes, Lambert Meredith ne'er broke his word to any man, and, God helping, he never will."

With a real struggle, the commissary held his anger in check. "I 'll talk of this later," he said, after a pause, "when I can speak less warmly than now I feel. As for ye, sir," he said, facing Mobray, "I will endeavour — the favour ye have done shall not be forgotten."

"Take what revenge you please, my Lord," replied Mobray, his voice shaking a little none the less, "I have done what as a gentleman I was compelled to do, and am ready for the consequences, be they what they may."

"A fit return for my lenience," remarked Clowes to the squire after Sir Frederick had made his exit. "He has long owed me money, for which I have never pressed him, yet now he would have it that if I but ask payment, 't is revenge."

One result of Mobray's outbreak was to give Janice another knight for the pageant.

"'Tis a crying shame," André told her; "but poor Fred has gone to the wall at last, and is to be sold up. Therefore he chooses to withdraw from the tourney, and begs me to make his apologies to you, for he is too dumpish to wish to see any one. 'Twill make no difference to you, save that you will have Brigade Major Tarleton in place of the baronet."

"Can nothing be done for him?" asked Janice.

"Be assured, if anything could be, his fellow-officers would not have allowed the army to lose him, for he is loved by every man in the service; but he is in for over eight thousand pounds."

"'Tis very sad," sighed Janice. "I thought him a man of property," she added aloud, while to herself she said, "Then it could not have been he who bought my miniature."

"Nay, he was sometimes in funds by his winnings, but he long since scattered his patrimony."

Janice's letter to Tabitha had long before, by its length, become in truth a journal, and to its pages were confided an account of the farewell *fête* to the British general: —

" 'The Mischianza,' as 't is styled, Tibbie, began at four o'clock in the afternoon with a grand regatta, all the galleys and flatboats being covered with awnings and dressed out with colours and streamers, making a most elegant spectacle. The embarkation took place at the upper end of the city, mommy and I entering the 'Hussar' which bore Sir William Howe. Preceded by the music boats, the full length of the town we were rowed, whilst every ship was decked with flags and ensigns, and the shores were crowded with spectators, who joined in 'God save the King' when the bands played it; and the 'Roebuck' frigate fired a royal salute. About six we drew up opposite the Wharton house, and landing, made our way between files of troops and sailors to a triumphal arch that ushered to an amphitheatre which had been erected for the guests, of whom, Tibbie, but four hundred were invited. Behind these seats spectators not to be numbered darked the whole plain around, held in check by a strong guard which controlled their curiosity. The fourteen

knights' ladies (selected, Tibbie, so 't was given out, as the foremost in youth, beauty, and fashion, and into a fine frenzy it threw those maids who were not asked) were seated in the front, and though 't is not for me to say it, we made a most pleasing display. Our costume was fancy, and consisted of gauze turbans, spangled and edged with gold and silver, on the right side of which a veil of the same hung as low as the waist, and the left side of the turban was enriched with pearls and tassels of gold or silver, crested with a feather. The jacket was of the polonaise kind, of white silk with long sleeves, and sashes worn around the waist tied with a large bow on the left side, hung very low and trimmed, spangled, and fringed according to the colours of the knight. But, wilt believe it, Tibbie, instead of skirts, 't was loose trousers, gathered at the ankle, we wore, and a fine to-do mommy made at first over the idea, till dadda said I might do as the other girls did; though indeed, Tibbie, 't is to be confessed I felt monstrous strange, and scarce enjoyed a dance through thought of them. And here let me relate that this was the ostensible reason for Mr. Shippen refusing to allow Margaret and Sarah to take part after they had their gowns made (and weren't they dancing mad at being forbid!), but 't is more shrewdly suspected that 't was because of a rumour (which no thinking person credits) that Philadelphia is to be evacuated, and so, being a man of no opinions, he chose not to risk offending the Whigs.

"Once seated, the combined bands of the army sounded a very loud and animated march, which was the signal for the beginning of the ceremony of the carousel. The seven knights of The Blended Rose, most marvellously dressed in a costume of the Henry IV. period of France (which, being so beyond description, I have endeavoured a sketch), on white horses, preceded by a herald and three trumpeters, entered the quadrangle, and by proclamation asserted that the ladies of The Blended Rose excelled in wit, beauty, and accomplishment those of the whole world, and challenged any knight to dispute it. Thereupon appeared the seven knights of The Burning Mountain, and by their herald announced that they would disprove by arms the vainglorious assertions of the knights of The Blended Rose and show that the ladies of The Burning Mountain as far excelled all others in charms as the knights themselves surpassed all others in prowess.

Upon this a glove of defiance was thrown, the esquires presented their knights with their lances, the signal for the charge was sounded, and the conflict ensued, until on a second signal they fell back, leaving but their chiefs in single combat. These fighting furiously, were presently parted by the judges of the field, with the announcement that they were of equal valour, and their ladies of equal beauty. Forming in single file, they advanced and saluted, and a finish was put to this part of the entertainment.

"We now retired to the house for tea, where the knights, having dismounted, followed us, and paid homage to their fair ones, from each of whom they received a favour. The ball then succeeded, which lasted till nine, when the company distributed themselves at the windows and doors to view fireworks of marvellous beauty, ending with a grand illumination of the arch. More dancing then occupied us, till we were summoned to supper, which was served in a saloon one hundred and eighty feet long, gaily painted and decorated, and made brilliant by a great number of lustres hung from the roof, while looking-glasses, chandeliers, and girandoles decked the walls, the whole enlivened by garlands of flowers and festoons of silk and ribbons. Here we were waited upon by twenty-four negroes in blue and white turbans and party-coloured clothes and sashes, whilst the most pathetic music was performed by a concealed band. Toasts to the king and queen, the royal family, the army and navy, with their respective commanders, the knights and their ladies, and the ladies in general, were drunk in succession, each followed by a flourish of music, when once again the dancing was resumed, and lasted till the orb of day intruded his presence upon us.

"Sir William left us at noon to-day, regretted by the whole army, and, as I write this, I can hear a salute of guns in honour of Sir Henry Clinton's assuming the command. Pray Heaven he does not remove dadda.

"At last I know, Tibbie, what court life must be like."

Three days after the departure of Howe, the squire came into dinner, a paper in hand, and with a beaming face. "Fine news!" he observed. "I am not to be displaced."

"Good!" cried the commissary, while Janice clapped her

hands. "I spoke to Sir Henry strongly in your favour, and am joyed to hear that it has borne fruit."

"How dost thou know, Lambert?" asked Mrs. Meredith.

"I have here an order to load the 'Rose' tender with such rebel property as the commissaries shall designate, and superintend its removal to New York. They 'd ne'er employ me on so long a job, were I marked to lose my employment, eh, Clowes?"

"Well reasoned. For 't is not merely a task of time, but one of confidence. But look ye, man, if ye 're indeed to make a voyage to York and back, which will likely take a month, 't is best that we settle this question of marriage ere ye go. I 've given Miss Janice time, I think ye 'll grant, and 't will be an advantage in your absence that she and Mrs. Meredith have one bound to protect them."

"I 'd say ay in a moment, Clowes, but for my word to Hennion."

"'T is a promise thou shouldst ne'er have made, and which it is now thy every interest to be quit of, let alone that 't is so distasteful to thy daughter."

"A promise is a promise," answered the father, with an obstinate motion of head.

"And a fool 's a fool," retorted Clowes, losing his temper. "In counsel and aid I 've done my best for ye; now go your gait, and see what comes of it."

A week later, Mr. Meredith bade farewell to wife and daughter.

"I wish you were n't going, dadda," Janice moaned. "'T is so akin to last summer that it frights me."

"Nay, lass, be grateful that I have the job to do, and that with good winds I shall return within a fortnight. Clowes has passed his word that ye shall want for nothing. I 'll be back ere ye know I 've gone."

There was a good cause, however, for the girl's fear of the future, for in less than a week from her father's sailing, on every street corner, in every tavern, and in every drawing-room of the town the news that Philadelphia was to be evacuated was being eagerly and anxiously discussed.

XLVII

THE EVACUATION

CONFIRMATION of the rumour, so far as Mrs. Meredith and Janice were concerned, was first received through the commissary.

"Ay," he told them, when questioned; "'t was decided at a council of war the very day Howe left us, and that was why we at once began transferring our stores and the seized property to New York, one cargo of which your husband was put in charge. 'T will tax our shipping to the utmost to save it all."

"But why didst thou not warn us, so that we might have embarked with him?" asked Mrs. Meredith.

"'T was a military secret to be told to no one."

"Can dadda return ere the evacuation begins?"

"'T is scarce possible, even if his orders permit it."

"Then what are we to do?"

"Thou hadst best apply at once to the deputy quartermaster-general for transports."

Mrs. Meredith acted on this advice the following day, but without success.

"Think you the king's ships and transports have naught to do but act as packet-boats for you Americans?" the deputy asked. "Hundreds of applications have been filed already, and not another one will we receive. If you 'd for New York, hire a passage in a private ship."

This was easier to recommend than to do, for such was the frantic demand for accommodation that the prices had been raised to exorbitant figures, quite beyond their means. So appeal was made once more to Clowes.

"'T is something of a quandary," he remarked; "but there is a simple way out."

"What?"

"I 'd have saved ye all worry over the matter but that I wished ye to learn the difficulties. I have never made pretence to doing favours out of mere kindness of heart, and ye know quite as well as I why I have given ye lodging and other aids. But for that very reason I am getting wearied of doing all and receiving nothing, and have come to the end. Give me Miss Janice, and my wife and mother shall have passage in the ship I sail in."

"You take a poor way, Lord Clowes, to gain your wish," said Janice. "Generosity —"

"Has had a six months' trial, and brought me no nearer to a consummation," interrupted the baron. "Small wonder I sicken of it and lose patience."

"'T is not to be expected that I would let Janice wed thee when her father has given thee nay."

"Because he has passed his word to another, and so holds himself bound. He said he 'd consent but for that, and by acting in his absence ye can save him a broken oath, yet do the sensible thing. He 'll be glad enough once done; that I 'll tie to."

"It scarce betters it in a moral sense," replied Mrs. Meredith. "However, we will not answer till we have had a chance to discuss it by ourselves."

"Janice," said her mother, once they were alone, "thy dread of that man is a just one, and I —"

"I know — I know," broke in the daughter, miserably; "but I — if I can make us all easy as to money and future —"

"Those are but worldly benefits, child."

"But, mommy," said the girl, chokingly, as she knelt at her mother's feet and threw her arms about Mrs. Meredith's waist, "since live we must, what can we do but — but — Oh, would that I had never been born!" and then the girl buried her head in her mother's lap.

"'T is most unseemly, child, to speak so. God has put us here to punish and chasten us for Adam's sin; and 't is not for us, who sinned in him, to question His infinite wisdom."

"Then I wish He 'd tell me what it is my duty to do!" lamented Janice.

"Thinkest thou he has nothing to do but take thought of thy affairs?"

"Wouldst have me marry him, mommy?" asked the girl, chokingly.

"Let us talk no further now, child, but take a night's thought over it."

They were engaged in discussing the problem the following afternoon, when Lieutenant Hennion burst in upon them.

"Why, Phil!" cried Mrs. Meredith; and Janice, springing from her chair, met him half-way with outstretched hand, while exclaiming, "Oh, Mr. Hennion, 't is indeed good to see an old friend's face."

"'T is glad tidings ter me ter hearn you say that," declared Philemon, eagerly. "Yestere'en General Lee and the other rebel prisoners came out from Philadelphia, and we, having been brought from Morristown some days ago, were at once set at liberty; but 't was too late ter come in, so we waited for daylight. I only reported at quarters, and then, learning where you lodged, I come — I came straight ter — to find how you fared."

Alternating explanation and commentary, the women told of their difficulties.

"I can't aid you to get aboard one of the ships, for I 've had ter draw my full pay all the time I was prisoner, the rebels nigh starving us, let alone freezing, so money 's as scarce with me as with you. But I 'll go ter — to my colonel, and see if I can't get permission that you may go with our baggage train."

"'T will be a benefit indeed, if you can do that," exclaimed Mrs. Meredith.

"Then I 'll not tarry now, but be off about it at once, for there was a rumour at brigade headquarters that three regiments had been ordered across the river this afternoon, and that it meant a quick movement." He picked up his hat as if to go, then paused, and haltingly continued, "I hope, Ja — Ja — Janice, that you 've come ter — to like — not to be so set against what I wants so much. It 's nigh a year since I seen — saw you last, but it 's only made me love you the better."

The girl, with a look of real contrition, answered, "Oh, Mr. Hennion, do not force — 'T would be wrong to us both if I deceived you."

"You can't love me?"

"I — oh, I believe I am a giddy, perverse female, for I seem able to care for no man."

"The world I 'd give ter win you, Janice; but I 'll not tease you now, the more that I can be doing you a service, and that 's joy enough."

Philemon went toward the door; but ere he had reached it Janice had overtaken him and seized his hand in both of hers. "You deserve to love a better maid," she said huskily, "and I wish you might; but perhaps 't will be some comfort to you to know that dadda holds to his promise, and — and that I am less wilful and more obedient, I hope, than once I was."

As Philemon opened his mouth to make reply, he was cut short by the entrance of the commissary, who halted and frowned as he took in the hand-clasp of the two.

"Humph!" he muttered, and then louder remarked, "Yet another! Ye 'll be pleased to know, sir, that Miss Meredith's favours mean little. But a month since I caught that fellow Brereton regaling himself with her lips."

"That 's a lie, I know," retorted Philemon, angrily; but as he glanced at the girl and saw her crimson, he exclaimed, "You just said you cared for no man!"

"It — it was at a moment when I scarce knew what I did," faltered Janice, "and — and — now I would not be kissed by him for anything in the world. I — I am — I was honest in what I said to you, Philemon."

"I 'll believe anything you say, Janice," impulsively replied the lieutenant, as with unprecedented boldness he raised her hand to his lips. Then facing Clowes he said: "And I advise you ter have a care how you speak of Miss Meredith. I 'll not brook hearing her aspersed." With this threat he left the room.

"I regret to have been an intruder on so tender a scene," sneered the commissary; "but I came with information that was too important to delay. Orders have been issued that all ships make ready to drop down the river with the tide at daybreak to-morrow, and 't is said that the army will begin its march across the Jerseys but a twenty-four hours later. So there is no time to lose if ye wish to sail with me. The marriage must take place by candle-light this evening, and we must embark immediately after."

"Philemon has promised us his aid, Lord Clowes," replied Mrs. Meredith, "and so we need not trouble thee."

"Hennion! But he must go with his regiment."

"He offers us a place in the baggage train."

"Evidently he has not seen the general orders. Clinton is too good an officer to so encumber himself; and the orders are strict that only the women of the regiments be permitted to march with the army. I take it ye scarce wish to class yourselves with them, however much it might delight the soldiery."

"They could scarce treat us worse than thee, Lord Clowes," said Mrs. Meredith, indignantly. "Nor do I believe that even the rank and file would take such advantage of two helpless women as thou art seeking to do."

"Tush! I may state it o'er plainly; but my intention is merely to make clear for your own good that ye have no other option but that I offer ye."

"Any insults would be easier to bear than yours," declared Janice, indignantly; "and theirs would be for once, while yours are unending."

"Such folly is enough to make one forswear the whole sex," the commissary angrily replied. "Nor am I the man to put up with such womanish humoursomeness. "I 've stood your caprice till my patience is exhausted; now I 'll teach ye what — "

"Heyday!" exclaimed André, as a servant threw open the door and ushered him in. "What have we here? I trust I am not *mal apropos?*"

"Far from it," spoke up Janice. "And thou 'rt welcome."

"I come laden with grief and with messages," said André, completely ignoring Clowes' presence. "Mr. Hennion, whom I met at headquarters, asked me to tell you his request was refused, that his regiment was even then embarking to cross the Delaware, and that therefore he could not return, whatever his wish. The Twenty-sixth is under orders to follow at daybreak to-morrow, and so we plan an impromptu farewell supper this evening at my quarters. Will you forgive such brief notice and help to cheer our sorrow with your presence?"

"With more than pleasure," assented Mrs. Meredith; "and if 't will not trouble thee, we will avail ourselves of thy escort even now."

"Would that such trouble were commoner!" responded André, holding open the door.

"Then we 'll get our coverings without delay."

Lord Clowes, with a deepened scowl on his face, intercepted them at the door. "One word in private with these ladies," he said to the captain. Then, as André with a bow passed out first, he continued, to the women: "I have warned ye that we must be aboard ship ere ten. Refuse me my will, and ye 'll not be able to rejoin Mr. Meredith. Take my offer, or remain in the city."

"We shall remain," responded Mrs. Meredith.

"With your husband a warden of the seized property of the rebels, and known to have carried away a ship-load of it? Let me warn ye that the rebels whom we drove out of Philadelphia will be in no sweet mood when they return and find what we have destroyed or carried off. Hast heard how the Bostonians treated Captain Fenton's wife and fifteen year-old daughter? Gentlewomen though they were, the mob pulled them out of their house, stripped them naked in the public streets, smeared them with tar and feathers, and then walked them as a spectacle through the town. And Fenton had done far less to make himself hated than Mr. Meredith. Consider their fate, and decide if marriage with me is the greater evil."

"Every word thou hast spoken, Lord Clowes," replied Mrs. Meredith, "has tended to make us think so."

"Then may you reap the full measure of your folly," raged the commissary.

"Come, Janice," said her mother; and the two, without a parting word, left him. Once upstairs, Janice flung her arms about Mrs. Meredith's neck.

"Oh, mother," she cried, "please, please forgive me! I have ever thought you hard and stern to me, but now I know you are not."

Strive as those at the supper might, they could not make it a merry meal. The officers, with a sense of defeat at heart, and feeling that they were abandoning those who had shown them only kindness, had double cause to feel depressed, while the ladies, without knowledge of what the future might contain, could not but be anxious, try their all. And as if these were not spectres enough at the feast, a question of Mrs. Meredith as to Mobray added one more gloomy shadow.

"Fred? alas!" one of the officers replied. "He was sold out, and the poor fellow was lodged in the debtors' prison, as you know. As we chose not to have them fall into the hands of the rebels, a general jail delivery was ordered this morning, which set him at large."

"And what became of him?" asked Janice.

"Would that I could learn!" groaned André. "As soon as I was off duty, I sought for him, but he was not to be heard of, go to whom I would. Bah! No more of this graveyard talk. Come, Miss Meredith, I'll give you the subject for a historical painting. I found of Franklin's possessions not a little which took my fancy, and such of it as I chose I carry with me to New York, as fair spoil of war. Prithee, draw a picture of the old fox as he will appear when he hears of his loss. 'T will at least give him the opportunity to prove himself the 'philosopher' he is said to be. I have taken his oil portrait, and when I get fit quarters again I shall hang it, and nightly pray that I may live long enough to do the same to the original. Heaven save me if ever I be captured, though, for I make little doubt that in his rage he would accord me the very fate I wish for him!"

When at last the evening's festivities, if such they might be termed, were over, it was André, preceded by a couple of soldiers with lanterns, who escorted them back to their home, and at Janice's request he ordered the two men to remain in the now deserted house.

"They must leave you before daybreak," the officer warned them; "but they will assure you a quiet night. I would that you were safe in New York, however, and shall rest uneasy till I welcome you there. Ladies, you have made many an hour happier to John André," ended the young officer, his voice breaking slightly. "Some day, God willing, he will endeavour to repay them."

"Oh, Captain André," replied Janice, "'tis we are the debtors indeed!"

"We 'll not quarrel over that at parting," said André, forcing a merry note into his voice. "When this wretched rebellion is over, and you are well back at Greenwood, and may that be soon, I will visit you and endeavour to settle debit and credit."

Just as he finished, the sound of drums was heard.

"'T is past tattoo, surely?" Mrs. Meredith questioned with a start.

"Ay," answered André. "'T is the rogue's march they are ruffling for a would-be deserter who was drum-headed this evening, and whom they are taking to the State House yard to hang. Brrew! Was not the gloom of to-night great enough without that as a last touch to ring in our ears? What a fate for a soldier who might have died in battle! Farewell, and may it be but a short *au revoir*," and, turning, the young officer hurried away, singing out, in an attempt to be cheery, the soldier's song:—

"Why, soldiers, why
    Should we be melancholy, boys?
Why, soldiers, why,
Whose business 't is to die?
What, sighing? fie!
    Drown fear, drink on, be jolly, boys.
'T is he, you, or I!"

XLVIII

A TIME OF TERROR

THE Merediths were awakened the next morning by sounds which told of the movements of troops, and all day long the regiments were marching to the river, and as fast as they could be ferried, were transferred to the Jersey side, the townspeople who, by choice or necessity, were left behind being helpless spectators meanwhile. Once again the streets of Philadelphia assumed the appearance of almost absolute desertion; for as the sun went down the prudent-minded retired within doors, taking good heed to bar shutters and bolt doors, and the precaution was well, for all night long men might be seen prowling about the streets, — jail-birds, British deserters, and other desperadoes, tempted by hope of plunder.

Fearful for their own safety, Mrs. Meredith and Janice failed not to use every means at hand to guard it, not merely closing and securing, so far as they were able, every possible entrance to the house, but as dark came on, their fear led them to ascend to the garret by a ladder through a trap, and drawing this up, they closed the entrance. Here they sat crouched on the bare boards, holding each other, for what seemed to them immeasurable hours; and such was the intensity of the nervous anxiety of waiting that it was scarcely added to, when, toward daybreak, both thought they detected the tread of stealthy footsteps through the rooms below. Of this they presently had assurance, for when the pound of horses' hoofs was heard outside, the intruders, whoever they might be, were heard to run through the hall and down the stairs with a haste which proved to the miserable women that more than they had cause for fear.

Hardly had this sound died away when a loud banging on the front door reached even their ears, and after several repetitions new fear was given them by the crashing of wood and splintering of glass, which told that some one had broken in a shutter and window to effect an entrance. Once again footsteps on the stairs were heard, and a man rushed into the room underneath them and came to a halt.

"Do you find them?" he shouted to some companion, whose answer could not be heard. "What ho!" he went on in stentorian voice. "Is there any one in this house who can give me word of a family of Merediths?"

Janice reached forward and raised the trap, but her mother caught her arm away, and the door fell with a bang.

"'T is all right, mommy," the girl protested. "Didst not hear the jingle of his spurs? 'T is surely an officer, and we need not fear any such."

Even as she spoke the trap was raised by a sabre from below. "Who 's above?" the man demanded, and as Janice leaned forward and peeked through the opening, he went on, "I seek — " There he uncovered. "Ah, Miss Meredith, dark as it is above, I could pick you from a thousand by Colonel Brereton's description. I was beginning to fear some misfortune had overtaken you. I am Captain McLane of the light horse. You can descend without fear."

With a relief that was not to be measured, the two dropped the ladder into place and descended.

"Is Colonel Brereton here?" asked Mrs. Meredith.

"Not he, or I suspect he 'd never have given me the thrice-repeated charge to make sure of your safety. He is with the main army, now in full pursuit of the British, and we 'll hope to come up with the rats ere they get safely to their old hole. Since you are safe I must not tarry, for there is much to — "

"Oh, Captain McLane, can't you stay?" beseeched Janice. "Do not leave us unprotected. I can't tell you what we have suffered through thought of possible violence, and even now — "

"I will station a trooper at the door," the officer promised; "but have no fear. Already patrols are established, and within an hour broadsides will be posted about the city warning all plunderers or other law-breakers that they will be shot or hanged on sight. General Arnold, who is given command of the city, intends there shall be no disturbance, and he is not the man to have his orders broke."

Set at ease as to their safety, the first concern of the women was a hastily improvised breakfast from the scantily supplied larder which Clowes' servants had abandoned to them. In the kitchen, as well as all over the house, they found ample signs that pilferers had been at work, for every receptacle had been thrown open, drawers dragged out, and the floor littered with whatever the despoilers elected not to take. A month before Janice would probably have been moved to tears at the discovery that her "elegant and dashy robing," as well as her Mischianza costume, had been stolen, but now she scarcely gave either of them a thought, so grateful was she merely to feel that they were safe from violence and insult.

In reinstating her own meagre possessions in their proper receptacles, which was the girl's after-breakfast occupation, she came upon an unfinished silk purse, and this served to bring an end for a time to the restoration of order, while she sat upon the floor in a meditative attitude. Presently she laid it on the bureau with a little sigh and returned to her task. Once this was completed, she again took the purse, and seating herself, set about its completion.

Afraid to stir out of doors, and with little to occupy her, the next three days served to complete the trifle, elaborate and complicated as the pattern was. Meantime, a steady stream of Whigs flooded into the city, and from Captain McLane, who twice dropped in to make sure of their well-being, they learned that the Continental Congress was about to resume its sessions in the city. Ocular proof that the rulers of America were assembling was very quickly brought home to the two, for one morning Janice, answering a rap of the knocker, opened the door to the Honourable Joseph Bagby.

"Well, miss, I guess you 're not sorry to see an old friend's face, are you, now that the dandiprat redcoats you 've been gallivanting with have shown that they prefer running away to fighting?" was his greeting, as he held out his hand.

Janice, divided in mind by the recollection of his treatment of them and by her fear of the future, extended her own and allowed it to be shaken, as the easiest means of escaping the still more difficult verbal response.

"Are n't you going to ask me in?" inquired the caller, "for I 've got something to say."

"I did n't know that you would want to," faltered Janice, making entrance for him. "Mommy will be gla — will be in the parlour," she said, leading the way to that room.

Without circumlocution, Bagby went at the object of his call the moment the equally embarrassing meeting with Mrs. Meredith was over.

"I came up to town," he announced, "to 'tend Congress, of which I 'm now a member;" and here the speaker paused as if to let the new dignity come home to his hearers. "Did n't I tell you I was a rising man? But I had another object in view in being so prompt, and that was to have a talk with you to see if we can 't arrange things. 'T is n't given to every girl to marry a Congressman, eh, miss?"

"I — I — suppose not," stammered Janice, frightened, yet with an intense desire to laugh.

"Before I say anything as to that," went on Bagby, "I want to tell you that I 've been a good friend of yours. Old Hennion, who 's come out hating your dad the worst way, was for introducing a bill in Assembly last session declaring his lands forfeited, but I told him I 'd not have it."

"'T is but a duty man owes to prevent evil deeds," said Mrs. Meredith.

"We are very grateful, Mr. Bagby," Janice thought it was necessary to add, with not a little surprise in her voice.

"That 's what I guessed you 'd be," said the legislator. "Says I to myself, 'They 've made a mistake as to the side they took; but when they see that the British is beat, they 'll do most anything to put themselves right again and save their property.' Now, if Miss Janice will marry me, there is n't any reason why you should n't all come back to Greenwood and live as fine as a fivepence."

"We should not be willing to give thee our daughter, Mr. Bagby, even were she."

"But I am — for the compliment you offer, sir, I thank you," interjected Janice.

"Now, you just listen to reason," protested Joe. "You must n't think it 's only the property I 'm set on. I 've made a swipe of money in the last year — nigh forty thousand dollars — Continental — so I can afford to marry whom I like; and though I own that thirty thousand acres is no smouch of land, yet I 'm really soft on Miss Janice, and would marry her even if she had n't money, now that I 've got some of my own."

"It can make no difference, Mr. Bagby," replied the mother. "Neither her father nor I would consent to her wedding thee, and I know her wishes accord with ours."

Joe, with a somewhat bewildered face and a decidedly awkward movement, picked up his hat. "It don't seem possible," he said, "that you 'll throw away all that property; for, of course, I 'm not going to stand between you and old Hennion when you show yourselves so unfriendly."

"'T is in the hands of One who knows best."

Bagby went to the door. "The Assembly meets on the twenty-eighth," he remarked, "and I promised some of the members I 'd quit Congress to 'tend the early part of the session, so I 've got to go back to Trenton in three days. If you change your mind before then, let me know."

"Oh, mommy," groaned the girl the moment the door closed, "I wish there were no such things in the world as lovers!" Then she told a yet greater untruth: "Or would that I had been born as plain as Tibbie's aunt!"

"'T is ingratitude to speak thus, child. Hast already forgot the help Philemon tried to give us, and what we owe to Colonel Brereton?"

The girl made no response for a little, then said hurriedly, "Mommy, dost think dadda, and wouldst thou wish me to wed Colonel Brereton, provided 't would save us our lands and let us live in peace at Greenwood?"

"I know not what to say, Janice. It would be a deliverance, indeed, from a future black with doubt and trouble; but thy father holds to his promise to Philemon, and I question if he 'd ever consent to have a rebel for a son-in-law. Nor do we know that Colonel Brereton was not but speaking in jest when he said what he did at Greenwood."

"He meant it, mommy," answered the daughter, "for — for

at grave risk he stole into Philadelphia last April to see me; and then he vowed he could save us from the Whigs if — if — "

"And wouldst thou wed him willingly?" asked the mother, when Janice lapsed into silence with the sentence unfinished.

With eyes on the floor and cheeks all aflame, the girl answered: "I — I scarce know, mommy. At times when I am with him I feel dreadfully excited and frightened — though never in the way I am with Lord Clowes — and want to get away; but the moment he is gone I — I wish him back, if only he would do but what I 'd have him — and yet I like him for — for having his own way — as he always does — though I know he 'd do mine if — if I asked him."

"Janice, canst thou not speak less lightly and foolishly?" chided Mrs. Meredith. "If thou lovest the man, say so without such silly maunderings, which are most unbefitting of thy years."

"But I — I don't love Colonel Brereton, mommy," protested the girl; "and I never could, after his — after knowing that he once gave his love to that — "

"And art thou so foolish, Janice," demanded her mother, "as to pretend that thou dost not care for him?"

"Really it — it would only be for you and dadda, and to save the property, mommy," persisted Janice.

"Then why didst thou draw back from Lord Clowes and Bagby?" asked the mother, sternly.

"But I — I could never have — have — Oh, mommy, there is a cart just stopped at the door, and I 'll see what is wanted," — an excuse conveniently present for the flustered maiden to escape an explanation.

As it proved, the arrival of the cart was of very material moment, for by the time Janice was at the door a lean-visaged woman had been helped from it, and her salutation was anything but promising.

"Who are you, that you are in my house?" she demanded, and then entered the hall, and, womanlike, would not listen to the explanations that both Janice and her mother sought to make. "Be off with you at once!" she ordered. "I 'll not have you here a minute. My son died of fever and starvation in a freezing prison last winter while you made free of his mother's home not a half-mile away. Be thankful I don't have you arrested for the rent, or hound the people into treating you Tory snakes as you deserve. No, you shall not stay to get your clothes; into the street I 'll bundle them when I have got them together, and there you 'll find them. Out with you!"

Janice was for obeying, but Mrs. Meredith refused positively to leave without packing. Hastily their scanty belongings were bestowed in the two little leathern trunks they had brought originally from Greenwood; these they dragged to the porch, and, sitting upon them, held debate as to their next step.

Ere they had been able to hit upon some escape from the nonplus, their attention was distracted by a rabble of men, women, and boys, who suddenly swept around a corner and flooded down the street toward them. With a premonition of coming evil, Janice sprang to the knocker, and rapped desperately, but their evictor paid no attention to the appeal. In a moment the mob, which numbered not less than a thousand people, reached the steps, hissing, hooting, and caterwauling, and from the din rose such cries as: "Tory, Tory!" "Turncoats!" "Where are the bloody-backs?" "Ain't we draggletails now?"

"Order!" shouted a man in a cart pulled by some of the crowd, for which a way was made by all so that it could be wheeled up to the sidewalk opposite where the two women, holding each other's hands, were despairingly facing the crowd. "Remember, I passed my oath to General Arnold that there 'ud be no violence; an' if we don't keep it, the troops will be down on us, an' some on you will spend a night in the guard-house."

"Hooray!" cheered some one, and the mass echoed the cry.

The spokesman turned to the Merediths. "We know'd the Fourth o' July ain't no joyous day to you-alls, so we 've done our bestest to keep you from thinkin' of it by bringin' some one to call on you. Ain't you glad to see again your old friend, Miss Shy Anna?"

As the speaker finished, he stepped to one side, bringing into view of the porch a woman seated upon the head of a barrel in the cart. A poor army drab, left behind in the evacuation, had been decked out in what Janice instantly recognised as her Mischianza costume; and with hair dressed so that it stood up not less than two feet above her forehead, splashed over with white paint, a drink-coloured face, doubly red in contrast, and bare feet, with an expanse of more than ankle in a similar nakedness below the trousers, she made up in all a figure so droll that under any other circumstances Janice would have laughed.

"We are escortin' Miss Shy Anna — who ain't really very shy — to see all her friends of The Blended Rose and of The Burning Mountain, an' as we hate airs an' pride, we demands that each give her a kiss. Just make a way for Miss Meredith to come and give her the chaste salute," he ordered of the throng.

"Thou wilt not insist on such a humiliation for my daughter," appealed Mrs. Meredith.

"Insult!" cried the leader. "Who dares to say 't ain't an honour to kiss one dressed in such clothes? Give the miss a little help, boys, but gently. Don't do her no harm."

A dozen men were through the gate before the sentence was finished, but outcries and a surge of the mob at this point gave a new bent to the general attention. A horseman from the direction opposite to that from which the crowd had come was spurring, with little heed, through the mass, and the clamour and movement were due to the commotion he precipitated.

In twenty seconds the rider, who was well coated with dust, and whose horse was lathered with the sweat of fast riding, had come abreast of the cart, and Janice gave a cry of joy. "Oh, Colonel Brereton," she called, "save us, I beg!"

"What are you about?" demanded the new-comer, sternly, of the crowd.

"We 're celebratin' independence," explained he in the cart, "and all we wants of this miss is that she buss her friend Miss Shy Anna. They both is British sympathisers."

"Be off with you, every doodle and rag-tail of you!" ordered the officer, angrily.

"And who are you?" demanded one; and another, emboldened by distance, recommended, "Pull him off his horse."

Twenty hands seized hold of Brereton; but as they did so,

the aide, realising his mistake, retrieved it by a sudden change of manner. "I am an aide of General Washington," he shouted, "and I bring news of a great battle."

An uproar of questions broke out, drowning every other sound, till, by raising his hand, the aide procured silence.

"I must carry the despatches to Congress; but come with me, and I'll give you the tale the moment they are safe delivered."

With a rush the crowd followed him, as he moved forward, deserting the cart and its occupants, who hastily descended, and hurried after the throng. But Jack was not so forgetful, and turning in his saddle, he called back, "I'll return as soon as I can."

XLIX

PLATO *vs.* CUPID

THE patience of the two homeless women was heavily taxed before Brereton returned, but finally, after nearly two hours' waiting, he came, almost running along the street.

"Neither the Congress nor the populace were to be put off," he began to explain, ere he was within the gate, "and I have had to retail again and again the story of the fight, and tell 'how our army swore in Flanders.' But I dared not break away from them through fear they would follow me back and force me to play hare to their hounds once more. 'T is a great relief to know that you are safe," Jack declared, as he shook their hands warmly.

"Thanks to you," replied Mrs. Meredith. "'T was indeed a mercy of God that thou cam'st when thou didst."

"Pray give my mare, who has done her seventy miles since daylight, some share," laughed the officer, heartily.

"Oh, Colonel Brereton, what do we not owe to you?" exclaimed Janice, warmly.

A few words told their champion of their plight and stirred him to hot anger.

"By heavens!" he growled; "I would that my general were here to curse the beldame, as he did Lee at Monmouth. Once you are cared for, I 'll return and see that she hear one's man's opinion of her. Follow me, and I 'll soon put you in comfort." Getting a trunk on each shoulder, he set off down the street.

"Did I understand thee aright in inferring that General Washington so far forgot himself as to use profane language?" asked Mrs. Meredith as they walked.

"Ay, Laus Deo!"

"I can't think of him as doing that," ejaculated Janice.

"'T was glorious to hear him, for he spoke with righteous anger as an angel from heaven might, and his every word was well deserved. Indeed, had I been in command, Lee should have had a file of soldiers before sundown for his conduct."

"What did he?"

"Everything that an honourable man should not," answered the aide, warmly. "Finding that Gates had lost favour with Congress, and had failed in his attempt to supplant Washington, he at once resumed his old intriguing. But, worse still, once we were across the Delaware and in full cry after the British, he persisted in the Council of War in asserting that 't would be madness to bring on a general engagement, and that we should keep at a comfortable distance and merely annoy them by detachment, — counsel that would have done credit to the most honourable Society of Midwives, and to them only, and which could mean naught but that he did not wish my general to reap the glory of defeating the British. Voted down, my fine gentleman at first refused the command of the advance; but once he saw that the attack had promise of success, he asserted his claim as senior officer to command it, only, it would seem, with the object of preventing its success, for at the moment of going into action he predicted to Lafayette that our troops could not stand against the British, and instead of supporting those engaged, he allowed them to be thrown into confusion and was the first to join in the retreat which he himself had brought about. 'T was at this moment, when he was actually heading the rout, that my general cantered up to him and demanded, 'By God, sir, what is the meaning of this disorderly retreat?' Lee began a stuttering explanation that did n't explain, so his Excellency repeated his question. 'You know that the attack was contrary to my advice and opinion,' stammered Lee, and then Washington thundered out, 'Then you should not have insisted on the command. You 're a damned poltroon!' And 't was what the whole army thought and wanted said."

"'T is too bad General Washington was beat," sighed Janice.

"That he was not," answered Brereton, triumphantly. "When we rode up, not a one of us but thought the day lost, but the general, with a quickness and decision I never before saw in him, grasped the situation, rallied the broken regiments, seized on a strong piece of ground, and not merely checked the British advance, but drove them back on their reserves, where, after nightfall, they were glad enough to sneak away, leaving their wounded and dead behind them. But for Lee's cowardice, or treachery, as I believe it to be, they 'd have never reached the protection of their fleet at Sandy Hook. Yet one benefit of his conduct will be that 't will end all talk of making him commander-in-chief. In seeking to injure his Excellency, he has but compassed his own discrediting, and the cabal against my general in Congress will break down for very lack of a possible successor. We did more than beat the English at Monmouth."

The tale served to bring the trio to the City tavern, where Brereton led the way at once to a room on the second floor, and deposited the two trunks.

"You 'll have no more than time to freshen yourselves for dinner, and we 'll leave talk till we 've eaten that," he suggested, as he picked up a pair of saddlebags and left the room.

"Oh, mommy," sighed Janice, rejoicefully, "is n't it a relief to be told what to do, and not have to worry one's self? He did n't make us think once."

Their self-chosen guardian was equally decisive as to the future, when the subject was taken up after the meal. "I must stay here two days for some despatches Congress wishes me to bear, and 't is fortunate, for I shall have time to procure a second horse and a pillion, so that you may journey with me."

"Whither?"

"To Brunswick."

"I suppose there is naught else left for us," said Mrs. Meredith, doubtingly, "but we have little reason to feel secure there."

"Do not give yourself a moment's discomposure or dolour. We shall find the army there; but, better still, I possess a means to secure your safety, whether it remains or no."

"And what is that?" inquired Mrs. Meredith, eagerly, while Janice, feeling her cheeks begin to burn, suddenly sprang to her feet, with a pretended interest in something to be seen from one of the windows, which enabled her to turn her back to the table.

"By good luck I have a hold over both Esquire Hennion and Bagby, and I 'll threat them that unless they let you live at peace I 'll use it."

Janice came back to the table. "'T was only the rounds," she remarked with a note of half surprise, half puzzlement, in her voice, which was not lost to her mother's ears.

"Art thou as sure as thou wert, Janice," Mrs. Meredith asked, once they were in their room again, "that Colonel Brereton wishes to wed thee?"

"I — I thought — he said he did," replied the girl, hanging her head with mortification; "but he may have changed his mind."

"I fear me, child, that thy vanity, which has ever led thee to give too much heed to the pretty speeches of men, has misled thee in this instance."

Janice's doubt grew in the next two days, for by not a word or act did the aide even hint that such a hope was present in his thoughts. Their every need was his care, and all his spare time was passed in their company; but his manner conveyed only the courtesy of the friend, and never the tenderness of the lover. Even when the maiden presented him with the silk purse to which she had given so many hours of toil, his thanks, though warm, were distinctly platonic. Both piqued and humiliated at his conduct, the girl was glad enough when, on the morning of the third day, they set out on their journey, and she almost welcomed the advent of Bagby, who overtook them as they were taking their noon baiting at Bristol, and who made the afternoon ride with them.

Another familiar face greeted them, as, toward nightfall, they rode into Trenton and drew rein in front of the Drinkers' house, whither the ladies had asked to be taken; for ere Janice had been lifted from the horse's back, or Mrs. Meredith had descended from the pillion, they were accosted by Squire Hennion.

"I hoped ez haow we wuz well quit of yer," he began; "an' yer need n't 'spect, after all yer goin's on, an' those of yer —— ole Tory husband, thet ye're goin' ter be allaowed ter come back ter Greenwood. I persume Joe 's told yer thet he an' I is goin' ter git a bill through this Assembly declarin' yer lands escheated."

"You have n't any right to talk for me, squire," protested Joe. "I can do my own talking; and my sympathies is always with the female sex."

"He, he!" snickered Hennion. "Ain't we doin' the gallant all of a suddint! An' ain't we foxy? Joe, here," he continued, turning to the ladies, "come ter me jest afore we left Brunswick, with a bill he 'd draw'd ter take yer lands, an' he says ter me he wuz a-goin' ter push it through Assembly. But by the time we gits ter Trenton, word come thet the redcoats wuz a scuttlin' fer York, so Joe he set off like a jiffy ter see, I persume, if yer wuz ter be faound. Did he offer ter buy yer lands cheap, or did he ask ter be bought off? Or is the sly tyke snoopin' araound arter yer darter?"

Bagby had the grace to grow a brick red at this revelation and home thrust, and he began an attempted explanation. But Brereton, who had helped both his charges to the ground, did not let them give ear to it. "I will bide at the tavern, and we 'll start to-morrow as soon after daybreak as we can," he said, as he escorted them to the door, then turned back to the two assemblymen, who were busy expressing frank opinions of each other. "Quarrel as you like," he broke in, "but understand one thing now. That bill must never be introduced, or the pair of you shall hear from me. I warn you both that I have in my possession your signed oaths of allegiance to King George, and if you dare to push your persecution of the Merediths I 'll ride from one end of Middlesex County to t' other, and prove to your constituents what kind of Whigs you are, over your own hands and seals." He took the two bridles and walked toward the tavern.

"Thet 'ere is a lie!" cried Hennion, yet following the officer.

"It is, if you never signed such a paper," remarked Jack, drily.

"I defy yer ter show it," challenged Hennion.

"If you want sight of it, introduce the bill," retorted the aide.

"Say, colonel," said Bagby, with a decided cringe, "you won't use those documents against your old friends, will you?"

"'T ain't fer a Continental officer ter injure them ez is ginooine

Whigs," chimed in Hennion, "an' only swore an oath cuz it seemed bestest jest then."

"If you don't want those papers known, stop persecuting the Merediths."

"So thet gal 's caught yer, too, hez she? Look aout fer them. They 'll use yer ter save theer lands, an' then they 'll send yer ter right-abaout, like they done with my Phil. I warns yer agin 'em, an' ef yer don't listen ter me, the day 'll come when yer 'll rue it."

Meanwhile the Drinkers had made the new arrivals most welcome; and the two girls, with so much to tell each other, found it difficult to know where to begin. They had not talked long, however, when Janice became conscious that there was a rift in the lute.

"My letter," she said, "would have told you better than ever I now can all about the routs and the plays, and everything else; but, alas! some one broke into our house the night the British left Philadelphia, and search as I would the next day, I could not find what I had written you."

"I should think thee 'd be glad," replied Tibbie; "for surely thou 'rt ashamed of having been so Toryish."

"Not I," denied Janice. "And why should I be?"

"Shame upon thee, Janice Meredith, for liking the enemies of thy country!"

"And pray, madam," questioned Janice, "what has caused this sudden fervour of Whigism in you?"

"I never was unfaithful to my country, nor smiled on its persecutors."

"Humph!" sniffed Janice. "One would think, to hear you talk, that you have given those smiles to some rebel lover."

"Better a Whig lover than one of your popinjay British officers," retorted Tibbie, crimsoning.

"Gemini!" burst from the other. "I believe 't is a hit from the way you colour."

"And if 't was — which 't is not — 't is naught to feel ashamed of," resentfully answered the accused.

The two girls had been spatting thus in lowered voices on the sofa, and as Tibbie ended, her disputant's arm was about her waist, and she was squeezed almost to suffocation.

"Oh, Tibbie, wilt tell me all about it — and him — once we are in bed to-night?" begged Janice, in the lowest but most eager of whispers.

Whether this prayer would have been granted was not to be known, for as it was uttered Mr. Drinker interrupted their dialogue.

"Why, Tabitha," he called from across the room, "here 's a great miscarriage. Mrs. Meredith tells me that Colonel Brereton rode with them from Philadelphia, but thinking to o'ercrowd us he has put up at the Sun tavern."

Had the daughter merely remarked that "'T was a monstrous pity," or suggested that her father should at once set off to the hostel to insist on his coming to them, Janice would have thought nothing of the incident; but in place of this Tibbie said, "'T is well," with a toss of her head, even as she grew redder still, and realising this, she pretended that some supper preparation required her attention, and almost fled from the room.

"Colonel Brereton," explained Mr. Drinker, "stopped with us last summer each time he rode through Trenton on public business, and we came to like him much; so glad were we when he was well enough from his wound this spring to once more drop in upon us."

"His wound!" exclaimed Janice.

"Ay," said Miss Drinker. "Didst thee not know that he was hit at Whitemarsh, and was weeks abed?"

Mr. Drinker gave a hearty laugh as the girl shook her head in dissent. "I 'll tell thee a secret, Jan," he said, "and give thee a fine chance to tease. There was a girl not a hundred miles from this house who was sorely wounded by that same British bullet, and who pilfered every goody she could find from our pantry, and would have it that I should ride myself to Valley Forge with them all, but that I found a less troublesome conveyance."

"'T was very good of her," said Janice, gravely. "I — I did not know that he had been wounded."

"Thou wert hardly in the way of it," replied Mr. Drinker. "British officers were scarce news sheets of our army."

However praiseworthy Miss Meredith may have thought her

friend's kindness to Brereton, one action conveyed the contrary import, for when the bed hour came she said to Tabitha: "I think I'll sleep with mommy, and not with thee, after all."

"Oh, Jan, and I have so much to tell thee!"

"We make so early a start," explained Miss Meredith, "that the sleep is more valuable to me." Then the girl, after a swallow, said: "And I thank you, Tibbie, for being so good to Colonel Brereton, to whom we owe much kindness; for even had we known he was injured, we could have done nothing for him." She kissed her friend and followed her mother.

When Brereton appeared the next morning, Janice mounted the horse which was to bear her while the aide was exchanging greetings with the Drinkers; and when these quickly changed into farewells, she heeded not Tabitha's protest that they had not kissed each other good-by.

"I thought to save time by mounting," explained Janice, "and for this once it does not matter." And during the whole morning's ride the aide found her strangely silent and unresponsive.

Both these qualities disappeared with marvellous suddenness once they were within the Greenwood gate. All along the Raritan the fields were dotted with tents and parks of artillery, and on Greenwood lawn stood a large marquee, from which floated the headquarters' flag, while groups of officers and soldiers were scattered about in every direction. But all this panoply of war was forgotten by the girl, as Sukey, who was carrying some dish from the house to the tent, dropped it with a crash on the ground, and with a screech of delight rushed forward. Janice slid, rather than alighted, from her horse; and as if there were no such things as social distinctions, mistress and slave hugged each other, both rendered inarticulate by their sobs of joy. Further to prove that hearts have nothing to do with the colour of the skin, Billy Lee, who had been following in Sukey's train with another dish, was so melted by the sight that he proceeded to deposit his burden of a large ham on the grass, and began a loud blubbering in sympathy. Their united outcries served to bring two more participants on the scene, for Peg and Clarion came running out of the house and with screams and yelps sought to express their joy.

While this spectacle was affording infinite amusement to the officers and sentinels, Brereton, after helping Mrs. Meredith alight, went in search of Washington and in a few moments returned with him.

"We have made free with your home, as you see, Mrs. Meredith," apologised the commander-in-chief, as he shook her hand, "and I scarce know now whether to bid you welcome, or to ask leave for us to tarry till to-morrow. May we not effect a compromise by your dining and supping with me, and, in return, your favouring me and my family with a night's lodging?"

"Thou couldst not fail of welcome for far longer, General Washington," said Mrs. Meredith, warmly, "but thou art doubly so if Lady Washington is with thee."

"Nay; I meant my military family," explained the general. "Mrs. Washington retreated, ere the campaign opened, to Mount Vernon." Then he turned to the daughter and shook her hand. "Ah, Miss Janice," he said, "sorry reports we 've had of thy goings on, and we greatly feared we had lost thee to the cause."

"Ah, no, your Excellency," protested the girl. "Though I did once pray that the British should capture Philadelphia, 't was not because I wished you beaten, but solely because it would bring dadda to us, and — and many a prayer I 've made for you."

The general smiled. "'T will be glad news to some," he said, with a sidelong look at Brereton, "that thy sympathies have always been with us. I presume thou hast simply been doing the British soldiery all the harm that thou couldst under guise of friendliness. I 'll warrant thou 'st a greater tale of wounded officers than any of Morgan's riflemen, sharpshooters though they be."

"I would I could say I had been ever faithful, your Excellency, but I must own to fickleness."

"These are times that test loyalty to the full," replied Washington, "and there has been many a waverer in the land."

"Of that I know full well, your Excellency."

"Nay, Miss Meredith, thou needest not pretend that thou hast any knowledge of inconstancy. From that particular failing of mankind I 'll agree to hold thee harmless."

"Your Excellency but compliments me," answered Janice, "in presuming me exempt from forgetfulness." And as she spoke the girl gave an unconscious glance at Brereton.

L

ROSES AND HONEYSUCKLE

DINNER, which was actually being placed on the table in the tent at the moment the ladies arrived, cut short further conversation with either Washington or Sukey. Utterly forgetful of her duties to spit and oven, nothing would do the former cook but to follow Janice to her old room, where she summarily ordered Billy to clear out the clothing and accoutrements of its military tenants.

"Don't you stay, Sukey," said Janice, "if you are needed in the kitchen. His Excellency — "

"Dat I ain't, chile. Gin'l Washington he trabell wid his own cook, an' Peg an' I 'se only helpin' Mr. Lee set de table and carry de dishes. Now I help ma honey."

"Oh, Sukey," carolled Janice, "it *is* so good to be home again!"

"Guess Missus Sukey tink dat too," said William, halting in his labours. "She dun talk about nuthin' else but her pooty young missus."

"And how 's Blueskin, Billy?" questioned Janice.

"Lor' bless us, miss, dyar ain't no restrainin' ob dat steed wid de airs he put on since he dun took part at Monmouth an' hear the 'gin'l say what he tink ob dat feller Lee. I tell him if he doan behave better, de next time dyar 's goin' to be a battle, I jus' saddle up Nelson an' leave him behind."

"Now youse stop a-talkin' an' tote dem men's tings somewhars else. Missy Janice gwine to change her gown, an' we doan want nuttin' ob dat sort in hyar."

"I 'll only smart myself a little and not change my frock, Sukey, because — "

"Dat youse must, honey, for I dun praise youse so dat I ain't gwine to have dem disappointed in youse. Who 'll be to dinner to-day, Mr. Lee?"

"Gen'l Greene an' Lord Sterlin', an' de staff, an' de field an' brigades major ob de day."

"Dere, chile, now doan youse depreciate yourself to all dem. Jus' youse put on de pootiest dress youse hab an' do ole Sukey proud." Then, as she helped Janice to bedeck herself, she poured out the story of their makeshift life, telling how, with what had been left of the poultry, and with the products of the small patch of the garden they had been able to till, the two slaves had managed to live the year through, taking the best care they could of their master's property, and hoping and praying daily for what had at last come to pass. The arraying would have been more speedy with the volunteer abigail out of the room; but not once did the mistress even suggest it, and, on the contrary, paused several times in the process to give the black a hug.

Finally, a call from her mother put an end to this frittering and hurried the girl downstairs. Washington gave his hand to Mrs. Meredith, and there was a contest of words among the numerous officers for the privilege of the girl's, till Lord Sterling asserted his prerogative of rank and carried her off. Her presence was indeed a boon to the twenty men who sat down at the table, and, accustomed as Janice was by this time to the attention of officers, she could not but be flattered by the homage and deference paid her, all the more, perhaps, that it was witnessed by Brereton. Nor did this cease with the withdrawal of the ladies, for a number of the younger blades elected for her society rather than for that of the bottle, and made themselves her escort in the tour of inspection which Janice insisted on making about the place; and had she needed to be helped or lifted over every fence, or even stone, they encountered, there would have been willing hands to do it. It is true she was teased not a little for her supposed British sympathies, but it was not done ill-naturedly, and the girl was now quick-witted and quick-tongued enough to protect herself.

This plurality of swains did not lessen as the afternoon advanced, for not one of the diners departed, and when tea-time had come, their ranks were swelled by a dozen new arrivals, giving both Mrs. Meredith and Janice all they could do to keep the assembly supplied with "dishes" of the cheerful but uninebriating beverage which had been so material a cause in the very embodying of this army. Then the officers idled about the lawn, each perhaps hoping for an invitation to stay on. to the supper which so quickly followed the tea-drinking; and those who were fortunate enough to attain their wish did not hurry away once the meal was concluded. Only when Mrs. Meredith excused herself and her daughter on the ground of fatigue, did the youngsters recollect that there were camp duties which called them away.

"I fear me, Miss Janice," said the commander-in-chief, as the good-nights were being said, "that discipline would be maintained with difficulty were we long to remain encamped here. Personally, I cannot but regret that we move northward to-morrow; but for the good of the service I think 't is fortunate."

Drum beat and bugle call, sounding reveille, brought Janice back to consciousness the next morning; and it is to be suspected that she took some pains with her morning toilet, for by the time she descended tents were already levelled and regiments and artillery were filing past on the road.

"We have reason to believe that Sir Henry meditates a move up the Hudson against our post of West Point," Washington explained to Janice; "and so it is our duty to put ourselves within protecting distance, though I myself think he will scarce venture a blow, the more that he is strengthening his lines about New York. 'T is not a little pleasing to us that, after two years' fighting and manœuvring, both armies are brought back to the very point they set out from, and that, from being the attacking party, the British are now reduced to the use of spade and pick-axe for defence."

"I wish you were not leaving us, your Excellency," sighed Janice.

"'T is one of the penalties of war," replied the general, "that we are doomed to see little of the fair sex, and must be content with an occasional sip of their society. Should we winter near here, as now seems possible, I trust you will honour Mrs. Washington and myself with your company at headquarters. And one word ere we part, Mrs. Meredith. You must not think that we make free with people's property, as we seem to have done in your case. Finding your home unoccupied, I made bold to take it for my headquarters; but the quartermaster-general will pay you before we leave for such use as I have made of it."

"We could not accept anything, your Excellency," protested the hostess. "The obligation is with us, and I beg — "

"Be off with you to your stations, gentlemen," ordered Washington, as he rose from the table; and having cleared the room, he continued: "Nay, Mrs. Meredith, Congress allows me my expenses, and 't is only just that you should be paid. And however well provided you may be, a little ready money will surely not be amiss?"

"Your Excellency is more thoughtful of our future than we are ourselves," responded Mrs. Meredith. "For a moment I had forgot our position; we will gladly accept payment."

"Would that I could as easily pay you for the pleasure you have given me," said the general, shaking her hand. "Miss Janice, we 'll do our best," he went on, "to tie the British soldiery into New York; but, whether we succeed or no, I wish to hear of no more philandering with their officers. 'T is hard enough to fight them in the field, without encountering them in our softer moments; so see to it that you save your smiles and blushes for us."

"I will, your Excellency," promised Janice, as she did both.

"Nay, nay, my child," he corrected, smiling. "I did not mean that thou shouldst blush and smile for me. I am a married man, and old enough to be thy father."

"'T is fortunate you are the first, your Excellency," laughed the girl in turn, "or the latter should not protect you." And as the general held out his hand she impulsively kissed it.

"I shall write Mrs. Washington that 't will never do for her to leave me during another campaign," replied the commander, reciprocating the salute. "Not but she will be very proud to think that so charming a maid honours her husband with such favours."

At the door the staff were already mounted and waiting their chief. Farewells were completed with all save Brereton, who for some reason had withdrawn a little from the group; and these done, the cavalcade trotted off.

No sooner was it upon the road than Brereton spurred up

alongside of his superior, and, saluting, said in a dropped voice: "Your Excellency, I had something of moment to say to the Merediths, but 't was impossible to get private word, with all the idlers and racketers and Jack-a-dandies of the army running in and out upon them. May I not turn back? I will overtake you ere many hours."

"Think you, sir," asked Washington, gravely, "I have no occasion for my aides, that you make such a request?"

Jack flushed with mortification and temper. "I supposed that, on the march, you could spare —"

"'I can, my boy," interrupted the commander-in-chief, with a change of manner, "and was but putting off a take-in on you. My own courting was done while colonel of the First Virginia regiment, and well I remember how galling the military duties were. 'T is to be feared I was not wholly candid in the reasons calling me from the regiment to Williamsburg, that I alleged to my superiors, for my business at the capital took few hours, and both going and returning I managed to stay many at 'White House.' May your wooing speed as prosperously," he finished, extending an arm and pressing his junior's hand warmly. "And if by chance you should not overtake us till to-morrow, I 'll think of twenty years ago and spare you a reprimand."

"God save you, sir!" exclaimed Jack, in an undertone of gratitude. "I — I love — She is — is so dear to me, that I could not bear the thought of waiting." Wheeling his horse, the rider gave him the spur.

The moment the general and staff had trotted away, Mrs. Meredith turned to her daughter and asked, "Hast thou refused Colonel Brereton, Janice?"

"No, mommy," faltered the girl.

"Then why did he ride off without a word to either of us?"

"I — 't is — I can only think that — that he has come to care for Tibbie — being in and out of love easily — and so is ashamed of the part he has played."

"'T is evident that I was right in my view that thy vanity had misled thee," replied the mother. "But we 'll not discuss its meaning now, for I must find out how we stand. Try to make thyself a task, child."

Her search for this took the maiden, closely followed by

Clarion, to the garden, where she found that weeds, if nothing else, had thriven, though the perennials still made a goodly show. Before beginning a war on the former, she walked to a great tangle of honeysuckle that clustered about and overtopped a garden seat, to pluck a bunch and stick it in the neckerchief that was folded over her bosom; then she went to her favourite rose-bush and kissed the one blossom July had left to it. "I'll not pick you," she said, "since you are the only one."

The sound of galloping caught her attention as she raised her head; and though she could not see the rider, her ears told her that he turned into Greenwood gate, even before the pace was slackened. Not knowing what it might bode, the girl stood listening, with an anxious look on her face. The cadence of the hoof-beats ended suddenly, and silence ensued for a time; then as suddenly, quick footsteps, accompanied by a tell-tale jingle and clank, came striding along the path from the kitchen to the port in the hedge. One glance Janice gave at the opposite entrance, as if flight were in her thoughts, then, with a hand resting on the back of the seat to steady herself, she awaited the intruder.

Brereton paused in the opening of the box, as his eyes rested on his love. "Would to Heaven," he exclaimed, "that I had my colours and the time to paint you as you stand!"

Both relieved and yet more frightened, Janice, in an attempt to conceal the latter feeling, remarked, "I thought you had departed, sir."

"Think you I'd rest content without farewell, or choose to have one with the whole staff as witnesses?" answered Jack, as he came forward. "Furthermore, I had some matters of which to speak that were not to be published to the world."

"Mommy is —"

"Where I'd have her," interjected the officer; "for what I have to say is to you. First: I put the screws on old Hennion and Bagby, and have their word that they will not push their forfeiture bill, or in any other way molest you."

"We thank you deeply, Colonel Brereton."

"I rode to Brunswick and saw Parson McClave yesterday afternoon, to bespeak his aid, and he says he is certain you may live at peace here, if you will not seek to be rigorous with your tenants, and that he will do his best to keep the community from persecuting you."

"'T is glad news, indeed."

"Knowing how you were circumstanced, I then rode about your farms and held interview with a number of your tenants and pleaded with them that they pay a part of their arrears in supplies; and several of the better sort gave me their word that you should not want for food."

"'T was most thoughtful of you."

"Finally, I wrote a letter to your father, and have sent it under a flag that was going to New York, telling him that you were safe arrived at Greenwood."

"Ah, Colonel Brereton, how can we ever repay your kindness?" murmured the girl, her eyes brightened and softened by a mist of unshed tears.

"'T was done for my own ease. Think you I could have ridden away, not knowing what risk or privation you might have to suffer in my absence?"

"'T is only the greater cause for gratitude that you make your ease depend on ours."

"That empties my packet of advices," said the aide; "and — and — unless you have something to tell me, I'll — we 'll say a farewell and I'll rejoin the army."

"Would that I could thank you, sir, as you deserve; but words mean so little that you have rendered me dumb," replied Janice, feelingly.

"Can you not — Have you nothing else to say to me?" he begged pleadingly.

"I — Indeed, I can think of nothing, Colonel Brereton," replied the maiden, very much flustered.

"Then good-by, and may God prosper you," ended Jack, sadly, taking her hand and kissing it gently. He turned with obvious reluctance, and went toward the house, but before he had reached the hedge he quickly retraced his steps. "I — I could not force my suit upon you when I found you in such helplessness — not even when you gave me the purse — though none but I can know what the restraint meant in torture," he burst out; "and it seems quite as ungenerous to try to advantage myself now of your moment's gratefulness. But my passion has its limits of control, and go I cannot without — without — Give me but a word, though it be a sentence of death to my heart's desire."

Janice, whose eyes had been dropped groundward during most of this colloquy, gave the pleader a come-and-go glance, then said breathlessly, "I — 'T is — Wha — wha — What would you wish me to say?"

"What you can," cried the officer, impetuously.

"I — I would — 'T is my desire to — to say what you would have me."

Both her hands were eagerly caught in those of the suppliant. "If you could — If — 'T would be everything on earth — more than life itself to me — could you but give me the faintest hope that I might win you. Have you such an abhorrence of me that you cannot give me the smallest guerdon of happiness?"

"You err in supposing that I dislike you," protested Janice.

"Then why do you refuse all that is dearest to me? Why turn from a devotion that would make your happiness its own?"

"But I have n't," denied the girl, her heart beating wildly and her breath coming quickly.

As the words passed her lips, she was impulsively yet tenderly caught in her lover's arms and drawn to him. "What have you done, then?" he demanded almost fiercely.

"I — I — oh! I don't know," she gasped.

"Then, as you have pity in you, grant my prayer?"

For a moment Janice, with down-bent head, was silent. Then she raised her eyes to Jack's and said, "I will marry you, Colonel Brereton, if dadda will let me."

LI

A FAREWELL AND A WELCOME

THERE was little weeding of the garden that forenoon, unless the brushing off with Jack's gauntlets of some green moss from the garden seat, about which clustered the honeysuckle, can be considered such. Possibly this was done that more sprays of the vine might be plucked, for when Sukey, after repeated calls from the entry, finally came to summon them to dinner, Jack had a bunch of it, and a single rose, thrust in his sword knot.

There was a pretence of affected unconsciousness at the meal on the part of the three, and even of Peg, though the servant made it difficult to maintain the fiction by several times going off into fits of reasonless giggles not easy for those at table to ignore. The repast eaten, Brereton drew Mrs. Meredith aside for a word, and Janice took advantage of the freedom to escape to her room, where she buried her face in the pillow, as if she had some secret to confide to it.

From this she was presently roused by her mother's entrance, and as the girl, with flushed cheeks and questioning look, met her eyes, Mrs. Meredith said: "I think, my child, thou hast acted for the best, and we will hope thy father will think so."

"Oh, mommy, dost think he'll consent?"

"I fear not, but that must be as God wills it. Go down now, for Colonel Brereton says he must ride away, and only tarries for a word with thee."

Janice gave one glance at the mirror, and put her hands to her hair, with a look of concern. "'T is dreadfully disordered."

"He will not notice it, that I'll warrant," prophesied the matron.

With his horse's bridle over his arm, the lover was waiting for her on the front porch. "Will you not walk with me down the road a little way?" he begged. "'T is so hard to leave you."

"I—I think I had better not," urged the girl, showing trepidation. "'T would surely delay you too—"

"Ah, Janice," interrupted the lover, "why—what have I done that you should show such fear of me?"

"I'm not afraid of you," denied Janice, hurriedly; "and of course I'll go, if—if you think it best."

"Then what is it frightens you, sweetheart?" persisted Jack, as they set off.

The maiden scrutinised the ground and horizon as if seeking an explanation ere she replied shyly, "'T is—'t is indeed no fear of you, but you—you never ask permission."

The officer laughed exultingly. "Then may I put my arm about you?" he requested.

"'T will make walking too difficult."

"How know you that?" demanded Jack.

"'T is—'t is easily fancied."

Brereton's free arm encircled the girl. "Try to fancy it," he entreated. "And never again say that I do not ask permission."

A mile down the road Jack halted. "I'll not let you go further," he groaned; "nor must I linger, for reminder of my wound still troubles me if I ride too quick."

"Why did you not tell me you had been wounded when you took me away from the ball?" asked Janice, reproachfully.

"'T was not once in my thoughts that evening, nor was anything else save you."

"I can make all sorts of preserves and jellies and pickles, and next winter I'll send you some to camp."

"That you shall not," asserted the aide; "for the day we go into winter quarters sees me back here to dance at your wedding."

"Hadst better wait till thou art invited, sir?" suggested Janice, saucily.

"What? A revolt on my hands already!" exclaimed the officer.

"'T is you are the rebel."

"Then you are my prisoner," retorted Jack, catching her in his arms.

"You Whigs are a lawless lot!"

"Toward avowed Tories, ay — and a good serve-out to them."

"But I gave my word to his Excellency that from henceforth I'd be Whiggish, so you've no right to treat me as one."

"Then I'll not," agreed the lover. "And since I plundered from you while you were against us, 't is only right that I should return what I took." He kissed her thrice tenderly. "Good-by, my sweet," he said, and, releasing her, mounted. "'T is fortunate I depend not on my own legs, for they 'd never consent to carry me away from you." He started his horse, but turned in his saddle to call back: "'T will not be later than the first of November, with or without permission," and throwing a last kiss with his hand, spurred away.

Till Jack passed from view, the girl's eyes followed him; then, with a look of dreaminess in her eyes, she walked slowly back to Greenwood, so abstracted by her thoughts that she spoke not a word to the attendant hound.

Whatever might be the inclination of the girl, her mother gave her little chance to dream in the next few days. Not merely was there much about house and garden to be brought into order, but Mrs. Meredith succeeded in bargaining their standing crop of grass in exchange for a milch cow, and to Janice was assigned both its milking and care, while the chickens likewise became her particular charge. From stores in the attic the mother produced pieces of whole cloth, and Janice was set at work on dresses and underclothes to resupply their depleted wardrobes. Not content with this, Mrs. Meredith drew from the same source unspun wool and unhatchelled flax, and the girl was put to spinning both into thread and yarn, that Peg might weave them into cloth, against the need of winter. From five in the morning till eight at night there was occupation for all; and so tired was the maiden that she gladly enough heard her mother's decree that their small supply of candles should not be used, but that they should go to bed with the sun.

They were thus already asleep by ten o'clock one August evening, when there came a gentle knocking on the back door, which, after several repetitions, ceased, but only to be resumed a moment later on the front one. Neither summons receiving any attention, a succession of pebbles were thrown against Janice's window, finally bringing the sleeper back to wakefulness. Her first feeling, as she became conscious of the cause, was one of fear, and her instinct was to pay no attention to the outsider. After one or two repetitions, however, of the disquieting taps, she stole to the window, and, keeping herself hidden, peeped out. All she could see was a man standing close to a shrub, as if to take advantage of its concealment, who occasionally raised an arm and tossed a pebble against the panes. Really alarmed, the girl was on the point of seeking her mother, when her eyes took in the fact that Clarion was standing beside the cause of her fright, and seeking, so far as he could, to win his attention. Reassured, the girl raised the sash, and instantly her father's voice broke upon her ears.

"Down with ye, Jan," he said, "and let me get under cover."

Both anxious and delighted, the girl ran downstairs and unbarred the door.

"I had begun to fear me that I had been misinformed and that ye and your mother were not hereabout," the squire began; "so 't is indeed a joy to find ye safe." And then, after Mrs. Meredith had been roused, he explained his presence. "Though I could not get back to ye in Philadelphia, no worry I felt on your account, making sure that Lord Clowes would look to your safety. An anxious week I had after the army reached New York, till I received Colonel Brereton's letter telling me of your safety, though that only assured me as to the past, and I knew that any moment the rascally Whigs might take to persecuting ye again."

"Nay, Lambert," said Mrs. Meredith, "not a one has offered us the slightest annoyance. On the contrary, some of thy tenants have tendered us food in payment of rent, though I own that they insist upon hard bargains."

"I would I had as little complaint to make," responded the husband. "No sooner did Clinton reach New York than my appointment was taken from me, and but for Phil's kindness I should like to have starved. Though with little money himself, the boy would let me want for nothing, and but for him I should not even have been able to be here to-night."

"How was that, dadda?" asked Janice.

"'T is not to be whispered outside, Jan, but some of these same rebel Jerseymen — ay, and the Connecticut Yankees — much prefer the ring of British guineas to the brustle of the worthless paper money of the Whigs, so almost nightly boat-loads of provisions and forage steal out of the Raritan for New York, but for which the British army would be on short commons. Phil, who knew of this traffic, secured me passage on one of the empty boats."

"Then the villagers know thou hast returned?" exclaimed Mrs. Meredith, anxiously.

"Not they, for those in the business are as little anxious to have it known they have been in New York as I am to have it advertised that I am here at Greenwood, and there is little danger that either of us will blab."

"Had Lord Clowes arrived in New York, Lambert?" inquired Mrs. Meredith.

"That he had, and in a mighty dudgeon he was at first against all of us: with ye for what he took offence at in Philadelphia, and with me because I hold to my promise to Phil. But when he had word that I was coming here, he sought me out in a great turn-over, and said if I brought ye back to New York his house should be at our service, and that we should want for nothing. There is no doubt, lass, that he loves ye prodigious."

The girl shivered, August night though it was, but merely exclaimed, "You 'd not think of making us go to New York when we are under no necessity?"

"Not I, now that I know ye to be well off, which I feared ye were not. The nut to crack is to know whether I hadst best find safety by returning to New York, to live like a pauper on Phil, or seek to lie hid here for a three-months."

"And why three months, Lambert?" asked his wife.

"'T is thought that will serve to bring about a peace. Have ye not heard how this much-vaunted alliance with France has resulted? The French fleet and soldiers, united to a force under Sullivan, attempted to capture the British post at Newport, but oil and vinegar would not mix. The Parley-voos wanted to monopolise all the honour by having the Americans play second fiddle to them, but to this they 'd not consent; and while the two were quarrelling over it, like dogs over a bone, in steps the British, drubs the two of them, and carries off the prize. That gone, they 've set to quarrelling as to whose fault it was. The feeling now is as bitter against the French as 't was against the British, and 't is thought that with this end to their hopes from the frog-eaters, they 'll be glad enough to make a peace with us, the more that their paper money, the only thing that has kept them going this long, loses value daily, and they will soon have nothing with which to pay bills and soldiers."

"Thou hadst best stay here, Lambert," advised Mrs. Meredith. "'T will be more comfortable for thee, and far happier for us."

"Remember that I run the risk of capture, wife."

"Thou canst be kept concealed from all but Peg and Sukey, who are as faithful as we."

"And I am sure if by chance you were discovered," suggested Janice, haltingly, "that Colonel Brereton would — would — save you from ill treatment."

"Colonel Brereton?"

"Ay, Lambert," spoke up Mrs. Meredith, as her daughter looked appealingly to her. "There is something yet to be told, which has won us a strong friend who would never permit thee to suffer. Colonel Brereton, to whom we owe all our present safety, has declared his attachment to Janice, and seeks her — "

"Small doubt he has," derisively interjected the squire. "I make certain that every rebel, seeing the game drawing to a close, is seeking to feather his nest."

"Nay, Lambert. 'T is obvious he truly loves our — "

"He may, but it shall not help him to her or her acres," again interrupted the father. "The impudence of these Whigs passes belief. I hope ye sent him off with a bee in his breeches, Matilda."

"That we did not," denied Mrs. Meredith. "Nor wouldst thou, hadst thee been with us to realise all his goodness to us."

"Well, well," grumbled the father, resignedly, "I suppose if the times are such that we must accept favours of the rebels, we must not resent their insults. But 't is bitter to think of our good land come to such a pass that rogues like this Brereton and Bagby should dare obtrude their suits upon us."

"Oh, dadda," protested Janice, pleadingly, "'t was truly no insult he intended, but the — the highest — he spoke as if — as if — There was a tender respect in his every word and action, as if I might have been a queen. And I could not — Oh, mommy, please, please, tell it for me!"

"'T is best thou shouldst know at once, Lambert, that Janice favours his wooing."

"What!" roared the squire, looking incredulously from mother to daughter, and then, as the latter nodded her head, he cried, "I 'll not believe it of ye, Jan, however ye may wag your pate. Wed a bondman! Have ye forgot your old pledge to me? Where 's your pride, child, that ye should even let the thought occur to ye?"

"But he is well born, dadda, far better than we ourselves, for he told me once that his great-grandfather was King of England," cried the girl, desperately.

"And ye believed the tale?"

"He would not lie to *me*, dadda, I am sure."

"Why think ye that?"

"Oh — he never — loving me, he never — can't you understand? He 'd not deceive me, dadda."

"Ye 're the very one he would, ye mean, and small wonder he takes advantage of ye if ye talk as foolishly to him as to me. Have done with all thought of the fellow and of his clankers concerning his birth. Whate'er he was, he is to-day a runaway bondservant and —"

"But, dadda, he is now a lieutenant-colonel and —"

"Of what? Where 's the honour in being in command of the riff-raff of the land? Dost not know that the most of their officers are made out of tapsters and tinkers and the like? Does it make a tavern idler or a bankrupt the less of either, that a pack of dunghills choose to dub him by another title? Once peace and law are come again, this same scalawag Brereton, or Fownes, or whatever he will then be, must return to my service and fulfil his bond, with a penalty of double time to boot. Proud ye 'd be to see your spouse ordered to field or stable work every morning by my overseer!"

"'T would grieve me, dadda," replied the girl, gently, "because I know how proud he is, and how it would make him suffer; but 't would not lessen my respect or — or affection for him."

"What?" snorted Mr. Meredith once more. "Dost mean to tell me that thy heart is in this?"

"I — indeed, dadda," stammered Janice, colouring, "until — until this moment I thought 't was only for yours and mommy's sakes — though at times puzzled by — by I know not what — but now —"

"Well, out with it!" ordered the squire, as his daughter hesitated.

Janice faltered, then hurried to where her father sat, and, throwing herself on her knees, buried her face in his waistcoat. Something she said, but very sharp ears it needed to resolve the muffled sounds into the words, "Oh, dadda, I 'm afraid that I care for him more than I thought."

"What!" for a third time demanded Mr. Meredith. "'T is not possible I hear ye aright, girl. Why, a nine-months ago ye were beseeching me, with your arms about my neck, to fulfil my word to Phil."

"But that was because I feared Lord Clowes," eagerly explained Janice, with her face withdrawn from its screen; "and then I did not love — or at least did not dream that I did."

"Pox me, but I believe Clowes is right when he says the sex are without stability," growled the squire, irascibly. "Put this fellow out of your thoughts, and remember that ye were promised long since."

"Oh, dadda, I want to be dutiful, and obedient I promise to be, but you would not have me marry with my heart given elsewhere. You could not be so cruel or —"

"Cease such bibble-babble, Jan. 'T is for your own good I am acting. Not merely is this fellow wholly beneath ye in birth and fortune, besides a rebel to our king, but there are facts about him of which ye have not cognisance that should serve to rouse your pride."

"What?"

"What say ye to an intimacy twixt this same Brereton and Mrs. Loring?"

With the question the girl was on her feet, yet with down-hung head. "He — I know he does not care for her," she declared.

"Ye know nothing of the kind," retorted the squire. "I bear in my pocket a letter from her to him of so private a nature that she would not trust it to a flag, because then it must be read, which Lord Clowes brought to me with the request that I would in some way smuggle it to him."

"That means little," said Janice.

"And what say ye to his meeting her in New York, for that is the purpose of her letter to him?"

"How know you that?" cried Janice.

"Because she writ on the outside that the commander at Paulus Hook had been sent orders to pass him to New York."

"That proves no wrong on his part," answered the girl, her head proudly erect. "Nor will I believe any of him." And without further words she went from the room. But though she went to bed, she tossed restless and wakeful till the sun rose.

LII

SCANT WELCOME FOR MAN AND BEAST

THE concealment of the master of Greenwood proved an easy affair, for it was now the harvest season and the neighbouring farmers were far too engaged by their own interests to have thought of anything else, while the four miles was distance sufficient to deter the villagers from keeping an eye on the daily household life. For their own comfort, a place of concealment was arranged for the squire in the garret behind the big loom; but thus assured of a retreat, he spent his time on the second floor, his only precautions being to avoid the windows in daylight hours and to keep Clarion at hand to give warning of any interloper.

In the next few days Mrs. Meredith twice reverted to the subject of their midnight discussion, but each time only to find her husband unyieldingly persistent that Janice was pledged to Philemon, and that if this bar did not exist, he would never countenance Brereton's suit. As for the girl, she shunned all allusion to the matter, taking refuge in a proud silence.

In September an unexpected event brought the difficulty to a crisis. One evening, after the work of the day was over, as they sat in Mrs. Meredith's room, waiting for the dusk to deepen enough for beds to become welcome, a creak of the stairs set all three to listening, and brought Clarion to his feet. Though no repetition of the sound followed, the dog, after a moment's attention, dashed out of the room and was heard springing and jumping about, with yelps betokening joyful recognition of some one. Reassured by this, yet wishing to know more, Janice hurried into the hall. Coming from the half-light, it was too dark for her to distinguish anything, so she was forced to grope her way to the stairs; but other eyes were keener, and Janice, without warning, was encompassed by a man's arms, which drew her to him that his lips might press an eager kiss upon hers.

"Who is it?" whispered the pilferer, after the theft.

"Oh, Colonel Brereton!" exclaimed the girl, in an undertone; "I knew at once, but —"

"Forgive me if I frightened you, sweetheart," begged the officer, softly. "I could not resist the impulse to surprise you, and so tied my horse down the road a bit, that I might steal in upon you unaware."

"But what brings you?" questioned the girl, anxiously.

Brereton, with a touch of irritation, answered: "And you can ask? Even my vanity is forced to realise you waste little love on me that you need explanation. Sixty miles and over I have rid to-day solely that I might bide the night here, and not so much as a word of welcome do you give me. But I vow you shall love me some day even as I love you; that you too shall long for sight of me when I am away, and caress me as fondly when I return."

"I did not mean that I was not glad to see you," protested the maiden; "but — I thought — I thought you could not leave the army."

"Know then, madam," banteringly explained the lover, "that the court-martial which has been trying Lee for his conduct at Monmouth has come to a verdict, which required transmission to Congress, for confirmation, and as I enjoy nothing better than two hundred and forty miles of riding in September heats and dust, I fairly went on my knees to his Excellency for permission to bear it. And now do you ask why I wished it? Do I not deserve something to lighten the journey? Ah, my sweet, if you care for me a little, prove it by once returning me one of my kisses!"

"With whom art thou speaking, daughter?" demanded Mrs. Meredith, losing patience at the continuance of the dialogue she could just realise.

"'T is I, John Brereton, Mrs. Meredith," spoke up the intruder, "come in search of a night's lodgings."

The information was enough to make the squire forget prudence, in the spleen it aroused. "Have done with your whispered prittle-prattle, Jan, and let me have sight of this fellow," he called angrily.

"Mr. Meredith! you here?" cried the officer, springing to the doorway, to make sure that his ears did not deceive him.

"Ay, and no wonder 't is a sad surprise to ye," went on Mr. Meredith, irascibly. "There shall be no more stolen interviews — ay, or kisses — from henceforth, ye Jerry Sneak! Come out of the hall, Janice, and have done with this courting by stealth."

"I call Heaven to witness," retorted Jack, hotly, "if once I have acted underhand; and you have no right — "

"Pooh! 't is not for a jail-bird and bond-servant and rebel to lay down the right and wrong to Lambert Meredith."

"Oh, dadda — " expostulatingly began Janice.

"What is more," continued the father, regardless of her protest, "I 'll have ye know that I take your behind-back wooing of my daughter as an insult, and will none of it."

"Is it prudent, Lambert, needlessly to offend Colonel Brereton?" deprecated Mrs. Meredith.

"Ay. Let him give me up to the authorities," sneered the husband. "'T will be all of a piece with his other doings."

"To such an imputation I refuse to make denial," said Brereton, proudly; "but be warned, sir, by the trials for treason now going on in Jersey and Pennsylvania, what fate awaits you if you are captured. Even I could not save you, I fear, after your taking office from the king, if you were caught thus."

"Wait till ye 're asked, and we 'll see who first needs help, ye or I," retorted the squire. "Meantime understand that I 'll not have ye at Greenwood, save as a bond-servant. My girl is promised to a man of property and respectability, and is to be had by no servant who dare not so much as let the world know who were his father and mother!"

It was now too dark to distinguish anything, so the others did not see how Brereton's face whitened. For a moment he was silent, then in a voice hoarsely strident he said: "No man but you could speak thus and not pay the full penalty of his words; and since you take so low an advantage of my position, further relations with you are impossible. Janice, choose between me and your father, for there can be but the one of us in your future life."

"Oh, Jack," cried the girl, imploringly, "you cannot — if you love me, you cannot ask such a thing of me."

"He puts it well," asserted Mr. Meredith. "Dost intend to obey me, child, or — "

"Oh, dadda," chokingly moaned Janice, "you know I have promised obedience, and never will I be undutiful, but — "

The aide, not giving her time to complete the sentence, vehemently exclaimed, "'T is as I might have expected! Lover good enough I am when you are in peril or want, but once saved, I am quickly taught that your favours are granted from policy and not from love."

"'T is not so," denied the girl, indignantly yet miserably; "I — "

"Be still, Jan," ordered the father. "Think ye, sir, Lambert Meredith's daughter would ever bring herself to wed a no-name and double-name fellow such as ye? Here is a letter I fetched to ye from that —— Mrs. Loring: take it and go to her. She 's the fit company for gentry of your breed, and not my girl."

"Beg of me forgiveness on your deathbed, or on mine, and I 'll not pardon you the words you have just spoken," thundered the officer; "and though you stand on the gallows itself, I will not stir finger to save you. Once for all, Janice, take choice between us."

"'T is an option you have no right to force upon me," responded the girl, desperately.

"Ay, pay no heed to what he says, Jan. Hand him this letter and let him go."

"If he wants it, he must take it himself," cried Janice. "I 'll not touch *her* letter."

The indignant loathing in the tone of the speaker was too clearly expressed not to be understood, and Brereton replied to it rather than to her words. "I tried to speak to you of her — to tell you the whole wretched story, when last I saw you, but I could not bring myself in such hap — at such an hour — the moment was too untimely — and so I did not.

Little I suspected that you already knew the facts of my connection with her."

"Despite the proof I myself had, I have ever refused to credit when told by others what you have just owned," declared the girl. "Nor will I listen to you. From the first I scorned and hated her, and now wish never to hear of the shameful creature again."

Without a word the officer passed into the hall, and began the descent. Before he had reached the foot of the stairs Janice was at its head.

"You'll not go without a good-by, Jack," she pleaded. "Obey dadda I ought—but— Oh, Jack—I will—if you will but come back— Yes, I will kiss you."

Brereton halted and clutched the banister, as if to prevent either departure or return, and could the girl have seen the look on his face she would have been in his arms before he had time to conquer himself. But in doubt as to what the pause indicated, she stood waiting, and after a moment's struggle Jack strode through the hallway and was gone. So long as his footsteps could be heard Janice stood listening to them, but when they had died out of hearing she went into her own room, and the parents heard the bolt shot.

There was something in the girl's eyes the next morning which prevented either father or mother from recurring to the scene, and time did not make it easier; for Janice, with a proudly sad face, did her tasks in an almost absolute silence, which told more clearly than words her misery. Probably the matter would have eventually been reopened, but two days brought a new difficulty which gave both Mr. and Mrs. Meredith something else for thought.

Its first warning was from the hound, who roused his master, as he dozed in an easy-chair one sleepy afternoon, by a growl, and the squire's own ears served to tell him that horsemen were entering the gate. The women on the floor below also heard the sounds, and with a call to make sure that the refugee was seeking his hiding-place, the mother and daughter hurried to the front door to learn what the incursion might portend.

From the porch they could see a half-dozen riders in uniform, who had drawn rein just inside the gateway, while yet another, accompanied by two dogs, rode up to where they were standing.

"'T is General Lee," exclaimed Mrs. Meredith, as he came within recognising distance. "Probably he wishes a night's lodging."

It was far from what the officer wanted, as it proved; for when he had come within good speaking distance he called angrily, "Ho! ye are there, are ye, hussy? Still busily seeking, I suppose, to be a pick-thanks with those in power by casting ridicule on those they are caballing to destroy."

"I know not the cause for thy extraordinary words, General Lee," replied Mrs. Meredith, with much dignity, "and can only conclude that a warm afternoon has tempted thee into a too free use of the bottle."

"Bah!" ejaculated Lee. "My bicker is not with ye, but with your girl, who, it seems, has a liking for mischief and slander."

"I am ignorant to what thee refers, sir, and cannot believe —" began the mother.

"Deny if you can that she limned the caricature of me which was handed about the theatre, and made me and my dogs the laugh of the town for a week?" interrupted Lee. "Only three days since I had a letter from a friend in Philadelphia, telling me a journal of hers had been examined by the council, and that therein she confessed it as her work."

"Indeed, General Lee," said Mrs. Meredith, apologetically, "the child meant no —"

"I tell you I 'm not to be mollified by any woman's brabble," blustered Lee. "I know 't is part and parcel of an attempt to ruin my character. Even to this silly witling, all are endeavouring to break me down by one succession of abominable, damnable lies. The very court that has been trying me would not believe that white was white as regards me, or that black was black as regards this G. Washington, whom the army and the people consider as an infallible divinity, when he is but a bladder of emptiness and pride. I am now on my way to get their verdict against me, and in favour of this Great Gargantua, or Lama Babek — for I know not which to call him — set aside, and I stopped in passing to tell you that I —"

What the general intended was not to be known, for at this point there came that which turned his thoughts. One of his dogs, an English spaniel, neither interested in Janice's caricature of Lee, nor in Lee's abuse of Washington, took advantage of his master's preoccupation to steal into the house, — a proceeding which Clarion evidently resented, for suddenly from within came loud yaps and growls, which told only too plainly that if there was no protector of the household from the anger of the general, there was one who objected to the intrusion of his dog. Scarcely had the sounds of the fight begun than shrill yelps of pain indicated that one participant was getting very much the worst of it, and which, was quickly shown by the general roaring an oath and a command that they stop the "murder of my Cæsar." The din was too great within, however, for Clarion to hear the order that both ladies shouted to him, though it is to be questioned if he would have heeded them if he had; and with another oath Lee was out of his saddle and into the house, his riding-whip raised to take summary vengeance.

Just as the general entered the hallway, the spaniel, wriggling free from the hound's onslaught, fled upstairs, closely pursued by the other dog, and after the two stamped the officer. On the second floor the fugitive faltered, to cast an agonised glance behind him, but sight of Clarion's open mouth was enough, and up the garret stairs he fled. At the top he once more paused, looking in all directions for a haven of refuge; and seeing a man in the act of retreating behind the loom in the corner, he fled to him for protection. When Lee entered the garret, only Clarion, every bristle on end, was in view, standing guard over a corner of the room; and striding to him, the general lashed him twice with his riding-whip ere the transgressor, with howls of surprised pain, fled. Then Lee peered behind the loom in search of his favourite.

"Devil seize me!" he exclaimed. "What have we here? Ho! a good find," he jeered, as he made out the squire. He rushed to one of the windows, threw it up, and called a summons to the group of horsemen, then came back as the squire crawled from his retreat. "Little did I reck," gloated Lee, "when I read at the tavern this very day the governor's proclamation attainting you, that ye 'd come to be my prize. And poetic justice it is that I should have the chance to avenge in you the insult of your daughter."

LIII

UNDER SHADOW OF THE GALLOWS

NO prayer the women could make served to sway Lee from his purpose, and without delay the prisoner was mounted behind one of the escort, taken to Brunswick, and handed over to the authorities. When Mrs. Meredith and Janice, who followed on foot, reached the town, it was to find that the squire was to be carried to Trenton the next morning. A plea was made that they should be permitted to accompany him, but it was refused, and a bargain was finally made with the publican to carry them.

The following evening saw them all in Trenton, Mr. Meredith in jail, and the ladies once more at the Drinkers'. It was too late for anything to be attempted that night; but early the next day Mrs. Meredith, with Mr. Drinker, called on Governor Livingston to plead for mercy.

"Had he come in and delivered himself up, there might have been some excuse for special lenience," the Governor argued; "but captured as he was, there can be none. The people have suffered so horribly in the last two years that they wish a striking example made of some prominent Tory, and will not brook a reasonless pardon. He must stand his trial under the statute and proclamation, and of that there can be but one outcome."

When the suppliants returned with this gloomy prediction, Janice, who held herself accountable for the calamity, primarily by having secured the appointment of her father, and still more by drawing the caricature which had brought such disaster, was so overcome that for a time the mother's anxieties were transferred to her. Realising this, after the first wild outburst of grief and horror were over, Janice struggled desperately to regain self-control; and when the two had gone to bed, she successfully resisted her longing to give way once more to tears, though no sleep came to her the night through. Yet, if she brought pale cheeks and tired eyes to the breakfast table, there was determination rather than despair in her face and manner, as if in her long vigil she had thought out some deliverance.

In what this consisted was shown by her whispered request to Mr. Drinker, the moment the meal had been despatched, to learn for her if Joe Bagby was in town, and to arrange for an interview. Within the hour her emissary returned with the member of Assembly.

"I suppose you have heard, Mr. Bagby, of my father's capture," she said, without even the preliminary of a greeting.

"Yes, miss," said Bagby, awkwardly and shamefacedly; "'t is news that did n't stop travelling, and 't was all over Trenton before he 'd been an hour in town. One way or another, he and I have n't got on well, but I did n't wish him or you any such bad luck, and I 'm real sorry it 's come about."

"I wished to see you to ask — to beg," went on the girl, "that you would persuade the Governor to set him free."

"But he 'd not have the right to do that," replied Joe. "He only can pardon the squire after the trial. And right now I want to say that if you have n't settled on any lawyer, I will take the case and do my best for your dad, and let you take your own time as to paying me."

"Oh, Mr. Bagby," pleaded Janice, "Mr. Drinker is sure that he will be convicted of treason. Can you not do something to stop it?"

"I am afraid he is right, miss. About his only chance will be for the Governor to pardon him."

"But only yesterday he said he should not," wailed Janice. "Can you not persuade him?"

"Guess 't would be only be a waste of my time," answered Joe. "He and I have disagreed over some appointments, and we are n't much of friends in consequence. But aside from that, he 's a great trimmer for popularity, and the people just now are desperate set on having the Tories punished."

"Don't say that," besought the girl. "Surely, if — if — if I promise to marry you, cannot you save him?"

"If 'twas a bridge to be built, or a contract for uniforms, or something of that sort, I 'd have real influence in the Assembly; but I am afraid I can't fix this matter. The Governor 's a consarned obstinate man most times, and I don't believe he 'll listen to any one in this. What I can do, though, if you 'll just do what you offered, miss, will be to save your property from all risk of being taken from you."

"Don't speak of it to me," cried Janice, wildly. "Do you think we could care for such a thing now?"

"Property 's property," said Joe, "and 't is n't a good thing to forget, no matter what happens. However, that can wait. Now, about my being your lawyer?"

"I will speak to my mother," replied the girl, sadly, "and let you know her wishes." And the words were so evidently a dismissal that Bagby took his departure.

Without pausing to mourn over the failure, Janice procured paper and pen, and set about a letter; but it was long in the writing, for again and again the pages were torn up. Finally, in desperation, she let her quill run on, regardless of form, grammar, erasures, or the blurs caused by her own tears, until three sheets had been filled with incoherent prayers and promises. "If only you can save him," one read, "nothing you ask of me, even to disobeying him, even to running off with you, will I refuse. I will be your very slave." If ever a proud girl humbled herself, Janice did so in this appeal.

The reading of the missive was begun the next day by an officer seated in the "public" of the City Tavern of Philadelphia, but after a very few lines he rose and carried it to his own room, and there completed it. Then folding it up, he thrust it into his pocket, once more descended the stairs, and inquired of the tavern-keeper: "'T was reported that General Lee came to town yesterday; dost know where he lodges?"

"I hearn he was at the Indian King."

"Thanks," responded the questioner, and then asked: "One thing more. Hast a stout riding-whip you can lend me for a few minutes?"

"Ay, Colonel Brereton. Take any that suits you from the rack."

The implement secured, the officer set out down the street, with a look that boded ill for somebody.

Five minutes later, with one hand held behind his back, he stood in the doorway of the public room of another ordinary, arriving just in time to hear a man proclaim in stentorian tones: —

"I tell ye, any other general in the world than General Howe would have beat General Washingion; and any other general in the world than General Washington would have beat General Howe."

"Hush!" said a man. "Here is one of his aides."

"Think ye I care?" roared Lee. "Colonel Brereton and all others of his staff know too well the truth of what I say to dare resent it. The more that hear me, the better."

Brereton strode forward to within three feet of Lee. "You owe your immunity," he said, struggling to speak quietly, "to the very man you are abusing, for not one of his family but would have challenged you after your insulting letters to him, had not General Washington commanded us all to refrain, lest, if any of his staff called you out, it should seem like his personal persecution. Your conduct to him was outrage enough to make me wish to kill you, but now you have given me a stronger reason, and this time there is no high-minded man to save you from my vengeance, you cur!" There was a quick motion of Jack's arm, a swishing sound, and the whip was furiously lashed full across the general's face.

Lee, white with rage, save where a broad red welt stretched from ear to chin, staggered to his feet, pulling at his sword as he rose, but his three companions united to restrain him.

"Take your satisfaction like a gentleman, sir," insisted one, "and not like a tavern broiler."

"I shall see Major Franks within the hour," remarked Brereton, "and have no doubt he will represent me. But if you wish a meeting, you must act promptly, for I shall not remain in the city later than noon to-morrow."

It was just after dawn the next morning that five horsemen turned off from the Frankford road into a meadow, and struck across it to a piece of timber on the other side. One of them was left with the horses, and the remainder took their way to an open spot, where the trees had been felled. Here the four paired off, and the couples held a brief consultation.

"I care not what the terms be," Brereton ended, "so long as you secure the privilege of advancing, for one of us goes not off the field unhurt."

The seconds held a conference, and then separated. Each gave his principal a pistol, and stationed him so that they stood some twenty paces apart.

"Gentlemen, with your weapons pointed groundward, on the word, you will walk toward each other, and fire when it pleases you," ordered Major Edwards. "Are you ready? Go!"

The duellists, with their pistol hands dropped, walked steadily forward, one, two, three, four, five strides.

"'T is murder, not satisfaction, they seek!" ejaculated Franks, below his breath.

Another and yet another step each took, until there was not twenty feet between the two; then Lee halted and coolly raised his arm; one more step Brereton took as he did so, and not pausing to steady his body, his pistol was swung upward so quickly that it flashed first. Lee's went off a second later, and both men stood facing each other, the smoking barrels dropped, and each striving to see through the smoke of his own discharge. Thus they remained for a moment, then Lee dropped his weapon, staggered, and with the words, "I am hit," went on one knee, and then sank to the ground.

Brereton walked back to his original position, and stood calmly waiting the report of his second, who, with Edwards, rushed to the wounded man's assistance.

"He is struck in the groin," Franks presently informed him; "and while not dangerous, 't will be a month before he 's good for anything."

"You mean good for nothing," replied Jack. "I meant to make it worse, but must rest content. As I told you, I ride north without delay, so will not even return to the city. Thank you, David, for helping me, and good-by."

Five hours later, Lee was lying in the Pennsylvania hospital, and Brereton was riding into Trenton. Without the loss of a moment, the aide sought an interview with the Governor, clearly with unsatisfactory results; for when he left that official his face was anxious, and not even tarrying to give his mare rest, he mounted and spurred northward, spending the whole night in the saddle. Pausing at Newark only to breakfast, he secured a fresh horse, and reached Fredericksburg a little before nightfall. Seeking out the commander-in-chief, he delivered certain papers he carried; but before the general could open them, he said: —

"Your Excellency, I wish speech with you on a matter of life and death. To no other man in the world would I show this letter, but I beg of you to read it, sir, and do what you can for my sake and for theirs."

Washington took the sheets held out to him and slowly read them from beginning to end. "'Tis a sad tale the poor girl tells," he said when he had finished; "but, my boy, however much I may pity and wish to aid them, my duty to the cause to which I have dedicated my life — "

"Ah, your Excellency," burst out Jack, "in just this one instance 't will surely not matter. A word from you to Governor Livingston — "

Washington shook his head. "I have ever refrained from interfering in the civil line," he said, "and one breaking of the rule would destroy the fabric I have reared with so much pains. If I have gained influence with the people, with the army, and with the State officials, it is because I have ever refused to allow personal considerations to shape my conduct; and that reputation it is my duty to maintain at all hazards, that what I advise and urge shall never be open to the slightest suspicion of any other motive than that of the public good. It is a necessity which has caused me pain in the past, and which grieves me at this moment, but I hold a trust. Do not make its performance harder than it need be."

"Do I not deserve something at your hands, sir? Faithfully I have served you to my uttermost ability."

"You ask what cannot be granted, Brereton; and from this refusal I must not recede. Now leave me, my boy, to read the despatches you have brought."

There was that in the general's manner which made impossible further entreaty, and the aide obeyed his behest. Yet such was the depth of his concern that he made a second appeal, two days later, when he brought a bunch of circular letters to the State governors, concerning quotas of provisions, which he had written, to his chief for signature.

"Will you not, sir," he implored, "relent and add a postscript to Governor Livingston in favour of mercy for Mr. Meredith?"

"I have given you my reasons, Brereton, why I must not, and all further petitions can but pain us both." Washington signed the series, and taking the sand-box, sprinkled the wet ink on each in turn. "Seal them, and see that they fail not to get into the post," he ordered calmly. Yet as he rose to leave the room, he laid his hand affectionately on Jack's shoulder, and said: "I grieve not to do it, my boy, for your sake and for hers."

The aide took the chair the general had vacated, and began mechanically the closing of the letters; but when that to the Governor of New Jersey was reached, he paused in the process. After a little, he took from his pocket Janice's frantic supplication, and reread it, his face displaying his response to her suffering. "And ten words would save him," he groaned. His eye sought once more the unsealed letter, and stared at it fixedly. "At worst it will be my life, and that is worth little to me and nothing to any one else!" He snatched a pen hastily, dipped it in the ink, but as he set the tip to the paper, paused, his brow clouded. "To trick him after all his generosity!" For a trice Jack hesitated. "He stands too high to be injured by it," he exclaimed. "It hurts not the cause, while 't will kill her if they hang him." Again he set pen to the paper, and wrote a postscript of four lines below Washington's name. "'T is the devil's work, or her good angel's, that I had the writing of the letters, so the penmanship agrees," he muttered, as he folded and sealed it. Gathering up the batch, he gave a reckless laugh. "I said I 'd not lift finger to save him from the rope, and here I am taking his place on the gallows. Well, 't is everything to do it for her, scorn and insult me as they may, and to die with the memory that my arms have held and my lips caressed her."

LIV

A GAIN AND A LOSS

IT was two days of miserable doubt which Janice spent after despatching her letter to Brereton. Then something Mr. Drinker told his daughter brought some cheer to the girl.

"Friend Penrhyn informed me that Colonel Brereton rode into town this afternoon, Tabitha," he said, at the supper table; "yet, though I went to the tavern to bespeak his company here this evening, I could not get word of him. 'Tis neglectful treatment, indeed, of his old friends, that three times in succession he should pass through without dropping in upon us."

"He may still come, father," suggested Tabitha; and more than she spent the evening in a state of expectancy. But bedtime arrived; and the morrow came and went without further news of him who had now become Janice's sole hope, and then she learned that he had ridden northward.

"I knew his temper was hot," she sobbed in her own room, "but never did I believe he could be so cruel as to come and go without word or sign."

From the trial, which occurred but three days after this crushing disappointment, the public were excluded, not even Mrs. Meredith and Janice being permitted to attend. The result, therefore, was first brought them by Bagby, who, though his services had been refused by Mr. Meredith, had succeeded in being present.

"The squire's lawyer," he told them, "was n't up to a trick or two that I had thought out, and which might have done something; but he made a pretty good case, if he could n't save him. Morris's charge was enough to convict, but every juryman was ready to vote 'Guilty' before the Chief Justice had so much as opened his mouth."

"Is there nothing to do?" cried Mrs. Meredith.

"I'll see the Governor, and I'll get my friends to see him," promised Bagby; "but don't you go to raising your hopes, for there is n't one chance in a hundred now."

Once again Mrs. Meredith sought interview with Livingston, but the Governor refused to even see her; and both Mr. Drinker's and Bagby's attempts succeeded little better, for they could only report that he declined to further discuss the matter, and that the execution was set for the following Friday.

Abandoning all hope, therefore, Mrs. Meredith wrote a letter, merely begging that they might spend the last night with Mr. Meredith in the jail; and when the next morning she received a call from the Governor, she only inferred that it was in relation to her plea.

"It has been far from my wish, Mrs. Meredith," Livingston said, "to bring suffering to you more than to any one else, and the position I have taken as regards your husband was only that which I deemed most for the good of the State, and most in accord with public opinion. The vipers of our own fireside require punishment; your husband had made himself one of the most conspicuous and unpopular of these by the office he held under the king, and no reason could I discover why he should not reap the punishment he fitly deserved. But this morning a potent one was furnished me, for I received a letter from General Washington, speaking in high terms of Mr. Meredith, and expressing a hope that we will not push his punishment to the extreme of the law. It is the first time his Excellency has ever ventured an opinion in a matter outside of his own concern, and I conclude that he believes stringent justice in this case will injure more than aid our cause; and as the use of his name furnishes me with an explanation that will satisfy the Assembly and people of this State, I can be less rigorous. That you should not endure one hour more of anxiety than need be, I have hurried to you, to tell you that I shall commute his sentence to imprisonment with the other political prisoners in Virginia."

The scene of gratitude and joy that ensued was not describable, and some hours passed before either mother or daughter became sufficiently composed to take thought of the future. Then, by permission of the jailer, they saw Mr. Meredith and discussed the problem before them. Neither wife nor daughter could bear the thought of again being separated from the squire, and begged so earnestly to be allowed to share the half-captivity, half-exile, that had been decreed him, that he could not deny them, the more that his own heart-strings in reality drew the same way, and only his better judgment was opposed to it.

"'T will be a hard journey, wife," he urged, "and little comfort we 're like to find at the end of it. For me there can be no escape, but 't is not necessary that ye should bear it, for 't is to be hoped ye can live on at Greenwood, as ye have already."

"We should suffer more, Lambert, in being separated from thee."

"Oh, dadda, nothing could be worse than that," cried Janice, her arms about his neck.

"Have your way, then," finally acceded their lord and master.

This settled, they set about such preparations as were possible. From Mr. Drinker a loan of five thousand dollars — equal to a hundred pounds, gold — was secured, and a bargain struck with a farmer to bring from Greenwood such supplies of clothes as Mrs. Meredith wrote to Sukey to pack and send. To most the prospect would not have been a cheering one, but after the last few days it seemed truly halcyon, and Janice was scarcely able to contain her happiness. She poured her warmest gratitude and thanks out in a letter to Washington, which would have surprised him not a little had he ever received it, but the mail in which it went was captured, and it was a British officer in New York who ultimately read it. Nor did this effusion satisfy her.

"Oh, mommy," she joyfully bubbled, as they were preparing for bed, "was there ever a greater or nobler or kinder man than General Washington?"

And though the first frost of the season was forming crystals on the panes, she knelt down in her short night-rail on a lamb's wool rug, so small that her little feet rested on the cold boards, and prayed for the general as he had probably never been prayed for, — prayed until she was shivering so that her mother interfered and ordered her to come to bed.

Her prayers were far more needed by some one else. From the commission of his wrong, Brereton made it a point to meet the post-rider as he trotted up to headquarters each afternoon, and on the third day after the action of the Governor, he found in the mail a letter which told him of the success of his trick. While he was still reading, Colonel Hamilton came to him with a message that Washington desired his presence and, squaring his shoulders and setting his mouth as if in preparation for an ordeal, Jack hastened to obey, though, as he came to the closed doorway he hesitated for a moment before he knocked, much as if his courage failed him.

Upon entrance, he found his superior striding up and down the room, a newspaper in his hand, and without preliminary word the general gave expression to his obvious anger.

"I would have you know, Colonel Brereton," sternly he began, "that I am not the man to overlook disobedience of my orders, nor pass over, without a rebuke, such disrespect as you have shown me."

"I do not deny that your Excellency has cause for complaint," replied Jack, steadily; "and in acting as I did I was fully prepared for whatever results might flow from it, even the penalty of life itself; but, believe me, sir, my chief grief will ever be the having deceived you, and my real punishment can be inflicted by no court-martial you may order, but will be in the loss of your trust and esteem."

"You speak in riddles, sir," responded Washington, halting in his walk. "Cause for anger I have richly, for, as I told my whole family, any challenge they might send General Lee would, by the public, be ascribed to persecution. But you know as well as I that your duel with him is no offence to submit to a court-martial, and that you should pretend that I have any such recourse is adding insincerity to the original fault. You have — "

"That, sir, is a charge I indignantly deny," interrupted Jack, warmly, "and I was referring — "

"No denial can justify your conduct, sir," broke in Washington, wrathfully. "You have exposed me to the criticism and misapprehension of the public. By your disregard of my orders and my wishes, you have deservedly forfeited all right to my favour or my affection."

"Your Excellency forgets —"

"I forget nothing," thundered the general. "'T is you have forgotten the respect and obedience due me from all my family and —"

"Think you an aide is but a slave," retorted Brereton, hotly, "and that he possesses no right of independent action? Nor did I conceive that your Excellency would ever judge me unheard. I did —"

"The case is too palpable for —"

"Yet misjudge me you have, for I did not challenge Lee because he had insulted you, but because he was shamefully persecuting the woman I love."

Washington, who had resumed his angry pacing of the room, once again halted. "Explain your meaning, sir."

"In your heat, your Excellency has clearly forgot the tale Miss Meredith's letter told of General Lee's conduct as regards herself and her father. With the feeling I bear for her, human nature could not brook such behaviour, and it was that for which I challenged him."

The general stood silent for a moment, then said, "I have been too hasty in my action, Brereton, and have drawn a conclusion that was not justified. I owe you an apology for my words, and trust that this acknowledgment will end the misunderstanding." He offered his hand, as he ended, to the aide.

"I thank your Excellency," answered Jack, "for your prompt reparation, but before accepting it and taking your hand, sir, it is my painful necessity to tell you that I have fully merited all the anger you have expressed. Guiltless as I am of fault as regards General Lee, I have committed a far greater offence against you,—a wrong, sir, which, done with however much deliberation, has caused me unending pain and remorse."

"Explain yourself, my boy," said Washington, kindly.

"Despite your decision, sir, I added a postscript in your letter to Governor Livingston touching upon the case of Mr. Meredith, and made you express a good opinion of him and a recommendation that he be dealt with leniently. I now hold in my hand a letter from a Trenton friend informing me that this recommendation induced the Governor to commute the death sentence into imprisonment. It is but the news I awaited before informing your Excellency of my breach of trust, and I should have made full confession to you within the hour, had you not sent for me, as I supposed, to charge me with this very treachery. And 't was this of which I was thinking when I spoke expectingly of a court-martial."

During the whole explanation, Washington had stood fixedly, his brows knit, and when the aide paused, he said nothing for a minute; then he asked: —

"Has there been aught in the past, sir, to have made me merit from you such a stab?"

"None, sir," answered Jack, gravely. "And whatever reason I can find for the action in my own heart, there is nothing I can offer in its defence to you."

Washington sat down at his desk and leaned his head on his hand. "Is it not enough," he said, "that Congress is filled with my enemies, that the generals on whom I must depend are scheming my ruin and their own advancement, but that even within my own family I cannot find those who will be faithful to me? My God! is there no one I can trust?"

"Your Excellency's every word," said Jack, with tears in his eyes, "cuts me to the heart, the more that nothing you can say can increase the blame I put upon myself. I beg of you, sir, to believe me when I say that, be your grief what it may, it can never equal mine. And I beg that if my past relations to you plead ever so little for a merciful judgment of my conduct, you will remember that my betrayal was committed from no want of affection for you, but because one there was, and but one alone, whom I loved better."

Washington rose and faced Brereton, his self-control regained. "Your lapse of duty to the cause we are engaged in, sir, and my sense of it, make it out of the question that I should ever again trust you; it is therefore impossible for me longer to retain you upon my staff. But your loyalty and past service speak loudly in your favour, and I shall not, therefore, push your public punishment further than to demand your resignation trom my family, and so soon as there is a vacancy among the officers of the line you will take your place according to the date of your commission. The wrong you have done me personally is of a different nature, and ends from this moment the affection I have borne you and such friendship as has existed between us."

LV

PRISONERS OF WAR

THE Governor had warned the Merediths that the removal to Charlottesville must await the chance of an empty army transport, or other means of conveyance, and for more than a month they waited, not knowing at what hour the order would come.

Finally they were told to be ready the following morning; and at daybreak the three, with a guard, were packed into a hay cart, the larger part of the townsfolk collecting to view their departure. Nor did Mr. Bagby, who had made a number of calls upon them in the interval, fail to appear for a good-by.

"Just you remember, miss," he urged, "that my arguments and General Washington's was what saved your dad, and that I can still do a lot to save your property. Don't forget either that I 'm going to go on rising. Only think it over well, and you 'll see which side your bread is buttered on, for, if you are mighty good-looking, you 're no fool."

"Thank you, Mr. Bagby, for everything you have done or tried to do," replied the girl; and the squire, who had heard the whole speech, said nothing, though the effort to remain silent was clearly a severe one.

"Whither do we go first?" asked Mrs. Meredith of the driver, after the ferry-boat had left the Jersey shore and the spectators both behind.

"Our orders is to take you to Reading, an' hand you over to the officer in charge of the Convention snogers, pervided the last detachment hev n't left theer; if they hev, we are to lick up till we overtake them."

"What regiment is that?" questioned Janice.

"Guess ye're a bit green on what's goin' on," chuckled one of the guard. "Them's poppy-cock, hifalutin, by-the-grace-of-God an' King Georgie, come-in-an'-surrender-afore-we-extirpate-yer, Johnny Burgoyne's army, as did a little capitulatin' themselves. We've kep' 'em about Boston till we've got tired of teamin' pork an' wheat to 'em, an' now we're takin' 'em to where the pigs an' wheat grows, to save us money, an' to show 'em the size of the country they calkerlated to overrun. I guess they'll write hum that that job's a good one to sub-let, after they've hoofed it from Cambridge to Charlottesville."

The departure had been well timed, for when they drove into Reading, about five, long lines of men, garbed in green or red uniforms, were answering the roll-call as a preliminary to having quarters for the night assigned to them in the court-house, churches, and school. After much search, the officer in command was found, and the prisoner turned over to him, to his evident displeasure.

"Heavens!" he complained, "is it not bad enough to move two thousand troops, a third of whom no man can understand the gibberish of, to say nothing of General de Riedesel's wife and children, but I must have other women to look out for? I wish that Governor Livingston would pardon less and hang more!"

Unpromising as this beginning was, it proved a case of growl and not of bite, for the colonel speedily secured a night's lodging for them in a private house, and the next morning made a place for the two women beside the driver of one of the carts of the baggage train, the squire being ordered to march on foot with the column.

The journey proved a most trying one. The November rains, which wellnigh turned the roads from aids into obstacles, so impeded them that frequently they were not able to compass more than six or seven miles in a day, and it sometimes happened, therefore, that they were not able to reach the village or town on which they had been billeted, and were compelled to spend the night in the open fields, often with scanty supplies of provisions as an additional discomfort. From the inhabitants of the villages and farms, too, they met with more kicks than ha'pence. Again and again the people refused to sell anything to those whom they considered their enemies, and some even denied them the common courtesy of a drink of water. The chief amusement of the children along the route was to shout opprobrious or derisive epithets as they passed, not infrequently accompanied with stones, rotten apples, and now and then the still more objectionable egg. The squire's opinion of Whiggism went to an even lower pitch, but his womenkind bore it unflinchingly and uncomplainingly, happy merely in the escape from greater suffering.

As for Janice, she took what came with such merriness and good cheer that she was soon friends not merely with a number of their fellow-companions in misery, the British and Brunswick officers, but with the officers of their escort of Continental troops, and they were all quickly vying to do the little they could to add to the Merediths' comfort and ease. Of the miserable lodgings, whether in town or field, they were sure to be given the least poor; no matter how short were the commons, their needs were supplied; at every halting-place they received the first firewood cut; and time and again some one of the officers dismounted that Mr. Meredith might take his place in the saddle for an hour.

The girl made a yet more fortunate acquaintance on a night of especial discomfort and privation, after they had crossed the Pennsylvania boundary and were well into the semi-wilderness of the Blue Ridge Mountains. A washed away bridge so delayed their morning progress that they had advanced only a little over five miles, and were still four miles from their appointed camping ground, when the first snowstorm of the season set in, and compelled them to bivouac along the roadside. The ration issued to each prisoner on that particular afternoon consisted of only a half-pound of salt pork and a handful of beans; and as she had frequently done before, Janice set out to make a tour of the straggling farms of the neighbourhood, in the hope of purchasing milk, eggs, or other supplies to eke the scanty fare. At the first log cabin she came to she made her request, and for a moment was hopeful, for the woman replied: —

"Yes. I have eggs and milk and chickens, and vegetables in a great plenty, but — "

"And what are your prices?"

"— But not a morsel of anything do you get. You come to our land to kill us and to waste our homes. Now it is our turn to torment you. I feed no royalists."

Her second application drew forth an even sterner rebuff, for the housewife, before Janice had said half of her speech, cried, "Be off with you, you Tory! think you I would give help to such nasty dogs?"

The third attempt was equally futile, for she was told: "Not for a thousand dollars would I give you anything, and if you would all die of hunger, 't would be so much the better."

The maiden was long since too accustomed to this treatment to let it discourage her, and in her fourth essay she was more fortunate. While the woman was refusing, the farmer himself appeared upon the scene, and moved by pity, or perhaps by the youth and beauty of the petitioner, vetoed his wife's decision, and not merely filled her pail with milk, but added a small basket of eggs and apples, declining to accept the one hundred dollars in Continental bills she tendered.

Her quest had taken Janice nearly two miles away from her quarters, and in returning with this wealth she was compelled to pass the length of the encampment. This brought her presently to a large tent, from which issued the sobs of a child, intermixed with complaints in French of cold and hunger, with all of which a woman's voice was blended, seeking to comfort the weeper.

On impulse, the girl turned aside and looked through the half-closed flap. Within she saw a woman of something over thirty years of age, with a decidedly charming face, sitting on a camp-stool with a child of about three years old in her arms and two slightly older children at her feet, from one of whom came the wails.

"We do not know each other, Madame de Riedesel," Janice apologised in the best French she could frame, "but Captain Geismar and others have told me so much about you that I — I —" There Janice came to a halt, and then in English, colouring as she spoke, she went on, "'T is mortifying, but though I thought I had become quite a rattler in French, the moment I need it, I lose courage."

"Ach!" cried Madame de Riedesel. "Nevair think. I speak ze Anglais parfaitement. Continuez."

"I was passing," explained Janice, mightily relieved, "and hearing what your little girl was saying, I made bold to intrude, in the hope that you will let me share my milk and eggs with the children." As she spoke, Janice held out to each of the three a rosy-cheeked apple, and the sobs had ended ere her explanation had.

"Ah!" cried the woman, "zees must be ze Mees Meredeez whom zay told me was weez ze waggons in ze rear, and who, zay assure me, was a saint. Zat must you be, to offer your leettle store to divide with me. Too well haf I learned how difficile it ees to get anyzing from zeese barbarians."

"They are hard, madame," explained Janice, "because they deem us foes."

"But women cannot be zare enemies, and yet ze women ze worst are. Ma foi! Weez ze army I kept through ze wilderness, ze bois, from Canada, and not one unkind or insult did I receef, till I came to where zere were zose of my own sex. Would you beleef it, in Boston ze femme zay even spat at me when I passed zem on ze street. And since from Cambridge we started, when I haf wished for anyzing, my one prayer zat it shall be a man and not a woman I must ask it has been. Ze women, I say it weez shame, are ze brutes, and ze men, zay seek to be gentle, mais, hélas! zay are born of ze women!"

Janice, pouring half her milk into an empty bowl that was on the table, and dividing her eggs, smiled archly as she said, "I fear, then, that my call is not a welcome one, since, hélas! I am a woman."

The baroness spilled the little girl from lap to floor as she sprang to her feet and clasped the caller in her arms. "You are une ange," she cried, "and I geef you my lofe, not for now, but for ze all time for efer."

The acquaintance thus begun ripened rapidly. In her gratitude for the kindness, Madame de Riedesel, who had a roomy calash and a light baggage waggon, insisted that Janice and Mrs. Meredith should quit the springless army van in the rear and travel henceforth with the advance in one or the other of her vehicles, giving them far greater ease and comfort.

Sometimes the children were sent with the baggage, and the three ladies used the calash, but more often Janice and Madame de Riedesel rode in it, with a child on each lap, and one sandwiched in between them, and the squire took the empty seat beside Mrs. Meredith in the waggon.

A second generosity of the new friend was her quickly offering to share with them the large officer's marquee that her husband's rank had secured for her, with the comfortable beds that formed a part of her camp equipment; and as they had hitherto been cramped into a small field tent, with only blankets and dead leaves laid on the frozen ground to sleep upon, the invitation was a still greater boon. Close packing it was, but the weather was now so cold that what was lost in space was made up for in warmth.

It was early in January that they finally reached their destination, — an improvised village of log huts, some two miles from Charlottesville, named Saratoga, from the capitulation that had served to bring it into being; but so far as the Merediths were concerned, it meant a change rather than a lessening of the privation. The cabin to which they were assigned consisted of one windowless room, and was without a chimney. They were necessarily without furniture, their sole stock beyond their own clothing being a few blankets and cooking utensils, which they had brought with them. Nor were they able to purchase much that they needed at the neighbouring town, for their cash had been seriously depleted by what they had bought in Trenton, and by the expenses of the march, while what was left had shrunk in value in the two months' march from fifty dollars to seventy-five dollars, paper, for one in gold.

Seeking to make the best of it, the three set to work diligently. From a neighbouring mill slabs were procured, which, being cut the right length and laid on logs, were made to do for beds, and others served to make an equally rough table. Sections of logs were utilised for chairs, and the squire built a crude fireplace a few feet from the doorway. At best, however, the discomfort was really very great. Even with the door closed, the cabin was cold almost beyond the point of endurance, and if it was not left open, the only light that came to them was through the chinks of the logs. Yet their suffering was far less than that of the troops, for many of the huts were unfinished when they arrived, and with three feet of snow on the ground, most of them were compelled to roof their own quarters and even in some cases entirely build them, as a first step to protection.

General de Riedesel, who had gone before his wife with the first detachment, that he might arrange a home in advance, had rented "Colle," the large house of Philip Mazzei, close to the log barracks. Madame de Riedesel was therefore at once in possession of comfortable quarters, and upon hearing from Janice how they were living, she offered her a home with them.

"Come to us, liebling," she begged. "Ze children zay lofe you so zat almost jealous I am; alreaty my goot husband he says ze Mees Meredeez ees charmant, and I — ah, I neet not tell it, for it tells itself."

"If it were right I would, Frederica, and I cannot thank you enough for wanting me; but ever since mommy had the fever she has not been really strong, and both she and dadda need me. Perhaps though, if you and the children — whom I dearly love — truly like me, you will help me in another way?"

"And how?"

"I heard you complaining to Baron de Riedesel yesterday of not being able to get a nurse. Will you not give me the place, and let my pay be for us all to live in your garret? We will make as little trouble — "

"Ach! Why deet I not it think before?" cried the baroness, boxing her own ear. "Cochon! Brute! You come, ma pauvre! Mais not as bonne, non, non."

"Indeed, Frederica, 't is the only way that we can. We could not live upon you without in some way making a return, and the paper money with which we furnished ourselves has gone on falling till now 't is worth but a threepence in the pound, so that we could not hope to pay for — "

"Bah! Who asks? You come as our guests; when you had ze plenty of milk and eggs you shared it weez us, and so now we share our plenty weez you. You, a proud girl, to be a nurse, indeet!"

"'T is that pride which asks it, my dear. Ah, if you only would let me! Mommy suffers so with the cold, and has such a frightful cough, that every day I fear to see it become a pneumonia, and —"

"Stop! I was ze wrong. Come as you please, à l'instant. Ah, ze leettle ones, zay will go craze for joy; ze baron he will geef no more eyes to ze wife who is losing her shape, and all ze officairs, zay will say, 'Gott! How I lofe children!' Mais, I will not angree be, but kiss you so, and so, and so. And to all will I say, 'Voilá, deet efer woman haf such a frent for herself and such a second mütter for her children?'"

LVI

A LIFE OF CAPTIVITY

THE removal to Colle was made the same day, and Janice assumed her new charge. It was, as it proved, not a very onerous one, for the children were well mannered for their years, and, young as they were, in the German method they were kept pretty steadily at tasks, while an old servant of the general, a German Yager, was only too delighted at any time to assume care of them. Janice herself slept in the nursery, and at first Mr. and Mrs. Meredith were given, as suggested, accommodation in the garret. But the baron, not content with the space at his command, as soon as the weather permitted, had built a large dining-room and salon, separate from the house, and this supplied so much more space that the parents were given a good room on a lower floor.

The new arrangement not merely brought them comfort, but also pleasure. Mr. and Mrs. Meredith were treated as guests; and Madame de Riedesel made Janice quite as much her own companion as an attendant on the children. With her, once her nervousness was conquered, Janice talked French entirely; and more for amusement than for improvement, she began the study of German, with her friend as instructor; and, having as well the aid of every Brunswick officer, who only too gladly frequented the house, she was soon able to both read and speak it, to the delight of the baron, who preferred his native tongue; though his wife, German-born as she was, could not understand how any one who could talk French would for a moment willingly use any other tongue. Furthermore, they taught each other the various stitches in embroidery and crocheting each knew; and the German, who was an excellent housewife, not merely made

Janice her assistant in the household cares, but, after expressing horror that the girl knew nothing of accounts, spent many hours inducting her into the mysteries by which she knew to a farthing how her money was expended.

Although these were all pastimes rather than labours to Janice, there were lighter hours in which she made a fourth at whist, learned chess from the general, and played on the harpsichord or sang to him. Once a week there was a musicale, at which all who could play on any instrument contributed a share, and dances and dinners were frequently given by the Riedesels and by General Phillips, the major-general in command of the British part of the Convention prisoners. Horses in plenty were in the stable, and the two ladies, well escorted by officers, took almost daily rides; the baroness making herself a figure of remark to the natives by riding astride her horse in a short skirt and long boots.

With the advent of summer, their pleasures became more pastoral. So soon as the weather permitted, the gentry of the neighbourhood came to call upon their foes, and this led to much dining about. Then, too, there were out-of-door *fêtes* and picnics, ofttentimes at long distances from the cantonment; so that ere many weeks the Riedesels and the Merediths had come to know both the people and the region intimately.

A sudden end came to these amusements by an untoward event. Janice and General de Riedesel had made the flower-garden at Colle their particular charge, working there, despite the heat, for hours each day, till early in August, when one day the baron was found lying in a pathway unconscious, his face blue, his hands white, and his eyes staring. He was hurriedly carried into the house, and when the army surgeon arrived, it was found to be a case of sunstroke. Though he was bled copiously, the sufferer improved but slowly, and before he was convalescent developed the "river" or "breakbone fever." Finally he was ordered over the mountains to the Warm Springs, to see whether their waters might not benefit him; and, leaving Mr. and Mrs. Meredith in charge, the baroness and Janice went with him, half as companions and half as nurses.

Upon their arrival there, they found the Springs so crowded that all the log cabins, which, by custom, fell to the first comers, were already occupied. Declining an offer from one of these to share lodgings, they set to work in a proper spot to make themselves comfortable; for, having foreseen this very possibility, they had come amply supplied with tents. Before they had well begun on their encampment, two negroes in white and red livery appeared, and the spokesman, executing a bow that would have done honour to a lord chamberlain, handed Madame de Riedesel a letter which read as follows: —

"*Mrs. Washington preasents her most respectful complements to the Barones de Reedaysell, and her sattisfacshon at being informed of her arival at the Springs. She beggs that if the barers of this can be of aney a sistance to the Barones in setling, that she will yuse them as long as they may be of sarvis to her.*

"*Mrs. Washington likewise bespeeks the honer of the Baroneses party to dinner today and beggs that if it will be aney conveenence to her, that she will sup as well.*"

Both offers Madame de Riedesel was only too glad to accept; and at the dinner hour, guided by the darkies, they made their way to Lady Washington's lodgings, to find a plump, smiling, little lady, who received them with much dignity, properly qualified with affability. The meal was spread underneath the trees, and they were quickly seated about the table and chatting genially over it.

Once the newness was taken off the acquaintance, the baroness made an appeal to the hostess for a favour. "Ah, Laty Washington," she begged, "ze surgeons, zay declare my goot husband he cannot recovair ze fevair in ze so hot climate, and zat ze one goot for him will be zat he to New York restores himself. I haf written ze prediction to Sir Henry Clinton, applicating zat he secure ze exchange of ze baron immediatement, mais, will you not also write to ze General Washington and ask him, also, zees zing to accomplish?"

"I would in a moment, gladly, baroness," replied Mrs. Washington, "but I assure you that the general would highly disapprove of my interfering in a public matter. Do not hesitate, however, to write yourself, for I can assure you he will do everything in his power to spare you anxiety or discomfort."

"Zen you zink he will my prayer grant?"

"I am sure he will, if it is possible, for, aside from his generous treatment of every one, let me whisper to you that 't is not a quality in his composition to say 'Nŏ' to a pretty woman."

"Oh, no, Frederika," broke in Janice; "you need not have the slightest fear of his Excellency. He is everything that is kind and great and generous!"

"What!" exclaimed Mrs. Washington. "You know the general, then?"

"Oh, yes," cried Janice, rapturously; "and if you but knew, Lady Washington, how we stand indebted to him at this very moment!"

The hostess smiled in response to the girl's enthusiasm. "'T is certain he refused you nothing, Miss Meredith," she said.

"Indeed, but he did," answered Janice, merrily. "Wouldst believe it, Lady Washington, though perhaps 't is monstrous bold of me to tell it, 't is he that has had to keep me at a distance, for I have courted him most outrageously!"

"'T is fortunate," replied the matron, "that he is a loyal husband, and that I am not a jealous wife, for 't is a way all women have with him. What think you a Virginian female, who happened to be passing through camp, had the forwardness to say to me but t' other day? 'When General Washington,' she writ, 'throws off the hero and takes up the chatty, agreeable companion, he can be downright impudent sometimes, Martha, — such impudence as you and I, and every woman, always like.'"

"Ah," asserted Madame de Riedesel, "ze goot men, zay all lofe us dearly. Eh, Janice?"

"What!" demanded the hostess. "Is your name Janice? Surely this is not my nice boy Jack's Miss Meredith?"

The girl reddened and then paled. "I beg, Lady Washington —" she began; but the baroness, who had noted her change of colour, cut her off.

"You haf a lofer," she cried, "and nevair one word to me told? Ach, ingrate! And your lofe I zought it was mine."

"Miss Meredith is very different, then, from a certain gentleman," remarked Mrs. Washington, laughingly. "I first gained his confidence when he lay wounded at headquarters winter before last; but once his secret was unbosomed, I could not so much as stop to ask how he did but he must begin and talk of nothing but her till he became so excited and feverish that I had to check or leave him for his own good."

"Indeed, Lady Washington," protested the girl, her lip trembling in her endeavour to keep back the tears, "once Colonel Brereton may have thought he cared for me, but, I assure you, 't was but a half-hearted regard, which long since died."

"'T is thy cruelty killed it, then," asserted Mrs. Washington, "for, unless my eyes and ears deceived me, never was there more eager lover than —"

"'T is not so; on the contrary, he won my heart and then broke it with his cruelty," denied the girl, the tears coming in spite of herself. "I pray you forgive my silly tears, and do not speak more of this matter," she ended.

"I cannot believe it of him," responded Lady Washington. "But 't was far from my thought to distress you, and it shall never be spoke of more."

The subject was instantly dropped; and though Janice saw much of Lady Washington during their three weeks' stay at the Springs, and a mutual liking sprang up between the two, never again was it broached save at the moment that they set out on their return to Colle, when her new friend, along with her farewell kiss, said, "I, too, shall soon leave the Springs, my dear, and journey ere long to join the general at headquarters for the winter. Have you any message for him?"

"Indeed, but I have," eagerly cried Janice. "Wilt take him my deepest thanks?"

"And no more?"

"If your ladyship were willing," said Janice, archly, "I would ask you to take him my love and a kiss."

"He shall have them, though I doubt not he would prefer such gifts without a proxy," promised Mrs. Washington, smiling. Then she whispered, "And can I not carry the same to some one else?"

"Never!" replied the girl, grave on the instant. "Once I cared for him, but such feeling as I had has long since died, and nothing can ever restore it."

Keenly desirous as the Merediths were for the well-being of the Riedesels, it was impossible for them not to feel a pang of regret when, one morning, the baroness broke the news to them that Washington had yielded to her prayer, that her husband and General Phillips had at last been exchanged, and that they were to set out within the week for New York. Yet, even in the departure, their benefactors continued their kindness; for, having rented Colle for two years, they placed the house at their disposal for the balance of the lease; and when, after tearful good-byes had been made and they were well started on their northern journey, Janice went to her room, she found a purse containing twenty guineas in gold as a parting gift from the general, a breastpin of price from the baroness, and a ring from Gustava, with a note attached to it in the English print which Janice had taught her, declaring her undying affection and her intention to ask God to change her to a boy that when she grew up she might return and wed her.

The months that drifted by after this departure were lean ones of incident. Succeeding as they did to the ample garden, poultry, pigs, and two cows which the baron had donated to them, they were quite at ease as to food. The junior officers who still remained in charge of the troops saw to it that they did not want for military servants, thus relieving them of all severe labour; and while they deeply felt the loss of the Riedesels, there was no lack of company.

The void the departure of the baroness and children made in Janice's life was partly filled by an acquaintance already made which now grew into a friendship. Soon after their settlement at Colle, Mrs. Jefferson, wife of the Governor, who lived but a few miles away at Monticello, had come to call on them, a visit which she was unable to repeat, owing to her breaking health, but this very invalidism, as it turned, tended to foster the intimacy. Her husband being compelled by public events to be at the capital, she was much alone, and often sent over an invitation to Janice to come and spend a few days with her. As a liking for the girl ripened, it induced an attempt to serve them.

"I have spoke to Thomas of your hard lot," she told Janice, "and repeated to him enough of the tale you told me to convince him that your father was not the active Tory he is reputed to be, and have at last persuaded him to write to Governor Livingston bespeaking a permission for you to return to your own home, if your father will but give his parole to take no part in public affairs."

"Oh, Mrs. Jefferson, how can we ever thank you?"

"I do not deserve it, believe me, Janice, for I long postponed what I knew I ought to do, through regret at the thought of losing your visits."

"That but deepens our thanks. If you —"

"I 'll not listen to them now," replied the friend, "for who can say that they will come to aught? 'T will be time enough when it has really accomplished something."

Distant as they were from the active operations of the war, the inmates of Collè were kept pretty well informed of its progress, for it was a constant theme of conversation, and the movements were closely followed on the military maps of the officers who frequented the house. From them Janice heard how Clinton, despairing of conquering the Northern colonies by force of arms, had resorted to bribery, but only to win the services of an officer he did not wish, and not the desired post of West Point; and with tears in her eyes she listened to the news that André, setting ambition above honour, had paid for the lapse with his life. Then, as the tide of war shifted, it was explained to her why the British general, keeping tight hold on New York as a base for operations, transferred a material part of his forces to the South, where, in succession, he captured Savannah and Charleston, and almost without resistance overran the States of Georgia and the two Carolinas.

"You see, Miss Meredith," she was told, "the yeomanry of the Northern States are so well armed that we have found it impossible to hold the country against their militia; but in the Southern States, aside from the difference between the energetic Northerners and the more indolent Southrons, the long distances between the plantations, and the fact that the gentry don't dare to trust their slaves with weapons, make them practically defenceless. The plan now seems to be, therefore, to wear the Northern colonies out by our fleet and by occasional descents upon the towns of the coast, while we meantime conquer the Southern States. Had it been adopted from the first, the strength would have been sapped out of the rebellion and it would have been ended two years ago; but the new strategy cannot fail, even at this late date, to bring them to their knees in time."

An evidence of the truth of this surmise, and an abrupt ending to the peaceful life at Saratoga, came to the little settlement in the first week of the year 1781, when a post rider spurred into Charlottesville with a despatch to the County Lieutenant of Albemarle announcing that a British fleet had entered the Capes of the Chesapeake and seized the town of Portsmouth, and summoning the militia to embody, for Virginia was threatened with the fate which had already befallen her sister States to the southward.

LVII

A PAPER MONEY AND MILITIA WAR

THE alarm of the British invasion was sufficient to throw the whole of Virginia into a panic, but especially the neighbourhood about Charlottesville, for it was inferred that one purpose of their coming was to attempt to liberate the Convention prisoners. The cantonment, therefore, was hastily broken up, and all the troops were marched over the mountains to Winchester, or northward into Pennsylvania, scarcely time for them to pack their few possessions being accorded to them. From this deportation the Merediths were excepted, for as political prisoners, no mention of them was made in the orders issued by Washington and the Virginia Council; and so Colonel Bland left them unmolested, the sole residents of the once overcrowded village of huts. The removal of the prisoners proved a needless precaution, for, after remaining but a few days, the British fleet retired, having effected little save to frighten badly the people, but the apprehension subsided as quickly as it had come.

The hope of quiet was a false one, for in a few months a second expedition, under the command of Arnold, sailed up the James River and captured and burned Richmond. To face this new enemy, to which the militia of the State were deemed inadequate, Washington detached a brigade under the command of Lafayette from the Northern army, supposing the movement, like the previous one, a mere predatory expedition, which could be held in check by this number of troops; and upon news that General Phillips, with reinforcements, had joined Arnold, he further despatched a second brigade under Wayne.

Meantime, the force under Cornwallis, after overrunning North Carolina, now suddenly swung northward and effected a juncture with the British force in Virginia, raising it to such strength that Lafayette dared not risk a battle, and was left no option, as the British advanced inland, but to fall back rapidly toward the mountains.

These latter events succeeded one another with such rapidity that the people of Charlottesville first heard of some of them by the arrival of Governor Jefferson and the members of the Assembly, to which place they had voted an adjournment just previous to their being forced to abandon the capital. Sessions had scarcely been begun, however, when word was brought that the enemy was within a few miles of the town, and once again they took to their heels and fled over the mountains into the Shenandoah valley, escaping none too soon, as it proved, for Tarleton's cavalry rode into the streets of Charlottesville so close upon what was left of the government of Virginia that some of the members were captured.

The Merediths, two miles away at Saratoga, first heard the news of these latter events from a captain of militia, who, accompanied by six sullen-looking companions, rode up early on the morning of the raid and sharply ordered the three to mount the led horses he brought with him.

"I 'm ridin'," he explained, "to collect the horses and alarm the hundreds towards Boswell's, and the county lieutenant ordered me to take you away from here. No, I can 't wait to have you pack."

"'T is surely not necessary that we should be treated so," pleaded Mr. Meredith. "My wife has not the strength to bear a long —"

"Can 't help that. Like as not the British horse ha'n't had word that the Convention troops have been sent away, and will ride this far, and we reckon we can't have you givin' them no information," answered the man. "I don 't want no talk. Into the saddle with you."

Protests and prayers were absolutely unavailing, and the whole party hurriedly set off at the best pace the horses were able to go. As they journeyed, a halt was made at each cabin and each plantation, and every white man found was summarily ordered by the captain to get his gun and join the party; while at each place all the horses were impressed, not merely to carry those unprovided with one, but to prevent their falling into the hands of the foe. Nor did the captain pay more heed to the expostulations and grumblings of the men, at being called away from their crops at the busiest farming season, nor of the women, at being deprived of their protectors in times of such danger, than he had to the weaker ones of the Merediths.

"The invasion law just passed by the 'sembly calls out every man as can fight, and declares every one as won't a traitor, so you can take your choice of shootin' at the British or bein' shot by us," was the captain's unvarying formula, be the complaints what they might.

As if to make the ill feeling the greater, too, he told the whole party at one point of the route, "If you-alls had been patriots and 'listed four weeks ago, you 'd every one of you 've got a bounty of five hundred dollars of the money my saddle-bags is filled with; but you had n't spunk, so it serves you-alls good and handsome that now you 've got to fight for 'nary a shillin'."

"We would n't have been a tinker's damn the richer if we had," snarled one of the unwilling conscripts. "I 'd rather have a pound of hay than the same weight in cursed state money, for you can feed the hay to a hoss, but I 'm consarned if t' other 's good for anythin'."

"Say, cap," asked a second, "has you ralely got them saddle-bags o' yourn filled with the stuff?"

"Ay. The presses were at Charlottesville busy strikin' it, and I was told to help save what was already printed from capture."

"Lord! the British would n't have seized that, with all the cord wood there is in Charlottesville, to say nothin' of grind-stones and ploughs and chimbleys built of brick and other things of value," asserted the original speaker.

"Might come handy along of all the terbacker they 've took down to Petersburg. Do to light a pipe with, I reckon," suggested another.

"Say, cap," again spoke up the second speaker, "the raison as why I asked that there question is that we 'll be gettin' to Hunker's ordinary at the four corners right smart off now, and I was calculatin' if you had enough of the rags with you to set us up a drink all round? 'T won't cost more 'n ten thousand dollars if Hunkers ain't in an avaricious mood."

The officer had been absolutely inattentive to the complaints and growls, but the quizzing made him lose his temper. "You-alls shut your jaws, the lot of you, or when we reach the roundyvous this evenin' I 'll report you to the kurnel and you 'll get the guard-house or worse," he threatened. "I 'm danged if I don 't believe every one of you-alls is a Tory at heart."

"A little more o' this 'll make me one," muttered a man who hitherto had been silent, but he spoke so low as to be heard by his fellow unfortunates only, and not by the captain.

"Don 't talk to me of the tyranny of Britain after this!" responded his immediate neighbour.

The militia officer would have done better to let the dissatisfaction find its vent in jokes; for, deprived of this outlet, the malcontents took to whispering among themselves in a manner that boded ill for something or somebody. But he was too busy securing each new recruit and each horse to give attention to the signs that might have warned him.

A rude awakening came to the captain when the motley cavalcade drew up at the ordinary at the cross-roads, for as he was in the act of dismounting, two of the party, who had been more expeditious in their movements, caught him by the leg as he swung it clear of the saddle, and brought him violently to the ground. He was held in that position while his hands and feet were tied with his own bridle, as many of the men as could get about him assisting in the operation, while the remainder, the Merediths excepted, kept up a chorus of approving remarks, or of gibing and mocking comments on the officer's half-smothered menaces and oaths. Once secured, he was dragged to the guide-post, and with his stirrup straps was fastened to it securely. This done, his saddle-bags were pulled off his horse and the paper money was emptied out and heaped about his feet. Meantime, and as an evidence of how carefully every detail of their revenge had been planned, one of the ring-leaders had disappeared into the tavern, and now returned with a lighted brand.

"You can threat and cuss all you hanker," he chuckled.

"If we ain't to have no bounty, we 'll give you some of ourn," he added malignantly, as he stooped and set fire to the pile of bills.

"Oh, don't!" screamed Janice. "Dadda, stop them!"

"For shame!" echoed Mr. Meredith, swinging out of his saddle, in which hitherto he had remained a passive spectator.

"Hands off," warned the torch-bearer, "if you don't want to be tied alongside of him."

There was nothing to do, and the ladies were only able to turn their backs on the sight; but they could not thus escape the howls of terror and pain that the miserable victim uttered, though the squire sought to save them from this by taking hold of the two bridles and leading their horses away.

This movement served to attract their attention to something hitherto not observed, and which the absorption of the militia in their revenge still prevented them from noting. On the road by which they had come arose a thick cloud of dust, out of which horsemen seemed to be riding, but, though they came on at a hand gallop, the screen, swept onward by the breeze, kept pace with the riders, and even at times hid now one, now all, from view, causing the squire, who first caught sight of the phenomenon, to rub his eyes, that he might have assurance that it was not a phantasm of his brain. Of this another sense furnished quick evidence, for even above the jeers of the torturers and the shrieks of the tortured sounded the clatter of hoofs. At the first warning, cries of alarm escaped from many mouths, and with the fright of guilt, there was a wild stampede for the horses; before the half of them were in the saddle, the thunder of a column of horse was close upon them, and as, mounted and unmounted, they scattered, there came a rush of red-coated troopers in amongst them. Loud above the tumult and uproar came the sharp order, —

"Capture what men you can, but don't let a horse escape!"

Mr. Meredith, the moment the militia had deserted the fire, rushed forward, and with three kicks scattered the flaming currency from about the man's legs, — a proceeding which attracted the attention of the officer who gave the order.

"What is the meaning of this?" he demanded, but all the reply he received was a startled exclamation which burst from the squire.

"What!" he ejaculated. "Why, this passes very belief! Pox me, if 't is not Phil Hennion."

LVIII

FROM BLUE RIDGE TO TIDE WATER

FOR a few moments the mingled exclamations, greetings, and questions were too broken and mixed to tell any of them much, but the first surprise over, the Merediths explained their presence.

"I knew from the baroness that you were at Colle, and bitter was the disappointment when I found you gone this morning. But my grief then makes me but the happier now."

"But how came ye here, lad?" questioned the squire.

"We were sent on a raid to Charlottesville, with orders to rejoin the main army at Point of Fork, and I was detached by Colonel Tarleton this morning to take this route, hoping to get more information concerning Lafayette's whereabouts and movements."

"I heard this fellow," said Mr. Meredith, indicating the still captive and moaning man, "who is a captain of militia, tell the men he was draughting that they were to march, as soon as embodied, to join the rebel army at Raccoon Ford."

"Hah! the junction with Wayne's force emboldens him to show us something more than his back at last. 'T is all I wish to learn, and we can now take the shortest road to rejoin Lord Cornwallis. Strap me! but 't was a heaven-sent chance that we should come just in the nick o' time to rescue you. There shall be no more captivity, that I can promise you." He turned to the now reassembled squadron, and ordered, "Parole your prisoners, Captain Cameron, and let them go. You, Lieutenant Beatty, bring up the best extra mount you have, and arrange as comfortable a place as possible for the ladies in one of the baggage-waggons."

"A suggestion, major," spoke up another officer. "Sergeant McDonald reports that there is a chaise in the tavern barn, and —"

"Put horse to it, and have it out before you set fire to the buildings," interrupted Hennion.

"What!" ejaculated Mr. Meredith. "Art thou a major, Phil?"

"Ay, squire. I 've fought my way up two grades since last we met."

There was a greater change in the officer than of rank, for his once long and ungainly frame had broadened and filled out into that of a well-formed, powerful man. His face, too, had lost its lankness, to its great improvement, for the features were strong, and, with the deep tan which the Southern campaigns had given it, had become, from being one of positive homeliness, one of decided distinction. But the most marked alteration was in his speech and bearing, for all trace of the awkward had disappeared from both; he spoke with facility and authority, and he sat his horse with soldierly erectness and ease.

The ladies were soon bestowed in the chaise, the bugle sounded, and the flying column resumed its movement. Little they saw of the commander all day, for he rode now with the foremost troop, and now with the rear one, keenly alert to all that was taking place, asking questions at each farmhouse as to roads, bridges, rivers, distances, the people, and everything which could be of value. Only when the heat of the day came, and they halted for a few hours' rest at a plantation, did he come to them, and then only for a brief word as to their accommodation. He offered Mrs. Meredith and Janice the best the house afforded, but, with keen recollections of their own sufferings, they refused to dispossess the women occupants from their home, and would accept in food and lodgings only what they had to spare. Indeed, though as far as possible it had been kept from their sight, the march had brought a realising sense to them, almost for the first time, of the full horror of the war, and made them appreciate that their own experience, however bad they had deemed it, was but that of hundreds. The day had been one long scene of rapine and destruction. At each plantation they had seen all serviceable horses seized, and the rest of the stock, young or old, slaughtered, all provisions of use to the army made prize of, and the remainder, with the buildings that held it, put to the torch, and the young crops of wheat, corn, and tobacco, so far as time allowed, destroyed. Under cover of all this, too, there was looting by the dragoons, which the officers could not prevent, try their best.

There was a still worse terror, of which, fortunately, the Merediths saw nothing. Large numbers of the negroes took advantage of the incursion, and indeed were encouraged by the cavalry, to escape from slavery by following in the rear of the column; and as the white men were either with the Virginia militia, or were in hiding away from the houses, the women were powerless to prevent the blacks from plundering, or from any other excess it pleased them to commit. The Old Dominion, the last State of the thirteen to be swept over by the foe, was harried as the Jerseys had been, but by troops made less merciful by many a fierce conflict, and by its own servitors, debased by slavery to but one degree above the brute. Only with death did the people forget the enormities of those few months, when Cornwallis's army cut a double swath from tide water almost to the mountains, and Tarleton's and Simcoe's cavalry rode whither they pleased; and the hatred of the British and the fear of their own slaves outlasted even the passing away of the generation which had suffered.

It was on the afternoon of the following day that the detachment effected a juncture with the main army, and so soon as Major Hennion had reported, Lord Cornwallis, who was quartered at Elk Hill, an estate of Jefferson's, sent word that he wished to see Mr. Meredith at once, and extended an invitation to them all to share the house. He questioned the squire for nearly an hour as to the whereabouts of the Convention prisoners, the condition of the State, and the feeling of the people.

"All you tell me tallies with such information as I have procured elsewhere," he ended; "and had I but a free hand I make certain I could destroy Lafayette and completely subjugate the State in one campaign."

"Surely, my Lord, you could not better serve the king. Virginia has been the great hot-bed of sedition, and if she were once smothered, the fire would quickly die out."

"Almost the very words I writ to Sir Henry, but he declares it out of the question to leave me the troops with which to effect it. As you no doubt are aware, a French force has been landed at Rhode Island, and is even now on its march to join Mr. Washington; and, by a fortunate interception of some of his despatches to Congress, we have full information that the united force intend an attack on New York. So I am ordered to fall down to a good defensive post on the Chesapeake and to send a material part of my army to his aid."

When finally the interview was ended, and Mr. Meredith asked one of the aides to take him to his room, it was explained that Mrs. Meredith and her daughter had been put in one and that he was to have a share of another.

"You 'd have had the floor or a tent, sir," his guide told him, as he threw open the door, "but for Lord Clowes saying he 'd take you in."

Surely enough, it was the commissary who warmly grasped the squire's hand as he entered, and who cried, "Welcome to ye, friend Meredith! I heard of your strange arrival from nowhere, and glad I was to be assured ye were still in the flesh and once more among friends."

"Ye 've clear surprised my breath out of my windpipe," returned the squire. "Who 'd have thought to find ye here?"

"And where else should I be, but where there 's an army to be fed, and crops to feed them? I' faith, never was there a richer harvest field for one who knows how to garner it. Why, man, aside from the captures of tobacco, now worth a great price, and other gains, over six thousand pounds I 've made in the last two years, by shipping niggers, who think they are escaping to freedom, to our West India islands, and selling them to the planters there. This war is a perfect gold mine."

"Little of that it 's been to me," lamented his listener.

"Ye can make it such, an' it please ye. She perceived me not, but I saw your daughter as ye rode up, and though I thought myself well cured of the infatuation, poof! one gloat was enough to set my blood afire, as if I were but a boy of eighteen again. Lord Clowes, with a cool ninety thousand, is ready to make her fortune and yours."

"Nay, Clowes, ye know I 've passed my word to Hennion, and — "

"Who 'll not outlive the war, ye may make sure. The fellow 's made himself known through the army by the way he puts himself forward in every engagement. Some one of these devilish straight-shooting riflemen will release that promise for ye."

"I trust not; but if it so falls, there 'd still be a bar to your wish. The girl dislikes ye very — "

"Dost not know that is no bad beginning? Nay, man, see if I bring her not round, once I have a clear field. I 've thought it out even now while I 've waited for ye. We 'll sail for New York on one of the ships that carries Lord Cornwallis's reinforcements to Clinton, and as 't will be some years still ere the country is entirely subdued, out of the question 't will be that ye go to Greenwood. I will resign my post, being now rich enough, and we 'll all go to London, where I 'll take a big house, and ye shall be my guests. Once let the girl taste of high life, with its frocks and jewels and carriages, and all that tempts the sex, and she 'll quickly see their provider in a new light."

"'T is little ye know of my lass, Clowes."

"Tush! I know women to the very bottom; and is she more than a woman?"

Their conference was ended by the call to supper, and in the hallway the baron attempted as hearty a greeting with the ladies as he had with the squire. Though taken by surprise, a distant curtsey was all he gained from them, and do his best, he could get little of their conversation during the meal.

On rising, Philemon, who had been a guest at table, drew the squire to one side. "The legion is ordered on a foray to destroy the military stores at Albemarle Court-house, and in this hot weather we try to do our riding at night, to spare our cattle, so we shall start away about eleven o'clock. His Lordship tells me that the army will begin to fall down to the coast in a day or two, so it may be a some time before I see you again. Have you money?"

"A bare trifle, but I 'll not further rob ye, lad, till I get to the end of my purse."

"Do not fear to take from me, sir. A major's pay is very different from a cornet's. 'T will make me feel easier, and, in fact, 't will be safer with you than with me," Phil said, as he forced a rouleau of coin into the squire's palm. Then, not waiting for Mr. Meredith's protests or thanks, he crossed to where Janice was talking with three of the staff, and broke in upon their conversation: "Janice, a soldier goes or stays not as he pleases, but as the bugle orders, and there is more work cut out for us, but this evening I am free. Wilt come and stroll along the river-bank for an hour?"

"Dash your impudence, Hennion!" protested one of the group. "Do you think you fellows of the cavalry can plunder everything? Pay no heed to him, Miss Meredith, I beg of you."

"Ay," echoed another, "'t is the artillery the major should belong to, for he 'd do to repair the brass cannon."

The girl stood irresolute for a breath, then, though she coloured, she said steadily, "Certainly, if you wish it, Philemon."

While they were passing the rows of camp-fires and tents, the major was silent, but once these were behind them he said:—

"'T would be idle, Janice, to make any pretence of why I wished to see you apart. You must know it as well as I."

"I suppose I do, Philemon," assented the girl, quietly.

"A long time we 've been parted, but not once has my love for you lessened, and — and in Philadelphia you held out a little hope that I 've lived on ever since. You said that the squire held to his promise, and that — did you — do you still think as you — "

"Have you spoken to dadda?"

"No. For — for I was afraid he 'd force you against your will. Once I was eager to take you even so, but I hope you won't judge me for that. I was an unthinking boy then."

"We all make mistakes, Philemon, and would that I could outlive mine as well as you have yours," Janice answered gently.

"Then — then — you will?"

"If dadda still — Before I answer — I — something must

be told that I wish — oh, how I wish, for your sake and for mine! — had never been. I gave — I tried to be truthful to you, Philemon, but, unknown to myself, some love I gave to — to one I need not name, and though I — though he quickly killed it, 't is but fair that you should know that the little heart — for I — I fear me I am cold by nature — I had to give was wasted on another. But if, after this confession, you still would have me for a wife, and dadda and mommy wish it, I will wed you, and try my best to be dutiful and loving."

"'T is all I ask," eagerly exclaimed Philemon, as he caught her hand, and drew her toward him. "Ah, Janice, if you but knew how I love —"

"Ho! there ye are," came the voice of the commissary not five paces away. "I saw ye go toward the river, and followed."

"My Lord, Miss Meredith and I are engaged in a private conversation, and cannot but take your intrusion amiss."

"Fudge, man, is not the night hot enough but ye must blaze up so? Nor is the river-bank your monopoly."

"Keep it all, then, and a good riddance to the society you enjoy it with. Come, Janice, we 'll back to the house."

At the doorway Philemon held out his hand. "We ride away while you will be sleeping, but 't is a joyous heart you let me carry."

"I am glad if I — if you are happy," responded the girl, as she let him press her fingers. Then, regardless of the sentry, she laid her free hand on Phil's arm impulsively and imploringly, as she added, "Oh, Philemon, please — whatever else you are, please don't be hard and cruel to me."

"I 'll try my best not to be, though 't is difficult for a soldier to be otherwise; but, come what may, I 'll never pain or deny you knowingly, Janice."

"'T is all I beg. But be kind and generous, and I 'll love you in time."

Rub-a-dub went the drums, sounding tattoo, and the beating brought several officers scurrying out of the house. Philemon kissed the girl's hand, and hurried away to his squadron.

Two days the army remained encamped at the Fork, then

by easy marches it followed the river down to Richmond, where a rest was taken. Once again getting in motion, it fell back on Williamsburg and halted, for it was now the height of summer, and the heat so intense that the troops were easily exhausted. Finally, the British retired across the James River, and took up a position at Portsmouth.

In the month thus spent, not once was Major Hennion able to get a word with Janice, for Lafayette followed closely upon the heels of the invaders until they were safe over the James, and there was constant skirmishing between the van and rear and two sharp encounters, which kept Tarleton's and Simcoe's cavalry, when they had rejoined, fully occupied in covering the retreat, while the Merediths and other loyalists who had joined the army travelled with the baggage in the advance.

The occupation of Portsmouth was brief, for upon the engineers reporting that the site was not one which could be fortified, the British general put his troops on board of such shipping as he could gather and transferred them bodily to Yorktown. Here he set the army, and the three thousand negroes who had followed them, leisurely to laying out lines of earthworks, that he might hold the post with the reduced number which would be left him after he detached the reinforcements needed at New York, and despatched a sloop-of-war to Clinton, with word that he but awaited the arrival of transports to send him whatever regiments he should direct.

If Hennion, by his constant service at the front, was helpless to assist his friends, Clowes, who was always with the baggage train, was unending in his favours. He secured them a stock of clothing, and assigned to them two admirable servants from the horde of runaway slaves; he promptly procured for them a more comfortable travelling carriage, and he made their lodgings a matter of daily concern, so that they always fared with the best, while his gifts of wine and other delicacies were almost embarrassingly frequent. At Yorktown, too, where the village of about sixty houses supplied but the poorest and scantiest accommodations for both man and beast, he managed to have the custom-house assigned for his own use, and then placed all the rooms the Merediths needed at their disposal. If Janice's preferences had been spoken and regarded, everything he did in their behalf would have been declined; but her mother's real need of the comforts of life, and her father's love of them, were arguments too strong for her own wishes, and by placing them under constant obligation to the baron made it impossible for her not to treat him with outward courtesy whenever he sought their company, which was with every opportunity. Yet it was in vain that the commissary plied her with his old-time arts of manner and tongue. Even the slow mind of the squire took note that he gained no ground with his daughter.

"'T is a tougher task ye 've undertaken even than ye counted upon," he said, one evening over the wine, as Janice left the table at the earliest possible instant.

"Tut! give me time. I 'll bring her around yet."

"I warned ye the maid had ye deep in her bad books."

"What 's a month? If a woman yields in that time, a man may save himself the parson's fee, and it please him."

"Still, though she is a good lass in most things, I must own to ye that she hath a strange vein of obstinacy in her, which she comes by from her mother."

"Then I'll use that same obstinacy to win her. Dost not know that every quality in a female is but a means by which to ensnare her? Let me once know a woman's virtues and frailties, and I 'll make each one of them serve my suit."

"'T is more than a month ye 've been striving to win her regard."

"Ay; but for some reason, in Philadelphia I could ne'er keep my head when with her, and as often went back as forward, curse it! 'Better slip with foot than with tongue,' runs the old saying, and I did both with her. I 've learned my lesson now, and once give me a clear field and ye shall see how 't will be."

The squire shook his head. "She 's promised to Major Hennion, and after much folly and womanishness at last she 's found her mind, and tells me she will cheerfully wed him."

"And how will the lot of ye live, man?" asked Clowes, crossly. "Hast not had word that Jersey has enacted a general act of forfeiture and escheatage 'gainst all Royalists?"

"That I 'd not," answered the squire, pulling a long face. "I suppose that has taken Greenwood from us?"

"Ay, for I saw the very advertisement of the sale, and have not told ye before merely to spare you distress. And 't will strip Hennion of his acres as well, I take it. Wilt deliberately marry her to a penniless man?"

"Boxely never was his, and I doubt not his scamp of a father will find some way to save it to him. I'll not tarry longer, for 't is ill news ye have just broke to me, and I must carry it to Matilda. It gives us but a black future to which to look forward."

Mr. Meredith gone from the room, the commissary took from his pocket a copy of Gaines' "New York Gazette and Weekly Mercury," which had come to him but that morning, and re-read an account it contained, taken from the "New Jersey Gazette," of the sale of Greenwood to Esquire Hennion. "'T is my devil's ill luck that he, of all men, should buy it," he muttered. "However, if I can but get them to New York, away from this dashing dragoon, and then persuade them to cross the Atlantic, 't will matter not who owns it." He rose, stretched himself, and as he did so, he repeated the words: —

"I and chance, against any two;
Time and I against chance and you."

LIX

TRAITORS IN THE REAR

ON a broiling August day in the year 1781, an officer rode along the Raritan between Middle-Brook and Brunswick. As he approached the entrance of Greenwood, he slowed his horse, and after a moment's apparent hesitation, finally turned him through the gateway. Once at the porch he drew rein and looked for a time at the paintless clap-boards, broken window-panes, and tangle of vines and weeds, all of which told so plainly the story of neglect and desertion. Starting his steed, he passed around to the kitchen door, and rapped thrice with the butt of a pistol without gaining any reply. Wheeling about, he was returning to the road when an idea seemed to come to him, for, altering direction, he pulled on his bridle, and turned his horse into the garden, now one dense overgrowth. Guiding him along one of the scarcely discernible paths, he checked him at a garden seat, and leaning in his saddle plucked half a dozen sprays of honeysuckle from the vine which surmounted it. He touched them to his lips, and gave his horse the spur. He held the sprays in his hand as he rode, occasionally raising them to his face until he was on the edge of Brunswick village, then he slipped them into his sword sash.

Giving his horse into the hands of the publican at the tavern, he crossed the green to the parsonage and knocked. "Is Parson McClave within?" he inquired of the hired girl.

"Come in, come in, Colonel Brereton," called a voice from the sitting-room; "and all the more welcome are you that I did not know you were in these parts."

"My regiment was ordered across the river to Chatham last week, to build ovens for the coming attack on New York, and I took a few hours off to look up old friends," Brereton answered in a loud voice. "Where can we safely talk?" he whispered.

"I'll leave my sermon even as it is," said the presbyter, "and it being hot here, let us into the meeting-house yard, where we'll get what breeze comes up the river. Eager I am to learn of what the army is about."

Once they were seated among the gravestones, the colonel said: "I need not tell you that five times in the last two months the continental post-riders have been waylaid 'twixt Brunswick and Princeton by scoundrels in the pay of the British. Only once, fortunately, was there information of the slightest importance, but 't is something that must be stopped; and General Washington, knowing of my familiarity with this neighbourhood, directed me to discover and bring the wretches to punishment. Because I can trust you, I come to ask if you have any information or even inkling that can be of service?"

"Surely, man, you do not suspect any one in my parish?" replied the clergyman.

Brereton smiled slightly. "There is little doubt that the secret Tories of Monmouth County are concerned; but there is some confederate in Brunswick, who, whether he takes an active share, supplies them with information concerning the routes, days, and hours of the posts. I see, however, you have no light to shed on the matter."

"'T is all news to me," answered the minister, shaking his head. "I knew that there was some illicit trading with New York, but that we had real traitors amongst us I never dreamed."

"Trap them I will, before many weeks," asserted the officer. "If in no other way, I'll—"

The sentence was interrupted by the clang of the church bell above them.

"Bless me!" cried McClave, springing to his feet. "Your call has made me forget the auction, which, as justice of the peace, I must attend."

"What auction?"

"For the sale of Greenwood under the statute."

The officer frowned. "I feared it when I read of the passing of a general act of forfeiture and escheatage," he muttered, "though I still hoped 't would not extend to them."

Together the two men crossed the green to the town hall, where now a crowd, consisting of almost every inhabitant of the village and of the outlying farms, was assembled. The officer, a scowl on his face, paused in the doorway and glanced about, then threaded his way to where two negresses stood weeping, and began talking to them. Meanwhile, the clergyman, pushing on through the throng, joined Esquire Hennion and Bagby, who for some reason were suspiciously eying each other on the platform.

"I intend to bid on the property, McClave," announced the Honourable Joseph, "so 't is best that the squire takes charge of the sale."

"Thet 'ere is jes what I'm a-calkerlatin' ter do, likewise," responded Hennion, with an ugly glance at Joe, "so I guess yer'll hev ter assoom the runnin' of the perseedins yerself, paason."

There was a moment's consultation, and then Justice McClave stepped forward and read in succession the text of an act of the New Jersey Assembly, a proclamation of the Governor, and an advertisement from the "New Jersey Gazette" by which documents, and by innumerable whereases and therefores, it was set forth that a state of war existed with Great Britain; that sundry inhabitants of the State, forgetful of their just duty and allegiance, had aided and abetted the common enemy; that by these acts they placed themselves outside of the laws of the commonwealth, their property became forfeited, and was ordered sold for the benefit of the State; that the property of one Lambert Meredith, who had been attainted, both by proclamation and by trial, of high treason, was therefore within the act; and, finally, that there would be sold to the highest bidder, at the court-house of the town of Brunswick, on the sixteenth day of August next ensuing, the said property of the said Lambert Meredith; namely, "Two likely negro women, who can cook and spin," and thirty thousand acres of choice arable farm and wood lands under cultivation lease, with one house, one stable, and corn-cribs and other outbuildings thereto appertaining.

It took not five minutes to sell the sobbing slaves, the tavern-keeper buying Sukey for the sum of forty-one pounds, and the clergyman announcing himself at the end of the bidding as the purchaser of Peg for thirty-nine pounds, six.

Then amidst a silence which told of the interest of the crowd, the auctioneer read out a description of the bounds and acreage of Greenwood, and asked for bids.

"Nine thousand pounds," instantly offered Bagby.

"Five hunded more," rejoined Hennion.

"Ten thousand," snapped Joe.

"Five hunded more," snarled his rival bidder.

"Eleven thousand," came Joe's counter bid.

"Thirteen thousand."

"And five hundred."

"Fifteen thousand."

Bagby hesitated, scowling, then said, "Sixteen thousand."

"Seventeen."

"Seventeen, five."

"Yer might ez waal quit, Joe," interjected Squire Hennion. "I hez more 'n' yer hev, an' I intends ter buy it. Nineteen 's my bid, pa'son."

"Twenty," burst out Joe, malignantly.

"Twenty-one."

"Twenty-five."

Hennion's face in turn grew red with anger, and he half rose, his fist clinched, but recollecting himself he resumed his seat.

"Going at twenty-five," announced McClave. "Will any one give more?"

A breathless pause came, while Bagby's countenance assumed a look of sudden anxiety. "I did n't say twenty-five," he quickly denied; "I said twenty-two."

A wave of contradiction swept through the hall.

Nothing daunted, the honourable Joseph repeated his assertion.

"He, he, he!" chuckled Hennion, "thet comes of biddin' more money than yers hev."

"We 'll call it twenty-two thousand," said McClave, "since Mr. Bagby persists. Will you give any more?"

"One hunded more," said Hennion; and nobody offering above him, it was knocked down at that price.

As the sale was declared completed, Bagby rose. "At least, I made you pay double for it," he growled spitefully to his competitor.

"Yer did, consarn yer," was Hennion's reply; but then a smile succeeded the angry look on the shrewd face. "I did n't pay more 'n a third of what 't is wuth, then."

"T will be a dear buy, that I warn you," retorted Joseph, angrily. "I 'll pay you off yet for bidding me out of it."

"Yer be keerful what yer do, or I 'll do some payin' off myself," warned Hennion.

Brereton, who had stayed through the sale, with a contemptous shrug of the shoulders, walked over to the ordinary. Here he ate a silent supper, and then mounting his horse set off on his evening ride back to his regiment.

Half-way between Brunswick and Greenwood, while his thoughts were dwelling on the day's doings, and on what effect it would have on those far away in the mountains of Virginia, he was brought back to the present by hearing his name called in a low voice from behind a wall.

"Who 's that?" he demanded, halting his horse.

"Are you alone?"

"Yes," replied the officer, as he drew out a pistol from the holster.

"No occasion for that, colonel," said Joe Bagby's unmistakable accents, as the man climbed over the stones and came forward. "It 's me," he announced. "Just walk your horse slow, so I can keep beside you, for I 've something to tell you, and I don't want to stand still here in the road."

"Well, what is it?" questioned Brereton, as he started his horse walking.

"I rather guess you came to town on business, did n't you?"

"Perhaps."

"Might be something to do with the sale of Greenwood."

"Possibly."

"But more likely 't was something to do with public matters?"

"Well?"

"What would you give to catch them as was concerned in the killing of the post-riders?"

Not a motion or sound did Jack give to betray himself. "That lies outside of my work," he said. "'T is the business of the secret service."

"Do you mean that, if I can put you in the way of laying hands on the whole gang, you won't do it?"

"If you choose to tell me what you know, I 'll report it, for what it 's worth, to headquarters, and General Washington will take such actions as he judges fit."

"There won't be time for that," asserted Joe. "It 's to-morrow the thing 's to be played."

"What thing?"

"The robbing of the mail."

"How know you that?"

"Well, being in politics, colonel, I make it my business to know most things that is happening in the county. Now, I 've been ferreting for some time to get at this post-riding business, and at last I 've found out how it 's done. And they 're going to do it again to-morrow night just this side of Rocky Hill."

For a moment Brereton was silent. "How is it done?" he asked.

"It 's this way. One of Moody's gang is working with Squire Hennion as hired man; and when Hennion knows that a rider is due, he drops into the ordinary, and, casual like, finds out all he can as to when he rides on, and by what road. Then he hurries off home and tells his man, and he goes and tells Moody, who gets his men together and does the business."

"I see. And how can we know where they set the ambush, so as to set a counter one?"

"It 's easy as can be. When they have the mail, it 's to Hennion's barn they all goes, where they cut it open and takes out everything as Clinton will pay for, and sends it off at once on one of the boats of provisions as old Hennion is stealing into New York two or three times a week."

"Ah, that 's where he 's got the money to buy Greenwood, is it?"

"Yes; I tell you he 's a traitor if there ever was one, colonel. But I guess he 'll be nabbed now. All you 've got to do is to hide your men in the barn to-morrow night, and you 'll take the whole lot red-handed."

"And I suppose you tell me this to get your revenge for this afternoon."

"Just a little, colonel; but don't forget I 'm a patriot, who 's always trying to serve his country. Now I 'll tell you how we 'll do it. You bring your men down t' other side of the river to Meegan's place; and as soon as it 's dark, I 'll come across the river in a sloop I own and will bring you right over to Hennion's wharf, from which it will be easy to steal into his barn without no one seeing us."

Brereton made no answer for a minute, then said, "Very well; I 'll adopt your plan."

"I suppose there 'll be some reward coming to me, colonel?"

"Undoubtedly," replied Jack, but with a twitch of contempt. "Is that all?"

"That 's enough to do the business, I guess," rejoined Joe. "About nine clock I 'll allow to be at Meegan's," he said.

Without a word of assent, Jack quickened his pace. When he had gone fifty feet he looked back, but already the informer had disappeared. "What dirty work every man must do on occasion!" he muttered. "I 'd suspect the scoundrel but for what I heard this afternoon, and he has it all so pat that he 's probably been in it himself more or less. However, it promises well; and 't will be a service of the utmost importance if we can but break up the murdering gang and bring them to justice, for 't is no time to have Clinton reading all our secrets."

It was midnight when Brereton trotted into Chatham and dismounting from his horse walked wearily into his tent.

His servant, sleeping on the floor, waked, and hastily rose. "A despatch, sir, from headquarters," he said, taking a paper from his pocket.

"When did it arrive?" demanded Jack, as he examined the seal, to make sure that it had not been tampered with, and then broke the letter open.

"Four hours ago, sir, by special courier."

What Brereton read was this: —

HEADQUARTERS, *August 16, 1781.*

SIR, — *Should you have already taken steps looking to the discovery and seizure of those concerned in the late robbing of the mails, you will hold all such proceedings in abeyance until further orders. For military reasons it is even desired that the post-bag which will be sent through to-morrow should fall into the hands of the enemy, and you will act accordingly. I have the honour to be,*

Yr. Obedt. hble Servt.

GO. WASHINGTON.

To COLONEL BRERETON,
Commanding the 3rd. New Jersey Regt.,
Stationed at Chatham.

Jack whistled softly, then smiled, "Joe will have a long wait," he chuckled. "I wonder what 's up."

He knew three days later, for orders came to him to put his regiment in motion and march for Philadelphia, and the bearer of the despatch added that the united forces of Washington and Rochambeau were already across the Hudson and would follow close upon his heels.

"We 've made Sir Henry Clinton buy the information that we intend to attack New York," the aide told him, "and now we are off to trap Cornwallis in Virginia."

LX

THE SPINNING OF THE WEB

OWING to the impossibility of the horses of Tarleton's and Simcoe's legions being ferried on the small boats which transported the foot troops from Portsmouth to Yorktown, they had been left behind the rest of the army, with directions to put themselves on board the frigate and sloops of war and effect a landing at Hampton or thereabouts. This gave the commissary still more time free from the presence of Major Hennion, but he had little reason to think it of advantage to him. At meal hours, since they had but one table, Janice could not avoid his company, but otherwise she very successfully eluded him. Much of each day she spent with her mother, who was ailing, and kept her room, and she made this an excuse for never remaining in those shared by all in common. When she went out of doors, which, owing to the August heats, was usually towards evening, she always took pains that the baron should not be in a position to join her, or even to know of her having sallied forth. With the same object, she generally, as soon as she left the house, hurried through the little village and past the rows of tents of the encampment on the outskirts and the lines of earthworks upon which the soldiery and negroes were working, until she reached the high point of land to the east, which opened on Chesapeake Bay, where, feeling secure, she could enjoy herself in the orchard of the Moore house, in the woods to the southward, or with sewing or a book, merely sit on the extreme point gazing off at the broad expanse of water.

She was thus engaged on the afternoon of the 28th of August, when the rustle of footsteps made her look up from her book, only to find that her precautions for once were futile, as it was the commissary who was hastening toward her.

"I needed this," he began, "to prove to me that you were not a witch, as well as a bewitcher, for, verily, I had begun to think that by some black art ye flew out of your window at will. Nay," he protested, as Janice, closing her book, rose, "call ye this fair treatment, Miss Meredith? Surely, if ye have no gratitude yourself, ye should at least remember what I am doing for your father and mother, and not seek to shun me as if I were the plague, rather than a man nigh mad with love for ye."

"'T is that very fact, Lord Clowes," replied Janice, gravely, "which has forced avoidance of you upon me. Surely you must understand that, promised now as I am to another, both by my father's word and by my own, your suit cannot fail to distress me?"

"Is 't possible that, to please others, thee intends, then, to force thyself to marry this long-legged dragoon?" protested Clowes. "Hast thy father not told thee of thy own loss of Greenwood and of his undoubted loss of Boxely?"

"Our loss of property, my Lord, but makes it all the more important that we save our good name; and if our change of circumstance does not alter Major Hennion's wishes, as I am certain it will not, we shall keep faith with him."

"Even though Lord Clowes offers ye position, wealth, and a home for your parents, not a one of which he can give?"

"Were I not promised, Lord Clowes, nothing could induce me to marry you."

"Why not?" questioned the baron, warmly.

"Methinks, if you but search the past, sir, you cannot for an instant be in doubt. Obligations you have heaped upon us at moments, for every one of which I thank you, but never could I bring myself to feel respect, far less affection for you."

The commissary, with knitted brows, started to speak, but checked himself and took half a dozen strides. Returning, he said: —

"Miss Meredith, 't is not just to judge the future by the past. Can ye not understand that what I did in Philadelphia, ay, every act of mine at which ye could take offence in our whole acquaintance, has been done on heated impulse? If ye but knew a man's feelings when he loves as I love, and finds no response to his passion in the object of it, ye would pardon my every act."

"'T is not alone your conduct to us, Lord Clowes, but as well that to others which has confirmed me in my conviction."

"Ye would charge me with — "

"'T is not I alone, my Lord, that you have deceived or injured, and you cannot plead for those the excuse you plead to me."

"'T is the circumstances of my parole of which ye speak?" demanded the baron.

"Of that and other things which have come to my knowledge."

Again the suitor hesitated before saying, with a suggestion of glibness: "Miss Meredith, every ounce of blame ye put upon my conduct I accept honestly and regretfully, but did ye but know all, I think ye would pity rather than judge me in that heart which seems open to every one but me. From the day my father died in the debtor's prison and I was thrown a penniless boy of twelve upon the world, it has been one long fight to keep head above water, till I got this appointment. The gentlemen of the army have told ye that I was a government spy, I doubt not. I wonder what they would have been in my straits! Think ye any man is spy by choice? Am I worse than the men who hired me to do the work, and who gained praise and rewards, even to the blue ribbon, by the information I had got for them, while only scorn and shame was my portion? Think ye a life given to indirection and worming, to prying and scheming, is one of self-choice? Hitherto I have done the dirty work of ministers, — ay, of kings; but from the day I leave this country, that is over and done with for ever, and their once tool, now rich, will take his place among the very best of England's peers, for money will buy a man anything in London nowadays. 'T is not alone that I love ye nigh to desperation that I beg your love; 't is that your love will help to make me the honest-living man

I ambition to be. But grant the longing of my life, and I'll pledge ye happiness. Ye shall write your own marriage settlement, a house, carriages, jewels — "

"Indeed, Lord Clowes, even were my feelings less strong, you ask for what is now impossible."

"Because your father, with a short-sightedness that is well-nigh criminal, has tied ye to this fellow! Can't ye perceive that the greatest service ye can render him will be to relieve him of the promise he has not the courage to end? In a six-months he'll bless ye for the deed, if ye will but do it."

Almost as if he had come to protect his rights, the voice of Major Hennion broke in upon them. "Everywhere have I sought you for upwards of an hour," he said, as he hurried toward them, "and began to fear that some evil had befallen you." He caught Janice's hand eagerly and kissed it.

"But when did you arrive?" exclaimed the girl.

"The legions were landed at Hampton Road this morning and reached camp an hour gone," explained the major. Still retaining her hand, he turned to Clowes and said, "If I understood you aright, my Lord, you told me you knew not where Miss Meredith was to be found?"

"And Miss Meredith will bear me out in the statement, sir, though I am quite willing that my word should stand by itself," retorted the commissary, tartly. "Nor am I in the habit of having it questioned by colonial striplings," he added insultingly.

"Nor am I —" began Philemon, heatedly; but Janice checked him by laying her free hand on his arm.

"'T is naught to take umbrage at, Phil," she said dissuadingly, "and do not by quarrelling over a foolish nothing spoil my pleasure in seeing you."

"That I'll not," acceded the major, heartily. "Ah, Janice," he cried, unable to contain himself even before the baron, "if you knew the thrill your words give me. Are you truly glad to see me?"

"Yes, Phil, or I would not say so," answered the girl, ingenuously.

Lord Clowes, a scowl on his face, turned from the two, to avoid sight of Hennion's look of gladness. This brought him gazing seaward, and he gave an exclamation. "Ho! What's here?"

The two faced about at his question, to see, just appearing from behind the curve of the land to the southward, a full-rigged ship, one mass of canvas from deck to spintle-heads, and with a single row of ports which bespoke the man-of-war.

"'T is a frigate," announced Clowes, "and no doubt sent to convoy the transports we have been awaiting. Yes; there comes another. 'T is the fleet, beyond question," he continued, as the first vessel having opened from the land, the bowsprit of a second began to appear.

The three stood silent as the two ships towering pyramids of sails, making them marvels of beauty, swept onward with slow dignity across the mouth of the York River, at this point nearly three miles wide, toward the Gloucester shore. Before they had gone a quarter of a mile, a third and larger vessel came sweeping into view, her two rows of ports showing her to be a line-of-battle ship. Barely was she clear of the land when a string of small flags broke out from her mizzen rigging, and almost as if by magic, the yard arms of all three vessels were alive with men, and royals, top gallants, and mainsails with machine-like precision were clewed up and furled, and each ship, stripped of all but its topsails, rounded to, with its head to the wind.

"That is a strange manœuvre," remarked Philemon. "Why stop they outside, instead of sailing up the river?"

"They 've hove to, no doubt, to wait a pilot, being strangers to the waters," surmised Clowes, wheeling and looking up the river townwards. "Ay, there goes some signal from the 'Charon's' truck," he went on, as the British frigate anchored off the town displayed three flags at her masthead.

Janice, thankful for the diversion the arrivals had caused, said something to Philemon in a low voice, and they set out toward the town. Not noticing the obvious attempt to escape from his society, or to outward appearance perturbed, the baron put himself alongside the two, and walked with them until the custom-house was reached.

"Will you come in, Philemon, and see dadda and mommy?" questioned the girl, as the three halted at the doorway.

As she spoke, an orderly, who a moment before had come out of headquarters, made towards the major, and, saluting, said, "Colonel Tarleton directs that you report at headquarters without delay, sir."

"My answer is made for me, Janice," sighed Philemon. "I fear me 't is some vidette duty, and that once again we are doomed to part, just as I thought my hour had come. Many more of such disappointments will turn me from a soldier into a Quaker. However, 't is possible his Lordship wants but to put some questions, and, if so, I 'll be with you shortly." He crossed the street and entered the Nelson house.

Shown by the orderly to the room where Cornwallis was, he found with him his colonel and a man in the uniform of a naval officer.

"Ah, here he is," said the British general. "Major Hennion, the three ships which have taken station at the mouth of the river pay no heed to the 'Charon's' signals, nor are theirs to be read by our book, so 't is feared that they are French ships. As 't is impossible to believe they would thus boldly venture into the bay if alone, we wish to know if there are others below. Furnish Lieutenant Foley with a mount, and, with an escort of a troop, guide him over the road you came to-day to some spot where a view of the roadstead at Old Point Comfort is to be commanded." Speaking to the naval officer, he enjoined, "You will carefully observe any shipping there may be, sir, and of what force, and report to me with the least possible delay."

It was a little after ten o'clock on the following day when a troop of hot and weary-looking horses and men clattered along the main street of the town and drew up in front of headquarters. Throwing himself from the saddle, Major Hennion hurried into the house. The moment he was in the presence of Cornwallis, he said: "'T is as you surmised, general. Between thirty and forty sail stretch from Lynnhaven Bay to the mouth of the James, and though 't was difficult to exactly estimate their force, they are mostly men of war, and some even three-deckers."

"Beyond question 't is the French West India fleet," burst

from Cornwallis. For a moment he was silent, then sternly demanded, "Where is Lieutenant Foley?"

"The gentlemen of the navy, sir, are more used to oak than to leather, and we set him such a pace that twelve miles back he could no longer sit his saddle, and we left him leading his horse, thinking this information could not be brought you too soon."

"It but proves the old saying that 'Ill news has wings,'" replied the earl, steadily, as he walked to the window and looked out into the garden. Here he stood silently for so long that finally Hennion spoke.

"I beg your pardon, general," he said, "but am I dismissed?"

All the reply Cornwallis made him was to ask, "When you first came amongst us, major, you spoke with the barbaric provincialism and nasal twang of your countrymen, but in your years with us you have lost them. Could you upon occasion resume both?"

"Indeed, my Lord," replied the officer, smiling, "'t is even yet a constant struggle to keep from it."

"The word you bring must be got to Clinton without question of fail and with the least possible delay. Are you willing to volunteer for a service of very great risk?"

"Does your Lordship for a moment question it?"

"Not I. To-night we will try to steal a small sloop out of the river with a despatch for Clinton; but we must not place our whole dependence on this means, and a second must be sent him overland. Get you a meal, sir, and a fresh horse, and from some civilian or negro procure such clothes as are fitting for a travelling peddler. I will order you a pack and a stock of such things as are appropriate from the public stores, and you shall at once be rowed across the river and must make your way as best you can northward to New York. Dost understand?"

"Ay, my Lord," replied Major Hennion, his hand already on the door-latch.

Left alone, Cornwallis stood for a moment, his lips pressed together, then summoning an aide, he gave him certain directions, after which, going to his writing-desk, he pulled out a drawer and from it took quite a batch of Continental and State currency. Seating himself at his desk, he laid one of the notes upon it, and taking his penknife he very neatly and dexterously split the bill through half its length. Taking from his pocket a wallet, he drew from it a sheet of paper covered with numbers and syllables, which was indorsed, "Cipher No. 1." Writing on a scrap of paper a few words, he then alternately looked at what he had penned and at the cipher, taking down on one of the inner surfaces of the bill a series of numbers. Scarcely had he done his task when a knock came at the door, and in response to his summons a negress entered.

"'Scuse me, your Lordship," she said with a bob. "De captain, he say youse done want a leetle flour gum."

"Yes. Give it to me and leave the room," answered the earl.

Touching his finger in the saucer she had brought, Cornwallis rubbed it inside the split along the three edges, and then laying the bill on his desk, he patted the edges where they had been split, together, wiping them clean with his handkerchief. Running over the pile of currency, he sorted out some fifty notes, then taking a sheet of paper, he began a letter.

Before the earl had finished what he was writing, he was again interrupted, and the new-comer proved to be Major Hennion, clothed in an old suit of butternut-coloured linen. And as if in laying aside his red coat, shorts, and boots he had as well laid aside military rank, he seemed to have already reverted to his old slouch.

"Good," exclaimed Cornwallis, as he rose. "Are your other preparations all made?"

"Every one, general; and my horse and pack are already at the river-side."

The earl took the pile of sorted bills from his desk and handed them to Hennion. "There is the money to pay your way," he said, "all Continental Loan office or Virginia currency, save one of North Carolina for forty shillings, which on no account are you to part with, even if any one in the States to the northward will accept it, for I have split it open and written within it to Sir Henry Clinton the news I have to tell. Say to him that a few moments in water will serve to part the edges where they have been gummed together. I give you the note, that if you are caught, you may still find some means to send it on. But lest by mischance it should be lost or taken from you, and you should yet be able to reach New York, I have here the words I have written in cipher within the bill. Have you a good memory?"

"For facts, if not for words, my Lord."

The general took up from his desk the little memorandum he had written before using his cipher and read out: "An enemy's fleet within the Capes. Between thirty and forty ships of war, mostly large." "Spare not your speed, sir, yet take no unnecessary risk," ended the earl, as he held out his hand.

As Hennion took it, he said: "I will endeavour not to fail your Lordship in either respect; in going, however, I have one favour to crave of you. I leave behind me my promised bride, Miss Meredith; and I beg of you that she shall not want for any service that your Lordship can render her, or that I could do were I but here."

"'T is given," promised the earl, and on the word Hennion hurried from the room. Crossing the street, he knocked at the custom-house, and of the servant inquired, "Is Miss Meredith within?"

"No, sir," replied the soldier.

"Where is she?"

"I know not, sir. She left the house an hour ago."

With something suspiciously like an oath, the major turned away and, hurrying along the street, descended that which sloped down the bluff to the river. Here stood an officer, while in the water lay a flatboat which already held, besides two rowers, a horse and a pair of fat saddle-bags. Without a word Phil jumped in and the rowers struck their oars into the water.

At the same time that Major Hennion's party had been despatched to gain news of the fleet, other troops of Tarleton's and Simcoe's cavalry had been thrown out on scouting parties across the peninsula to the James, and the following day they brought word that the French were busily engaged in landing troops from their ships at Jamestown, with the obvious intention of effecting a junction with Lafayette's brigades, which were at Williamsburg. A council of war was held that evening to debate whether the British force should not march out and attack them; but it was recognised that even if they completely crushed the French and Americans, they had themselves made escape southward impossible by the care with which they had destroyed the bridges and ferries in their march into Virginia, while if they fled northward, they would certainly have to fight Washington's army long before they could reach New York. It was therefore unanimously voted that the least hazardous course was to remain passive in their present position.

Five days after this decision, a deserter from Lafayette's camp came into the British lines, bringing with him the news that it was openly talked in Williamsburg that Washington and Rochambeau, with their armies, were coming to join the troops already in Virginia. Nor were the British long able to continue their doubting of his assertions, for a Tory brought in the same tale, and with it a copy of the "Baltimore Journal," which printed the positive statement that the Northern army was on the march southward and was already arrived at Wilmington. A second council of war was therefore summoned to debate once again their difficulties; but ere the general and field officers had met, a schooner, eluding the French vessels which blockaded the mouth of the river, arrived from New York, bringing a despatch from Sir Henry Clinton, in which he assured the encircled general that the British fleet would quickly sail to relieve him, and that he himself, with four thousand men, would follow close upon its heels. The order for the council was therefore recalled; and Cornwallis turned the whole energies of the force under his command to strengthening his lines and in other ways making ready to resist the gathering storm.

LXI

IN THE TOILS

ON the morning of the 6th of October, twelve thousand American and French soldiers lay encamped in the form of a broad semi-circle almost a mile from the British earthworks about Yorktown. Still nearer, in a deep ravine, above which were some outworks that had been abandoned by the British on the approach of the allies, were the outposts; and these, lacking tents, had hutted themselves with boughs. Intermittently came the roar of a cannon from the British lines, and those in the hollow could occasionally see and hear a shell as it screeched past them overhead; but they gave not one-tenth the heed to it that they gave to the breakfast they were despatching. Indeed, their sole grumblings were at the meagreness of the ration which had been dealt out to them the night before ere they had been marched forward into their present position; and as a field officer, coming from the American camp, descended into the ravine, these found open expression.

"'T is mighty fine fer the ginral ter say in the ginral orders that he wants us if attacked ter rely on the bagonet," spoke up one of the murmurers loud enough to make it evident that he intended the officer to overhear him; "but no troops kin fight on a shred o' salt pork and a mouthful of collards."

The officer halted, and speaking more to all those within hearing than to the man, said: "You got as good as any of the Continental regiments, boys, and better than some."

"That may be, kun'l," answered the complainant, "but how about the dandies?"

"Yes," assented the officer. "We sent the French regiments all the flour and fresh meat the commissaries could lay hands on, I grant you. Is there one of you who would have kept it from them for his own benefit?"

"P'raps not," acknowledged another, "but that don't make it any the less unfairsome."

"Remember they come to help us, and are really our guests. Nor are they accustomed to the privation we know too well. General Washington has surety that you can fight on an empty stomach, for you 've done it many a time, but he is not so certain of the French."

The remark was greeted with a general laugh, which seemed to dissipate the grievance.

"Lord!" exclaimed a corporal; "them fine birds do need careful tending."

"'T ain't ter be wondered at thet the Frenchies is so keerful ter bring their tents with 'em," remarked a third. "Whatever would happen ter one o' them Soissonnais fellers, with his rose-coloured facings an' his white an' rose feathers, if he had ter sleep in a bowery along o' us? Some on 'em looks so pretty, thet it don't seem right ter even trust 'em out in a heavy dew." As he ended, the speaker looked down at his own linen overalls. "T ain't no shakes they laughs a bit at us an' won't believe we are really snogers."

"'T is for us to make them laugh the other way before we 've done Cornwallis's business," remarked the officer. "But make up your minds to one thing, boys, if their caps are full of feathers and their uniforms more fit for a ball-room than for service, these same fine-plumaged birds can fight; and there must be no lagging if we are to prove ourselves their betters, or even their equals."

"We 'll show 'em what the Jarsey game-cocks kin do, an' don't you be afeared, kun'l."

As the assertion was made, a group of officers appeared on the brow of the ravine, and the colonel turned and went forward to meet them as they descended.

"How far in advance are your pickets, Colonel Brereton?" one of them asked.

"About three hundred paces, your Excellency."

"And is the ground open?" demanded a second of the party, with a markedly French accent.

"There is some timber cover, General du Portail, but 't is chiefly open and rolling."

"We wish, sir, to advance as far as can be safely effected," said Washington, "and shall rely on you for guidance."

"This way, sir," answered Brereton; and the whole party ascended out of the hollow through a side ravine which brought them into a clump of poplars occupied by a party of skirmishers, and which commanded a view of the British earthworks. Halting at the edge of the timber, glasses were levelled, and each man began a study of the enemy's lines. Scarcely had they taken position when a puff of smoke rose from one of the redoubts, and a shell came screeching towards them, passing high enough to cut the branches of the trees over their heads, and bringing them falling among the group. A minute later a solid shot struck directly in their front, causing all except the commander-in-chief to fall back out of sight among the trees; but he, apparently unmoved by the danger, calmly continued observing the enemies' works, and though directly in their view, for some reason they did not fire again.

When Washington finally turned about and rejoined the group, he said to Brereton: "Keep your men, sir, as they are at present disposed, out of sight of the batteries, till evening; then push your pickets forward as close to the town as they can venture, with orders to fall back, unless attacked, only with daylight. Last night the British put outside their lines a number of blacks stricken with the small-pox; you will order your skirmishers, therefore, to fire on them if they endeavour to repeat the attempt, for even the dictates of humanity cannot allow us to jeopardise the health of our army. Hold your regiment in readiness to move out at nightfall in support of the pioneers who will begin breaking ground this evening. Further and specific orders will reach you later through the regular channels."

It was already dark when Brereton, guiding General du Portail and the engineers, once more came out upon the plain. Following after them were a corps of sappers and miners, regiments detailed as pioneers, carrying intrenching tools, regiments armed as usual, to support them if attacked, and carts loaded with bags of sand, empty barrels, fascines, and gabions.

Advancing cautiously, each man keeping touch with the one in front of him, they went forward until within six hundred yards of the British position. Without delay, by means of lanterns which were screened from the foe by being carried in half-barrels, the engineering tapes were laid down, and with pick and shovel the fatigue party went to work, the eagerness of the men being such that, despite of orders, the men from the supporting regiments, leaving their muskets in charge of their fellow-soldiers, would join in the toil. Nor did their colonels reprove them for this; but, on the contrary, Brereton, finding six men from one company engaged in rolling a large rock out of the ditch and to the top of the rapidly waxing pile of earth in its rear, said approvingly: "Well done, boys. I've a wager with the Marquis de Chastellux that an American battery fires the first shot, and I see you intend that I shall win the bet."

"Arrah, 't is in yez pocket aready, colonel," cried one of the sappers. "Sure, how kin a Frinchman expect to bate us whin nary ground-hog nor baver, the aither av thim, is theer in his counthry to tache him how to work wid earth an' timber?"

So well was the night spent that when morning dawned the British found a long line of new earthworks stretched along their front; and though instantly their guns began cannonading them, the men were now protected and could dig on, unheeding of the fire. Indeed, such was the enthusiasm that when at six o'clock the order came for the regiments to fall in, and it was found that they were to be replaced by fresh troops, there was open grumbling. "'T is we did the work," complained a sergeant, "and now them fellows who slept all night will steal the glory."

"Not a bit of it, boys," denied Brereton, as he was passing down the lines preparatory to giving the order of march. "There are still redoubts to be made and the guns are not up yet. 'T will come our turn in the trenches again before they are."

Their commander spoke wittingly, for two days it took to get the trenches, and the redoubts thrown out in advance of them, completed, and the heavy siege-guns were not moved forward until after dark on the 8th. All night long and the most of the following morning the men toiled, placing them in position, paying no attention to the unceasing thunder of the British guns, unless to stop momentarily and gaze with admiration at the shells, each with its tail of fire, as they curved through the air, or to crack a joke over some one which flew especially near.

"Bark away," laughed one, as he affectionately patted a twenty-four pounder just moved into its position, while shaking his other fist toward Yorktown. "Scold while ye kin, for 't is yer last chance. Like men, we 've sat silent for nine days, an' let ye, like women, do the talkin', but it 's to-morrow mornin' ye 'll find that, if we 've kept still, it 's not been for want of a tongue."

It was noon when Brereton came hurrying into the battery to find the men sleeping among the guns, where they had dropped after their hard labour.

"How is it, Jack?" questioned the officer in command.

"General du Portail has reported the battery completed, and he tells me we 've beat the French by at least two hours."

A wild yell of joy broke from one of the apparently unconscious men, bringing most of the sleepers scrambling to their feet and grasping for their weapons. "I said they could never dig in them clothes!" he cried.

"'T is however to be another 'Gentlemen of the guards, fire first,'" went on Brereton. "General Washington, as a compliment to the French, has decided that their guns shall fire the first shot."

A growl came from the captain of the nearest cannon. "I promised the old gal," he muttered discontentedly, his hand on his thirty-two pounder, "that she should begin it, an' she 's sighted to knock over that twelve pounder that 's been teasin' us, or may I never fire gun agin."

"She 'll do it just as well on the second shot," said Colonel Lamb, "and who cares which fires first, since we 've beat them."

It was three o'clock when Washington and Rochambeau, accompanied by their staffs, came out of the covert-way which permitted entrance and egress to a French redoubt, from the trenches in its rear, and infantry and gunners came to the "present."

"Votre Excellence," said Colonel d'Aboville, saluting, "mes

cannoniers vous implorent de leur donner l'honneur immortel en mettant feu au premier coup de cannon."

Washington, realizing that the speech was addressed to him, turned to Rochambeau with a helpless and questioning look.

"Zay desire zat your Excellency does zem ze honneur to fire ze first gun," explained the French general.

Washington removed his hat and bowed. "Try as we will, count," he said, "we cannot equal your nation in politeness." In silence he stepped forward to the gun the colonel indicated, and the captain of the piece handed him the loggerhead with a salute and then fell back respectfully.

Washington touched the red-hot iron to the port fire; there was a puff of smoke, a deafening crash; and the great gun gave a little jump, as if for joy. A thousand pairs of eyes strained after the solid shot as it flew, then as it disappeared over the British earthworks and was heard to go tearing its way through some wall a great shout went up from one end of the lines of the allies, to the other.

Instantly came the roar of the other five cannon, and two ten-inch mortars echoed their thunder by sending ten-inch shells curving high in the air. Ere they descended one of the guns peeping from a British redoubt rose on end and disappeared; raising another cheer. At last the siege was begun.

As if to prove that the foe was nothing daunted, a solid shot, just topping the redoubt, tore through the middle of the group of generals, scattering sand and pebbles over them. Colonel Cobb, who stood nearest Washington, turning impulsively, said, "Sir, you are too much exposed here. Had you not better step back a little?"

"If you are afraid, Colonel Cobb," quietly answered Washington, "you have liberty to step back."

By dark three batteries were firing, and all through the night the guns on both sides rained shot and shell at each other. Two more batteries of thirty-two pounders opened fire on the 10th, and by hot shot set fire that evening to the "Charon" frigate, making a sight of marvellous grandeur, for the ship became one mass of fire from the water's edge to her spintle-heads, all her ports belching flame and each spar and every rope ablaze at the same moment. The morning of the 11th found fifty-two pieces of artillery mounted and hurling a storm of projectiles into the British lines; and that evening, a second parallel was opened, bringing the guns of the besiegers less than three hundred yards from their earthworks, and putting all parts of the town within range. After this was completed, the defensive fire slackened, for every gun with which the garrison sought to make reply was dismounted the moment it was advanced into the embrasure, compelling their withdrawal during daylight hours; and though each night as soon as dark screened them from the accurate gunnery of the Americans, they were restored and the firing renewed, it was done with a feebleness that bespoke discouragement and exhaustion. For two days shot and shell splintered and tore through abattis and fraising, and levelled parapet and ditch, almost unanswered.

To the right of the new parallel, and almost enfilading it by their fire, were two detached redoubts of the British, well in advance of their main lines. To end their destructive cross fire, as well as to complete the investiture, it was determined to carry them by assault; and as dark settled down on the evening of the 14th, two storming parties, one of French grenadiers and chasseurs, drawn from the brigade of the Baron de Viomenil and under the command of the Comte de Deuxponts, and the second, of American light infantry, taken from the division of the Marquis de Lafayette and commanded by Alexander Hamilton, were moved out of the trenches, and, followed by strong supporting battalions, were advanced as far as was prudent.

It was while the American forlorn hope was standing at ease, awaiting the signal, that Colonel Brereton came hurrying up to where Hamilton and Laurens were whispering final details.

"I could n't keep out of this," he explained; "and the marquis was good enough to say I might serve as a volunteer."

"The more the merrier," responded Laurens. "Come along with me, Jack. We are to take the fort in the rear, and you shall have your stomach full of fighting, I 'll warrant you. Here, put this paper in your hat, if you don't want to be stuck by our own men."

Hamilton, turning from the two, addressed the three battalions. "Light infantry," he said, "when the council of war reached the decision to carry the works in our front, Baron de Viomenil argued that both should be left to his troops, as the American soldiery could not be depended upon for an assault. The commander-in-chief would not disgrace us by yielding to his claim, and 't is for us to prove that he was right. We have shown the French artillerists that we can serve our guns quicker and more accurately; now let us see if we cannot prove ourselves the swifter and steadier at this work. Let the sergeants see to it that each man in his file has a piece of paper in his hat, and that each has removed the flint from his gun. I want you to carry the redoubt without a shot, by the bayonet alone."

A murmur of assent and applause passed along the lines, and then all stood listening for the signal. It was a night of intense darkness, and now, after ten days of unending bombardment, the cannonading had entirely ceased, giving place to a stillness which to ears so long accustomed to the uproar seemed to have a menacing quality in it.

Suddenly a gun boomed loud and clear; and as its echo reverberated out over the river, every man clutched his musket more firmly. Boom! went a second close upon the first, and each soldier drew a deep breath as if to prepare for some exertion. Boom! went a third, and a restless undulation swept along the lines. Boom! for a fourth time roared a cannon, and some of the men laughed nervously. Boom! rolled out yet a fifth, and the ranks stood tense and rigid, every ear, every sense, straining.

Boom! crashed the sixth gun, and not a man needed the "Forward, light infantry!" of the commander, every one of them being in motion before the order was given. Steadily they advanced in silence, save only for muttered grumbles here and there over the slowness of the pace.

Without warning, out of the blackness came a challenge, "Who goes there?"

Making no answer, the stormers broke into a run and swept forward with a rush.

"Bang!" went a single musket; and had it been fired into

a mine, the tremendous uproar that ensued could not have come more instantaneously, for twenty cannon thundered, and the redoubts fairly seemed to spit fire as the defenders' muskets flashed. High in the air rose rockets, which lit up the whole scene, and for the time they lasted fairly turned the night into day.

As the main and flanking parties swept up to the redoubt, the sappers and miners, who formed the first rank, attacked the abattis with their axes; but the troops, mad with long waiting and fretted by the galling fire of the foe, would not wait, and, pushing them aside, clambering, boosting, and tumbling went over the obstruction. Not pausing to form in the ditch, they scrambled up the parapet and went surging over the crest, pell-mell, upon the British.

Brereton, sword in hand, had half sprung, half been tossed upon the row of barrels filled with earth which topped the breastworks, only to face a bayonet which one of the garrison lunged up at him. A sharp prick he felt in his chest; but as in the quick thought of danger he realised his death moment, the weapon, instead of being driven home, was jerked back, and the soldier who had thrust with it cried:—

"Charlie!"

"Fred!" exclaimed Jack, and the two men caught each other by the hand and stood still while the invaders poured past them over the barrels.

It was Mobray who spoke first. "Oh, Charlie!" he almost sobbed, "one misery at least has been saved me! My God! You bleed."

"A pin-prick only, Fred. But what does this mean? You! and in the ranks."

"Ay, and for three years desperately seeking a death which will not come!"

"And the Fusileers?"

"Hold this redoubt. Oh, Charlie, to think that your sword should ever be raised against the old regiment!"

As Mobray spoke, came a cry from the garrison, "We yield!" and the clatter of their weapons could be heard as they were grounded, or were thrown to the earth.

"Quick!" cried Brereton, fairly hauling Sir Frederick to

where he stood. "Run, Fred! At least, you shall be no prisoner." Jack gave him a last squeeze of the hand and a shove, which sent his friend fairly staggering down into the ditch.

Mobray sprang through a break in the abattis, but had not run ten feet when he turned and shouted back something which the thundering of the artillery prevented Brereton from entirely hearing, but the words he distinguished were sufficient to make him catch at the barrels for support, for they were: —

"Janice Meredith . . . Yorktown . . . point of death . . . small-pox."

For a moment Brereton stood in a kind of daze; but as the full horror of Mobray's words came home to him, he groaned. Turning, he plunged down into the fortress with a look of a man bereft, and striding to the commander cried, "For God's sake, Hamilton, give me something to do!"

"The very man I wanted," replied the little colonel. "Carry word to the marquis that the redoubt is ours, and that the supports may advance."

Dashing out of the now open sally port, Jack ran at his top speed, and within two minutes delivered the report to General de Lafayette.

"Ah, mes braves," ejaculated the marquis, triumphantly. "My own countreemen they thought they would not it do, and now my boys, they have the fort before Deuxponts has his," he went on, as he pointed into the darkness, out of which could be seen the flash of muskets. "Ah, we will teach the baron a lesson. Colonel Barber," he ordered, turning to his aide, "ride at your best quickness to General Viomenil; tell him, with my compliments, that our fort, it is ours, and that we can give him the assistance, if he needs it."

The help was not needed, for in five minutes the second outpost was also in the possession of the allies. Working parties were at once thrown forward, and before morning the two captured positions were connected with and made part of the already established parallel.

The fall of these two redoubts in turn opened an enfilading fire on the British, and in desperation, just before dawn on the 15th a sortie was made, and the French were driven out of one of the batteries, and the guns spiked; but the advantage could not be held against the reserves that came up at the first alarm, and they were in turn forced out at the point of the bayonet.

On the morning of the 16th almost a hundred heavy guns and mortars were in position; and for twenty-four hours the whole peninsula trembled, as they poured a torrent of destructive, direct, and raking fire, at the closest range, into the weakened defences and crumbling town, with scarcely pretence of resistance from the hemmed in and exhausted British, every shot which especially told being greeted with cheers from the trenches of the allies.

One there was in the uniform of a field officer, who never cheered, yet who, standing in a recklessly exposed position, staringly followed each solid shot as it buried itself in the earthworks, or, passing over them, was heard to strike in the town, and each shell, as it curved upwards and downwards in its great arc. Sometimes the explosion of the latter would throw fragments of what it destroyed in the air, — earth, shingles, bricks, and even human limbs, — raising a cry of triumph from those who served the piece, but he only pressed his lips the more tightly together, as if enduring some torture. Nor could he be persuaded to leave his place for food or sleep, urge who would, but with careworn face and haggard eyes never left it for thirty hours. Occasionally, when for a minute or two there would come an accidental break in the firing, his lips could be seen to move as if he were speaking to himself. Not one knew why he stood there following each shot so anxiously, or little recked that, when there was not one to fasten his attention, he saw instead a pair of dark eyes shadowed by long lashes, delicately pencilled eyebrows, a low forehead surmounted by a wealth of darkest brown hair, a little straight nose, cheeks scarcely ever two minutes the same tint, and lips that, whether they spoke or no, wooed as never words yet did. And as each time the vision flashed out before him, he would half mutter, half sob a prayer: —

"Oh, God, rob her of her beauty if you will, but do not let disease or shot kill her."

It was he, watching as no other man in all those lines

watched, who suddenly, a little after ten o'clock on the morning of the 17th, shouted: —

"Cease firing!"

Every man within hearing turned to him, and then looked to where his finger pointed.

On the top of a British redoubt stood a red-coated drummer, to the eye beating his instrument, but the sound of it was drowned in the roar of the guns. As the order passed from battery to battery, the thunder gradually ceased, and all that could be heard was the distant riffle of the single drum, sounding "The Parley." Once the cessation of the firing was complete, an officer, whose uniform and accoutrements flashed out brilliantly as the eastern sun shone on them, mounted the works, and standing beside the drummer slowly waved a white flag.

LXII

WITHIN THE LINES

ONE there was in Yorktown whose suffering was to the eye as great as he who had watched from the outside. A sudden change came over Clowes with the realisation of their danger. He turned white on the confirmation of the arrival of the French fleet; and when the news spread through the town that a deserter had arrived from the American camp with word of Washington's approach, he fell on the street in a fit, out of which he came only when he had been cupped, and sixty ounces of blood taken from him. Not once after that did he seek out Janice, or even come to the custom-house for food or sleep, but pale, and talking much to himself, he wandered restlessly about the town, or still more commonly stood for hours on the highest point of land which opened a view of the bay, gazing anxiously eastward for the promised English fleet.

Janice was too occupied, however, with her mother even to note this exemption. The exposure and fatigue of the long, hot march to Yorktown had proved too great a tax upon Mrs. Meredith's strength, and almost with their arrival she took to her bed and slowly developed a low tidal fever, not dangerous in its character, but unyielding to the doctor's ministrations.

It was on the day that the videttes fell back on the town, bringing word that the allies were advancing, that the girl noticed so marked a change in her mother that she sent for the army surgeon, and that she had done wisely was shown by his gravity after a very cursory examination.

"Miss Meredith," he said, "this nursing is like to be of longer duration than at first seemed probable, and will overtax your strength. 'T is best, therefore, that you let us move

Mrs. Meredith into the army hospital, where she can be properly tended, and you saved from the strain."

"I could not but stay with her, doctor," answered Janice; "but if you think it best for her that she be moved, I can as well attend her there."

The surgeon bit his lip, then told her, "I'll try to secure you permission, if your father think it best." He went downstairs, and finding the squire said: "Mr. Meredith, I have very ill news for you. It has been kept from the army, but there has been for some days an outbreak of small-pox among the negroes, and now your wife is attacked by it."

"Don't say it, man!" implored the squire.

"'T is, alas! but too true. It is necessary that she be at once removed on board the hospital ship, and I shall return as quickly as possible with my assistants and move her. The more promptly you call your daughter from her bedside, the better, for 't will just so much lessen the chance of contagion."

Before the father had well broken the news to Janice, or could persuade her to leave the invalid, the surgeon was returned, and, regardless of the girl's prayers and tears, her mother was placed upon a stretcher, carried to the river-side, and then transferred to the pest-ship, which was anchored in mid-stream. Against his better judgment, but unable to resist his daughter's appeals, the squire sought out Cornwallis with the request that she might be allowed to attend Mrs. Meredith on the ship, but the British general refused.

"Not only would it be contrary to necessary rules, sir, but it would merely expose her needlessly. Fear not that Mrs. Meredith will lack the best of care, for I will give especial directions to the surgeons. My intention was to send a flag, as soon as the enemy approached, with a request that I might pass you all through the lines, out of danger; and this is a sad derangement to the wish, for General Washington would certainly refuse passage to any one sick of this disease, and all must justify him in the refusal. I still think that 't would be best to let me apply for leave for you and Miss Meredith to go out, but — "

"Neither the lass nor I would consider it for a moment, though grateful to your Lordship for the offer."

"Then I will see that you have room in one of the bomb-proofs, but 't will be a time of horror, that I warn you."

He spoke only too truly, and the misery of the next twenty days are impossible to picture. The moment the bombardment began, father and daughter were forced to seek the protection of one of the caves that had been dug in the side of the bluff; and here, in damp, airless, almost dark, and fearfully over-crowded quarters, they were compelled to remain day and night during the siege. Almost from the first, scarcity of wood produced an entire abandonment of cooked food, every one subsisting on raw pork or raw salt beef, or, as Janice chose, eating only ship biscuit and unground coffee berries. Once the fire of the allies began to tell, each hour supplied a fresh tale of wounded, and these were brought into the bomb-proofs for the surgeons to tend, their presence and moans adding to the nightmare; yet but for them it seemed to Janice she would have gone mad in those weeks, for she devoted herself to nursing and feeding them, as an escape from dwelling on her mother's danger and their own helplessness. Even news from the pest-ship had its torture, for when her father twice each day descended the bluff to get the word from the doctor's boat, as it came ashore, she stood in the low doorway of the cave, and at every shot that was heard shrieking through the air, and at every shell which exploded with a crash, she held her breath, full of dread of what it might have done, and in anguish till her father was safe returned with the unvarying and uncheering bulletin the surgeons gave him of Mrs. Meredith's condition.

Yet those in the bomb-proofs escaped the direst of the horrors. Above them were enacted scenes which turned even the stoutest hearts sick with fear and loathing. The least of these was the slaughter of the horses, baggage, cavalry, and artillery, which want of forage rendered necessary, one whole day being made hideous by the screams of the poor beasts, as one by one they were led to a spot where the putrefying of their carcasses would least endanger the health of the soldiery, and their throats cut. All pretence of care of the negroes disappeared with the demand on the officers and soldiers to man the redoubts, and on the surgeons to care for the sick and wounded soldiers, who soon numbered upwards of two thousand. Naked and half starving, they who had dreamed of freedom were left for the small-pox and putrid fever and for shot and shell to work their will among them. In the abandoned houses and even in the streets, they lay, sick, dismembered, dying, and dead, with not so much as one to aid or bury them.

On the morning of the 17th a fresh number of wounded men were brought into the already overcrowded cave; and though Janice was faint with the long days of anxiety, fright, bad air, poor food, and hard work, she went from man to man, doing what could be done to ease their torments and lessen their groans. The last brought in was in a faint, with the lower part of his face and shoulder horribly torn and shattered by the fragments of a shell, but a little brandy revived him, and he moaned for water. Hurriedly she stooped over him, to drop a little from a spoon between the open lips.

"Janice!" he startled her by crying.

"Who are — ? Oh, Sir Frederick!" she exclaimed. "You! How came you here?"

"They let me out of the prison Clowes me put in," Mobray gasped; "and having nothing better, I enlisted in the ranks under another name." There he choked with blood.

"Doctor," called Janice, "come quickly!"

"Humph!" growled the surgeon, after one glance. "You should not summon me to waste time on him. Can't you see 't is hopeless?"

"Oh, don't —" began Janice.

"Nay, he speaks the truth," said Mobray; "and I thank God 't is so. Don't cry. I am glad to go; and though I have wasted my life, 't is a happier death than poor John André's."

For a moment only the sobs of the girl could be heard, then the dying man gaspingly resumed: "A comrade I once had whom I loved best in this world till I knew you. By a strange chance we loved the same girl; I wish I might die with the knowledge that he is to have the happiness that was denied to me."

"Oh, Sir Frederick, you must not ask it! He —"

"His was so bitter a story that he deserves a love such as yours would be to make it up to him. I can remember him the merriest of us all, loved by every man in the regiment, from batman to colonel."

"And what changed him?" Janice could not help asking.

"'Twas one evening at the mess of the Fusileers, when Powel, too deep in drink to know what he was saying, blurted out something concerning Mrs. Loring's relations with Sir William. Poor Charlie was the one man in the force who knew not why such favouritism had been shown in his being put so young into Howe's regiment. But that we were eight to one, he 'd have killed Powel then and there. Prevented in that, he set off to slay his colonel, never dreaming he was his own father. He burst in on me late that night, crazed with grief, and told me how he had found him at his mother's, and how she had robbed him of his vengeance by a word. The next day he disappeared, and never news had I of him until that encounter at Greenwood. Does he not deserve something to sweeten his life?"

"I feel for him deeply," replied the girl, sadly, "the more that I did him a grave wrong in my thoughts, and by some words I spoke must have cut him to the quick and added pain to pain."

"Then you will make him happy?"

"No, Sir Frederick, that I cannot."

"Don't punish him for what was not his fault."

"'Tis not for that," she explained. "Once I loved him, I own. But in a moment of direst need, when I appealed to him, he failed me; and though now I better understand his resentment against my father and myself, I could never bring myself to forgive his cruelty, even were my love not dead."

"I will not believe it of him. Hot and impulsive he is by nature, but never cruel or resentful."

"'Tis, alas! but too true," grieved Janice.

Once again the baronet choked with blood and struggled for a moment convulsively. Then more faintly he said: "Wilt give him my love and a good-by?"

"I will," sobbed the girl.

Nothing more was said for some time, then Mobray asked faintly: "Is it that I am losing consciousness, or has the firing ceased?"

Janice raised her head with a start. "Why, it has stopped," she exclaimed. "What can it mean?"

"That courage and tenacity have done their all, and now must yield. Poor Cornwallis! I make no doubt he 'd gladly change places with me at this instant."

Here Mr. Meredith's voice broke in upon them, as standing in the mouth of the cave he called: "Come, Janice. The firing has ceased, to permit an exchange of flags with the rebels. Up with ye, and get the fresh air while ye can."

"I will stay here, father," replied the girl, "and care for —"

"Nonsense, lass! Ye shall not kill yourself. I order ye to come away."

"Go, Miss Meredith," begged Mobray. "You can do naught for me, and — and — I would have — Do as he says." His hand blindly groped until Janice placed hers within it, when he gave it a weak pressure as he said, "'T is many a long march and many a sleepless night that the memory of you has sweetened. Thank you, and good-by."

Reluctantly Janice came out of the bomb-proof, blinking and gasping with the novelty of sunlight and sea breeze, after the darkness and stench of the last weeks; and her father, partly supporting, led her up the bluff. It was a strange transformation that greeted her eyes, — ploughed-up streets and ruins of buildings dismantled by shot or left heaps of ashes by the shell, everywhere telling of the fury of the siege.

"Keep your eyes closed, lass," suggested the squire, "for there are sights of horror. In a moment I 'll have ye at headquarters, where things have been kept more tidy. There, now ye can look; sit down here and fill your lungs with this good air."

Silently the two seated themselves on the steps of the Nelson house, now pierced in every direction by the shot of the allies, though less damaged than many others. Presently Janice's attention was caught by the sound of shuffling footsteps, as of one with only partial use of his legs, and glancing up she gave a slight cry of fear. And well she might, for there stood the commissary, with his face like one risen from the dead, it was so white and staring.

"Meredith," he whispered, as if his larynx were parched

beyond the ability to speak aloud, while with one hand he held his throat in a vain attempt to make his speech less weak and raucous, "they say 'The Parley' has been beat and a flag sent out, and that the post is to be surrendered. Tell me that Cornwallis will never do that. He 's a brave man. Tell me it is n't so."

"Nothing else is there for him to do, Clowes. He 's made a splendid defence, but now scarce a gun is left mounted and powder and shot are both exhausted; to persist longer would be useless murder."

"No, no! Let him hold out a few days longer. Clinton will relieve us yet. He must n't give up. God! Meredith, they 'll hang me! He must n't surrender. I can't die just as life is worth something. No, no! I can't die now. I 'm rich. Ninety thousand pounds I 've made. To be caught like a rat! He must n't surrender the post." And muttering to himself, the miserable man shambled away, to repeat the same hopes and expostulations to the next one he found.

"He had another fit last night," remarked the squire; "and no one has seen him eat or sleep in four days, nor can he be persuaded to either, but goes wandering unceasingly about the town, quite unminding of shot and shell. Ho! what 's here?" he ended, pointing up the street.

Three officers were coming towards them, arm in arm, the two outsiders in red coats, and the middle one in a blue one, with buff facings. Occasionally as they advanced, he in the blue uniform swerved or stumbled slightly, as if he might be wounded or drunk. But one look at his face was sufficient to show the cause, for across his eyes was tied a broad white band.

"Oh, dadda," murmured Janice, suddenly paling, "'t is Colonel Brereton they have captured!"

"Nonsense, Jan! 't is impossible to know any man, so covered."

The girl attempted no reassertion, and as the three officers marched up to the headquarters, the two hastily rose from the steps.

"Ha!" exclaimed one of the British officers. "Here stands Miss Meredith now, Colonel Brereton, as if to end your doubting of my assurances of her being alive."

The blindfolded man, with a quick motion, withdrew the hand passed through the arm of his guide and raised it impulsively to the bandage.

"Hold," warningly said the British officer, as he caught the hand. "Small wonder the handkerchief becomes intolerable, with her to look at, but stay on it must till you are within doors."

Jack's hand clutched the officer's arm. "God! man, you are not deceiving me?"

"Speak up, Miss Meredith, and convince the sceptic that General O'Hara, though Irish, is yet a truth-teller on occasion."

"Oh, Colonel Brereton," said Janice, "I have just left Sir Frederick, who is at the point of death, and he gave me a message of farewell to you. Can you not go to him for a moment? 'T would be everything to him."

Jack hesitated. "My mission is so important — General O'Hara, wilt deliver this letter with a proper explanation to his Lordship, while I see this friend?"

"Certainly. If Miss Meredith will guide you and Lord Chewton to where he lies, I 'll see that Lord Cornwallis gets the letter."

In the briefest possible time Brereton stood beside Mobray. Yet when the officer in charge of him untied the handkerchief and stepped back out of hearing, Jack's eyes did not seek his friend, but turned instead to the face of the girl standing beside him. For a moment they lingered in a gaze so steadfast, so devouring, that, try as she would not to look at him, Janice's eyes were drawn to his, despite herself. With a long breath, as if relieved of some dread, Jack finally turned away and knelt beside his friend. "Fred, old comrade," he said, as he took his hand.

"Charlie!" gasped Mobray, weakly, as his eyes opened. "Is 't really you, or am I wandering?"

"'T is I, Fred, come into town with a flag."

"You 've beat old Britain, after all, have n't you?"

"No, dear lad," replied Jack, gently. "'T is the old spirit of England that has conquered, as it ever will, when fighting for its rights against those who would rob it of them."

"True. We forgot 't was our own whelps, grown strong, we sought to subjugate. And you had the better man to lead you, Jack."

"Ay, and so we ever shall, so long as Britain makes men generals because they are king's bastards."

"Nay, Charlie, don't let the sore rankle through life. 'T is not from whence you came that counts; 't is what you are. I 'd take your shame of birth, if I could rid myself of mine. Fortune, position, and opportunity I 've wasted, while you have won rank and glory."

"And now have not one thing to make life worth the while."

"Don't say it, Charlie. There 's something for you to live for still. Put your hand into my shirt — yes — to the left — now you have it."

Brereton drew forth a miniature set with brilliants; and as his eyes lit upon it, he gave an exclamation of surprise.

"'T is the one thing I concealed from my creditors," moaned Sir Frederick, "and now I leave it to you. Watch over and care for her for the sake of your love and of mine, Charlie."

Brereton leaned down and kissed Mobray on the cheek, as he whispered, "I will."

"Is — is Miss Meredith here, Charlie?" asked the dying baronet.

"Yes, Sir Frederick," replied Janice, with a choke.

"I — I — I fear I am a ghastly object," he went on, "but could you bring yourself — Am I too horrible for one kiss of farewell from you? Charlie will not grudge it to me."

The girl knelt beside Brereton, and stooping tenderly kissed the dying man on the same spot that Jack had kissed. Mobray's left hand feebly took hers, and, consciously or unconsciously, brought the one which still held Jack's to it. Holding the two hands within his own so that they touched, he said chokingly: —

"Heaven bless you, and try to forgive him. Good-by both. I have served my term, and at last am released from the bigger jail." A little shudder, a twitch, and he was dead.

For a minute the two remained kneeling, then Brereton said sadly: —

"He was the only friend left me in the world, and I know not why he is taken and I am left." He withdrew his hand from contact with the girl's, and rose. "I cannot stay, for my mission is not to be slighted, but I will speak to O'Hara, and see that he gets a funeral befitting his rank." Brereton squared his shoulders and raised his voice, to say: "Lord Chewton, I am —"

With a quick motion, the girl rose to her feet and said: "I have no right to detain you, Colonel Brereton, but — but I want you to know that neither dadda nor I knew the truth concerning Mrs. Loring when we said what we did on that fatal night. We both thought — thought — Your confession to me that once you loved her, and her looking too young to be your mother, led me into a misconception."

"Then you forgive me?" he cried eagerly.

"For the words you spoke then I do not even blame you, sir. But what was, can never be again."

"Ay," said the officer, bitterly. "You need not say it. You cannot scorn me more than I scorn myself."

Not giving her time to reply, he crossed to where the officer with the bandage stood waiting him, and once again was blindfolded, and led to headquarters.

"This way," directed General O'Hara, leading him into a room where stood Cornwallis.

"Are you familiar, sir, with the contents of General Washington's letter?" asked the earl.

"No, my Lord; I was its bearer only because I begged the Marquis de Lafayette to secure me the service."

"He grants a suspension of hostilities for two hours from the delivery of this, for me to put my proposals in writing. Did he say aught to you, sir, of the terms he would grant?"

"I am no longer on General Washington's staff," answered Brereton, "so I know not his expectations."

"From all I hear of him," said the general, "he is not a man to use a triumph ungenerously. He fought bravely under the British standards, and surely will not now seek to bring unnecessary shame on them." Seating himself at the table, he wrote a few lines, which he folded and sealed. "Will you not, sir, use your influence with him to grant us the customary honours, and spare the officers from the disgrace of giving up their side arms?"

"I no longer possess influence with or the confidence of his Excellency," replied Brereton, gravely; "but he is a generous man, and I predict will not push his advantage merely for your humiliation."

"Will he not forbear making our surrender a spectacle?"

"If the talk of the camp be of value, my Lord, 't is said you are to be granted the exact terms you allowed to General Lincoln at Savannah; and you yourself cannot but acknowledge the justice of such treatment."

"'T was not I who dictated the terms of that surrender."

"Your observation, my Lord, forces the reply that 't is a nation, not an individual, we are fighting."

The proud face of the British general worked for a moment in the intensity of his emotion. "We have no right to complain that we receive measure for measure," he said; "and yet sir, though the *lex talionis* may be justified, it makes it none the less bitter."

Colonel Brereton took the letter, his eyes were blindfolded again, and he was led back beyond the lines.

With the expiration of the two hours, the firing was not resumed; and all that day and the next flags were passing and repassing between the lines, with the result that on the afternoon of the latter, commissioners met at the Moore house and drew up the terms of capitulation, which were signed that evening.

At twelve o'clock on the 19th, the English colours were struck on the redoubts, and the American were hoisted in their stead. Two hours later the armies of the allies took up position opposite each other on the level ground outside the town, and the British troops, with shouldered arms, cased colours, and bands playing, as stipulated, an English air, "The World Turned Upside Down," came marching out of their lines. As they advanced, Washington turned to an officer behind him and ordered, "Let the word be passed that the troops are not to cheer. They have fought too well for us to triumph over them." In consequence not a sound came from the American ranks as the British regiments marched up and with tears in many a brave man's eyes grounded their arms and colours. But the officers, through Washington's generosity, were allowed to retain their swords, sparing Cornwallis the mortification of having to be present in person; and it was General O'Hara who spoke the formal words of surrender, and who led the disarmed and flagless regiments back into the town, once the formalities had been completed. By nightfall twenty-four standards and over eight thousand prisoners were in the possession of the allied forces.

But one had escaped them, for in a cellar, hidden behind a heap of refuse and boxes, his body already stripped of its clothes by pilfering negroes, his face horribly distorted, and with froth yet on his lips, lay the commissary, dead.

And at the very moment the next day that two companies, one of British Fusileers, and one of New Jersey Continentals, were firing a volley over a new-made grave, in which, wrapped in the flag of his country, and buried with every military honor, had been deposited the body of him who had been Sir Frederick Mobray, a fatigue party were rolling into a trench, and carelessly covering with earth from the battered redoubts, along with the bodies of negroes and horses, and of barrels of spoiled pork and beef, the naked corpse of him who had been John Ombrey, Baron Clowes.

LXIII

ON BRUNSWICK GREEN

ON a pleasant June afternoon in the year 1782, the loungers about the Continental Tavern in the village of Brunswick were discussing the recent proclamations of the governor and commander-in-chief forbidding illicit trading with New York, both of which called forth general condemnation, well voiced by Bagby, when he remarked: —

"A man with half an eye can see what they are working for, and that their objections to our supplying the Yorkers is only a blind. What they really wants is that we patriots, who don't spend our days idling about in camp all winter at Rocky-Hill and now at Middle-Brook, doing nothing except eat the people's food, and spend the people's money, but who earn a living by hard work, sha' n't have no market but the continental commissaries, and so will have to take whatever they allow to offer us for our crops."

"'T aint the proclamations ez duz the rale injoory," asserted Squire Hennion; "fer printed orders duz n't hurt nobody, but when the gin'ral sends a hull brigade of sogers ter pervent us sellin' our craps then I consarned ef it aint tyranny ez every freeman is baound ter resist, jest ez we did in '65 an' '74."

Bagby, with a sour look at Hennion, said: "That 's one of the biggest grievances, but not the way some pretended friends of the people would have us think. What do your fellows say to officers having been fixed, so that pickets are only put where they 'll stop us from sending boats to New York, while there 's one right here is allowed to send cargoes just when he likes?"

"Does yer mean that, Joe?" demanded a farmer.

"That I does," asserted Bagby, looking meaningly at Hennion. "I was told as a chance was given to the army to catch the man deepest in the business — and in worse — red handed. But what 's done? Instead of laying a trap, and catching him, they don't stir a finger, but wait ten months and then sends the very officer who did n't do nothing to put a stop to it. For weeks that high cock-a-lorum Brereton 's been smelling about this town, and lining the river at night with his pickets, when all the time he could have come here any afternoon, and arrested the traitor."

"Thet 'eres lucky fer yer," snarled Hennion viciously. "yer ain't the only one ez kin tell tales, I warns yer."

"I have n't done no bribing, and it was n't *me* as the information was lodged against," retorted Joe, rancourously.

"You can't mean as General Brereton 's winking at the trade, when scarce a boat 's got out of the river since his brigade camped there," demanded one of the loungers, indicating with his thumb Brunswick Green, whitened by rows of tents.

"I mean as Brereton could lay hands any time he pleased on one traitor, and why he has n't done so is what I want to know. What 's more, I 'd like to know, why Washington does n't take any notice of the charges that I 've been told was preferred against Brereton nigh six months ago for this very matter. I tell you, fellows, that money 's being used, and that some of those who hold themselves highest, is taking it."

"Don't seem like his Excellency 'ud do anythin' ez sneaky ez that," observed the publican, glancing upwards with pride at his signboard, now restored to its former position. "Folks says he 's a 'nation fine man."

"I 'm just sick of all this getting on the knees to a man," grumbled Joseph, "just because he went and captivated Cornwallis. Washington is n't a bit better than some of us right here and it won't be long before you 'll find it out."

"How do you make that, Joe?"

"Is n't he trying to bully Congress into paying the army, just as if he was king, as I suppose he hopes to be some day. You wait till he gets his way, and I guess the tax collectors will make the people sing a different tune about him. If I 'm elected to the Assembly this spring, I calculate to make some ears buzz and tingle a bit, once the legislature meets. I 'll teach some of these swaggering military chaps — who were n't nothing but bond-servants once yet who some of you fellows is fools enough now to talk of sending to Congress — that this is a nation of freemen, and that now that the British is licked, we don't have no more use for them, and — "

"Waal, I declare, if thet don't favour Squire Meredith, an' his darter," interjected a farmer, suddenly, pointing with his pipe to where an army waggon was approaching on the Princeton post-road.

"Swan, ef yer ain't right," cried Hennion. "I did hope we wuz quit of them fer good an' all."

"Wonder what the gal 's in black fer?" observed a lounger.

"My nigger cook Sukey," said the landlord, "told me that Gin'ral Brereton told her the ole lady wuz mortal sick o' the small-pox an' that when he went aboard the pest-ship, she wuz so weak it did n't seem like she could be moved, but he an' the doctor got her safe ashore, an' when he last hearn, 'bout the first o' the year, she wuz gainin'."

The publican rose and went forward as the van stopped in front of his door. "Glad tew see yer, squire," he said, "an' yer, too, Miss Janice. Seems most like ole times. Hope nuthin 's wrong with Miss Meredith?"

The squire slowly and heavily got down from the box seat. "We have her body in the waggon," he said wearily and sadly.

"I vum, but that 's too bad!" exclaimed the landlord, and, for want of words of comfort, he hesitatingly held out his hand, but recollecting himself, he was drawing it back, when Mr. Meredith, forgetful of rank, caught and squeezed it.

"She never really rallied," went on the squire, with tears in his eyes, "and though she lived on through the winter, she did n't have the strength to mend. She died three weeks ago, and we have come back here to bury her."

"Naow yer an' Miss Janice come right intew my place, an' I 'll fix yer both ez comfortable ez I kin," invited the publican, warmly, once again forgetting himself so far as to pat Mr. Meredith on the back. Then as he helped Janice down, he shouted, "Abram, mix a noggin o' sling, from the bestest, an' tell Sukey that she 's wanted right off, no matter what she 's doin'."

The last direction was needless, for the slave, in some way informed of the arrival, had Janice in her arms ere the landlord well completed his speech, and was carrying more than leading her into the hotel and up the stairs to the room reserved for people of quality only, where she lifted her on to the bed and with her arms still clasped about the girl wept over her, half in misery, and half in an almost savage joy, while repeating again and again, "Oh, my missy, my Missy Janice, my young missy, my pooty young missy, come back to ole Sukey."

"Oh, Sukey," sobbed Janice, "but mommy is dead."

"Doan young missy pine," begged the slave. "De Lord he know best, an' he bring my chile, dat I dun take care ob from de day he dun gib her, back to ole black Sukey."

Meantime, the squire, after a question as to where the coffin could be temporarily placed, and a direction to the driver of the wagon, asked the publican: "We had word in Virginia that Greenwood was sold by the state; is 't so?"

"Yes, squire, it wuz auctioned last August an' wuz bought by ole squire Hennion, an' jes naow his Excellency 's usin' it fer headquarters, till the army moves north'ard."

A sadder look came on Mr. Meredith's face. "That 's worse news yet," he grieved, with a shake of his head; "but perhaps he 'll not carry his hatred into this." He walked over to where the all-attentive loungers were sitting, and going up to Hennion, said humbly: "We were once friends, Hennion, and I trust that such ill feeling as ye bear for me will not lead ye to refuse a request I have to make."

"An' what 'ere is thet?" inquired Hennion, suspiciously.

"'T was Matilda's — 't was my wife's dying prayer that we should bring her back here, and lay her beside her four babies, and to let her die happy I gave her my word it should be done. Ye 'll not refuse me leave, I 'm sure, man, to bury her in the private plot at Greenwood."

"Yer need n't expect ter fool me by no sich a story. I ain't goin' ter let yer weaken my title by no sich a trick!"

"For shame!" cried Joseph, and a number of others echoed his words.

"Yelp away," snarled Hennion, rising; "If 't 't wuz yer

bull ez wuz ter be gored yer 'd whine t' other side of yer teeth." With which remark he shuffled away.

Not stopping to listen to the expressions of sympathy and disgust that the idlers began upon, Mr. Meredith entered the public of the tavern.

"Here yer be, squire, jus' mixed from my very bestest liquor, an' it 'll set yer right up," declared the landlord, offering him a pewter pot.

The squire made a motion of dissent, but seeing the publican's look of disappointment, he took the cup and drained it. "Ye 've not lost your skill, Simon," he remarked kindly, as he returned it. "Canst tell me if 't is possible for me to get a letter into New York quickly?"

"'T aint ez easy ez it wuz afore the soldiers come here fer they pervent the secret trade, but if yer apply tew Gin'ral Brereton, ez lodges with the paason, I calkerlate he kin send it in with a flag if he hez a mind tew."

Mr. Meredith shook his head in discouragement. "It seems as if all I ask must be begged of enemies. However, 't is small grief, after what has passed. Wilt give me pen and ink, man?"

While he was writing, Bagby came into the public, and interrupted him.

"I did n't offer to shake hands, squire," he said, "seeing as you were in trouble, and took up with other things, but I 'm glad to see you and Miss Janice back, and there 's my hand to prove it."

Mr. Meredith laid down his pen, and took the proffered handshake. "Thank ye, Mr. Bagby," he said, meekly.

"I would n't stop what you 're at now," went on Joseph, sitting down at the table, "if I had n't something in my mind as I think 'll interest you big, and may make some things easier that you want."

"What 's that?"

"If I put you on to this, I guess you 'll be so grateful that I don't need to make no terms beforehand. You 'd give me about what I asked, would n't you, if I can get you Greenwood back again?"

"How could ye e'er do that?"

"It 's this way. That general act was n't drawn very careful, and when old Hennion bid the place in, I looked it over sharp, and I concluded there was a fighting chance to break the sale. You see, the act declares certain persons traitors, and that their property is forfeited to the state. Now what we must do is to make out that Greenwood was Mrs. Meredith's and that as she was n't named in the act, of course the sale was n't valid and is void."

The squire wagged his head despondingly. "By the colony law it became mine the moment she inherited it."

"You see if I can't make a case of it," urged Bagby. "I 've come out a great hand at tieing the facts up in such a snarl as no judge or jury can get them straight again, and this time the jury will be with us before we begin. You see old Hennion 's been putting the screws on his tenants tight as he can twist them, and glad enough they 'd be if they could only have you again, 'stead of him. The whole country 's so down on him that I 've been planning to prevent his being re-elected to Assembly this spring. Now, you know, as well as I, what I would like, and I guess you won't be so set against it now, for I 've got nigh to twenty thousand pounds specie, laid out in all sorts of ventures, so even if we don't get Greenwood, I 'll be all the better match, but we won't say nothing about all that till we 've seen what comes."

"Nay, Mr. Bagby, I 'll not gain your aid by a deceitful silence. I owe ye an apology for the way I treated your overture before, but I must tell you that both my own, and my girl's word is given to Major Hennion, and so — "

"But he 's been attainted, an' 'll never be able to come back here."

"Aye, and we too expect to accept exile with him. When we left Williamsburg, we planned once we had buried our dead, to go to New York, where the two will marry, and then I shall follow them to wherever his regiment is ordered."

"But you don't need to go, now that General Brereton's persuaded the governor to pardon you," protested Joseph, "and you — "

"Was it Brereton did that?" demanded Mr. Meredith.

"Between you and me, squire, I 'd been at Livingston ever

since you was sent away, and had about won him over, when Brereton got back from Virginia and went to see him."

"I'm glad to hear he's willing to do me a kindness, for not once at Yorktown did he come nigh us, and so I feared me he would refuse a favour I must shortly ask of him."

"What's that?"

"I'm writing to Phil Hennion, begging him to intercede with his father and get me permission to bury my wife at Greenwood."

"You would n't need to do no asking if you'd only let me get the property back."

"You're right, man, and if it does nothing more, we'll perhaps frighten him into yielding us that much."

"'T will take time, you understand, squire, and it can't be done if you go to York or out of the country."

"We'll stay here as long as there's nothing better to do."

"That's the talk. And don't you wherrit about your lodgings, if you're short of cash. I'll fix it with Si, and chance my getting paid somehow. I'll see him right off, and fix it so you and Miss Janice has the best there is." He started to go; then asked, "I hope — there is n't any danger — I suppose — she'll keep, eh, squire?"

The husband winced. "Yes," he replied huskily. "The Marquis de Lafayette, quite unasked, ordered the commissaries to give us all we needed of a pipe of rum."

"That was mighty generous," said Bagby, "for I suppose he had to pay for it. Even a major-general, I take it, can't draw no such a quantity gratis."

"I writ him, asking that I might know the cost, but he answered that 't was nothing. 'T is impossible to say what we owe to him. 'T was he, so Doctor Craik told me, who asked him to bring Mrs. Meredith off the pest-ship, and 't was he who furnished us with the army-van in which we've journeyed from Virginia. Had we been kinsmen, he could not have been kinder."

"Now that only shows how a man tries to take credit for what he has n't had a finger in. Brereton, who, since he was made a general and got so thick with the governor, has put on airs enough to kill a cat, told your Sukey, as now is cook here, that 't was he went aboard the pest-ship with the doctor, and brought her off."

"'T is the first I 've heard of it," averred Mr. Meredith, incredulously yet thoughtfully.

"I tell you that Brereton is a sly, sneaky fellow, as needs watching in more than one matter. Nigh ten months ago I showed him how he could nab old Hennion, so that like as not he'd have gone to the gallows, but he did n't stir a finger, durn him! Oh, here 's Si, now. Say, I want you to treat Mr. Meredith and Miss Janice real handsome, and don't trouble them with no bills, but leave me to square it," he said to the landlord, who had come bustling in.

"Lor, Joe, yer duz n't think I wuz goin' tew make no charge fer this? Why, the squire lent me the money ez started me, an' I calkerlate he kin stay on here jus' about ez long ez he elects tew." Then the publican laughed. "Like ez not there won't be no supper tew-night, squire. That 'ere Sukey hez got yer gal tucked in my best tester bed, an' is croonin' her tew sleep jes' like she wuz a baby ag'in. She most bit my head off when I went in tew tell her supper-time wuz comin'. 'Stonishin' haow like white folks niggers kin feel sometimes, ain't it?"

"I bought her when our first baby was coming, and she saw four born and buried, and nigh broke her heart over each one in turn," said the squire, huskily; "so when Janice came, 't was as if she was her own child." He rose, his letter completed, and with a word to explain his movements, walked across the green to the parsonage, where his knock brought Peg to the door, and resulted in a series of wild greetings and exclamations. At last, however, the old-time master was permitted to make known the object of his call, and was ushered into a room where Brereton was sitting writing.

"Mr. Meredith!" exclaimed Jack, starting to his feet. "How are you all — that — how is Miss Meredith?"

"She 's stood the grief and — I know not if ye have heard of Mrs. Meredith's death?"

"Yes; a friend in Virginia wrote me."

"She 's borne up under that and under the hard journey wonderfully, and has been braver and more cheerful, I fear, than I myself. I 've come to ye, General Brereton, to ask if ye could send a letter for me, under flag, to New York?"

"Certainly, if 't is of a character that makes it allowable."

"I 've not sealed it, that you might read it," answered the squire, holding out his letter.

Brereton read it slowly, as if he was thinking between the words. "It shall be sent in at once," he promised, his lips set as if to conceal some emotion. Then he asked, "You write to Colonel Hennion as if — are he and — you intend to give Miss Meredith to him?"

"Yes."

Jack wheeled and looked out of a window for an instant; without turning he said, "Is she — does she — she is willing?"

"Ay, the lass has at last found she loves him, and is as ready now as I ever was."

Again Brereton was silent for a breathing space. "When will they wed?" he questioned finally.

"Once we can get to York."

"And that will be?"

"The burial of Mrs. Meredith and other matters will keep us in Brunswick for an uncertain length of time."

"And you will lodge where?"

"At the tavern."

"'T is no place for Miss Meredith."

"Beggars cannot be choosers, sir."

For a moment Brereton said nothing; then remarked as he faced about, "If I can serve you in any other way, Mr. Meredith, hesitate to ask nothing of me."

"My thanks to ye, general," answered Mr. Meredith, gratefully. "I fear me I little merit courtesy at your hands."

"'T is a peace-making time," replied Jack, "and we 'll put the ill feeling away, as 't is to be hoped Great Britain and our country will do, once the treaty is negotiated and ratified."

"'T is no country I have," rejoined the squire, sadly. "One word, sir, and I will be gone. I was but just told that 't was ye who got Mrs. Meredith off the pest-ship; and if — "

Brereton held up his hand. "'T was the Marquis who gave

the order, Mr. Meredith, and the Surgeon-General who superintended the removal."

"So I was told at the time, but I feared that I might have been misinformed. None the less, general, I am your present debtor;" with which words the squire bowed himself out.

Left alone, Brereton stood like a stone for some minutes ere he resumed his seat. He glanced down at the sheet, on which was written: —

BRUNSWICK, *June 13th, 1782.*

"SIR, —*After three months' test, I can assure your Excellency that it is possible to very materially if not entirely check the illicit trade with New York, but only by the constant employment of a considerable force of men in a service at once fatiguing to them and irritating to the neighbourhood. I would therefore suggest, in place of these purely repressive measures, that others which will at once bring to justice those most deeply concerned in the trade, and terrify by example those who are only occasionally guilty, be employed, and therefore beg to submit for your consideration the following plan of action.*

Shoving the paper to one side, Brereton took a fresh sheet, and wrote a hurried letter, which, when sealed, he addressed to "Lady Washington, Headquarters at Greenwood Manor." This done, he finished his official letter, and going to the rows of tents on the green, he delivered the two into the hands of an officer, with an order to ride with them at once.

On the following day a coach drew up in front of the Continental Tavern, and with much dignity a negro in livery alighted from the seat beside the driver.

"You will deliber Lady Washington's an' my deferential complimen's to Miss Janice Meredith; likewise dis letter from his Excellency," he said grandly to the tavern-keeper.

"Waal, of all airs fer a nigger!" snorted mine host. "Duz his Excellency run yer jobs fer yer ter hum? Guess yer ain't so fat, be yer, that yer keant carry that inter the settin'-room yerself."

With a glance of outraged dignity that should have annihilated the publican, the man went across the hall, and after a knock, entered.

"Why, Billy!" exclaimed Janice, starting up from her chair, her arm outstretched.

The intense dignity melted away in a breath, and the darky chuckled and slapped himself with delight as he took the hand. "Der, now!" he cried, "I dun assure her Ladyship dat Missy would remember Billy. Here am a letter from his Excellency, Miss."

Opening it, Janice read it out to her father: —

HEADQUARTERS, *14 June, 1782.*

DEAR MISS JANICE, — *In writing this I but act as Mrs. Washington's scribe, she having an invincible dislike to the use of a pen. She hopes and begs that you will favour us with the honour of your company for a time at Headquarters, and to this I would add my own persuasions were I not sure that hers will count above mine. However, let me say that it will be a personal gratification to me if you give us now the pleasure I have several times counted upon in the past. Thinking to make more certain of your granting this request, and that you may make the journey without discomfort, Mrs. Washington sends her coach.*

I most sincerely regretted not seeing you at Yorktown, the more that Lord Cornwallis assured me when he dined with me on the evening after the surrender, that he would secure your presence at the banquet he tendered to the French and American officers; but I was still more grieved when told the reason for your refusal to grace the occasion by your presence. The sudden sickness of poor Mr. Custis, which compelled me to hasten away from York, and the affecting circumstance of his untimely death threw Mrs. Washington and Mrs. Bassett, who were both present, into such deep distress that I could not find it in my heart to leave Eltham, once the funeral rites were performed. The Marquis has since assured me that nothing was neglected which could be of comfort or service to your mother, and I trust that he speaks informedly. I have just learned of your loss, and hasten to tender you both Mrs. Washington's and my own sympathy on this melancholy occasion.

Be assured that your company will truly gratify both me and the partner of all my Domestic enjoyments, and that I am, my dear young lady, with every sentiment of respect and esteem,

Yr most obed.t h.ble serv.t

G.o WASHINGTON.

" 'T is the very thing I 'd have for ye, Jan," exclaimed the squire.

" Oh, dadda, I 'll not leave you."

" That ye shall, for I 'll be busy with this scheme of Bagby's, and the tavern is no place for ye, child, let alone what ye 'll be forever dwelling on if ye have no distraction."

" An' his Excellency," said the messenger, " done tell me to say dat he done holds you' parole ob honour, an' dat, if you doan' come back with me in de coach, he done send de provost gyard to fotch youse under arrest. What 's mo, Miss, dat big villin, Blueskin, will be powerful joyed to see youse again."

LXIV

A SETTLING OF OLD SCORES

ON a night of the most intense darkness a strange-looking craft was stealing slowly up the Raritan, quite as much helped in its progress by the flood-tide as by the silent stroke of the oars, about which were wound cloths where they rubbed against the thole-pins. The rowers knelt on the bottom of the boat, so that nothing but their heads projected above the gunwale, which set low in the water, and to which were tied branches of trees, concealing it so completely that at ten feet distance on any ordinarily clear night it would have been difficult to know that it was not a drifting limb.

Lying at full length in the bottom of the boat were two men, one of whom from time to time moved impatiently.

"Will we never get there?" he finally whispered.

"Slow work it is," replied the other, in the lowest of voices, "but it has to be done careful."

"I understood you the river was open once more."

"Ay. We had word the regiments had been withdrawn, to go north with the main army; but this is only the second night the boats have ventured in, and cautious we 've always had to be."

The note of a crow came floating over the water, and at the sound the last speaker raised himself on his elbow and deliberately began counting in a low voice. As he spoke the number "ten," once again came the discordant "caw, caw," and instantly the counter opened his mouth and sent forth an admirable imitation of the cry of a screech-owl. Counting once again to ten, he repeated the shriek, then listened.

In a moment the first splash of oars reached them.

"This way," softly called the man, and put out his hand to prevent a small boat colliding with the larger one.

"Thought I heard a bird just now," remarked the solitary occupant.

"If you did, 't was a king bird."

"I have n't much to-night," announced the new arrival, as he handed a small packet into the boat. "It contains a paper from No. 2, giving the decisions of the last council of war, and the line of march they have adopted for next week."

The one in the larger boat pulled up a cleverly fitted board in the bottom of the boat, and taking out a letter, slipped the just received parcel into the cavity and dropped the plank back into place. "There 's a letter for you," he said, passing it to the new-comer. Without another word the stranger shoved off, and in a moment was lost in the darkness.

"Was n't that Joe Bagby?" questioned the man's companion.

"'Sh! We don't mention no names, if it can be avoided."

"You need not fear me. I am in the general's confidence, and know as well as you that No. 2 is Major-General Parsons of the Connecticut line."

"That 's more than I knew," muttered the boatman; "so you see, Colonel Hennion, 't is as well not to mention names."

In silence the boat drifted onward, save for an order presently given that the rowers turn in toward the left bank.

"Seems like I hearn suthin'," suddenly came a voice out of the darkness.

"'T is only we, fishin' for what 's to be caught!" said the boatman.

"No danger of yer catchin' nuthin' here," asserted the unseen speaker.

"Pull into the pier, boys! We 're got your son aboard, Hennion."

A low exclamation came from the man standing on the rude wharf that suddenly loomed into view. "Yer duz n't mean my Phil!"

"Ay, dad," answered the colonel, as he rose and climbed out of the boat; "'t is me."

"Lordy me, if I ever expected ter see yer ag'in, Phil," cried the father, as he threw his arms about him. "This is a surprise ez duz my ole bones a heap of good. Naow say yer 've come ter tell me thet I may make yer peace with the state, an' yer 'll come back ter Boxely fer good. Terrible lonesome I 've bin, lad, all these years yer 've bin off."

"Nay, dad, my heart 's too much in the service to ever let me get interested in turnips or cabbages again. What I 've come for is to make you yield to Mr. Meredith's request, and if possible to get a word with Janice. Tell me he 's mistaken, dad, in what he wrote. You never refused —"

"Look here, Hennion," growled the boatman, "we can't waste all night while you —"

He was in turn interrupted by a sharp click, the spit of a port fire sounded, and instantly came a glare of red light, which brought those on the pier into full view, and showed to them two boats full of soldiers on the river, and another party of them rising from behind a fence a few rods away.

With a scream of terror, Squire Hennion started down the wharf, hoping to escape before the troops closed in.

"Halt!" commanded some one; and when the old man still ran, he ordered "Fire."

"Bang!" went a musket on the word; but Hennion reached the end of the pier, and turned down the river bank. "Bang, bang," went two more; and the runner staggered, then pitched forward on his face.

"I surrender," announced Philemon, as the soldiers came crowding on to the wharf. "Where is your commander?"

"I am sorry to see you here, Hennion," said Brereton's voice. "You are the last man I wanted to take prisoner under such circumstances."

"Wilt let me go to my father?" steadily requested the British colonel. "I give my word not to escape."

"Let him go free," ordered Brereton; and together they walked down to the prostrate body, which an officer had already turned on its face, so that he might search the pockets.

As the two came up, the squire opened his eyes. "They 've dun fer me, Phil," he moaned. "Yer ole dad 's gone ter the well once too offen, an' a durn fool he wuz ter go on, when he know'd they wuz arter them ez wuz consarned in it."

As he spoke, the keel of one of the boats which had rowed in, grated on the river bottom. An officer, springing ashore, joined the group, and saluting, reported: "General Brereton, when you fired the light, it revealed, close upon us, a small boat stealing up the river, in which we captured Mr. Bagby. He declares he was out fishing; but he had no tackle, and the bowsman swears that as we approached he saw him put something into his mouth and swallow it."

"Bring him here," ordered the commander; and Bagby, his hands and feet tied, was more speedily than politely spilled into the shallow water and dragged ashore.

"I'll pay you military fellows up!" he sputtered angrily. "Attacking and abusing citizens as is engaged in lawful occupations. You wait till the Assembly meets. Hello! Well, I'm durned, what's happened to Squire Hennion?" he ejaculated. "You don't mean to say he's got his deserts at last? Now, I guess you see what your buying of Greenwood's brought you. No man makes an enemy of Joe Bagby but lives to regret it."

A look of intense malignity came on the dying man's face, and pushing his son, who was kneeling beside him, away, he raised himself with an effort on one elbow. "So it wuz yer ez betrayed me, wuz it," he cried, "yer ez took yer share in it daown ter the time ez we split over Greenwood, an' naow goes an' plays the sneak? Duz yer hearn that, Phil? Ef yer care fer me one bit, boy, bide yer chance an' pay him aout fer what he's done ter —" He beat the air wildly with his free arm, in a vain attempt to steady himself, and then once more pitched forward on his face, the blood pouring from his mouth.

The sun had been up an hour when three companies of Continentals, guarding five prisoners, marched into Brunswick, and at the word of command halted on the green. The sight was enough to draw most of the villagers to doors or windows; but when the rumour spread like wild-fire that among those prisoners were Joseph Bagby and Philemon Hennion, every inhabitant who could, promptly collected about the troops, where, as the soldiers and officers paid no attention to their questions, they spent their time in surmises as to what it meant, and in listening to the Honourable Joseph's threats and fulminations against the military power.

Among those who thus gathered was Mr. Meredith; and the moment he appeared Colonel Hennion called to Brereton, who was busily engaged in conferring with the officer in actual command of the half battalion.

"General Brereton," he requested, "may I have a few words in private with Squire Meredith?"

"Withdraw your guards out of ear-shot, Captain Blaisdell," ordered Brereton.

"Why, Phil, this is a sad plight to find ye in," said the squire, regretfully, as he held out his hand, forgetful that the prisoner's cords prevented his taking it.

"'T is worse than you think, squire," answered Philemon, calmly; "I came but to see my father about your wish, but, caught as I was, they will never believe it, and will doubtless hang me as a spy the moment a court-martial has sat."

"Nay, lad, 't is not possible they — "

"'T is what we should do in the same circumstances, so 't is not for me to complain. 'T was not this, however, of which I desired to speak. My father was killed this morning, and his death makes it possible for me to end your difficulties. We had word in New York that the governor had pardoned you; is 't so?"

"Ay."

"Then 't is all right, if we but act quick enough to complete it, ere I am sent to the gallows. Find a justice of the peace without delay, and let him draw deeds from me to — to Janice, of both Greenwood and Boxely, and bring them to me to sign — "

"Surely, Phil, 't is — " protestingly began the squire.

"Waste not a moment," importuned Philemon. "If 't is delayed till I am convicted, the state may claim that they were in escheat, but for these few hours I have a good title, and if ever they seek to invalidate the deeds, set up the mortgages on Boxely that you hold, as the consideration."

"But — "

"In God's name, squire, don't lose the opportunity by delay! 'T is best, whatever comes; for even if by the most marvellous luck I can convince the court that I am no spy, and so go free, the moment the legislature meets, they will vote a bill of forfeiture against me; so 't is the one means to save the property, whatever comes."

"Ye have the sense of it, lad," acceded Mr. Meredith, "and I 'll do as ye tell me, this instant. But I 'll do all that 's possible to save ye as well, and if ye but go free, ye shall be not a penny the worse off, that I swear to ye."

"And if not, 't is what I would do with the lands, were I dying a natural death, squire."

"Don't lose hope, lad," said the squire, his hand on Phil's shoulder. "Once the parson has drawn the deeds, I 'll see Washington himself, and we 'll save ye yet." Then he hurried away towards the parsonage.

During this dialogue other occurrences had been taking place, which very much interested yet mystified the crowd of spectators. When the conference between the general and major had ended, Brereton walked to the doctor's house and entered it. The major meantime went over to the constable, and in response to something he said, the town official took out his keys, and unlocked the stocks, a proceeding which set both soldiers and townsfolk whispering curiously.

"Free the prisoner Bagby's hands and feet, Corporal Cox, and set him in," commanded the major.

"What in the 'nation is comin'!" marvelled one of the observers. "Of all rum ways o' treatin' a suspect, this 'ere is the rummiest."

Another pause followed, save for a new outburst from Joe, concerning the kinds of vengeance he intended to shortly inaugurate; but presently Brereton and the doctor came across the green, the latter carrying a bottle and spoon in his hand.

"This is the one," said the general; and then, as the doctor stepped forward and poured the spoon full from the bottle, he ordered, "Open your mouth, Mr. Bagby."

"This is tyranny," shrieked Joe, "and I won't do no such thing." He shut his mouth with a snap and set his jaws rigidly.

"Hold his head," commanded Brereton; and the corporal

took it firmly and bent it back so that the helpless man looked skyward. "Snuff," said Jack, and a second officer, pulling out a small box, stepped forward, and placed a pinch in Bagby's nose.

"A-chew!" went Joe, and as his mouth flew open, the officer inserted the barrel of his pistol, so that when he tried to close his jaws again they only bit on steel. Instantly the spoon was put to his lips, and the contents emptied down his throat.

"How long will it take?" the general asked.

"The lobelia ought to act in about five minutes," replied the doctor.

Silence ensued, as soldiers and crowd stared at the immovable Joseph, whose complexion slowly turned from ruddy to white, and from white to greenish yellow, while into his eyes and mouth came a hang-dog look of woebegone misery and sickness.

LXV

PEACE IN SIGHT

THE occupants of Greenwood were still at breakfast that same morning, when word was brought to the commander-in-chief that Mr. Meredith desired speech with him.

"Set another place, Billy, and bid him to come in," ordered the hostess.

"I'll tell him, Lady Washington," cried Janice, springing up, and after she had nearly throttled her father on the porch, he was led in.

"My thanks to ye, Lady Washington," said the squire, once the introduction was made, "but I have broken fast already, and have merely come to intercede with his Excellency on a sad matter." In the fewest possible words he explained Philemon's situation. "The lad assures me that he came but to serve me, and with never a thought of spying," he ended. "I trust therefore that ye'll not hold him as one, however suspiciously it may appear."

"The matter shall have careful consideration at my hands, Mr. Meredith," replied Washington.

"All the more, I trust, that ye are good enough to take an interest in my Jan, who is his promised bride."

Both Washington and his wife turned to the girl, and the former said, —

"What, Miss Janice, is this the way thou hast kept thy promise to me to save thy smiles and blushes for some good Whig?"

"Janice Meredith! you are the most ungrateful creature that ever I knew!" asserted Mrs. Washington, crossly.

The girl only looked down into her lap, without an attempt at reply, but her father took up the cudgels.

"Nay!" he denied, "many a favor we owe to Mr. Hennion, and now he has topped them all by signing deeds within the hour that gives to the girl both Greenwood and Boxely."

Janice looked up at her father. "'T is like him," she said, chokingly. "Oh, General Washington, will you not be merciful to him?"

"What is done must depend wholly on General Brereton's report, Miss Janice," answered Washington, gravely.

"Oh, not on him!" besought the girl. "He has reason to dislike Major Hennion, and he is capable of such bitter resentments."

"Hush, child, have you no eyes?" cried Mrs. Washington, and Janice faced about to find Brereton standing behind her.

Not a feature of Jack's face showed that he had heard her, as he saluted and began, —

"The manœuvre was executed last night, your Excellency, and I have the honour to hand you my report."

Washington took the document and began an instant reading of it, while the new arrival turned to give and receive a warm greeting with the hostess. "You'll eat some breakfast, Jack," she almost begged, with affectionate hospitality.

"Thank you, Lady Washington, I — I — some other morning," answered the officer.

An awkward silence fell, yet which no one attempted to break, as the commander-in-chief slowly conned each page of the report. Once finished, he turned to the squire, and said, "I must ask, Mr. Meredith, that you go into the parlour, where later I will see you. I have certain questions to put to General Brereton." Mr. Meredith gone, he asked, —

"What was the paper you recovered from this Bagby?"

"'T was a slip of tissue silk, which proves beyond doubt that he has been supplying the British with information, though unluckily there is nothing to show from whom in our army he received his information."

"'T is unfortunate, for we have long known that a leak existed in our very councils. However, 't is something gained to have broken the channel of communication, and to have brought one traitor to the gallows. You will deliver the prisoners into the hands of the provost-marshal, sir, and be at headquarters at two this afternoon, prepared to give your testimony and papers to the court I shall order."

Brereton saluted, and made a movement of departure, but Washington spoke again, —

"In this report, sir, you speak of having taken Lieutenant Colonel Hennion a prisoner of war. Under the circumstances in which he was captured 't is a strange definition to give to his footing."

Jack's bronzed face reddened slightly. "I so stated it, your Excellency, because I overheard the colonel tell his father that he had but stolen within our lines to do Mr. Meredith a service, and having myself read the letter that induced him to take the risk, I had every reason to believe that he spoke nothing but the truth. Yet I knew that no court-martial would take such a view, and so gave him that quality in my report, to save him from a fate he does not merit."

"Once, sir, you were guilty of a deceit," said Washington, sternly, "and the present conditions are enough similar to make me suspicious. Are you certain that the fact that Miss Meredith's happiness is concerned in this officer's fate, has had nothing to do with the quality you have given to his status?"

Despite the tan, General Brereton's cheeks paled. "My God, your Excellency!" he burst out. "It has been one long struggle from the moment I found him my prisoner, until my report was safe in your hands not to — not to send him to the gallows, as I could by mere silence so easily have done. That I reported so promptly was due to the fact that I dared not delay, lest the temptation should become too strong."

Washington's eye had never left Brereton during his outbreak, and at the end he said: "You will remain at headquarters, and report to me again, sir, in half an hour, after I have duly considered the facts."

Making no reply, Jack saluted, and passed out of the room. As he reached the doorway, Janice, who had risen, said:

"I pray you, General Brereton, to forgive me the grave wrong I have just done you in both thought and speech."

Silently Jack bowed, and closed the door.

"I should think thee 'd be well ashamed of thyself, miss," declared Mrs. Washington, fretfully.

"I am, Lady Washington," replied the girl, humbly, "but believe me, that wrong as I was in this instance, I am not so wholly to blame as I seem, for one example of General Brereton's temper which he gave me, proves that he can carry his resentment to all lengths, and — "

"And is it because the man has a temper that you have slighted his suit?" interrupted the matron, peevishly. "Child, child, don't you know that every man that is worth his salt has a warm constitution? Why, the tales and warnings that were brought to me of the general's choleric nature when he was wooing me were enough to fright any woman. And true they were, for once roused, his wrath is terrible. Yet to me he has ever been the kindest and most amiable of husbands."

Washington smiled, as he said, "Miss Janice will know who deserves the credit for that. But my wife is right. A man is not apt to vent his wrath on the woman he loves, unless she gives him extreme cause."

"Bitter cause we gave to General Brereton, I own, but — but I can never think that had he truly loved me he would have refused his aid in our extremity."

"Refused thee aid!" snapped Jack's partisan. "Has he done anything but help thee in every way he could? Who was it brought thy poor mother off that dreadful ship? Who was it has teased General Lafayette with such unending favours for thee, that the marquis asked me what was the source of General Brereton's interest in one Mr. Meredith? Who only last week wrote me a letter that would have melted a stone — anything, I believe, but thy heart — begging me to offer thee a home, that thou might'st escape the tavern discomfort and crowd? I declare, thy ingratitude nigh makes me regret my having wasted any liking upon thee."

"Oh, Lady Washington," cried Janice, "not a one of these did I know of, and if you but knew what gladness it brings me to learn that, once he knew we had insulted him unwittingly, he forgave us, and put his resentment away."

"Then you 'll reward him as he deserves?" delightedly exclaimed the match-maker.

"I am promised, Lady Washington," replied the girl, gravely, "and were I not, I could never forget his once cruelty —"

"What did he?"

"I cannot bear to tell, now he has, by his kindness, endeavoured to atone for it."

"I make no doubt 't is more of his masked generosity. Never will I believe that loving you as I know he does, he could be hard-hearted or cruel to you."

"'T was not — 't was worse than if his anger had fallen on me, Lady Washington. He refused to aid my father, and but for his Excellency's untellable generosity and —"

Washington, who had been rereading the report, looked up, and interrupted: "Did General Brereton tell you that it was my act, Miss Janice?"

"No, your Excellency, 't was from Governor Livingston that we learned of the debt we owed to you, for which no thanks can ever —"

Once again Washington interrupted. "There are no thanks due to me, Miss Janice," he said, "for, much as I may have wished to service you, my public duties made it unwise. Your gratitude is wholly due to Brereton."

"I do not understand — What do you mean?" exclaimed the girl. "He — 't was your letter, so the governor said —"

"'T was my letter, but his act," replied Washington; and in a few words explained. "General Brereton expected, and should have been court-martialled and shot for what he did," he ended; "but he had served me faithfully, and so I refrained from making his misconduct public, and punished him no further than by demanding his resignation from my staff. You lost me a good friend and servant, Miss Janice, but now, with the war in effect ended, I scarce feel regret that his action, however blamable, spared you the loss of your father."

"Now, what do you say, miss?" inquired Mrs. Washington, triumphantly.

All the reply Janice made was to let her head fall forward on the table, as she burst into tears.

"There, there, my child!" cried the matron, putting her arms about and raising the girl, so that the down bent head might find a resting-place on her bosom. "I did not mean to pain thee."

"Oh, Lady Washington," sobbed Janice, as she threw her arms about the dame's neck, "I — I am so miserable, an — an — and so happy!"

Ten minutes later, Janice, with pale cheeks, but determined air, sought her father in the parlour, and going on her knees at his feet, said, —

"I have that to tell, dadda, which I fear will anger and pain you greatly." Then in a few words she repeated to him what Washington had told her.

"And why should that hurt me, lass? I own I treated the general somewhat scurvily, and that he has repaid it in different kind, but 't will be no grief to apologise and thank him for what he did."

"'T was not that of which I am apprehensive, but when I wrote to General Brereton, and besought his aid, I promised that I would wed him if he would but save you, and — and, oh, dadda, please be not angry with me, but I — I feel I must fulfil my pledge, if he asks it of me."

"And how of your promise — and mine — to Phil?"

"I came to you, ere seeking to see him, to explain — "

The squire shook his head doubtingly. "I can't lay blame on ye, Jan, since I owe my very life to what ye did. Yet 't is bitter to me to break faith with Philemon."

"I feel as guilty, dadda, but I think he will be generous, and give us back our promise, when I tell him all the facts."

"And 't is nigh as hard," went on the father, "to think of letting ye wed General Brereton, though I do owe my life to him."

"Ah, dadda, you will not punish him for the wrong his parents did him?"

"'T is not that, Jan, but because he is a rebel to — "

The girl gave a little laugh, as if a weight were taken from her thoughts, and she flung her arms about her father's neck and kissed him. "Why, dadda," she cried, with the old roguishness, "how can he be a rebel, now that they've won?"

The squire pulled a wry look. "Little I dreamed I'd

ever break faith, or make friends of the enemies of my king, but the times are disloyal, and I suppose one must go with them. If ye can persuade Phil to release us, Jan, have your way."

Again his daughter kissed him, but this time tenderly, with all the archness gone. "Thank you, dadda, for yielding," she said, "for 't would have been horrible to me had you not."

The squire kissed her in return. "Better one rebel in the family than two," he responded with a laugh, which suggested that whatever his compunctions, he knew at heart that the outcome was for the best, and was already reconciled to it. "Thou 'rt too good a lass, Jan, to make into more of a rebel than this same Brereton will no doubt make thee."

"He 'll make no rebel of me to my darling dadda, that I promise," asserted Janice, joyfully.

Mr. Meredith laughed still more heartily. "I 'll rest content if ye don't declare independence of your old dad, and allegiance to him, within one month of marriage, Jan."

As he ended, came a knock on the door and an officer entered. "His Excellency directs me to say, Miss Meredith," he announced, "that the provost-marshal has orders to bring Colonel Hennion to you, whenever you are ready to see him."

"I 'll see him now," replied the girl.

"Poor lad!" lamented the squire.

"Oh, dadda, what can I say to him?" grieved Janice.

"I know not, lass," replied the father, as he hastened to leave the room.

It was a hard interview the girl had with Colonel Hennion, but she went through with it bravely, telling all the circumstances. "'T is not merely that I owe him the fulfilment of the promise I made him before that to you was given, Phil," Janice ended, "but though I thought my love for him was dead, the moment I heard of how he had risked life and station to spare me grief, I — I —" There she ceased speaking, but her eyes and cheeks told eloquently what her tongue refused to put in words.

Philemon, with a sad face, took her hand. "I 'll not make it the harder for you by protests or appeals, Janice," he said, "for, however it may pain me, I wish to spare you."

"Oh, don't, please," she sobbed. "If you — if you would only blame me."

"I can't do that," he replied simply. "And — and 't is as well, perhaps. General Washington just sent me word that I am only to be treated as a prisoner of war, but even when I am exchanged I must henceforth be an exile, with only my sword to depend upon; so it would have been no life for you."

"Oh, Phil, you 'll take back Greenwood and Boxely, won't — "

"Only to have them taken by the state? Keep them, as I would have you, Janice, and if ever I am invalided, and the laws will let me, I 'll come back and ask you for Boxely, provided I can bear the thought of — of — of a life of rust. Till then God prosper you and good-by."

For some time after Philemon left the room the girl wept, but by degrees the sobs ended, and she became calmer. Yet, as the tears ceased, some other emotion replaced them, for thrice, as she sat musing, her cheeks flushed without apparent reason, several times her brows wrinkled, as if some question were puzzling her; and once she started forward impulsively, some action determined, only to sink back, as if lacking courage. Suddenly she sprang to her feet, and, apparently afraid to give herself time for consideration, she ran, rather than walked, into the garden. Here she picked a single blossom from a rose bush, and such sprays of honeysuckle as she could find, and made them into a bunch. Kissing the flowers as if they were the dearest thing in the world, she hurried out of the garden, and glanced about. Seeing a soldier on the road, she hailed him and asked him whither he was going.

"Nowhere in pertickerler, miss."

"Dost know where General Brereton is to be found?" she asked boldly, though blushing none the less for some reason.

"I just seen him down ter Colonel Daytou's quarters."

"Wilt favour me by taking him these flowers?" Janice requested, holding them out with one hand, while her other tendered a Spanish milled dollar, her eyes dropped groundward, as if to hide something.

"Calkerlate I might; and who 'll I say sent 'em?"

"I — say nothing at all — but just give him the bunch."

"Don't hardly worth seem carryin'," said the soldier, glancing at the flowers with open contempt, "an' sartin it ain't worth no sich money ter take 'em." Lest she would agree with him, however, he set off with celerity. "Like as not he 'll give me a reprimand fer troublin' him with a gal's nonsense," he soliliquised, as he walked. "Swan ef I ain't most tempted ter throw 'em in the ditch."

Fortunately he did not commit the breach of faith, though there were distinct qualities of shame and apology in his voice and manner, when he walked up to a group of officers sitting under a tree, and said to one of them, —

"A gal gave me this, general, ter take ter you, an' she would hev it, though I told her she 'd no business ter be botherin' yer with sich plumb foolishness."

The flowers were snatched rather than taken from his hand. "Where was she when she gave them to you?" demanded Brereton.

"I seen her go back inter the garding over ter Headquarters House, sir."

The general, without a word of explanation or apology to his fellow officers, started away almost at a run. Halting suddenly after he had gone some fifty feet, he fumbled in his pocket, and pulling out three or four coins, he tossed back a gold piece to the man; then hastened away.

"Waal!" ejaculated the soldier, as he stooped and picked it up. "A hard dollar from a gal was bad enough, but I did n't expect ter see the general go clean crazy like that. A louis, as I 'm a livin' sinner!"

When Jack entered the hedge, one glance he took, and then strode to the garden seat. "I know you would not torture me with false hopes, yet I — I dare not believe the message I would give the world to read in these," he said hoarsely.

The girl put her hand gently on his arm. "They say, Jack," she replied, her eyes upturned to his, "whatever you would wish they might."

On the words, her lover's arms were about her.

"Then they say that I am forgiven and —"

"Oh, Jack," cried Janice despairingly, "can you ever forgive me — "Can I ever atone — ever thank you for all — "

"Hush, my sweet. Put the past, as I will, out of mind for ever."

"I will, I will — but, oh, Jack, I must tell you how I have suffered — how my heart nearly broke — so that you may know how happy I am!"

"Oh, sweetheart," cried Brereton, clasping her tightly. "Do you mean — can the flowers truly say that you really love me?"

"They can, but never how much."

"Then tell me yourself."

"No words can."

"Ah, sweetheart, try," besought Brereton.

"Then stoop and let me whisper it," said the girl, and obediently Jack bent his head. But what she had to tell was told by her lips upon his.

. . . .

It was Billy Lee who finally interrupted them. "You 'll 'scuse me, Gen'l an' Missy Janice," he called, apologetically, from the opening in the hedge, "but Lady Washington dun send me to 'splain dat if she delay de dinner any mo' dat Gen'l Brereton suttinly be late at de cote-martial." And as a second couple made a hurried if reluctant exodus from paradise, he continued, "I dun tender youse my bestest felicitations, sah. Golly! Won't Missis Sukey and dat Blueskin dun be pleased."

"She will be when she and Peg are bought and safe back at Greenwood, Billy, as they soon will be," predicted Brereton.

In the dining room stood the commander-in-chief and Mrs. Washington, and as Jack and Janice entered it through one of the windows, the latter caught the girl in her arms, and kissed her warmly.

"Oh, Lady Washington," cried the maiden, ecstatically, "how can I ever thank you!"

"That is my duty, Janice, not yours," asserted Brereton, taking the matron's hand and kissing it.

Janice, her eyes starry with happiness, crossed to General

Washington. "Oh, your Excellency," she begged, her hand on his arm, "there is but one flaw in my gladness, and 't is that for my sake he lost your trust and affection. Will you — oh, won't you forgive him, as he has me, and let my joy be perfect?"

Washington smiled indulgently into the winsome face, and turning to Brereton, held out his hand. "You have secured an able pleader," he said, "and I cannot find it in my heart to give her nay at any such time. Indeed," he added, as Jack eagerly took the proffered peace-offering, "'t is to be feared, my boy, that had she but made her prayer to me instead of you, I should have found it difficult not to be equally faithless to my duty."

Janice stooped and kissed the two hands as they clasped each other, then, as her father entered the room, she sped to him, and throwing her arms about his neck, kissed him as well.

"Mr. Meredith," said Jack, tendering his hand a little doubtfully, "a bondservant of yours ran off while yet there was four years of service due to you. He is ready now to fulfil the bond, nor will he complain if you enforce the legal penalty of double time."

"'T is lucky for me, general," answered the squire, heartily, "that ye acknowledge my claim, for I take it that, my lass having sworn a new allegiance, I shall need a hold on you, if I am to retain any lien on her."

"Nay, Mr. Meredith," said Washington, "you need not fear that the new tie will efface the old one. We have ended the mother country's rule of us, but 't is probable her children will never cease to feel affection for the one who gave them being; and so you will find it with Miss Janice."

THE END

Emily's Adventures
in Wonderland

Ryan & Julia

CPSIA information can be obtained at www.ICGtesting.com
Printed in the USA
BVOW08s2230040814

361679BV00013B/217/P

9 781313 430524